# SERVIN' IT UP

## Favorite Recipes from Region 16 Telephone Pioneers

# *Dedication*

This book is dedicated to those who have taught us how to **serve** and to those who will **serve** the needs of our local communities in the future.

This cookbook is a collection of favorite recipes, which are not necessarily original recipes.

Published by: Telephone Pioneers of America Region 16


600 North 19th Street, 24th Floor
Birmingham, Alabama 35203

Library of Congress Number: 94-61713
ISBN: 0-87197-418-5

Designed, Edited and Printed by: Favorite Recipes® Press
P.O. Box 305142
Nashville, Tennessee 37230
1-800-358-0560

Manufactured in the United States of America
First Printing: 1994, 21,500 copies

# *In Acknowledgement*

The Region 16 Telephone Pioneers of America wish to express appreciation to all the Pioneers and especially to those individuals who have assisted in selecting the recipes and providing information and photographs for ***Servin' It Up***.

Linda Morrison, Alabama Chapter No. 34

Patti DeBrown, Florida Gold Coast Chapter No. 83

Carmel Dean, Dixie Chapter No. 23 and
Dogwood Chapter No. 84

Judi Cooper, Kentucky Chapter No. 32

Judy Arceneaux, Louisiana Chapter No. 24

Betty Byrd, Mississippi Chapter No. 36

Loma Purkes, North Florida Chapter No. 39

Wilma Burleson, North Carolina Chapter No. 35

Joan Steele, South Carolina Chapter No. 61

Ella Chadwell, Tennessee Chapter No. 21

Jean Smith, Region 7 Assistant

Bonnie Browning, Region 16 Assistant

R. E. Nelson, Region 16 Vice President

# *Sweet Sixteen*

Pioneering in the Southeastern Region of the United States began in the early 1920s with the Southern Bell Telephone Company. By 1942, the Pioneer Association was divided into twelve sections for greater efficiency. The Southern Bell Telephone Company was designated as Section 7 and later became known as Region 7.

In 1968, Southern Bell was divided and South Central Bell was born. With it came the creation of a new Pioneer Region, called Lucky 13. On July 1, 1994, Regions 7 and 13 combined to become Region 16, or Sweet Sixteen! This completed a full circle bringing Region 16 back to the original nine state area.

The states which make up the "Sweet Sixteen" Region are: Alabama, Florida, Georgia, Kentucky, Louisiana, Mississippi, North Carolina, South Carolina and Tennessee. There are currently eleven chapters representing more than 150,000 members both active and retired employees who are responsible for this new cookbook.

The Telephone Pioneers of America is the community service organization of our sponsoring company, BellSouth Corporation. Our volunteers are dedicated to service both from our industry roots as well as through our corporate value of Community Mindedness. ***Servin' It Up*** was therefore selected as an appropriate title because of our commitment to our local communities throughout our region. Pioneers are called "TO ANSWER THE CALL OF THOSE IN NEED" through **Service** and **Serving** others.

The many community service projects through which our chapters become involved are funded by the sale of cookbooks just like this one. At the onset of these two regions (7 and 13) merging, the administrators agreed that the first major region project should be to pull all our famous recipes together to make a "Best of the Best" cookbook. We are proud to belong to the Southeastern Region and hope that this cookbook will bring you many happy and successful meals to share with your family, neighbors, and most probably, those in need.

Thank you for purchasing this cookbook. May it bring you many years of enjoyment to your table and to your hearts.

# Table of Contents

# Alabama Chapter No. 34

The clubs and councils of Alabama Chapter No. 34 are all active supporters of many individual projects in their areas, as well as state-wide projects. Here are a few of those projects:

## Alabama the Beautiful

The Telephone Pioneers, Alabama Chapter No. 34, have entered into a partnership with the National Tree Trust, and spearheaded a project to help centralize the growing of 15,000 trees at the Alabama Forestry Commission Miller Nursery in Autaugaville, Alabama. The project has been so successful that the National Tree Trust is viewing the Alabama partnership as a model for other states around the nation.

## Abused Children Committees

The Abused Children Committees of the Telephone Pioneer Birmingham Councils help abused and needy children in Blount, Jefferson, and Shelby counties. The councils help to provide clothing, sponsor children from group homes and shelters, visit, have parties, provide arts and crafts festivals, play and talk with the kids, and educate adults about child abuse.

## Camps for Adults and Children

Camp Bluebird is a camp for adult cancer patients. Within Camp Bluebird's secure and medically supervised environment, cancer patients are offered an opportunity to rebuild their weakened self-esteem. Camp ASCCA, (Alabama Special Camp for Children & Adults), is the world's largest year-round barrier-free camp for people with disabilities.

## Battery Saturday

Alabama Pioneers distributed some 14,000 magnets urging Alabamians to change your clock and change your battery. This annual event known as Battery Saturday is a safety and educational day performed in conjunction with area fire departments and school systems to make everyone aware of fire safety and encourage all Alabamians to change the batteries in their smoke detectors when they change their clocks to or from daylight saving time.

### *Have A Heart and Hug-A-Bears*

Thanks to the Tuscaloosa Life Members, having heart surgery will be a little easier for patients in Druid City Hospital. Through their efforts, heart pillows are made and delivered to anyone having open-heart surgery. This helps to ease the discomfort of surgery; a patient presses the pillow against the chest when coughing or sneezing. Hug-A-Bears are provided for children involved in accidents or disasters.

### *Greenhouse Repaired*

With the help of the other Councils across the state, the Anniston Council raised money to help rebuild the Calhoun/Cleburne County Mental Health Center's Greenhouse located at Duke School. The Greenhouse was severely damaged by the 1993 snowstorm. Fund-raising efforts produced $4000. This center serves 70 handicapped adults and helps to mainline them into the community.

### *Clowning is More Than Fun*

Clowning is a favorite project of the Birmingham South Council, with involvement of many participants. The Clown Corps organized a sign language class to learn American Sign Language, and with their newly-acquired talents the clowns will entertain hearing-impaired children through skits and songs. Also, the moneys collected as fees for class attendance provided a TDD for use by deaf children enrolled at a local elementary school.

### *Lending a Helping Hand*

Alabama Pioneers have been available any time disaster strikes. In 1992 during the terrible aftermath of Hurricane Andrew, this group raised funds, bought supplies to sustain the hurricane victims, and sent two packed eighteen wheelers to Florida and Louisiana. Aid to the hurricane victims continued throughout the fall and through the Christmas holidays. When tragedy struck with the Mid-West floods, Pioneers were among the first to send to the region money and aid, as well as Hug-A-Bears, the homemade teddy bears that have become so much of a tradition with the Telephone Pioneers.

# *Dixie Chapter No. 23*

The Dixie Chapter was granted, and the organization completed, on May 23, 1923. It initially drew it's membership from all 10 Southern Bell States. This was a brief allegiance however, and members in states other than Georgia transferred to new chapters in their own states. The establishment of councils began in 1938 when the membership in Georgia grew too large to handle. Now there are 15 Councils and 9 Life Member Clubs. Total membership is 8,057, with 4,740 active and 3,317 life members. Today the Dixie Chapter still covers the major part of Georgia.

## *Make-a-Wish*

We strive to grant the wishes of terminally ill children—frequently even more abundantly than their initial request.

We will continue throughout the year to assist in the granting of these wishes with the hope of providing some happiness for these youngsters in their often short and very painful lives.

## *CHEER UP*

The 1994–95 Pioneer year for Dixie Clowns is bringing on a new challenge. They will be working closely with the Educational and Community Service chairpersons on a "CHEER-UP" Project—Clowns Help Educate Everyone Responsibly Using Pioneers. Our clowns will be used to educate all ages in a variety of concerns, such as drug awareness, nutrition, 911 use, safety and many others. We will be performing in schools, nursing homes, hospitals, parades, festivals and anywhere the opportunity arises.

## *Georgia Sheriffs' Youth Home Pineland Camp Grounds*

During Pioneer years '92–'93, '93–'94 the Dixie Chapter and Georgia Sheriffs' Youth Homes joined hands for a 2-year Community Service Project. Dixie Pioneers committed $140,000 to this project. During the '92–'93 year, Dixie Chapter Pioneers supported the Georgia Sheriffs' Youth Home Pineland Campus in LaGrange Georgia by establishing

Camp Pioneer. Pioneers cleared land, built an access road to campgrounds, built 17 campsites that included benches, tent pads, barbecue grills, fire rings, and picnic tables, and built a bathhouse with restrooms and showers. During the '93–'94 Pioneer year, Dixie Pioneers built a 60-foot cooking and eating pavilion behind the campground. The projects exceeded the commitment by $18,000.

During the '94–'95 Pioneer year, Dixie Chapter Pioneers plan to continue their relationship with the Georgia Sheriffs' Youth Home Pineland Campus in LaGrange by reconstructing a lake on the grounds, stocking it with fish and establishing a family recreational area around the lake as part of our Chapter Environmental Project, with a projected cost of approximately $39,000.

## *Adopt a State Park*

The Augusta Council and Life Member Club adopted Mistletoe State Park, located in Appling, Georgia. This was a Dixie Chapter Environmental project for the 1993–94 Pioneer Year. The quality of life and the environment is something very important to this Council and Club. Together they built the only barrier-free fishing dock for the handicapped in the state. The dimensions of the ramp are 18-foot by 30-foot dock and 140-foot walkway. The project was started in November of 1993 and completed in April of 1994. The dedication took place on April 30, 1994, with the Southeastern Paralyzed Veterans, state park officials, Pioneers, and Life Members.

## *Flag (Freedom and Liberty for Americans in Georgia)*

We, the Dixie Chapter of the Telephone Pioneers of America, are involved in a beautification of the state of Georgia by bringing back feelings of true patriotism and recognizing the privilege of being Americans through one of our environmental projects, FLAG (Freedom and Liberty for Americans in Georgia).

This project consists of placing flagpoles at the rest areas throughout the state of Georgia on major interstate highways maintained by the Department of Transportation.

There is a granite stone at the foot of each pole with the inscription, "Donated by the Telephone Pioneers of America Dixie Chapter No. 23." We are proud of this project and feel it will show travelers that we are proud to be Americans.

This project is ongoing and will be continued through the years as rest areas are added around the state.

# Dogwood Chapter No. 84

The Dogwood Chapter was chartered on July 1, 1974 with 4,500 members. The chapter territory encompasses the Metropolitan area of Atlanta, which has been a part of the Dixie Chapter. The dogwood tree is native to this area and the blossom is considered a symbol of Atlanta. Consequently this was adopted as the chapter name and emblem.

## FODA—Friends of Disabled Adults

Friends of Disabled Adults is a Christian Ministry that serves the needs of the sick and disabled throughout Georgia and the Southeast—regardless of age, creed or location—with wheelchairs, mobility assistance equipment, and sickroom equipment and supplies including: hospital beds, patient lifters, ostomy supplies, oxygen supplies and bathroom equipment.

## Habitat for Humanity

Dogwood Chapter will fund and construct one house in 1995.

*Habitat for Humanity house.* (Dogwood Chapter No. 84)

*Environmental cleanup and development project.* (Dogwood Chapter No. 84)

## *Georgia Sheriffs' Youth Homes*

Dogwood Chapter will fund and develop a nature center, nature trail and a number of sites for outdoor camping to benefit the youth of the Metro Atlanta area.

## *Mobile Youth Resource Center*

Dogwood Chapter will fund and equip a motor home-style vehicle that will be staffed with volunteers from the community and government agencies to administer to the needs of troubled youth in the inner city area of Atlanta.

*Pioneer Clowns liven the Taste of Atlanta festival.* (Dogwood Chapter No. 84)

# Florida Gold Coast Chapter No. 83

Florida Gold Coast Chapter No. 83 was chartered on July 1, 1972 with 3,061 members. The chapter territory encompasses the southern part of Florida, starting with Sebastian on the east coast and south to Key West, and extending to the territory south of Sarasota on the west coast. Today, the chapter has almost 13,000 members, comprised of 7,500-plus active Pioneers and 5,000-plus Life Member Pioneers.

Florida Gold Coast Pioneers regularly volunteer with hundreds of wonderful projects. Our focus areas include: Education, Homeless/Hungry, AIDS and Other Chronic Diseases, Disabled, Elderly, Crime Prevention, and Environmental Issues.

## Education

*Under the Education umbrella, we:*

- tutor; provide school supplies to the disadvantaged; and,
- organize walk-a-thons to benefit scholarships.

## Homeless/Hungry

*Under the Homeless/Hungry umbrella, we:*

- feed hundreds of homeless in 3 counties monthly by raising funds through penny drives; raise money for and help build Habitat for Humanity homes; and,
- also fund-raise to help support missions for the hungry and homeless.

## Disabled

*Under the Disabled umbrella, we:*

- help with Special Olympics; hold Easter Egg Hunts for the visually impaired; work with disabled vets; and,
- build ramps for Easy Access.

## Elderly

*Under the Elderly umbrella, we:*

- support various senior service agencies in 5 counties with holiday visits to nursing homes; make home repairs for the aged and indigent; and,
- conduct bingo at nursing homes.

## Crime Prevention

*Under the Crime Prevention umbrella:*

- the chapter is involved with domestic violence issues; with centers for abused and abandoned; and,
- with organizations to help children affected by violence.

## Environmental Issues

*Under the Environmental Issues umbrella, we:*

- recycle; adopt highways and beaches; collect flip tops from aluminum cans to help Ronald McDonald Houses; and,
- clean parks.

## AIDS and Other Chronic Diseases

*With regard to AIDS and other diseases, we:*

- organize and participate in walks/runs to benefit AIDS awareness; cancer research; and,
- United Cerebral Palsy and Multiple Sclerosis.

Our clown troupe is very active in supporting all chapter goals. All projects have the full support of our active, retired, and Pioneers Partners.

## Dedication

Chapter 83 wishes to thank all the Pioneers, their Partners and families who give so much of themselves—in fact, who volunteer about ONE MILLION hours annually to help those in need throughout the communities in South Florida. Further, we appreciate the ongoing support of our sponsor company: BellSouth. Finally, we wish to dedicate this to our Life Members—those Pioneers who have come before us and set the high ideals, goals, and standards which make this organization as great as it is.

# Kentucky Chapter No. 32

The Kentucky Chapter was chartered September 24, 1924, as the J. B. Speed Chapter. It had 27 charter members.

Mr. Speed was an ambitious industrialist. He brought the first telephone to Kentucky and installed it in Louisville in 1877. Also he established the first telephone company and opened an exchange in Louisville in 1879.

In 1944, the name of the chapter was changed to Kentucky Chapter. The trend at this time was to name or rename chapters after states rather than individuals. The chapter territory is coterminous with the South Central Bell Telephone Company's Kentucky Area. Its membership had grown to 3,675 as of June 30, 1980. To date, we have over 6,000 members with a total of eight councils and eleven clubs.

*Building playground.* (Kentucky Chapter No. 32)

*Building playground.* (Kentucky Chapter No. 32)

## *Camp Bluebird*

Over 40-plus campers shared fellowship and warmth of our two campers when brought together at Camp Loucon in October and April of 1994. The Kentucky Pioneers concluded each event with a wonderful feeling of helping cancer patients.

## *Christmas Wish— Pennyrile Council in Owensboro, Kentucky*

Life Member Clubs brought in nearly $100,000 during the Christmas holiday. Wishes were granted and many Pioneers felt the real blessings of Christmas. TDD's are being placed in the Purchase Area as a direct result of the Earl Dodds Grant. The Paducah Life Member Club is well on its way to exceeding the matching grant for this year.

## *Annual Assembly Project*

Approximately 100 Kentucky Pioneers built an entire playground and landscaped a local center during the 69th Annual Assembly in Owensboro, Kentucky.

# *Louisiana Chapter No. 24*

Louisiana Chapter No. 24 was formed June 5, 1923 and consists of 14 Councils and 17 Life Member Clubs numbering over 14,000 members. In the spirit of Telephone Pioneers everywhere, Chapter No. 24 is active in many projects in which members provide food, clothing, shelter, education, therapy, environmental and many other comforts, necessities and the extras that make life better for the community via the following projects:

- Adopt-A-School
- Camp Bluebird for cancer patients, a three-day camp for autistic children, and helping with a camp for blind children
- Hug-A-Bears for local hospitals as well as disaster victims
- Lap robes for senior citizen nursing home residents, as well as nursing home visits to provide bingo games and monthly birthday parties. Color-Me-Beautiful provides female residents with manicures, makeup and hair-styling assistance.
- Disaster Relief for hurricane and flood victims
- Walk-A-America
- ABC Quilts
- Shelter of Hope and other shelters for abused women and children
- AIDS NAMES quilt project
- Habitat for Humanity houses
- Holiday parties for area children and senior citizens
- Multiple Sclerosis
- Huck Finn Fishing Rodeo
- Spina Bifida bikes
- Hunter safety courses
- Happy Trails Riding Camp recreational and developmental assistance for physically and mentally challenged individuals
- Mothers Against Drugs
- MS Tour for Cure
- BAT-RAY mobiles
- Light-Up-A-Life
- Children's Miracle Network

- Kids Can Change the World
- Drug Free Youth in Town
- Blood pressure screenings and other health-related tests for the Council on Aging
- HOOP (Helping Our Own People), a program of activities for members who are shut-ins or have no nearby family or friends to lend assistance
- Pioneer Clowns
- Talking Books
- Special Olympics
- Senior Olympics
- Sickle Cell Anemia
- Carville Hanson's Disease Center

*Huck Finn Fishing Rodeo.* (Louisiana Chapter No. 24)

# Mississippi Chapter No. 36

The Mississippi Chapter was chartered on September 25, 1925, as the Magnolia Chapter. The Chapter had 25 charter members, and the membership has grown to 6,357 as of the end of June 30, 1994.

On July 1, 1973, the chapter name was changed to the Mississippi Chapter. It is comprised of eight councils and 16 Life Member Clubs in the state. The Chapter has a dedicated program in service to the Mississippi communities, fellowship with active and retired employees and loyalty to the industry that sponsors the organization. The Mississippi Chapter contributed over 760,000 community service hours and over $261,000 in "ANSWERING THE CALL OF THOSE IN NEED" during the 1993–94 Pioneer year.

## *Adopt A Highway*

Pioneers have adopted over 80 miles across our state with the pledge to clean the roadside of trash.

## *Mobile Mammography Service*

The Mississippi Chapter No. 36, in partnership with Forrest General Hospital, is providing Mississippi's first mobile mammography unit, serving the rural areas of the state.

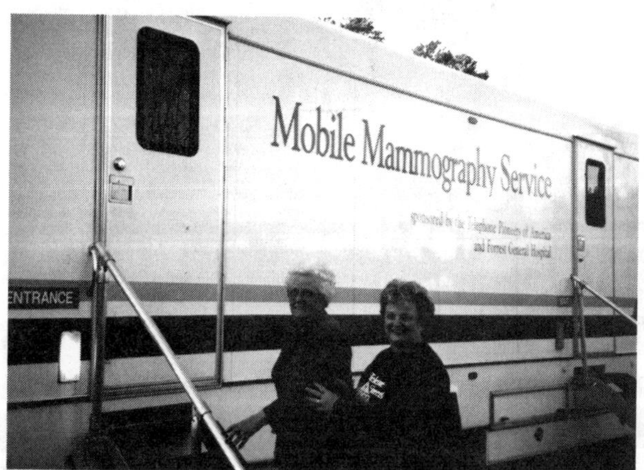


*Mobile Mammography Service.* (Mississippi Chapter No. 36)

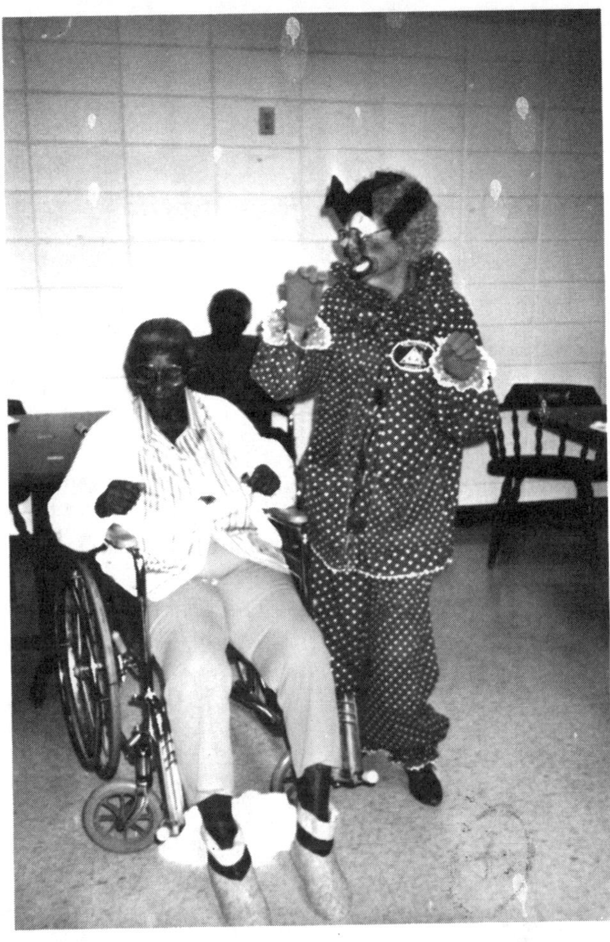

*Clowning.* (Mississippi Chapter No. 36)

## *Read to Me*

Pioneers assemble "Read to Me" packets to be donated to area hospitals. Reading is the "door to the world," and Mississippi Pioneers wish to open this door to all children.

## *Clowning*

Clowns cheer the day for those less fortunate. Pioneer Clowns are very special.

## *Camp Bluebird*

Mississippi Pioneers sponsor six camps each year, some for adult cancer patients and some for children.

# North Carolina Chapter No. 35

On July 1, 1925, a charter was granted by Mr. Ben S. Read, President of the Telephone Pioneers of America, authorizing organization of the J. Epps Brown Chapter No. 35 (No. 35 because the chapter was the 35th to be organized in the Association).

Prior to the formation of Chapter No. 35, North Carolina and South Carolina Pioneers were members of Dixie Chapter No. 23. Members were employees of Southern Bell as well as employees of the independent telephone companies. The suggestion that such a chapter be organized originated with John C. McManus. The organizational meeting, with 49 chapter members, was held on July 24, 1925, in the Chamber of Commerce Hall in Charlotte, North Carolina. The Chapter was named in honor of J. Epps Brown, Southern Bell President and a native of Newberry, South Carolina.

*Share a hug and learn to read.* (North Carolina Chapter No. 35)

As early as 1949, it became evident that there was a need to split the J. Epps Brown Chapter. Prior to 1949, Southern Bell was organized so that North Carolina and South Carolina were part of the Carolinas Division. Due to the rapid growth in telephone business following World War II, Southern Bell found it necessary to divide the Carolinas Division into two separate divisions. In October, 1949, a petition signed by thirty-one members of the J. Epps Brown Chapter No. 35 residing in Columbia, South Carolina, requested that consideration be given to the establishment of a South Carolina Chapter. A charter was granted on January 31, 1950, but the official announcement was withheld until June 10, 1950, to coincide with the Silver Anniversary of the J. Epps Brown Chapter No. 35, which was being celebrated by Pioneers in Charleston, South Carolina. The North Carolina Pioneers retained the original charter and the original chapter number 35, but adopted the new name "North Carolina Chapter No. 35."

North Carolina Chapter No. 35 is made up of active and retired members from AT&T, BellSouth, and Northern Telecom. There are 10 councils and 15 life member clubs with a membership of more than 12,000.

Evelyn Newman is the only person to have served more than one term as Chapter President, serving from 1980–1981 and 1983–1984.

North Carolina Chapter No. 35 has had four members to serve as Region 7 Vice Presidents. They are Margaret Jackson, Larry Morgan, Joe Clontz, and George Harmon.

The real "movers and shakers" of the Pioneer organization are the hundreds and hundreds who so graciously agree to take on leadership roles in the Councils. They devote untold personal hours to ensure that Pioneer programs in their Council territory carry out the Purpose of Pioneering.

# North Florida Chapter No. 39

The North Florida Chapter was chartered on October 28, 1928, with 25 members. The Chapter is a spin-off of the Dixie Chapter in Georgia, and was originally named the David Laird Chapter. Meetings were held annually until 1939, when the Association authorized the formation of councils in five of the most populated areas of the state. It took 22 years to reach a membership of 1,000. The membership today is 8,929 active members, 5,961 life members, and 6,624 affiliate members, for a total of 21,514 members.

## First Life Member Club

The first Life Member Club was formed in St. Petersburg in 1937. The influx of retirees from other states resulted in rapid growth of clubs for affiliate life members in the central and west coast areas. Today we have 34 Life Member Clubs in North Florida.

## St. Augustine School

North Florida is currently involved with the St. Augustine School for the Deaf and Blind, building them a playground area which is built to scale for a blind child, to help them better understand their community. For example, there is a small bank, McDonalds, phone center store, and grocery store, all of which will be in miniature and called the Pioneer Village.

## Habitat for Humanity

We also are involved with Habitat for Humanity in most of our communities.

## Pick an Angel

We provide over 5,000 toys in our "Pick an Angel" project for underprivileged children each Christmas season, as well as stuff thousands of Christmas stockings for the Salvation Army.

## *Adopt a Tree*

We provide trees for state highway medians, public parks, and schools thru our "Adopt a Tree" project.

## *Tel a Pal*

We help hundreds of children with our "Tel a Pal" program, which links a BellSouth employee with a child in elementary school on a one-to-one basis.

## *Easy Access*

We are involved with the federal parks in providing an easy access walkway at Fort Matanzas in St. Augustine, Florida.

## *Clown Corps*

We also have developed clown corps in the middle schools in order to get at-risk children involved in school and their communities.

# South Carolina Chapter No. 61

The South Carolina Chapter was initially chartered with 31 members on January 31, 1950, as the J. Epps Brown Chapter. Mr. Brown was a former president of the Southern Bell Telephone and Telegraph Company and a native of Newberry, South Carolina. On July 16, 1970, the Chapter was renamed the South Carolina Chapter No. 61.

As of July 1, 1994, the membership was 7,984. South Carolina Chapter No. 61 consists of eight Councils and nine Life Member Clubs throughout the state.

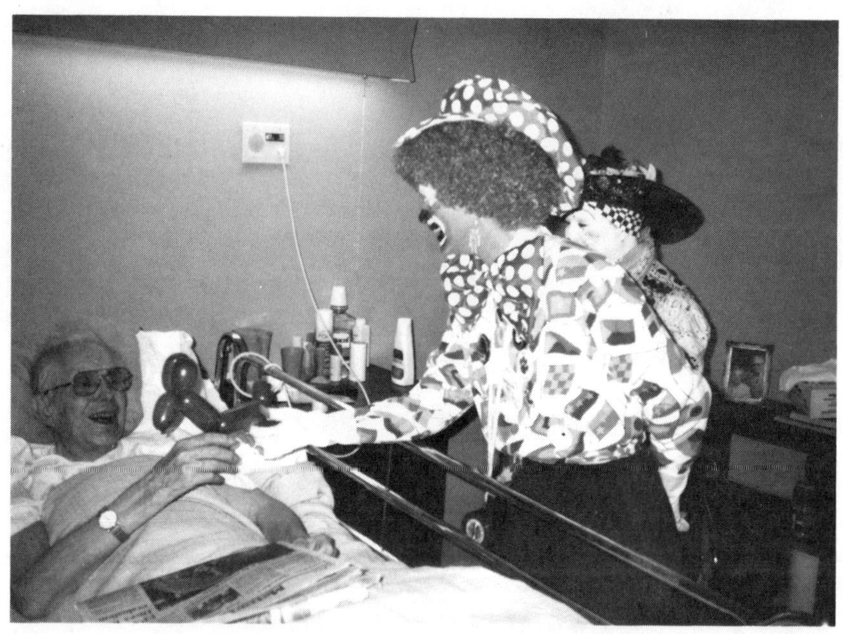

*Clowns visit nursing home in Bamberg.*
(South Carolina Chapter No. 61)

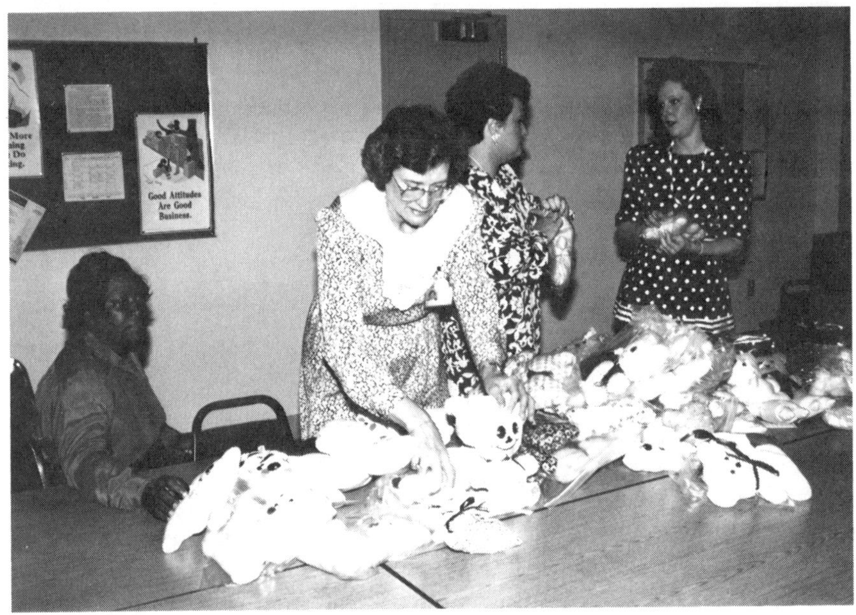


*Distributing Hug-A-Bears.* (South Carolina Chapter No. 61)

## *Projects*

Current and past chapter projects consist of: working with the elderly through Project H.O.P.E. (Helping Older People Excel); establishing the South Carolina Adam Walsh Child Resource Center; working and supporting the South Carolina School for the Deaf, Blind, and Multihandicapped; and supporting the Wil Lou Gray Opportunity School for at-risk students by funding an indoor nature center and an outdoor ropes course for the purpose of building self-esteem and trust.

## *Dedication*

To all South Carolina Telephone Pioneers, Active, Life Members, and Partners, who continually give of their time and talents to help answer the call of those in need.

# Tennessee Chapter No. 21

Tennessee Chapter 21 was chartered January 18, 1923. Pioneers motivated active employees to acquire a hobby; mentioning frequently how important it is, after so many years of service to the Company, to keep active and interested in life for one's own well-being. Tennessee Pioneers early-on expressed favor of doing something for the betterment of humanity. By the mid-1930s, Pioneers were active in service among the sick and afflicted and in rendering aid and comfort to those who were in need of good cheer. By 1941, Pioneers were active in the sale of stamps and bonds, China relief work, medical dressings for the Red Cross, raffles to purchase wheelchairs for partially paralyzed service men and in all activities associated with War work. Following the War, the Pioneers felt their opportunities were never broader and responsibilities never greater.

## Life Member Clubs

Life Member Clubs were formed for the association of retirees and the company. An organized effort of community service became a major role of the Pioneers. It was manifest in Cancer Crusades, benefits for the March of Dimes polio effort, Christmas parties for orphaned children and in helping the blind through the Talking Book Maintenance Project. And yes, there is record about 1955 of the Cookbook project, which netted a "tidy sum"—financial books indicate $102.65—which supported the Pioneers volunteer efforts.

## Our Future—The Children

Today, Pioneers in Tennessee are concerned with the growing issues of our society, especially within the communities where we live, work and raise our children. All across Tennessee you can meet some Pioneer who may be tutoring a child because of our concern for literacy.

## Pioneer Klown Korp

Pioneers team up with others to encourage kids to say NO to drugs—"Don't Follow Me" stories teach kids there is more to life than drugs. Pioneers bring joy and laughter through the Pioneer Klown Korp, our awareness programs have restored dignity to victims of child abuse, and domestic violence can be prevented and even stopped if we are willing to help—that's how Pioneers think and dedicate themselves to these pressing issues.

## *Service to Others*

Our Pioneers know that victims of AIDS need hugs and understanding; Pioneers build relationships and homes through Habitat For Humanity; and our camp for adult cancer patients, known as Camp Bluebird, provides a place where a person can relax in the midst of a tragic disease.

## *Ecology*

Pioneers are concerned with the Earth and her future. All along the highways you can see Pioneers picking up litter, feeding the birds in the dead of winter, cleaning up after a severe ice storm. Pioneers know it is important to give to others.

## *Dedication*

To those who have come before us and to those who will continue after us.

> "The 'Spirit of Service' of our industry was not found in the byways and hedges of life. It was made. And it was made, not by chance, but through brain, brawn, character, energy and sacrifice, and that indescribable something which comes from the devotion of men's souls to the dignity and worth of work, which is of service to others. Life is a bridge—we older Pioneers who are beyond the center of the span have the responsibility of walking back to meet the on-coming Pioneers and of giving to them that strength and that purpose which the ideals and traditions of the industry have always given us."
>
> —N. R. Powley, 1941

# *Recipe Finder*

| Recipe Title | Page No. |
|---|---|
| | |
| | |
| | |
| | |
| | |
| | |
| | |
| | |
| | |
| | |
| | |
| | |
| | |
| | |
| | |
| | |
| | |
| | |
| | |
| | |
| | |
| | |
| | |
| | |
| | |
| | |
| | |
| | |
| | |
| | |
| | |
| | |
| | |
| | |
| | |

# *Recipe Finder*

| Recipe Title | Page No. |
|---|---|
| | |
| | |
| | |
| | |
| | |
| | |
| | |
| | |
| | |
| | |
| | |
| | |
| | |
| | |
| | |
| | |
| | |
| | |
| | |
| | |
| | |
| | |
| | |
| | |
| | |
| | |
| | |
| | |
| | |
| | |
| | |
| | |
| | |
| | |
| | |

# *Recipe Finder*

| Recipe Title | Page No. |
|---|---|
| | |
| | |
| | |
| | |
| | |
| | |
| | |
| | |
| | |
| | |
| | |
| | |
| | |
| | |
| | |
| | |
| | |
| | |
| | |
| | |
| | |
| | |
| | |
| | |
| | |
| | |
| | |
| | |
| | |
| | |
| | |
| | |
| | |
| | |
| | |

# Appetizers & Beverages

## Chipped Beef Ball

**3 (8 oz.) cream cheese**
**1 small jar chipped beef**
**1 small can chopped ripe olives**
**1 small bunch green onions**
**1 small jar mushrooms**
**3 tsp. Accent**

Soften cream cheese. Chop remaining ingredients. Add to cheese. Shape into 2 balls. Wrap in Saran Wrap. Freezes well.

Mrs. Ralph E. Anderson, *Bell's Best 3*, Mississippi Chapter No. 36

## Beer Cheese

**1 lb. sharp Cheddar cheese**
**1/2 tsp. cayenne**
**1/4 c. beer (or a little less; just enough to moisten)***
**8 oz. pkg. Philadelphia cream cheese**
**1/2 tsp. garlic juice**

Have cheeses at room temperature. Grate Cheddar cheese, then add cream cheese and other ingredients; mix thoroughly. Shape into log and roll in a mixture of 1 tablespoon chili powder, 1 teaspoon cayenne and approximately 1/2 cup paprika. Wrap in wax paper and store in refrigerator. Will keep a week or longer.

*Olive juice can be substituted for beer if preferred.

*Kentucky Kitchens, Volume I*, Kentucky Chapter No. 32

## Tootsie's Chipped Beef Ball

**1 (3 oz.) pkg. chopped beef**
**1 (8 oz.) pkg. cream cheese, softened**
**1/4 c. Parmesan cheese, grated**
**1/4 c. chopped olives**
**2 tbsp. horseradish (or less)**
**2 c. crushed potato chips for topping**

In large mixing bowl blend first 5 ingredients. Form a ball of cheese mixture. Roll in potato chips. Serve with sesame seed crackers.

Joyce Bauer
*A Tablespoon of Pioneering and a Teaspoon of Horses and the Handicapped*
Florida Gold Coast Chapter No. 83

## *Beer-Cheese Pine Cones*

16 oz. cream cheese, softened
1/3 c. beer
2 Tbsp. finely snipped parsley
1 tsp. paprika
3 c. shredded, smoked, sharp Cheddar cheese
Sliced almonds
Apple slices*
Pear slices*
Assorted crackers

In a large bowl, beat together the softened cream cheese, beer, parsley and paprika till well blended. Stir in the shredded Cheddar cheese. Cover and chill mixture 1 hour. Divide mixture in half. With hands, mold each portion into a pine cone shape; place on a baking sheet. Insert sliced almonds in rows over molded cheese to resemble pine cones. Cover and chill several hours. To serve, transfer pine cones to board or platter with wide metal spatula. Serve with apple slices, pear slices and assorted crackers. Makes 4 cups spread.

*Dip apple and pear slices in a mixture of water, lemon juice or ascorbic acid color keeper to prevent the fruit from darkening.

Patti Headrick, *Dogwood Delights*, Dogwood Chapter No. 84

## *K. O.'s "Bet Me" Cheese Ball*

1/4 c. milk
1 tsp. Worcestershire sauce
1 sm. onion wedge, grated
8 oz. sharp Door County Cheddar cheese, grated
3 oz. bleu cheese
1 pkg. cream cheese, softened
1/2 to 1 c. chopped nuts
1/2 c. parsley, chopped

In a bowl mix all ingredients, except nuts and parsley. Mix well. Cover and refrigerate overnight.

The next day roll and form cheese mixture into a ball.

Mix together nuts and parsley. Roll cheese ball in nuts and parsley, pressing the mix into the surface of the cheese ball. Serve with crackers and cocktails!!

Kathy O'Hara
*A Tablespoon of Pioneering and a Teaspoon of Horses and the Handicapped*
Florida Gold Coast Chapter No. 83

## Party Cheese Ball

2 (8 oz.) pkg. cream cheese, softened
1 (8 oz.) pkg. sharp Cheddar cheese, shredded
1 Tbsp. chopped pimento
1 Tbsp. chopped green pepper
1 Tbsp. finely chopped onion
2 Tbsp. Worcestershire sauce
1 tsp. lemon juice
Dash of cayenne
Dash of salt
Finely chopped pecans

Combine cream cheese and Cheddar cheese, mixing well. Stir in remaining ingredients, except pecans. Shape into a ball and roll in chopped pecans. Chill. Serve at room temperature. Yield: about 3 cups.

Mrs. Ralph E. Anderson, *Bell's Best 3*, Mississippi Chapter No. 36

## Pimento Cheese Spread

2 lb. aged Hoop cheese
1 (7 oz.) jar red pimentos
4 large sour pickles
1 small sweet onion
6 to 8 oz. cottage cheese
3 Tbsp. mayonnaise
1/2 tsp. black pepper
1 tsp. Worcestershire sauce

Cut pickles and onion into chunks. Place in blender with pimentos. Blend until liquid and pour over cheese grated into a large bowl. Add mayonnaise and stir mixture while adding other ingredients until smooth and creamy.

Best after marinating overnight in refrigerator.

Louis W. Harmon, *Bell's Best 3*, Mississippi Chapter No. 36

# Pineapple Cheese Ball

- 1/4 cup chopped green bell pepper
- 1/4 cup shredded carrot
- 1 8-ounce can juice-pack crushed pineapple, drained
- 8 ounces Neufchâtel cheese, softened
- 1/2 cup unsalted sunflower seed

Combine green pepper, carrot, pineapple and Neufchâtel cheese in bowl; mix well. Chill, covered, for 1 hour or until firm. Shape into ball on waxed paper. Roll in sunflower seed, coating well. Chill, covered, until serving time. Place on serving plate. Serve with wheat crackers or Melba toast rounds. Yield: 48 tablespoons.

**Approx Per Serving:** Cal 24; Prot 1 g; Carbo 1 g; Fiber <1 g; T Fat 2 g; Chol 4 mg; Sod 19 mg.
**Dietary Exchanges:** Fat 1/2

"*Answering the Call of Those in Need*," Tennessee Chapter No. 21

# Crab Spread

1st layer:

*Mix:*

- 8 oz. softened cream cheese
- 2 T. Worcestershire sauce
- 2 T. mayonnaise
- 1 sml. onion, grated
- dash garlic

Spread on platter.

2nd layer:

*Spread:*

- 1 1/2 oz. crab meat

*Pour:*

- 1/2 bottle chili sauce

Sprinkle with parsley.

Edna Daniel, *Taste of Dixie*, Dixie Chapter No. 23

## Crabmeat Appetizer

- 1/2 lb. peeled crabmeat
- 1 pkg. Philadelphia Cream cheese
- 1 stick butter
- 1/2 c. green shallots
- 1/2 tsp. garlic powder
- 1 tsp. lemon juice

On HIGH in microwave, soften cheese and butter. Add shallots, crabmeat, lemon juice and garlic powder. Melt till creamy. Serve hot and use crackers or chips to dip.

Mary Bird, *Pots, Pans and Pioneers, Volume IV*
Louisiana Chapter No. 24

## Salmon Party Ball

- 2 cups flaked salmon
- 8 ounces cream cheese, softened
- 1 tablespoon lemon juice
- 2 teaspoons horseradish
- 1 teaspoon minced onion
- 1/4 teaspoon salt
- 1/4 teaspoon liquid smoke
- 3 tablespoons chopped parsley
- 1/2 cup chopped pecans

Combine salmon, cream cheese, lemon juice, horseradish, onion, salt and liquid smoke in bowl; mix well. Chill, tightly covered, for several hours. Shape into ball. Roll in mixture of parsley and pecans. Chill until serving time. Serve with crackers. Yield: 20 servings.

**Approx Per Serving:** Cal 92; Prot 6 g; Carbo 1 g; Fiber <1 g; T Fat 7 g; Chol 24 mg; Sod 187 mg.

Shirley T. Hinson, *Carolina Cooking*, North Carolina Chapter No. 35

### A Helpful Hint

For a large party, arrange small attractive plates of appetizers, which can be refilled easily, rather than a large one which loses its attractiveness as guests enjoy it.

# *Salmon Party Log*

**1 (1 lb.) can salmon**
**1 (8 oz.) pkg. cream cheese, room temperature**
**1 Tbsp. lemon juice**
**2 tsp. grated onion**
**1 tsp. prepared horseradish**
**1/4 tsp. salt**
**1/4 tsp. liquid smoke**
**1/2 c. chopped pecans**
**3 Tbsp. snipped parsley**

Drain and flake salmon. Remove skin and bone. Combine salmon with next 6 ingredients. Mix thoroughly. Chill several hours.

Combine nuts and parsley. Shape salmon mixture into a slender log. Roll in mixture of nuts and parsley.

Serve with crackers.

Debbie Boyette, *Pioneers Pots and Pans—1985 Cookbook*
North Florida Chapter No. 39

*Packing more than 500 Hug-A-Bears for children affected by the 1993 floods.* (Alabama Chapter No. 34)

## Shrimp Mold

**1 can tomato soup**
**1 (8 oz.) pkg. cream cheese**
**1/4 tsp. salt**
**3/4 c. celery**
**3/4 c. onion**
**1 envelope unflavored gelatin**
**1/4 c. boiling water**
**1 c. mayonnaise**
**2 cans tiny shrimp**

Blend together soup and cream cheese over low flame; add salt and finely chopped celery and onion. Mix gelatin in hot water and stir into mixture. Rinse shrimp very well and also add mayonnaise. Pour into mold and let set overnight.

Serve with crackers.

Mary Jane Clary, *Pioneers Pots and Pans—1985 Cookbook*
North Florida Chapter No. 39

## Shrimp Mold

**1 large or 2 small cans shrimp**
**1 can tomato soup**
**3 small packages cream cheese**
**1 1/2 tbsp. unflavored gelatin**
**Salt and pepper to taste**
**Dash of tabasco**
**1 cup mayonnaise**
**3/4 cup finely chopped celery**
**3/4 cup finely chopped spring onions**

Soak gelatin in 1/4 cup cold water. Add 1/2 cup of water to soup and heat to boiling. Add gelatin and heat to dissolve. Add cream cheese and stir until blended well. Let this mixture cool. In another bowl, mix celery, onions and shrimp (crumble shrimp with hand very fine). Add mayonnaise, salt, pepper and tabasco. Pour cooled mixture of tomato soup and cream cheese over this. Mix well. Refrigerate in mold desired.

Martha Herrington, *Secret Recipes of Telephone Pioneers, Volume II*
South Carolina Chapter No. 61

## Molded Shrimp Spread

**8 ounces cream cheese, softened**
**1 cup mayonnaise**
**1 10-ounce can tomato soup, heated**
**2 envelopes unflavored gelatin**
**1/2 cup cold water**
**2 cups coarsely chopped, cooked, peeled shrimp**
**1 cup minced celery**
**1/3 cup minced onion**
**Salt to taste**
**Lemon juice to taste**

Blend cream cheese and mayonnaise in bowl. Stir into hot soup. Soften gelatin in cold water. Add to soup mixture, stirring constantly until dissolved. Stir in shrimp, celery and onion. Season with salt and lemon juice. Spoon into mold. Chill, tightly covered, in refrigerator for 24 hours or more. Unmold onto serving plate. Serve with crackers or rye bread. Yield: 50 servings.

**Approx Per Serving:** Cal 60; Prot 2 g; Carbo 1 g; Fiber <1 g; T Fat 5 g; Chol 16 mg; Sod 89 mg.

Becky Adams, *Carolina Cooking*, North Carolina Chapter No. 35

## David's Cheese Dip

**Origin:** Unknown.

**8 oz. cream cheese, softened**
**Beer**
**8 oz. aged Cheddar cheese, diced**
**1 clove garlic**

Into container of an electric blender, put 8 ounces softened cream cheese and 1/2 cup beer. Cover and blend on high speed for 20 seconds.

Add 1/4 cup beer, 8 ounces aged Cheddar cheese (diced) and 1 clove garlic. Cover and blend for 20 seconds, or until smooth, stopping to stir down if necessary. Empty into bowl and chill. Makes 3 cups.

**Preparation time:** 15 minutes.

Kathy Paganini, *A Taste of Pioneering*
Florida Gold Coast Chapter No. 83

## Chili con Queso

1 pound ground beef
1 pound hot pork sausage
32 ounces Velveeta cheese
1 can cream of mushroom soup
3 jalapeños, seeded, chopped
1 small onion, chopped
1 tomato, chopped

Brown ground beef and sausage in skillet, stirring until crumbly; drain. Combine ground beef mixture, cheese, soup, jalapeños, onion and tomato in Crock•Pot; mix well. Heat until cheese is melted. May add a small amount of milk if desired. Serve warm with tortilla chips. Yield: 128 servings.

**Approx Per Serving:** Cal 41; Prot 2 g; Carbo 1 g; Fiber <1 g; T Fat 3 g; Chol 10 mg; Sod 140 mg.

Susan M. Perry, *Carolina Cooking*, North Carolina Chapter No. 35

## Spicy Cheese Dip

1 can Cheddar cheese soup
1 can Ro-Tel tomaotes
1 lb. sausage

Brown sausage in skillet; remove and drain off fat. In saucepan, heat soup, stirring until smooth. Add tomatoes and sausage. Serve hot or at room temperature. Great on taco chips.

Debbie Hemphill, *Bell's Best*, Mississippi Chapter No. 36

## Crab Dip

2 8-oz. pkg. cream cheese
1 cup sour cream
1 cup grated cheese
1 tsp. dry mustard
1 Tbsp. Worcestershire sauce
4 Tbsp. mayonnaise
1/2 tsp. lemon juice
3 dashes garlic
3/4 lb. chopped crab meat—can use imitation extra grated cheese for top

Blend all ingredients except crab. Stir in chopped crab meat. Pour into greased casserole dish. Top with extra grated cheese. Bake for 30 minutes at 350 degrees. Serve with assorted crackers.

Paul Wickensimer, *Secret Recipes of Telephone Pioneers, Volume III*
South Carolina Chapter No. 61

## Crabmeat Dip

**Country:** U.S.A.; **City:** Palm Beach. **Recipe obtained from:** Friend.

12 oz. frozen crabmeat
16 oz. cream cheese
1/4 c. Hellmann's mayo
1/8 c. white wine
1 clove garlic, crushed
1 tsp. Dijon mustard
2 tsp. powdered sugar
Salt to taste
Fresh pepper to taste
Tabasco sauce to taste
Worcestershire sauce to taste
Horseradish to taste
Lemon juice to taste
1/3 c. slivered almonds
1/4 c. fresh parsley, minced

Combine all ingredients, except crabmeat and almonds. Fold in crab and heat. Top with toasted almonds. Bake 15 minutes at 350°. Serve warm with Melba rounds.

**Preparation time:** 30 minutes.
**Cooking time:** 15 minutes.

Ruthann Woodbury, *A Taste of Pioneering*
Florida Gold Coast Chapter No. 83

## Hot Crab Dip

8 oz. cream cheese
1 c. crabmeat — frozen or canned
1 Tbsp. milk
1/2 tsp. horseradish
1/4 c. slivered almonds

Soften cream cheese and mix all ingredients together except almonds. Spread in casserole. Sprinkle with almonds. Bake 30 minutes at 350°. Serve with crackers.

Beverly Egan, *Pioneers Pots and Pans—1985 Cookbook*
North Florida Chapter No. 39

### A Helpful Hint

Vary dips by substituting yogurt for sour cream or Neufchâtel cheese for cream cheese. Cottage cheese processed in a blender until smooth and creamy can be substituted for either sour cream or yogurt to reduce calories.

# Dill Dip

1 c. sour cream
1 c. mayonnaise
2 Tbsp. dill weed
2 Tbsp. parsley
2 Tbsp. finely minced onion

Mix together and let chill a few hours before serving. Best if sits overnight.

Serve with raw vegetables—broccoli, cauliflower, celery, carrots, squash, cucumbers, green peppers.

Margie Kearney, *Pioneers Pots and Pans—1985 Cookbook*
North Florida Chapter No. 39

# Fruit Dip

1 (8 oz.) pkg. cream cheese
1 small jar marshmallow cream
1 (8 oz.) Cool Whip

Mix well and dip your fruits. *It is delicious.*

Georgann Downs, *Bell's Best 3*, Mississippi Chapter No. 36

# Jezebel Dip

1 (18 oz.) jar pineapple preserves
5 Tbsp. horseradish
1 (18 oz.) jar apple jelly
1 Tbsp. cracked black pepper
5 oz. dry mustard
Cream cheese, chopped in hunks

Combine all ingredients, except cream cheese. Mix and refrigerate. Serve over chopped cream cheese as needed. Serve with party crackers.

Mrs. Johnny Cole, *Pots, Pans and Pioneers III*, Louisiana Chapter No. 24

# *Mock Sour Cream*

**1 cup low-fat cottage cheese**
**2 tablespoons skim milk**
**1 tablespoon lemon juice**

Combine cottage cheese, skim milk and lemon juice in blender container. Process at medium speed until smooth. Use as sour cream substitute. Yield: 16 servings.

**Approx Per Serving:** Cal 11; Prot 2 g; Carbo 1 g; Fiber <1 g; T Fat <1 g; Chol 1 mg; Sod 58 mg.

Addie F. Vance, *Carolina Cooking*, North Carolina Chapter No. 35

# *Nacho Dip*

**8 ounces cream cheese, softened**
**1 cup sour cream**
**1 10-ounce can jalapeño bean dip**
**1 envelope chili seasoning mix**
**10 drops of Tabasco sauce**
**1/4 cup taco sauce**
**1 1/4 cups shredded Cheddar cheese**
**1 1/4 cups shredded Monterey Jack cheese**

Blend cream cheese and sour cream in bowl. Stir in bean dip, seasoning mix, Tabasco sauce, taco sauce and half of each cheese. Spoon into 8x12-inch baking dish. Top with remaining cheeses. Bake at 325 degrees for 15 to 20 minutes or until cheese is melted. Serve with tortilla chips. Yield: 96 servings.

**Approx Per Serving:** Cal 31; Prot 1 g; Carbo 1 g; Fiber <1 g; T Fat 2 g; Chol 7 mg; Sod 80 mg.

Darlene Fulton, *Carolina Cooking*, North Carolina Chapter No. 35

## Nacho Dip

2 cans refried beans
1/2 lb. each ground beef and sausage (hot)
2 medium onions, chopped
3/4 tsp. salt
1/4 tsp. pepper
1 1/4 tsp. chili powder
1 tsp. garlic
2 cans green chilies
16 oz. extra sharp cheddar cheese, shredded
1 jar taco sauce—hot or mild

Layer all and chill for a while. Cook at 375 degrees for 45 minutes until bubbly. Serve with nachos or large dip fritos.

Linda Richardson, *Secret Recipes of Telephone Pioneers, Volume III*
South Carolina Chapter No. 61

## Shrimp Fondue

(Microwave)

1 (10 3/4 oz.) can condensed cream of shrimp soup
1 c. shredded Swiss cheese
1/4 c. white wine
1/2 tsp. Worcestershire sauce
French bread, cut into 1 inch cubes

In 1 quart casserole dish, combine soup, cheese, wine, and Worcestershire sauce. Heat for 7 to 8 minutes until cheese is melted, stirring every 2 minutes. Serve hot with French bread. Yield: 4 servings.

Serene Schwartz, *Dogwood Delights Volume II*
Dogwood Chapter No. 84

## Spinach Dip

1 (10 oz.) pkg. chopped spinach
1 1/2 c. sour cream
1 c. mayonnaise
1 pkg. Knorr vegetable soup mix
1 (8 oz.) can water chestnuts, chopped
3 green onions, chopped

Thaw spinach and squeeze until dry. Stir together with remaining ingredients. Blend well. Cover and refrigerate for 2 hours. Stir before serving.

Mary Ann Goodson, *Bell's Best 3*, Mississippi Chapter No. 36

## Spinach Dip

1 (10 oz.) pkg. chopped spinach (uncooked)
1½ c. sour cream
1 c. Hellmann's mayonnaise
1 pkg. Knorr vegetable soup mix
1 (8 oz.) can water chestnuts, chopped
3 green onions, or 1 small white onion, chopped

Thaw and squeeze out water from chopped spinach until dry. Stir together spinach, sour cream, mayonnaise, soup mix, water chestnuts, and onions; mix well. Cover and refrigerate about 2 or 3 hours. Stir before serving.

Real good with Waverly or Escort crackers.

Judy Sporl, *Pots, Pans and Pioneers, Volume IV*
Louisiana Chapter No. 24

## Tuna Dip

1 pkg. cream cheese, softened
1 can tuna
¼ medium onion, finely diced
1 dash Tabasco

Cream together all ingredients in medium size bowl. Delicious.

Makes 6 to 8 servings.

Pam Jolly, *Pioneers Pots and Pans—1985 Cookbook*
North Florida Chapter No. 39

*Easy Access Project for Physically Challenged at Big South Fork National Park.* (Tennessee Chapter No. 21)

## Alligator Balls

1 lb. alligator meat, ground
$1^{1}/_{3}$ c. flour
2 tsp. baking powder
$^{1}/_{2}$ tsp. salt
$^{1}/_{3}$ c. milk
1 egg, beaten
$^{1}/_{2}$ tsp. celery seed
1 tbsp. minced onion
2 bird peppers or $^{1}/_{4}$ tsp. Tabasco

Place ground gator in large bowl. Sift together flour, baking powder and salt. Add to meat.

In small bowl combine milk, eggs and the rest of the ingredients. Add to meat and mix thoroughly. Form into balls. Fry in deep fat or in skillet turning to brown all surfaces. Makes 16 tasty Gator Balls.

Conch may be substituted for alligator, but needs to be washed and marinated in fresh lime juice for 30 minutes to remove slime before grinding.

Jean points out that tame, marshmallow fed alligators are inappropriate for this recipe; first, the marshmallows alter the taste of the meat, and second, no one should ever feed marshmallows to alligators. They are wild creatures and might recognize humans as a food source!!

Jean Smith
*A Tablespoon of Pioneering and a Teaspoon of Horses and the Handicapped*
Florida Gold Coast Chapter No. 83

## Asparagus Rolls

20 slices bread
1 egg, beaten
1 cup shredded sharp Cheddar cheese
8 ounces cream cheese
1 14-ounce can asparagus spears, drained
1 cup melted margarine

Trim crusts from bread. Flatten with rolling pin. Combine egg, softened Cheddar cheese and cream cheese in bowl; mix well. Spread evenly on bread. Place 1 asparagus spear on each slice of bread. Roll to enclose asparagus; secure with wooden picks. Dip in margarine; place on ungreased baking sheet. Freeze until firm. Let stand at room temperature until partially thawed. Cut each roll into 3 pieces. Bake at 375 degrees for 15 minutes or until golden brown. Serve immediately. May substitute 3 ounces bleu cheese for Cheddar cheese. Yield: 60 appetizers.

Pat Hodges, *Lawfully Good Eating*, Dixie Chapter No. 23

# *Asparagus-Cream Cheese Roll-Ups*

**1 package (3 oz.) cream cheese**
**8 pieces bacon, cooked and crumbled**
**12 slices Roman Meal bread, trimmed**
**1 can (14 oz.) asparagus spears**
**Melted Butter**

Flatten bread slightly with a rolling pin. Mix crumbled bacon with cream cheese and spread mixture on each slice of bread. Roll bread around 1 spear. Place on baking sheet. Brush with melted butter and broil until slightly brown. Cut each roll into three pieces and serve hot. Recipe makes 36.

Janie Peach, *Secret Recipes of Telephone Pioneers, Volume II*
South Carolina Chapter No. 61

# *Bacon Rollups*

**1/4 c. butter**
**1/2 c. water**
**1 egg, beaten**
**1 1/2 c. Pepperidge Farm herb stuffing mix**
**1/4 lb. sausage**
**1 lb. bacon, cut in thirds**

Melt butter in water. Remove from heat and stir in stuffing mix. Add egg; mix in raw sausage. Chill. Shape into oblong balls about the size of a walnut. Wrap with bacon strips. Cook on rack in 400° oven until bacon is done, turning once.

Mavis W. O'Rourke, *Pots, Pans and Pioneers III*
Louisiana Chapter No. 24

## *A Helpful Hint*

Wrap thin slices of smoked salmon around cucumber slices or thin slices of prosciutto around melon slices for easy and elegant appetizers.

# Baked Cheese Balls

12 oz. New York sharp cheese, grated
2 sticks margarine, melted
2 c. sifted flour
1/2 tsp. salt
3/4 tsp. red pepper
2 large jars of small green stuffed olives

Mix grated cheese and flour. Add melted margarine and seasonings. Mix well (with hands if needed). Make small balls, putting olive in center. Cook at 450° for 5 minutes on bottom shelf of oven, then 5 minutes on top shelf. Balls may be frozen. Makes 4 to 5 dozen.

*Pots, Pans and Pioneers, Volume I*, Louisiana Chapter No. 24

# Cheese Tempters

1 stick margarine
1/2 pound grated sharp cheese
1/4 teaspoon salt
1 cup and 2 teaspoons self-rising flour
Dash red pepper
1/2 cup chopped nuts

Let margarine soften. Add grated cheese, salt and red pepper. Mix well, adding flour and nuts. Shape into 3 long rolls. Chill several hours or freeze. Cut into thin slices. Bake on ungreased cookie sheet at 350° until lightly browned, approximately 10 to 12 minutes.

Mrs. J. H. Dunn, *Secret Recipes of Telephone Pioneers, Volume I*
South Carolina Chapter No. 61

# Sesame and Cheddar Sticks

1 1/2 cups flour
2 teaspoons sesame seed
1/2 teaspoon salt
4 ounces sharp Cheddar cheese, shredded
1/2 cup butter, softened
3 tablespoons Worcestershire sauce
2 teaspoons cold water

Combine flour, sesame seed and salt in bowl; mix well. Cut in cheese and butter until crumbly. Add mixture of Worcestershire sauce and water; mix well. Shape into ball. Roll to 1/4-inch thickness on floured surface. Cut into 3 1/2-inch strips. Place strips on baking sheet. Bake at 450 degrees for 6 to 8 minutes or until golden brown. Remove to wire rack to cool. Yield: 6 dozen.

Trudi Gadjen, *Kentucky Kitchens, Volume II*, Kentucky Chapter No. 32

# Jalapeño Cheese Squares

4 cups shredded Cheddar cheese
4 eggs, beaten
4 jalapeños, peeled, seeded, chopped
1 teaspoon minced onion

Combine cheese, beaten eggs, jalapeños and onion in bowl; mix well. Spread in ungreased 8-inch square baking dish. Bake at 350 degrees for 45 to 60 minutes or until knife inserted near center comes out clean. Let stand for 10 minutes. Cut into squares. Yield: 36 servings.

**Approx Per Serving:** Cal 61; Prot 4 g; Carbo 1 g; Fiber <1 g; T Fat 5 g; Chol 37 mg; Sod 86 mg.

Cheryl Griffin, *Carolina Cooking*, North Carolina Chapter No. 35

# Golden Chicken Nuggets

4 chicken breast filets
1/2 cup dry bread crumbs
1/4 cup Parmesan cheese
1 teaspoon basil
1 teaspoon thyme
1/2 cup melted margarine

Rinse chicken and pat dry. Cut into bite-sized pieces. Combine bread crumbs, cheese, basil and thyme in bowl; mix well. Dip chicken in margarine; coat with crumb mixture. Place on foil-lined baking sheet. Bake at 400 degrees for 10 minutes. Arrange on serving plate. Yield: 20 servings.

**Approx Per Serving:** Cal 113; Prot 12 g; Carbo 2 g; Fiber 0 g; T Fat 6 g; Chol 30 mg; Sod 120 mg.
**Dietary Exchanges:** Meat 1 1/2; Fat 1

"*Answering the Call of Those in Need*," Tennessee Chapter No. 21

## A Helpful Hint

Help your family select nutritious snacks: keep cut-up raw vegetables in the refrigerator with a supply of yogurt or bean dip; make frozen juice pops in an ice cube tray or freeze grapes, pineapple, banana chunks or other fresh fruit; stock up on snacks high in carbohydrates and low in fat, such as bagels, pretzels and English muffins.

## Rumaki

**12 chicken livers**
**12 water chestnuts**
**12 slices bacon**
**1/4 cup lemon juice**
**1/4 cup soy sauce**
**1/4 cup oil**
**3 tablespoons catsup**
**1 teaspoon liquid garlic**
**1/2 teaspoon pepper**
**1/2 cup packed brown sugar**

Cut chicken livers, water chestnuts and bacon slices into halves. Wrap each liver half and water chestnut half together with 1/2 bacon slice, securing with pick. Place in shallow dish. Combine lemon juice, soy sauce, oil, catsup, garlic and pepper in bowl; mix well. Pour over chicken livers. Marinate in refrigerator overnight, turning occasionally. Coat each appetizer with brown sugar. Place on rack in baking pan. Bake at 450 degrees for 10 minutes. Turn appetizers over. Bake for 15 minutes longer. Yield: 2 dozen appetizers.

Peggy Posante, *Kentucky Kitchens, Volume II*, Kentucky Chapter No. 32

## Cheese Wafers

**1 lb. sharp Cheddar cheese**
**1 lb. butter**
**1/4 tsp. salt**
**4 c. flour**
**1/4 tsp. cayenne**

Grate Cheese and mix with butter at room temperature. Add flour, salt and cayenne. Mix well, using hands. Make small balls, rolling in palms of hands. Place on ungreased baking sheet. Press half a pecan in center of each ball, mashing in well. Bake at 425° for 20 to 25 minutes.

These do not get brown. These freeze really well.

Barbara C. Hendrick, *Kentucky Kitchens, Volume I*
Kentucky Chapter No. 32

### A Helpful Hint

Freeze chicken livers and wings until you have enough for a party appetizer. Livers make excellent paté and wings are delicious cooked in a barbecue sauce.

# Crab Stuffed Snow Peas

- 1/2 lb. fresh snow peas
- 2 6 oz. pkgs. frozen crabmeat—thawed and well chilled
- 3 Tbsp. mayonnaise
- 1 Tbsp. lemon juice
- 3 dashes bottled red pepper sauce
- 2 hard cooked eggs, finely chopped
- 3 Tbsp. finely chopped celery
- 1 tsp. capers

Wash and trim snow peas. Split on top side, leaving bottom intact to form a little boat. Blanch in lightly salted water 10 seconds, then submerge in cold water. Remove, drain, cool (may be covered and refrigerated up to 24 hours). Combine all ingredients. Stir gently and stuff with one teaspoonful of filling. Refrigerate up to 6 hours. Recipe makes 60. (15 calories each)

Martha Lemond, *Secret Recipes of Telephone Pioneers, Volume III*
South Carolina Chapter No. 61

# Marinated Crab Claws

(Exact duplicate from Ernest's supper club)

- 1 c. onions, minced
- 1/2 c. parsley, minced
- 2 ribs celery, minced
- 2 garlic cloves, pressed
- 1 c. olive oil
- 1/2 c. tarragon vinegar
- 2 Tbsp. lemon juice
- Crab claws, either fresh or canned

Mix ingredients and pour over crab claws. Marinate 2 or 3 hours. Mixture may be placed in tightly sealed container in refrigerator until ready for use. When serving, have hot crusty bread and butter to "sop" with.

Marilou Bridges, *Pots, Pans and Pioneers, Volume I*
Louisiana Chapter No. 24

# Easy Stuffed Crabs

**1 lb. crabmeat**
**3/4 to 1 stick butter or oleo**
**1 medium chopped onion**
**1/3 c. parsley**
**3 toes chopped garlic**
**1/3 c. chopped celery**
**6 Tbsp. plain bread crumbs**
**1 beaten egg**

Melt butter or oleo. Sauté all seasonings, except parsley. Add crabmeat. Mix with seasonings. Add plain bread crumbs. Mix well. Throw in parsley and cook 5 to 10 minutes. Add salt, pepper, and cayenne to taste.

Marian Alcantara, *Pots, Pans and Pioneers, Volume IV*
Louisiana Chapter No. 24

# Hanky Pankys

**1 lb. sausage (hot)**
**1 1/2 lb. ground beef**
**1 lb. Velveeta cheese**
**Hot sauce to taste**
**1 small loaf cocktail rye bread**
**Worcestershire sauce to taste**

Fry sausage and beef together; drain fat, put cheese in and stir till melted. Add hot sauce and Worcestershire sauce. Spread on bread. Place on cookie sheet and broil for 2–3 minutes.

Elaine Taylor, *Dogwood Delights*, Dogwood Chapter No. 84

# Foolproof Mushrooms

**3 tbsp. grated Parmesan cheese**
**1 pkg. (4 to 5 oz.) garlic-herb cheese spread, softened**
**32 sm. mushrooms, stems removed**

Preheat oven to 400 degrees. Spray a cookie sheet or jelly roll pan with no-stick spray.

In a small bowl combine 2 tablespoons of Parmesan with cheese spread. Blend well. Spoon a small amount (or more if you want) into each mushroom cap. Sprinkle remaining Parmesan over tops of mushrooms. Bake at 400 degrees 8 to 10 minutes until lightly browned on top.

This easy to make appetizer can be made well ahead of time. Just cover and refrigerate up to 4 hours before baking. Should be served hot.

Sue Gerry
*A Tablespoon of Pioneering and a Teaspoon of Horses and the Handicapped*
Florida Gold Coast Chapter No. 83

# Hot Mushroom Turnovers

**Cream Cheese Pastry:**

**8 oz. cream cheese**
**1/2 cup margarine**
**1 1/2 cups flour**

Mix well. Wrap in wax paper and refrigerate 1 hour or overnight.

**Filling:**

**3 Tbsp. margarine**
**3 Tbsp. minced shallots**
**1/2 lb. mushrooms, finely minced**
**1/2 tsp. salt**
**1/4 tsp. nutmeg**
**1/4 tsp. thyme**
**2 Tbsp. flour**
**1/4 cup sour cream**

Melt margarine and sauté shallots and mushrooms. Stir in seasonings and flour. Blend in sour cream. Let cool. Bring dough to room temperature. Roll out one-half dough at a time on floured board. Roll thin and cut 2 inch circles with cookie cutter or glass. Brush edge of circles with beaten egg. Place 1/2 tsp. mushroom on each circle. Fold in half. Press edges together with fork. Prick tops of tarts. Brush with beaten egg. Place on ungreased sheet and bake at 450 degrees for 12–15 minutes. Best when turnovers are baked and frozen, then reheated just before serving. Serve warm.

Martha Lemond, *Secret Recipes of Telephone Pioneers, Volume III*
South Carolina Chapter No. 61

*Clowns with Cancer Clinic children.* (South Carolina Chapter No. 61)

## Nachos Supreme

2 to 3 doz. Tostitos crispy round tortilla chips (traditional flavor)
1 c. grated sharp Cheddar cheese
1 c. grated Monterey Jack cheese
1 to 2 small onions, chopped
1 to 2 medium green peppers or hot peppers, chopped
2 to 3 Tbsp. chopped green onions (with tops)
1 to 2 tomatoes, chopped
12 to 24 Spanish olives, sliced
1 to 4 tsp. hot or mild taco sauce (optional)
2 to 4 Tbsp. sour cream (optional)

Place 6 to 8 Tostitos on each of 4 to 6 paper plates or microwave-safe glass plates. Top each with approximately 1 tablespoon grated cheeses; sprinkle with green peppers and both onions. Microwave on HIGH (10) for 30 seconds. Top with tomatoes and sliced olives; microwave another 15 to 30 seconds or until cheese is completely melted. Do not overcook! Remove from oven. Top with taco sauce or a small dollop of sour cream and an olive slice. Serves 3 to 4.

Conventional cooking instructions: Can also be prepared by baking for 5 to 7 minutes in a 500° oven.

"As good as the ones in restaurants! So Easy!"

Bev Brodie, *Dogwood Delights Volume II*, Dogwood Chapter No. 84

## Onion Squares

3 cups bisquick
1 cup beer
3/4 cup sour cream
1 (0.56) package green onion dip mix
1 egg

Combine bisquick and beer; stir well. Spoon dough into well greased 9-inch square baking dish. Combine sour cream and onion dip mix and eggs. Spread mixture over bisquick mixture.

Bake for 20 minutes in 9-inch square pyrex pan at 400°. Cut into 3-inch squares and serve warm. Recipe serves 6–8.

Edna Gray, *Secret Recipes of Telephone Pioneers, Volume II*
South Carolina Chapter No. 61

## *Potato Skin (Like Bennigan's)*

potatoes
bacon, cooked well and crumbled
cheddar cheese, grated
sour cream
chives or green onions

Bake or microwave desired amount of potatoes until done. Cut in half and scoop out center, leaving about 1/4 inch of potato around the skin. Deep fry potato skin until light brown and crispy. Drain well. Sprinkle grated cheese in the center of each and place in oven just until cheese melts. Top with crumbled bacon and serve with sour cream and chives.

Betty Poland, *Pioneers Pots and Pans—1985 Cookbook*
North Florida Chapter No. 39

## *Bite-Sized Salmon Balls*

1 small (7 3/4 oz.) can salmon
1 egg, beaten
1/4 c. mayonnaise
1/4 c. Cheddar cheese
1 c. crushed cheese crackers
1/4 c. each chopped dill pickles and olives

Mix well. Shape into 1-inch balls. Place on baking sheet. Bake at 375° F. for 10–15 minutes until golden brown. Makes 5 dozen.

Helen Henderson, *Dogwood Delights*, Dogwood Chapter No. 84

## *Sausage Balls*

1 pound hot or mild sausage
10 ounces sharp Cheddar cheese, shredded
3 cups buttermilk baking mix

Combine sausage, cheese and baking mix in bowl; mix well. Shape into small balls. Place on baking sheet. Bake at 350 degrees for 25 to 30 minutes or until brown. Drain. May add milk or water and beef bouillon granules for variation. May be frozen and reheated.
Yield: 80 sausage balls.

*Kentucky Kitchens, Volume II*, Kentucky Chapter No. 32

## Sweet and Sour Sausage

2 Tbsp. cornstarch
1/2 c. sugar
1/2 c. vinegar
1 Tbsp. soy sauce
1 green pepper, chopped
1 large can pineapple chunks
2 pkg. Oscar Meyer smoky links

Simmer sausage in small amount of water for 20 minutes. Drain. Cut meat into 4 or 5 pieces. Add other ingredients and simmer for 1 hour.

Mrs. Ralph E. Anderson, *Bell's Best 3*, Mississippi Chapter No. 36

## Marinated Shrimp

5 to 6 lb. shrimp, boiled and peeled
4 pkg. Good Seasons Italian dressing
4 pkg. Good Seasons herb and garlic dressing
1 to 2 purple onions, chopped large
1 to 2 yellow onions, chopped large
1 jar jalapeño pepper slices, drained
1 jar sweet banana pepper slices (undrained)
Olive oil
Vinegar

In large container, place shrimp, onions, and peppers. Mix dressings, one at a time, by directions, except use 1/2 olive oil. Add to mixture till covered. Place in airtight container and store in refrigerator. Stir or shake every day. Good after 6 days. Better every day. Keeps for months.

Quida Rawls, *Bell's Best 3*, Mississippi Chapter No. 36

## Marinated or Pickled Shrimp

2 1/2 pounds cooked shrimp (small)
1/2 cup celery tops (chopped)
1/4 cup mixed pickling spices
3 1/2 tablespoons salt
2 cups sliced onions
7 bay leaves

Place all of the above in a large bowl, and add:

1 1/4 cups salad oil
1 cup white vinegar
2 1/2 tablespoons capers
2 1/2 tablespoons celery salt
Dash of Tabasco
1/2 tablespoon mustard

Pour over shrimp, cover and chill for 5 or 6 days. Stir once daily. Serves 20.

Mrs. Jennie Lancaster, *Secret Recipes of Telephone Pioneers, Volume I*
South Carolina Chapter No. 61

# Party Turnovers

1 env. onion soup mix
1 c. shredded Cheddar cheese
1 lb. ground beef
3 pkg. crescent rolls

Preheat oven to 375°. In medium skillet, combine onion soup mix and meat; brown well. Blend in cheese. Separate crescent rolls according to package directions. Cut in halves. Place spoonful of meat mixture in center of each triangle, fold over and seal edges. Place on greased cookie sheet and bake 15 minutes or until golden brown.

Pam Cown, *Dogwood Delights*, Dogwood Chapter No. 84

# Veggie Bites

2 8-count cans crescent rolls
1 egg, beaten
16 ounces cream cheese, softened
1 cup mayonnaise
1 envelope ranch salad dressing mix
1/2 cup finely chopped cauliflower
1/2 cup finely chopped broccoli
1/2 cup finely chopped mushrooms
1/2 cup finely chopped green bell pepper
1/2 cup finely chopped tomato
3/4 cup shredded Cheddar cheese

Unroll crescent roll dough. Spread in 10x15-inch baking sheet, sealing perforations. Brush with egg. Bake at 375 degrees for 11 to 13 minutes or until light brown. Cool. Beat cream cheese, mayonnaise and salad dressing mix in mixer bowl until smooth. Spread over baked layer. Sprinkle with next 5 ingredients. Top with cheese. Chill for 2 hours. Cut into 1x1 1/2-inch pieces. Yield: 96 servings.

**Approx Per Serving:** Cal 53; Prot 1 g; Carbo 3 g; Fiber <1 g; T Fat 4 g; 73% Calories from Fat; Chol 10 mg; Sod 95 mg.

Jim Meeks, *Calling All Cooks three*, Alabama Chapter No. 34

## A Helpful Hint

Substitute tortillas, split pita rounds, English muffins or split French loaves for the traditional crust for quick and easy pizza snacks.

# Vegetable Pizza

2 (8 oz.) pkgs. crescent rolls
1 (8 oz.) pkg. cream cheese, softened
1 c. mayonnaise
2 tsp. dill (dried)
1 or 2 tsp. garlic powder or garlic salt
2 or 3 green onions
Broccoli (cut into flowerets)
1 tomato, peeled and chopped
1 green and/or red pepper
Yellow squash, sliced
Mushrooms, sliced

Unroll crescent rolls and flatten dough onto cookie sheet and bake as directed on package. Let cool completely.

In a medium sized bowl, mix cream cheese, mayonnaise, dill weed and garlic powder until smooth. Spread mixture evenly over cooled crust. Sprinkle chopped vegetables over crust. Press down slightly, so vegetables will adhere to cream cheese. Refrigerate and cut into squares to serve.

Laurie Moegenburg
*A Tablespoon of Pioneering and a Teaspoon of Horses and the Handicapped*
Florida Gold Coast Chapter No. 83

# Vegetable Squares

2 cans Pillsbury Crescent Rolls
2 (8 oz.) pkgs. cream cheese
1 pkg. Hidden Valley Ranch dressing
1 c. mayonnaise
1 c. shredded Cheddar cheese
3/4 c. each any of the following raw vegetables: carrots, broccoli, cauliflower, squash, zucchini, onion, green pepper, tomato, mushrooms, etc.

Press crescent rolls out flat on bottom of cookie sheet, then bake according to package directions. Let cool completely.

Mix together softened cream cheese, Ranch dressing and mayonnaise and spread over cooled crust. Then, top with any combination of the raw vegetables chopped very fine. Top with shredded cheese.

Terri Parker
*A Tablespoon of Pioneering and a Teaspoon of Horses and the Handicapped*
Florida Gold Coast Chapter No. 83

# *Banana Punch*

6 c. water
4 c. white sugar
3 c. pineapple juice
4 large *ripe* bananas
3 c. orange juice (6 oz. can frozen plus 2 cans water)
1 can frozen lemonade (or 4–5 lemons)
2 bottles lemon-lime beverage

Put orange juice and bananas (chopped) and lemonade in blender and liquefy. In large bowl or pot, mix sugar and water until sugar dissolves. Add pineapple juice and orange, lemon and banana mixture. Mix well. Freeze in small containers (1 pound butter dishes). When ready to serve, let thaw 1 hour. Chop semi-thawed punch into punch bowl and add 2 bottles of lemon-lime beverage.

Jane Roe, *Dining with Pioneers, Volume II*, Tennessee Chapter No. 21

# *Champagne Punch*

1/5 champagne
1/2 (#4) can pineapple juice
1 small can frozen orange juice
1/5 sauterne
16 oz. pkg. strawberries
1/2 bottle sparkling water

Mix ingredients together and stir lightly. Pour over decorative ice mold.

Linda Angley, *Pioneers Pots and Pans—1985 Cookbook*
North Florida Chapter No. 39

# *Perky Cranberry Punch*

2 32-ounce bottles of cranberry juice cocktail
1 46-ounce can unsweetened pineapple juice
2 cups water
1 1/3 cups packed brown sugar
2 tablespoons allspice
1 to 2 tablespoons whole cloves
12 2-inch cinnamon sticks

Mix cranberry juice, pineapple juice, water and brown sugar in 30-cup percolator, stirring until brown sugar dissolves. Place allspice, cloves and cinnamon sticks in percolator basket. Perk through complete cycle of electric percolator. Serve hot. Yield: 20 servings.

**Approx Per Serving:** Cal 141; Prot <1 g; Carbo 36 g; Fiber 1 g; T Fat <1 g; 1% Calories from Fat; Chol 0 mg; Sod 8 mg.

Glenda K. Beck, *Calling All Cooks three*, Alabama Chapter No. 34

# Fruit Punch

- 1 12-ounce can frozen orange juice concentrate
- 1 12-ounce can frozen lemonade concentrate
- 1 46-ounce can pineapple juice
- 4 cups strong sweetened tea
- 1 4-ounce jar maraschino cherries

Combine juice concentrates, pineapple juice, tea and maraschino cherries in large pitcher; mix well. Chill, tightly covered, until serving time. Pour into punch bowl. Yield: 20 servings.

**Approx Per Serving:** Cal 118; Prot 1 g; Carbo 30 g; Fiber 1 g; T Fat <1 g; Chol 0 mg; Sod 2 mg.

Madelon Haskin, *Carolina Cooking*, North Carolina Chapter No. 35

# Golden Fruit Punch

- 1 (12 oz.) can frozen orange juice concentrate, thawed (undiluted)
- 1 (12 oz.) can frozen lemonade concentrate, thawed (undiluted)
- 1 (46 oz.) can unsweetened pineapple juice
- 1 qt. apricot nectar
- 2 c. unsweetened grapefruit juice
- 2/3 c. sugar
- 1 (33.8 oz.) bottle ginger ale, chilled
- Orange slices (optional)
- Lemon slices (optional)

Combine juices and sugar in a punch bowl; stir until sugar dissolves. Chill. To serve, add ginger ale and ice cubes or ring. Garnish with orange and lemon slices if desired. Yield: About 4½ quarts. *Good.*

Served at Mask Ball.

Dot Trinkner, *Bell's Best 3*, Mississippi Chapter No. 36

# *Kahlua*

4½ c. water
3½ c. sugar
1 c. dry instant coffee (eg. 2 oz. of Yuban or Maxwell House)
1 quart vodka
1 vanilla bean, split lengthwise

Boil sugar and water together for 5 minutes. Remove from heat. Stir in coffee, a little at a time. Return to heat; bring to a boil. Remove from heat; let cool. When cool, add vodka. Pour into a gallon container over the vanilla bean. After 10 days, remove the bean and bottle.

P.S. You can drink it any time after this, but it gets better as it ages a little.

G. W. Sitgreaves, *Pioneers Pots and Pans—1985 Cookbook*
North Florida Chapter No. 39

# *Lemon Champagne Punch*

1 (12 oz.) can frozen lemonade (undiluted)
1 (46 oz.) can unsweetened pineapple juice
1 fifth Rhine wine
Ice mold (frozen with whole strawberries inside)
2 fifths inexpensive champagne

Mix lemonade, pineapple juice, and Rhine wine in punch bowl. Add ice mold. Add champagne just before serving. Makes 35 to 40 punch cups. (If cups are small, you can easily get 50.)

Very refreshing for a summer open house or patio party.

Mrs. W. Boone Nall (Carmen), *Dogwood Delights Volume II*
Dogwood Chapter No. 84

### *A Helpful Hint*

Freeze fruit or edible flowers in ice cube trays to serve in drinks.

# *Party Punch*

- 2 large cans orange juice, chilled
- 2 large cans pineapple juice, chilled
- 2 large bottles ginger ale, chilled
- 1/2 gal. pineapple sherbet or your favorite

Pour chilled juices and ginger ale in large container. Add sherbet. Ice if desired.

Mary Weekes, *Pots, Pans and Pioneers, Volume IV*
Louisiana Chapter No. 24

# *Tea Punch*

- 1 large bottle of concentrated lemon juice
- 6 small cans frozen orange juice (not diluted)
- 3 cups strong tea (brew 2 teaspoons tea and 1 cup water)
- 3 cups sugar into hot tea
- 4 quarts Ginger Ale

Mix well. Makes approximately 2 gallons.

Mrs. Mary E. Robinson, *Secret Recipes of Telephone Pioneers, Volume I*
South Carolina Chapter No. 61

# *River Commission Punch*

- 18 fresh lemons
- 18 fresh oranges
- 1 large (2 lb.) can sweetened pineapple juice
- 3 c. sugar
- 5 qt. ginger ale

Squeeze juice from lemons and oranges, saving rind from 2 lemons and 2 oranges. Cut up and cook rinds in approximately 1 cup water for 3 to 4 minutes. Remove rind and strain juice into large container. Add lemon, orange, and pineapple juices. If necessary, add enough water to make 5 quarts. Mix well. Freeze in quart containers. Thaw frozen mixture for 1 to 3 hours.

Margie Sasser, *Bell's Best 3*, Mississippi Chapter No. 36

# Shower Punch

*Mix together:*

½ gallon water
2 c. sugar
4 regular packs Kool-Aid (any flavor desired)

*Then add:*

1 (46 oz.) can pink grapefruit juice
1 (46 oz.) can grapefruit and pineapple drink
½ gallon Farmbest cherry nugget ice cream or any flavor desired

Add enough ice to float in punch bowl just to chill. This is better if you will mix the ingredients all except the ice cream the day before, as this will cause the flavors to blend together.

Makes approximately 50 to 75 servings.

Ethel Boone, *Pioneers Pots and Pans—1985 Cookbook*
North Florida Chapter No. 39

# Slush Punch

1 3-ounce package any flavor gelatin
2 cups sugar
3 cups boiling water
1 46-ounce can pineapple juice
1 6-ounce can frozen lemonade concentrate
1 tablespoon almond extract
5 cups cold water

Dissolve gelatin and sugar in boiling water in bowl. Combine gelatin mixture with pineapple juice, lemonade concentrate, almond extract and cold water in large freezer container. Freeze for 3 to 4 days. Let thaw for 6 hours before serving; stir. Pour into punch bowl; ladle into punch cups. Yield: 20 servings.

**Approx Per Serving:** Cal 154; Prot 1 g; Carbo 39 g; Fiber 1 g; T Fat <1 g; <1% Calories from Fat; Chol 0 mg; Sod 12 mg.

Betty C. Gray, *Calling All Cooks three*, Alabama Chapter No. 34

## A Helpful Hint

Sweeten beverages with sugar stored in a jar with lemon or orange zest.

# *Smoothie*

**1/2 frozen banana**
**2 large frozen strawberries**
**1 1/2 c. apple juice**
**2 ice cubes**

Blend in blender until fruits are all liquid and drink is bubbly.

**Helpful Hint:** Peel bananas and cut in halves; place in Ziploc freezer bags. Clean strawberries and pull off tops. Drain on paper towel. Place berries (whole) in Ziploc freezer bags. Keep these frozen and you'll always be ready for a smoothie.

Doris Beeler, *Kentucky Kitchens, Volume I*, Kentucky Chapter No. 32

# *Tangy Tutti-Fruitti Punch*

**1/2 c. fresh lemon juice**
**1 c. pineapple juice**
**2 cans (6 oz.) frozen orange juice**
**1/4 c. maraschino cherry juice, optional**

Mix. Add 2 quarts ginger ale. Yield: 25 punch cups.
To "Punch-Up," add 1 1/2 quarts light rum or champagne.

Mrs. Charles Toops, *Pioneers Pots and Pans—1985 Cookbook*
North Florida Chapter No. 39

# *Tropical Fruit Punch*

**juice of 5 oranges**
**juice of 3 lemons**
**2 large bananas, sliced**
**1/2 c. rum**
**1/2 c. honey**
**1/4 c. crushed pineapple, drained**
**1/4 c. banana-flavored liqueur**
**2 Tbsp. grenadine syrup**

Combine all ingredients in a large bowl, stirring well. Pour half of punch mixture into container of electric blender. Process until smooth. Repeat process with remaining punch mixture. Serve over ice.
Yield: 5 1/2 cups.

Margaret Stalling, *Pioneers Pots and Pans—1985 Cookbook*
North Florida Chapter No. 39

# *Crock•Pot Wassail*

**2 quarts apple juice**
**1 pint cranberry juice**
**3/4 cup sugar**
**1 teaspoon aromatic bitters**
**2 cinnamon sticks**
**1 teaspoon whole allspice**
**1 small orange, peeled**
**Whole cloves**
**1 cup rum (optional)**

Pour apple juice, cranberry juice, sugar, bitters, cinnamon and allspice into Crock•Pot. Stud orange with cloves. Add to juice mixture. Add rum. Cook on High for 1 hour. Simmer on Low for 4 to 8 hours. Serve warm. May substitute apple cider for apple juice. Yield: 12 cups.

Dennis Bryan, *Kentucky Kitchens, Volume II*, Kentucky Chapter No. 32

# *Corned Beef Sandwiches*

**3 cups sharp grated cheese**
**1/2 jar mustard (small size)**
**1 stick butter**
**1 can corned beef**

Preheat oven at 350°. Melt butter, add to cheese. Chop corned beef and mix with butter and cheese; add mustard. Spread on thin fresh sliced bread. Roll sandwiches corner to corner and roll in wax paper. Twist ends to secure roll. Store in refrigerator overnight or freeze. Toast for 30 minutes or until brown. Makes 25 or 30. For fancy sandwiches, trim bread ends. For hearty man-pleasers, leave crust on.

Mrs. Harry R. Marsh, *Secret Recipes of Telephone Pioneers, Volume I*
South Carolina Chapter No. 61

# *Chicken Salad Sandwich Filling*

**3 chicken breasts, cooked and finely chopped**
**3/4 c. finely chopped celery**
**1/2 c. pickle relish, drained well**
**3 hard cooked eggs***
**3/4 c. mayonnaise**
**Salt and pepper to taste**

Mix all ingredients together and spread on bread. Decorate with bits of hard cooked egg, parsley, and pimento. Yield: 100 small sandwiches.

*Use 2 1/2 eggs finely chopped in the salad; save 1/2 egg to decorate sandwiches.

Beth Harbour, *Bell's Best 3*, Mississippi Chapter No. 36

# Open-Face Cucumber Sandwiches

½ pkg. Good Seasons Italian salad dressing mix
2 level Tbsp. mayonnaise
8 oz. cream cheese
1 loaf party rye
Cucumber and dill

Mix cream cheese, Italian dressing mix, and mayonnaise. Whip until creamy. Spread on slices of party rye. Lay 2 very thin slices of cucumber on top. Sprinkle with dill weed.

Frances P. Breeden, *Bell's Best 3*, Mississippi Chapter No. 36

# Egg Salad Sandwiches

2 hard-cooked eggs, chopped
¼ c. finely chopped celery
2 tsp. chopped parsley
¾ tsp. chopped pimento
⅛ tsp. salt
Dash of pepper
3 Tbsp. mayonnaise or salad dressing
6 slices buttered toast
1 tomato, sliced
4 slices bacon, cooked
2 lettuce leaves

Combine chopped eggs, celery, parsley, pimento, salt and pepper; add mayonnaise and mix well. Spread 2 slices of toast with egg mixture; top each with another slice of toast. Arrange tomato slices, bacon and lettuce on top of toast. Top with remaining toast. Cut each sandwich into quarters to serve, using wooden picks to hold layers together. Yield: 2 servings.

Eurcle Culipher, *Bell's Best 2*, Mississippi Chapter No. 36

# Vegetable Sandwich

1 large pkg. cream cheese (8 oz.)
1 small cucumber (peeled)
3 Tbsp. Mayonnaise
cayenne pepper
3 small carrots
1 small onion
1 tsp. salt

Grind or grate vegetables. Drain well. Add mayonnaise to cheese and mix well. Add vegetables and mix well. Add salt and cayenne pepper (two shakes and taste!). Makes 12 sandwiches. May be refrigerated a couple days before spreading, or sandwiches may be frozen for several days after they are made.

Mary Strickland, *Secret Recipes of Telephone Pioneers, Volume III*
South Carolina Chapter No. 61

# Sandwiches

**Combine Cheese With:**

- Grated American cheese, dried beef, chili sauce
- Blue cheese with turkey or ham, sliced
- Swiss cheese slices, deviled ham, pickles
- Cottage cheese, celery and green pepper
- Sharp cheese spread, sliced salami, mustard.

**Mix Hard-Cooked Eggs With:**

- Grated raw carrot, sliced ripe olives, mayonnaise
- Chopped chicken, celery, onions, mayonnaise
- Deviled ham, chopped pickles, mustard, mayonnaise
- Tuna or salmon, celery, pickle relish, mayonnaise.

**Use Meat or Poultry With:**

- Apple, celery, mayonnaise, with chopped cooked chicken
- Nuts, green olives, mayonnaise with chopped cooked chicken
- Celery, grated onion, chili sauce, and mayonnaise with chopped roast beef
- American cheese, dill pickle, and mayonnaise with ground ham
- Green pepper, celery, mayonnaise with chopped roast pork

**Use peanut Butter With:**

- Chopped crisp bacon, raw apple
- Grated raw carrot, chopped raisins, or celery
- Chopped dates or figs, lemon juice
- Deviled ham, chopped dill pickles, mayonnaise.

**Use Raw Vegetables:**

- Chopped cabbage, dried apricots, nuts, mayonnaise
- Chopped cabbage, peanuts, grated carrots, mayonnaise
- Grated carrot, minced celery, green pepper, mayonnaise
- Grated carrot, raisins, chopped peanuts, mayonnaise.

**Use Softened Cream Cheese With:**

- Chopped cooked dried prunes and apricots
- Chopped crisp bacon, pickle relish
- Dried beef, minced onion, chili sauce
- Chopped dates or figs, peanuts
- Chopped green pepper, olives, and celery
- Finely chopped peanuts, minced onion, mayonnaise.

Mae Jeter, *Secret Recipes of Telephone Pioneers, Volume II*
South Carolina Chapter No. 61

# Oyster Cracker Snacks

**1 large envelope ranch salad dressing mix**
**2/3 cup oil**
**2 teaspoons dillweed**
**2 11-ounce packages oyster crackers**

Combine salad dressing mix and oil in bowl; mix well. Stir in dillweed. Pour over crackers in large bowl. Mix by hand until all liquid is absorbed by crackers. Store in airtight container. Will keep for 1 week. Yield: 16 servings.

**Approx Per Serving:** Cal 244; Prot 4 g; Carbo 28 g; Fiber 1 g; T Fat 14 g; Chol 0 mg; Sod 489 mg.
Nutritional information does not include salad dressing mix.

Priscilla Wise, *Carolina Cooking*, North Carolina Chapter No. 35

# Quick Snack

**1/2 cup margarine**
**1 6-ounce package chocolate chips**
**1 cup peanut butter**
**1 17-ounce package Rice Chex cereal**
**1 pound confectioners' sugar**

Melt margarine, chocolate chips and peanut butter in saucepan, stirring constantly. Place cereal in large bowl. Pour chocolate mixture over top, stirring until cereal is well coated. Add confectioners' sugar; mix well. Store in airtight container. Yield: 1 recipe.

Pat Cole, *Kentucky Kitchens, Volume II*, Kentucky Chapter No. 32

# Glazed Almonds

**1 c. whole, blanched almonds**
**1/2 c. sugar**
**2 Tbsp. butter**
**1/2 tsp. vanilla**

Heat almonds, sugar and butter in heavy saucepan or skillet over medium heat. Stir constantly until almonds are toasted and sugar is golden brown, 15 minutes. Add vanilla; spread nuts on foil, sprinkle with salt. Cool; break into clusters.

Sherry Marks, *Dogwood Delights*, Dogwood Chapter No. 84

# *Irresistible Cinnamon Nuts*

(Warning: these are dangerously good!)

**4 c. (1 lb.) mixed, fresh shelled, unsalted nuts (select from pecans, walnuts, almonds or hazelnuts; do not use peanuts)**
**6 tbsp. unsalted butter, cut into pieces**
**2 egg whites**
**Pinch of salt**
**½ to 1 tsp. ground cinnamon**
**6 tbsp. granulated sugar**

Shake nuts in a colander to remove pieces of shell, nut skin or small pieces of nuts that might burn when roasting. Spread nuts on a rimmed baking sheet, such as a jelly roll pan, and roast in a 325 degree oven for 15 to 20 minutes or until lightly browned, stirring occasionally. Remove from oven and set aside until completely cooled. Transfer nuts to a bowl. Wipe can clean.

Line the same rimmed baking sheet with heavy duty foil. Melt butter on pan in a 325 degree oven.

Meanwhile, in a large mixing bowl (preferably stainless steel), with electric mixer on high speed, beat egg whites and the pinch of salt until stiff. Stir cinnamon into sugar (using the greater amount if it's your favorite spice). Gradually beat sugar mixture into the egg whites 1 tablespoon at a time, beating well after each addition. Continue beating until it becomes a very thick meringue.

Fold cooled nuts into meringue, making sure they are well coated. Spread nuts over top of melted butter. Bake in a 325 degree oven 25 to 30 minutes, stirring every 10 minutes with a wooden spoon. (This is important if nuts are to brown evenly.)

During the final 10 minutes of baking, nuts may be sufficiently browned; watch closely. Remove from oven to wire rack and let cool completely. Store in an airtight container. Makes enough for 2 delicious gifts.

Ann Hemingway
*A Tablespoon of Pioneering and a Teaspoon of Horses and the Handicapped*
Florida Gold Coast Chapter No. 83

## *A Helpful Hint*

At parties, set up the drink station away from the food to avoid overcrowding.

# Roasted Pecans

**1/2 cup melted margarine**
**3 tablespoons Worcestershire sauce**
**1 1/2 teaspoons garlic salt**
**1/2 teaspoon onion salt**
**4 cups chopped pecans**

Combine melted margarine, Worcestershire sauce, garlic salt and onion salt in large bowl; mix well. Stir in pecans. Spread on lightly greased baking sheet. Bake at 350 degrees for 45 minutes, stirring frequently. Drain on paper towel. Yield: 16 servings.

**Approx Per Serving:** Cal 252; Prot 2 g; Carbo 6 g; Fiber 2 g; T Fat 26 g; Chol 0 mg; Sod 287 mg.

Amanda Tucker, *Carolina Cooking*, North Carolina Chapter No. 35

# Special Toasted Pecans

**1 egg white, beaten**
**1 tablespoon water**
**2 cups pecan halves**
**1/2 cup sugar**
**1 teaspoon cinnamon**
**3/4 teaspoon salt**
**1/4 teaspoon ground cloves**
**1/4 teaspoon nutmeg**

Combine beaten egg white, water and pecans in bowl; mix well. Spread in lightly greased baking dish. Combine sugar, cinnamon, salt, cloves and nutmeg in bowl; mix well. Sprinkle over pecan mixture; stir until pecans are coated. Bake at 300 degrees for 30 minutes, stirring 3 times. Yield: 10 servings.

**Approx Per Serving:** Cal 184; Prot 2 g; Carbo 14 g; Fiber 1 g; T Fat 15 g; Chol 0 mg; Sod 165 mg.

Joanne Tallent, *Carolina Cooking*, North Carolina Chapter No. 35

# Soups & Salads

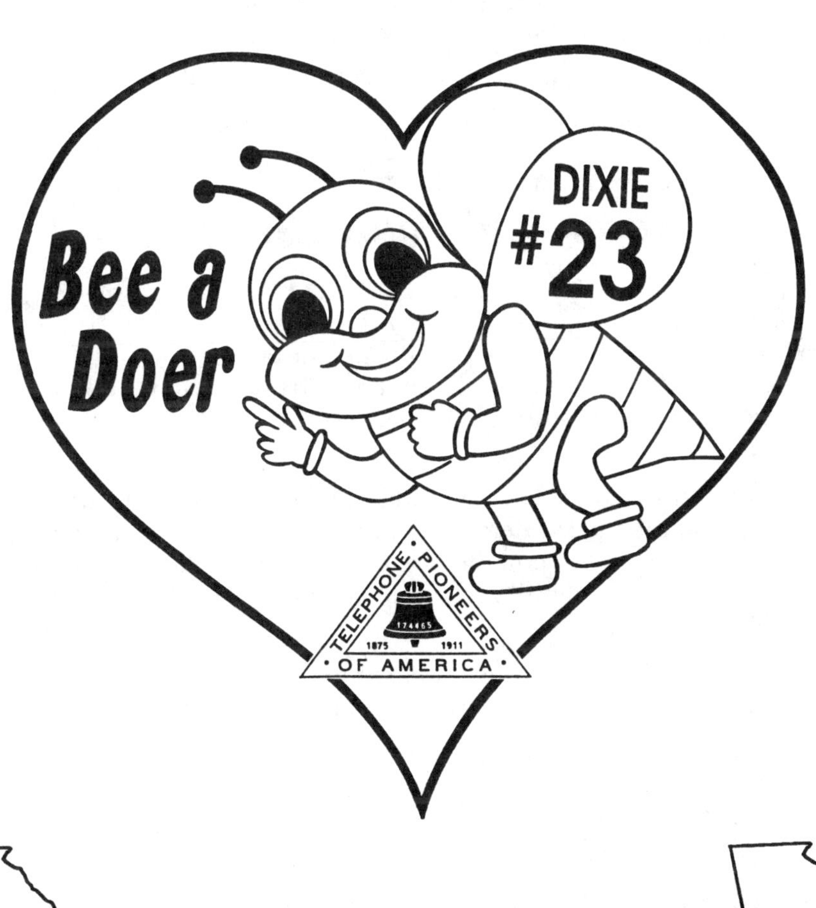

## Cream of Artichoke Soup

1 stick butter
4 Tbsp. flour
1 c. hot water
3 chicken bouillon cubes
1 can artichokes, chopped (save water)
2 c. warm milk
4 shallots or green onions, chopped fine
1 Tbsp. finely chopped parsley
No salt

On a low fire, melt butter; sauté onions in butter. Add flour and artichoke water. Cream until well blended. Add the hot water in which the chicken bouillon cubes have been dissolved and the artichokes. Cook 10 minutes; then, add warm milk and cook 10 minutes. If too thick, add a little more milk. I use skim milk. If you let this stand overnight, it tastes better. Sprinkle parsley over top.

Mary Weekes, *Pots, Pans and Pioneers, Volume IV*
Louisiana Chapter No. 24

## Bacon and Potato Soup

8 slices bacon, fried crisp
1 c. onions, chopped
2 c. cubed potatoes
1 c. water
1 can cream of chicken soup
1 3/4 c. milk
1 (4 oz.) ctn. sour cream
1/2 tsp. salt
Pepper to taste
2 Tbsp. fresh parsley, chopped
Bacon fat

In bacon fat, sauté onions 2 to 3 minutes. Drain. In a pot with sautéed onions, add potatoes and water; bring to a boil. Cover and simmer for about 15 minutes, or until potatoes are tender. Stir in soup, sour cream and crumbled bacon. Add milk, salt, pepper and parsley. Heat to serving temperature. Do not boil.

Mildred Mattingly (submitted by Brownie-Lois Bruner)
*Kentucky Kitchens, Volume I*, Kentucky Chapter No. 32

# Cheese Soup

(Serves 4)

1 large potato, finely diced
1 medium onion, finely diced
1/2 c. carrots, finely diced
1/4 c. celery, finely diced
1 c. water
2 c. chicken broth
8 oz. grated sharp Cheddar cheese
1/2 c. cream
Dash of salt
Tabasco sauce to taste
6 slices Canadian bacon, cooked and diced

In a 2-quart covered saucepan, simmer vegetables in water until tender. Add chicken broth and heat. Slowly add cheese, stirring constantly, so it melts and doesn't stick. When cheese has melted, add other ingredients. Heat, but do *not* boil. Serve immediately.

*Dogwood Delights*, Dogwood Chapter No. 84

# Beer-Cheese Soup

2 cans beer
1 c. whole corn
1 c. chopped celery
1/2 c. carrot slices
1/2 c. chopped onions
2 beef bouillon cubes
1/2 tsp. Tabasco sauce
1 (16 oz.) jar Cheez Whiz

Meatballs:

1 lb. ground beef
1/4 c. bread crumbs
1/2 tsp. Tabasco sauce
1 egg
1 tsp. salt

Put meatballs and everything, except cheese, in a kettle. Bring to a boil. Cover and simmer on low heat for 2 hours. Add Cheez Whiz and heat. Add cornstarch and water to thicken and absorb grease.

*Dogwood Delights Volume II*, Dogwood Chapter No. 84

# Fish Soup

**1 c. chopped onions**
**1 c. parsley, chopped**
**1 c. chopped green onions**
**1 c. chopped carrots**
**1 tsp. cayenne pepper**
**1/2 tsp. garlic powder**
**1 tsp. dried crushed thyme**
**About 1 1/2 lb. catfish fillets**

Add water to almost cover. Bring to a boil. Add about 4 teaspoons salt. Cover and simmer on low heat for about 2 hours.

Sam Templeton, *Dogwood Delights Volume II*, Dogwood Chapter No. 84

# 3-Bean Soup

**1/2 lb. dried Great Northern beans**
**1/2 lb. dried red kidney beans**
**1/2 lb. dried pink or pinto beans**
**Water**
**2 Tbsp. butter or margarine**
**1 medium onion, finely chopped**
**1 1/2 lb. smoked neck bones or ham hocks**
**1 bay leaf**
**1/2 lb. smoked sausage or kielbasa, sliced**

1. Rinse beans; discard any stones. In large saucepot or kettle, heat beans and 8 cups water to boiling. Boil for 2 minutes. Remove from heat; cover and let stand for 1 hour. Drain beans in colander and rinse with water.

2. In same saucepot, heat butter and cook onion until tender, stirring occasionally. Add smoked neck bones or ham hocks, bay leaf, and 7 cups water. Heat to boiling. Add drained beans. Return to boiling.

3. Cover and simmer beans for about 1 hour or until almost tender, stirring occasionally. Add smoked sausage and cook for 15 minutes more or until beans are soft. Remove bay leaf and neck bones or ham hocks. Cool slightly and trim meat from bones; add to soup. Discard bay leaf and bones. Add salt and pepper to soup to taste. Makes about 8 servings.

Sheila Moore, *Bell's Best 3*, Mississippi Chapter No. 36

# *Tuscan Bean Soup*

8 ounces dried Great Northern beans
8 ounces dried pinto beans
1 1/2 cups chopped ham
2 leeks, thinly sliced
2 stalks celery, finely chopped
1 onion, chopped
2 cloves of garlic, finely chopped
3 tablespoons olive oil
1/2 teaspoon dried rosemary
1/4 teaspoon red pepper
9 cups beef broth
1 14-ounce can whole tomatoes, chopped
2 zucchini, cut into 1/2-inch cubes
13 1/2-inch thick slices Italian bread
Olive oil
Freshly grated Parmesan cheese

Soak beans in water to cover overnight; drain and set aside. Sauté ham, leeks, celery, onion and garlic in olive oil in large saucepan over medium heat for 5 minutes. Add beans, rosemary, red pepper, beef broth and chopped undrained tomatoes; mix well. Bring to a boil; reduce heat to medium. Simmer, partially covered, for 2 hours or until beans are tender, stirring occasionally. Stir in zucchini. Simmer, covered, for 30 minutes longer. Brush bread slices with olive oil; place on baking sheet. Bake at 375 degrees until toasted on both sides. Ladle soup into heated serving bowls. Float toast in each bowl; sprinkle with Parmesan cheese. Yield: 13 servings.

Margaret Casalino, *Lawfully Good Eating*, Dixie Chapter No. 23

*The only barrier-free fishing dock for the handicapped in Georgia, built at Mistletoe State Park.* (Dixie Chapter No. 23)

# Tuscan Bean Soup

1 bunch (1 lb.) Swiss chard or escarole
1 tbsp. olive oil
1 c. chopped onions
1 tbsp. minced garlic
3 cans (10½ oz.) chicken broth and 1½ cans water
1 can (14 oz.) tomatoes, chopped—no juice
2 carrots, sliced
½ tsp. rosemary
¼ tsp. freshly ground pepper
1 can (16 oz.) cannellini beans, drained
¼ c. uncooked orzo pasta
¼ c. chopped parsley
Grated Parmesan cheese

1. Slice chard or escarole stalks ¼ inch thick. Slice leafy tops 1 inch thick. Set aside.

2. Heat oil in saucepan over medium heat. Add onions, sauté until transparent. Add garlic and cook 30 seconds. Add chard stalks, chicken broth, tomatoes, carrots, rosemary and pepper.

3. Bring to boil. Reduce heat and simmer 10 minutes.

4. Stir in beans, macaroni, parsley and chard tops. Return to boil, reduce heat and simmer 10 minutes.

5. Serve with Parmesan cheese and Italian bread.

Anne Caulfield
*A Tablespoon of Pioneering and a Teaspoon of Horses and the Handicapped*
Florida Gold Coast Chapter No. 83

# Tennessee Cheddar Soup

½ c. margarine
1 c. finely chopped onion
1 c. finely chopped carrots
1 c. finely chopped celery
1 c. flour
1 qt. chicken stock or bouillon
1 qt. milk
3 c. grated Cheddar cheese
1 tsp. salt
½ tsp. white pepper

Sauté vegetables in margarine until soft. Add flour and mix until smooth. Add chicken stock. Bring to a boil; reduce heat and simmer for 15 minutes. Add cheese; cook 10 minutes longer. Add milk, salt and pepper. Heat to serving temperature. Makes 2 quarts, approximately 12 servings.

Sandy Allen, *Dining with Pioneers, Volume II*, Tennessee Chapter No. 21

## Corn Chowder

2 cans whole kernel corn
1 can cream style corn
1 can cream of celery soup
1–2 cups potatoes, diced
1 onion, chopped very fine
4 or 5 strips bacon
1¾ cups milk
1 stick butter or margarine

In frying pan, cook bacon and drain. Add enough water to pan to simmer onion. Put corn, potatoes and celery soup in crock pot with enough liquid to rinse out cans. Add onions and liquid from frying pan. Salt and pepper to taste. Cook on medium to high from 20–30 minutes until potatoes are done. Add 1¾ cups milk when ready to serve. Crumble bacon on top and add pat of butter to each bowl. Recipe serves 8 to 10.

Von Dean Parker, *Secret Recipes of Telephone Pioneers, Volume III*
South Carolina Chapter No. 61

## Cheesy Vegetable Chowder

2 (14 oz.) cans chicken broth
1 c. sliced celery
1 c. cubed potatoes
1 c. sliced carrots
1 small onion, chopped
1 clove garlic, chopped
¼ c. butter
¼ c. flour
2 c. milk
⅛ tsp. paprika
1 Tbsp. prepared mustard
2 Tbsp. pimento
¼ tsp. pepper
2 c. shredded cheddar cheese

Bring first 6 ingredients to a boil and simmer, covered, for 15 minutes, until tender. Melt butter in heavy skillet, add flour, stir until thick and bubbly. Add milk slowly, cook until milk mixture is thick.

Add remaining ingredients into milk mixture, mix well. Pour cheese mixture into vegetable pot. Mix well. Simmer for 15 minutes, uncovered. Makes about 2 quarts.

Deborah J. DuBost, *Pioneers Pots and Pans—1985 Cookbook*
North Florida Chapter No. 39

## Clam Chowder

6 slices bacon, chopped
1 cup chopped onion
1 cup chopped celery
1/2 cup chopped green bell pepper
1 21-ounce can minced clams
1 28-ounce can tomatoes
3 cups water
1/2 teaspoon thyme
1 bay leaf
1 teaspoon salt
1/4 teaspoon pepper
3 cups chopped potatoes
1 16-ounce can Shoe Peg corn
2 tablespoons margarine

Cook bacon in heavy saucepan until nearly crisp. Add onion, celery and green pepper. Cook over low heat for 10 minutes or until tender, stirring occasionally; drain. Drain clams, reserving liquid. Add clam liquid, tomatoes, water, thyme, bay leaf, salt and pepper to saucepan. Bring to a boil; reduce heat. Simmer, covered, for 1 hour. Add potatoes. Cook for 30 minutes or until potatoes are tender. Add clams and corn. Simmer for 15 minutes. Stir in margarine; discard bay leaf.
Yield: 8 servings.

**Approx Per Serving:** Cal 249; Prot 12 g; Carbo 39 g; Fiber 4 g; T Fat 11 g; Chol 51 mg; Sod 743 mg.

Kathy E. Beam, *Carolina Cooking*, North Carolina Chapter No. 35

## Nassau Conch Chowder

1 1/2 lb. ground conch
8 oz. potatoes, diced
4 oz. onion, diced
4 oz. celery, diced
4 oz. bacon, diced
6 oz. tomatoes
4 oz. green pepper
2 oz. lime juice
1/2 tsp. salt
1/2 tsp. hot pepper
1 tsp. thyme
2 oz. bread crumbs

Marinate ground conch in lime juice, hot pepper and salt for 1 to 2 hours. Add bacon, let fry until light brown. Add onions. Fry for 3 to 5 minutes on low flame. Add marinated conch, celery, tomatoes, green pepper, thyme and potatoes. Simmer for 15 minutes. Add 2 quarts hot water and bread crumbs. Steep and let boil for 30 minutes. Stir occasionally so chowder would not burn. Simmer for 15 minutes and serve hot with rolls or bread.

Claire Quashie, *Pioneers Pots and Pans—1985 Cookbook*
North Florida Chapter No. 39

# Crab Soup

1 lb. crab meat
1/2 chopped onion
1/3 c. butter or margarine
1/3 c. flour
1 c. half and half
2 quarts milk
2 Tbsp. Worcestershire sauce
1 Tbsp. salt and pepper
3 Tbsp. dry sherry

Sauté onions in butter and add flour; mix. Add cream and milk. Mix well. Add remaining ingredients. Simmer 10 minutes. Serve.

8 servings.

Nancy Kersey, *Pioneers Pots and Pans—1985 Cookbook*
North Florida Chapter No. 39

# She Crab Soup

1/2 stick salt-free butter
1 onion, finely chopped
4 cans cream of celery soup
1 lb. crabmeat, frozen or fresh
2 1/2 soup cans milk
1 tsp. Worcestershire
1/4 tsp. mace
1/3 cup egg yolk (crab roe would be best, if you had it)
1/2 cup sherry
pepper to taste

Sauté butter and onion. Add other ingredients. Cook over low, stirring frequently for about 45 minutes. Always better the second day. This is a short-cut recipe and it's great! You'll think you're at Pawley's Island. Serves 6–8.

Lee Zobel, *Secret Recipes of Telephone Pioneers, Volume III*
South Carolina Chapter No. 61

## A Helpful Hint

Make a quick soup by adding a rounded tablespoon of shredded crab meat for each serving to hot chicken broth and seasoning lightly with soy sauce or dry sherry and chopped green onions.

## *Shrimp and Corn Soup*

$1/2$ c. oil
3 c. onions, chopped
$1/3$ c. Bell pepper, chopped
1 can creamed corn, large
$1\ 1/2$ qt. water
2 lb. cleaned raw shrimp
$1/2$ c. green onions, chopped
$1/2$ c. flour
1 c. celery, chopped
$1/2$ c. fresh tomato, chopped
1 small can whole kernel corn
Salt, pepper, garlic salt and sugar to taste

Make roux of oil and flour. Stir until golden brown over low heat. Add onions, celery, Bell pepper and tomato. Cook about 10 minutes to slightly wilt; stir often. Add corns, water and seasonings. Simmer 30 minutes, then add shrimp and green onions. Cook 20 minutes. Serve.

Marie Reeves, *Pots, Pans and Pioneers, Volume I*
Louisiana Chapter No. 24

## *Easy Egg Drop Soup*

4 cups water
2 teaspoons instant chicken bouillon
1 green onion, chopped
2 teaspoons reduced-sodium soy sauce
2 eggs, beaten

Bring water, bouillon, green onion and soy sauce to a boil in large saucepan. Pour eggs gradually into boiling broth. Serve immediately. Yield: 4 servings.

**Approx Per Serving:** Cal 46; Prot 4 g; Carbo 1 g; Fiber <1 g; T Fat 3 g; Chol 137 mg; Sod 739 mg.
**Dietary Exchanges:** Meat $1/2$; Fat $1/2$

"*Answering the Call of Those in Need,*" Tennessee Chapter No. 21

# *Seafood Gumbo*

1/2 c. bacon grease
2/3 c. flour
4 or 5 ribs celery
2 large onions
3 pods garlic
1 bell pepper
1 lb. cut okra, or 1 (10 oz.) pkg. frozen okra
2 1/2 Tbsp. Worcestershire sauce
1/4 c. catsup
3 bay leaves
1 can tomato sauce
2 Tbsp. A.1. Sauce
1 can Ro-Tel tomatoes and chili peppers
1 Tbsp. sugar
1/2 lemon, juiced
1 can tomatoes
1 qt. water
1 Tbsp. loose crab boil
Salt to taste
1 lb. can crabmeat, or meat of 12 crabs
2 1/2 lb. shrimp (best raw)
2 Tbsp. gumbo filé

Make dark mahogany roux of the bacon grease and flour. Chop the celery, onions, garlic and bell pepper; add to the roux and sauté. Then add the okra and cook until slime is gone. Add the remaining ingredients, except the crabmeat, shrimp and filé. Cook slowly at least 3 hours. The last 15 or 20 minutes, add the crabmeat, shrimp and filé. It is good to peel shrimp and boil hulls to obtain the quart of water to be used. This also freezes well, but gumbo filé should be added only to the amount to be eaten and to other after freezing.

Chris Callahan, *Bell's Best* 2, Mississippi Chapter No. 36

*Serving meals at Camp Carefree, camp for the terminally ill in North Carolina.* (North Carolina Chapter No. 35)

# Shrimp and Oyster Gumbo

1 lb. raw, shelled shrimp
12 oysters, medium sized
4 Tbsp. butter
1/2 lb. fresh okra, thinly sliced
1/2 c. onion, finely chopped
1/4 c. green pepper, finely chopped
1/2 tsp. garlic, minced
1 Tbsp. flour
2 c. chicken stock
3 medium sized firm, ripe tomatoes, chopped
3 fresh parsley sprigs
1 bay leaf
1/4 tsp. crumbled dried thyme
1 tsp. salt
1/4 tsp. black pepper, freshly ground
1 tsp. lemon juice
1 tsp. Worcestershire sauce
1/4 tsp. red pepper
2 c. cooked rice

In a heavy skillet, melt the butter. When it begins to froth, add okra and cook for 3 or 4 minutes, stirring constantly. Lower heat; add onions, green pepper and garlic. Cook about 5 minutes or until vegetables are soft but not brown. Add the flour, stir evenly for a minute or two. Pour in chicken stock slowly. Now, add chopped tomatoes, parsley, bay leaf, thyme, salt and pepper. Bring to a boil, reduce heat to low and simmer covered for 30 minutes. Add the shrimp and simmer for 5 minutes; add oysters and continue to simmer for 3 more minutes or until the edges begin to curl. Discard parsley and bay leaf. Stir in lemon juice, Worcestershire sauce and red pepper. Serve over cooked rice.

Serves 6.

Evelyn Carney, *Pioneers Pots and Pans—1985 Cookbook*
North Florida Chapter No. 39

# Black-Eyed Jambalaya

*Sauté in oil in heavy pot:*

**1 onion, chopped**
**1 bell pepper, chopped**
**2 stalks celery, chopped**

Parboil 1 pound Frey "hot" smoked sausage, sliced (approximately 20–30 minutes).

*Add to wilted vegetables:*

**Sausage**
**1 can Ro-Tel tomatoes**
**3 cans Trappey's black-eyes with jalapeño**
**1 env. Lipton onion soup**
**1 Tbsp. Al's green chow chow**

Simmer 20 minutes. Add 2 cups raw rice and 2 cups water. Simmer, covered, 30 minutes or until rice is done.

Roland Begnaud, *Pots, Pans and Pioneers, Volume IV*
Louisiana Chapter No. 24

# Lobster Bisque

**1 10-ounce can cream of asparagus soup**
**1 10-ounce can cream of mushroom soup**
**1½ soup cans light cream**
**1 8-ounce can lobster meat**
**3 to 4 tablespoons sherry**
**Sliced lemon**

Combine first 4 ingredients in double boiler; mix well. Heat over simmering water, stirring frequently. Stir in sherry. Ladle into soup bowls. Garnish with lemon slices. Yield: 4 to 6 servings.

Judy Moody, *Lawfully Good Eating*, Dixie Chapter No. 23

## A Helpful Hint

Chill soup stock before using it. The congealed fat can then be easily skimmed off the top. Each tablespoon of fat removed eliminates about 100 calories.

# Hearty French Onion Soup

**1/4 cup butter**
**5 medium yellow onions, thinly sliced**
**1/8 teaspoon sugar**
**2 tablespoons flour**
**5 cups low-sodium beef broth**
**1/2 teaspoon thyme, crumbled**
**1 bay leaf**
**1/4 teaspoon pepper**
**8 1/2-inch slices French bread, toasted**
**1 cup shredded Swiss cheese**
**1/4 cup Parmesan cheese**

Melt butter in large saucepan over medium heat. Add onions. Cook for 10 to 15 minutes or until golden, stirring gently. Stir in sugar and flour. Cook for 3 minutes longer, stirring constantly. Add broth, thyme, bay leaf and pepper; mix well. Bring to a boil over medium-high heat, stirring constantly. Boil for 6 minutes, stirring constantly; reduce heat. Simmer, loosely covered, for 30 minutes. Remove and discard bay leaf. Ladle into ovenproof bowls. Top with French bread; sprinkle with Swiss and Parmesan cheese. Broil 4 to 6 inches from heat source for 2 minutes or until golden. Yield: 4 servings.

**Approx Per Serving:** Cal 375; Prot 18 g; Carbo 26 g; Fiber 4 g; T Fat 23 g; Chol 62 mg; Sod 1328 mg.

Phyllis Jones, *Carolina Cooking*, North Carolina Chapter No. 35

# Creamy Potato Soup

**8 slices bacon**
**1 large stalk celery, chopped**
**1 onion, chopped**
**4 small carrots, thinly sliced**
**8 small potatoes, peeled, cubed**
**6 cups milk**
**Salt and pepper to taste**
**1 cup sour cream**
**2 tablespoons flour**

Fry bacon in soup pot until crisp; drain, reserving 2 tablespoons pan drippings. Sauté celery, onion and carrots in reserved pan drippings over medium heat until tender. Add potatoes. Cook until slightly browned, stirring frequently. Add milk. Bring to a boil; reduce heat. Add salt and pepper. Cook over low heat for 30 to 40 minutes or until potatoes are tender. Mix sour cream and flour in small bowl. Stir into soup. Cook over low heat for 5 to 10 minutes or until of desired consistency. Ladle into serving bowls; sprinkle with crumbled bacon. Yield: 8 servings.

Sandra Stalvey, *Lawfully Good Eating*, Dixie Chapter No. 23

## Last Days of Winter Soup

1 lb. lean ground beef
1 Tbsp. vegetable oil
1 cup thinly sliced carrots
1/2 cup chopped onion
1/2 cup thinly sliced celery
2 Tbsp. flour
1 can (13 3/4 or 14 1/2 oz.) beef broth
1 can (14 oz.) Italian tomatoes, cut up
1 cup water
1 tsp. Worcestershire sauce
1/2 tsp. each salt and pepper
1/2 cup frozen peas
2 Tbsp. parsley

Brown beef in medium saucepan over medium-high heat for 5 minutes. Remove with slotted spoon to plate and set aside. Add oil to pan and then carrots, onion and celery. Cover and cook 5 minutes, until vegetables are softened. Stir in flour and cook 1 minute more. Gradually add tomatoes chopped with juice, water, sauce, salt and pepper. Return ground beef to soup and bring to a boil. Reduce heat and simmer 25 minutes. Stir in frozen peas and parsley. Simmer 5 minutes more.

Barbara Morgan, *Secret Recipes of Telephone Pioneers, Volume III*
South Carolina Chapter No. 61

## Hamburger-Vegetable Soup

Brown and drain approximately 1 pound hamburger. Add 1 can (medium) chopped tomatoes.

*Add:*

2 cans water
1 can tomato soup
2 beef bouillon cubes
salt to taste
2 stalks celery—take out after transparent
1 can cream corn (must be cream)
1 can string beans
cut-up potatoes
tiny macaroni

Cook until potatoes are done.

Joanne Henderson, *Pioneers Pots and Pans—1985 Cookbook*
North Florida Chapter No. 39

## Applesauce Salad

**1 6-ounce package raspberry or strawberry gelatin**
**1 16-ounce can applesauce**
**1 10-ounce can diet cola**
**1 8-ounce can crushed pineapple**
**1 cup chopped pecans**
**1 cup chopped cherries**
**Miniature marshmallows**

Combine gelatin and applesauce in saucepan. Heat until gelatin is dissolved, stirring constantly. Cool for 15 to 20 minutes. Add diet cola, pineapple, pecans and cherries, stirring to mix. Pour into serving bowl; cover top with miniature marshmallows. Chill in refrigerator for 2 hours or until congealed. Yield: 6 to 8 servings.

Ruth Bracewell, *Lawfully Good Eating*, Dixie Chapter No. 23

## Blueberry Salad

**1 large can blueberries**
**2 (3 oz.) pkg. raspberry jello**
**2 c. boiling water**
**1 large can pineapple tidbits**
**½ c. chopped nuts**
**Cool Whip**

Dissolve jello in boiling water. Add pineapple, nuts and blueberries. Refrigerate. When jelled, top with Cool Whip.

Una Mize, *Pots, Pans & Pioneers II*, Louisiana Chapter No. 24

*A playground area landscaped and built by Kentucky Pioneers for the Daniel Pitino Center, a homeless shelter in Owensboro, Kentucky.* (Kentucky Chapter No. 32)

# Blueberry Congealed Salad

1 can blueberry pie filling
2 regular boxes Concord grape jello
1 large can crushed pineapple in heavy syrup
1 (8 oz.) pkg. Philadelphia cream cheese
1 (8 oz.) ctn. sour cream
2 Tbsp. sugar
1/2 c. crushed pecans
1 c. chopped pecans

Put dry jello into large bowl; add 2 cups boiling water. Stir in pie filling, pineapple with syrup and crushed pecans (optional). Pour in oblong dish; cover and let congeal overnight in refrigerator. Next day, blend cream cheese, sour cream and sugar until smooth. Spread this on top of salad, then sprinkle chopped pecans on top.

Nancy Peete, *Dining with Pioneers, Volume I*, Tennessee Chapter No. 21

# Low-Fat Blueberry and Pineapple Salad

2 3-ounce packages grape gelatin
2 cups boiling water
1 20-ounce can crushed pineapple
1 21-ounce can blueberry pie filling
1 envelope whipped topping mix
1/2 cup milk
1/2 cup sugar
8 ounces cream cheese, softened
1 teaspoon vanilla extract

Dissolve gelatin in boiling water in bowl. Stir in pineapple and pie filling. Spoon into serving dish. Chill until set. Combine whipped topping mix, milk and sugar in mixer bowl. Beat until stiff peaks form. Add cream cheese and vanilla; mix well. Spread over congealed layer. Chill until serving time. Yield: 15 servings.

**Approx Per Serving:** Cal 230; Prot 3 g; Carbo 39 g; Fiber 1 g; T Fat 8 g; 30% Calories from Fat; Chol 18 mg; Sod 95 mg.

Edith Dixon, *Calling All Cooks three*, Alabama Chapter No. 34

## A Helpful Hint

Oil molds lightly for easier unmolding of congealed salads.

# Buttermilk Salad

**Origin:** Cordele, Georgia. **Relative obtained from:** Aunt Eddie Bell Ray. **Brief history:** Georgia country cookin' at its best is from my Aunt Eddie Bell Ray's kitchen. Nothing comes out of it that isn't finger licking good. Believe me, these are great recipes.

**2 small pkg. strawberry jello**
**1 large can crushed pineapple**
**2 c. buttermilk**
**1 medium container Cool Whip**

Drain juice from pineapple; put in boiler and heat. Dissolve jello in juice. Pour in bowl and stir in 2 cups buttermilk. Refrigerate until it begins to gel. Take out and stir in pineapple and Cool Whip. Pour in mold and return to refrigerator. Dress up with a teaspoon of salad dressing and strawberries.

Charlene S. Monser, *A Taste of Pioneering*
Florida Gold Coast Chapter No. 83

# Cherry Salad

**2 small pkg. cherry Jello**
**1 can red cherries (unsweetened)**
**1 (No. 2) can crushed pineapple**
**3/4 c. sugar (scant)**
**1 small (8 oz.) bottle Coke**

Heat cherries until almost boiling. Add 3/4 cup sugar and stir until dissolved. Pour over Jello and stir until dissolved. Add can of pineapple (juice and all). Add Coke last. Refrigerate until completely set.

Jewell Hundley, *Kentucky Kitchens, Volume I*, Kentucky Chapter No. 32

## A Helpful Hint

For a layered congealed salad for the Fourth of July, use cherry and blueberry gelatins separated by a cream cheese layer. Use strawberry and lime gelatins for Christmas.

## Coca-Cola Salad

1 pkg. cherry jello
1 pkg. strawberry jello
1 large can crushed pineapple
1 can Bing cherries, pitted
1 c. chopped nuts
1 (3 oz.) pkg. cream cheese
2 regular Cokes, or 12 oz.

Drain and save juice from pineapple and cherries. Heat juice and pour over jello to dissolve. Mix nuts, pineapple, cherries and cream cheese and pour over jello. (Chip cheese; do not melt.) Blend well and add Coke. Stir several times while congealing to even out fruit and nuts. Serve on lettuce leaf.

Fay Lambert, *Bell's Best* 2, Mississippi Chapter No. 36

## Creamy Cranberry Salad

1 16-ounce can whole cranberry sauce
1 14-ounce can sweetened condensed milk
1 tablespoon lemon juice
1 7-ounce can crushed pineapple, drained
1 cup chopped pecans
10 ounces whipped topping

Combine first 5 ingredients in bowl; mix well. Fold in whipped topping. Chill until serving time. Yield: 6 servings.

**Approx Per Serving:** Cal 626; Prot 8 g; Carbo 84 g; Fiber 3 g; T Fat 31 g; 43% Calories from Fat; Chol 22 mg; Sod 119 mg.

Mamie Parmer, *Calling All Cooks three*, Alabama Chapter No. 34

## Fresh Cranberry Salad

2 cups cranberries
1/4 cup sugar
1 cup nuts
2 cups diced apples
1 medium container of Cool Whip
3 cups miniature marshmallows

Combine crushed cranberries, sugar and miniature marshmallows and let stand overnight in refrigerator. Add nuts, apple, and Cool Whip and mix together. Serves 8.

Carolyn Kolcz, *Secret Recipes of Telephone Pioneers, Volume III*
South Carolina Chapter No. 61

## Cranberry Waldorf Salad

**1 cup cranberry juice**
**1 3-ounce package lemon gelatin**
**1 cup cranberry juice, chilled**
**1 cup chopped apple**
**1/2 cup chopped celery**
**1/4 cup chopped walnuts**

Bring 1 cup cranberry juice to a boil in saucepan. Add gelatin, stirring to dissolve completely. Stir in chilled cranberry juice. Chill until partially set. Fold in apple, celery and walnuts. Pour into greased ring mold. Chill until firm. Unmold onto lettuce-lined serving plate. Yield: 8 servings.

**Approx Per Serving:** Cal 101; Prot 2 g; Carbo 21 g; Fiber 1 g; T Fat 2 g; Chol 0 mg; Sod 43 mg.
**Dietary Exchanges:** Fruit 1; Bread/Starch 1/2; Fat 1/2

"*Answering the Call of Those in Need,*" Tennessee Chapter No. 21

## Thanksgiving Cranberry Relish Mold

**1 medium orange**
**12 ounces fresh cranberries**
**1/2 cup sugar**
**1 3-ounce package black cherry gelatin**

Cut orange into small sections; remove seeds. Process orange, cranberries and sugar in food processor until fruit is coarsely chopped. Prepare gelatin, using package directions. Chill until partially set. Add chopped fruit; mix well. Pour into large mold. Chill until set. Unmold onto serving plate. Garnish with orange slices and parsley. Chill until serving time. Yield: 8 servings.

**Approx Per Serving:** Cal 116; Prot 1 g; Carbo 29 g; Fiber 2 g; T Fat <1 g; Chol 0 mg; Sod 35 mg.

Wilhelmena Wallace, *Carolina Cooking*, North Carolina Chapter No. 35

## Christmas Fruit Bowl

- 1 3-ounce package lime gelatin
- 1 3-ounce package cherry gelatin
- 8 ounces whipping cream
- Sugar to taste
- 8 ounces seedless grapes, cut into halves
- 3 apples, chopped
- Sections of 2 grapefruit
- Sections of 3 oranges
- 1 16-ounce can peaches
- 1 8-ounce can pears
- 1 16-ounce can pineapple chunks
- 1 cup chopped pecans

Prepare each gelatin according to package directions using 1½ cups boiling water for each flavor. Pour into separate 8x9-inch dishes. Chill until firm. Whip cream in small bowl, adding sugar. Chill in refrigerator. Combine fresh fruit in bowl. Drain canned fruit; chop peaches and pears. Add to fresh fruit. Add pecans. Cut gelatin into squares. Fold gelatin and whipped cream into fruit mixture gently. Chill for 30 minutes. Yield: 20 servings.

Charlene P. Atkinson, *Kentucky Kitchens, Volume II*
Kentucky Chapter No. 32

## Doris' Fruit Salad

- 1 large (30 oz.) can fruit cocktail, drained
- 1 medium (20 oz.) can crushed pineapple, drained
- 1 can condensed milk
- 1 (8 oz.) Philadelphia cream cheese, softened
- 1 (12 oz.) Cool Whip
- 3 to 4 tsp. lemon juice
- Coconut and pecans (optional)

Soften cream cheese and mix with condensed milk. Add lemon juice and mix. Add fruit. Fold in whip cream. Put in bowl and refrigerate overnight. Add coconut and pecans, if desired, separately.

Doris Barrios, *Pots, Pans and Pioneers, Volume IV*
Louisiana Chapter No. 24

# Hawaiian Delight Salad

*1 small:*
pkg. orange Jello
pkg. cream cheese
can crushed pineapple, drained
container Cool Whip

*Remaining ingredients:*
2 c. miniature marshmallows
1 c. chopped pecans

Soften cream cheese and cream with dry Jello. Add marshmallows to 2 c. hot water; then, add to jello mixture. Add pineapple and nuts. Chill until slightly thick; then, stir Cool Whip into mixture. Let congeal. May be used as salad or dessert.

Sybil A. Mills, *Taste of Dixie*, Dixie Chapter No. 23

# Millionaire Salad

2 c. cooked rice
2 Tbsp. sugar
1 (8 oz.) pkg. cream cheese
1 medium can crushed pineapple
1 Tbsp. salad dressing
1 c. whipping cream
1 c. pecans
1 pkg. miniature marshmallows

Combine cream cheese and sugar. Mix everything else, except whipping cream. Add it last.

Virginia Stith, *Kentucky Kitchens, Volume I*, Kentucky Chapter No. 32

# Pineapple Marshmallow Salad

*Place in a large bowl:*
1 large can chunk pineapple, drained
3 sliced bananas or orange slices
1 pkg. large marshmallows, cut in pieces

Dressing:

1 Tbsp. flour or cornstarch
1 egg, beaten
juice drained from the pineapple
1/2 c. sugar
dash salt

Cook until thick and let cool. Cover and toss salad.

Cynthia Gailey, *Pioneers Pots and Pans—1985 Cookbook*
North Florida Chapter No. 39

# *Rich Man's Jello*

**1 large pkg. lime Jello**
**1 large can crushed pineapple**
**1 pt. whipping cream**
**Pecans to suit taste**
**1 large pkg. cream cheese**

Drain pineapple; add water to juice to make 4 cups. Mash cream cheese; add to water and Jello. Cook until it is like buttermilk. Pour into 2 oblong dishes; chill until firm. Add pineapple, nuts and whipped cream. Place in refrigerator. Serve as salad or dessert.

Shirley Lawrence, *Pots, Pans and Pioneers III*, Louisiana Chapter No. 24

# *Euna's Sawdust Salad*

First layer:

**2 boxes mixed fruit gelatin**
**$1^1/_2$ c. cold water**
**1 large can fruit cocktail (drained)**
**2 c. hot water**
**3 bananas**
**2 c. miniature marshmallows**

Dissolve Jello in hot water, add cold water and fruit cocktail. Pour in pan. Slice bananas on top, then put marshmallows on top of bananas. Set til firm.

Second layer:

**2 eggs, well beaten**
**5 T. flour**
**2 c. pineapple juice**
**1 c. sugar**

Combine all ingredients, cook til thick. Spread on top of set Jello. Cool.

Third layer:

**2 pkg. Dream Whip**
**1 c. milk**
**1 8 oz. pkg. cream cheese**

Mix Dream Whip and milk, whip til thick. Add cream cheese, whip thoroughly. Spread on top of cooled layer. Sprinkle with coconut and nuts. . .ENJOY.

Euna S. Nuss, *Taste of Dixie*, Dixie Chapter No. 23

## *A Helpful Hint*

Use thawed orange juice concentrate as a quick dressing for chilled fruit.

## Strawberry Pretzel Salad

1 stick butter
2 c. broken pretzels
8 oz. cream cheese
1 c. sugar
2 c. whipped topping
2 c. water
6 oz. strawberry gelatin
2 (10 oz.) pkg. frozen strawberries

**First layer:** Melt butter in 9x13 inch pan. Spread pretzels evenly in bottom of pan. Bake at 350° for 10 minutes. Cool completely.

**Second layer:** Cream sugar and cream cheese. Add whipped topping. Spread over cooled crust. Chill for 30 to 60 minutes.

**Third layer:** Dissolve strawberry gelatin in 2 cups boiling water. Add thawed strawberries with its juice. Allow to gel some. Pour on top of cream cheese layer. Congeal.

Carol Bass, *Dogwood Delights Volume II*, Dogwood Chapter No. 84

## Strawberry Pretzel Salad

1 to 2 cups crushed pretzel sticks
3/4 cup melted butter
1/4 to 1/2 cup sugar
8 ounces cream cheese, softened
1 cup sugar
8 ounces whipped topping
1 6-ounce package strawberry gelatin
2 cups boiling water
1 16-ounce can crushed pineapple (optional)
2 10-ounce packages frozen strawberries

Combine pretzel crumbs, butter and 1/4 to 1/2 cup sugar in bowl; mix well. Press into 9x13-inch baking dish. Bake at 350 degrees for 12 minutes. Cool. Combine cream cheese, 1 cup sugar and whipped topping in mixer bowl; beat well. Spread in baked crust. Chill until firm. Dissolve gelatin in boiling water in bowl. Add pineapple with juice and frozen strawberries. Stir until strawberries thaw. Spread over cream cheese layer. Chill until firm. May use 2 cups pineapple juice instead of pineapple. Yield: 12 servings.

*Kentucky Kitchens, Volume II*, Kentucky Chapter No. 32

## *Sweet and Sour Salad*

1 (3 oz.) pkg. lime jello
1 c. boiling water
1 c. mayonnaise
1 c. chopped celery
½ c. chopped onion
½ c. chopped green pepper

Mix jello and boiling water until dissolved. When mixture starts to thicken, whip in mayonnaise. Add celery, onion and green pepper.

Great with meats, especially ham. This salad is different from most congealed salads and one of our favorites.

Emory and Virginia Reeves, *Dogwood Delights Volume II*
Dogwood Chapter No. 84

## *Twenty-Four Hour Salad*

(Serves 10)

2 eggs, beaten
4 Tbsp. vinegar
2 Tbsp. butter
1 c. whipped cream or Cool Whip
2 c. white cherries, cut in halves
2 c. pineapple, cut in pieces
2 oranges, cut in pieces
2 c. small marshmallows

Put eggs in double boiler; add vinegar and beat constantly until thick and smooth. Remove from heat, add butter and cool. When cool, fold in whipped cream or Cool Whip and fruit mixture. Put in refrigerator for 24 hours before serving.

Mary Jo Rainey, *Dogwood Delights*, Dogwood Chapter No. 84

### *A Helpful Hint*

For a quick and easy salad, fill the hollows of peach halves with blueberries and serve with honey-yogurt, or roll cored pears in mayonnaise and finely chopped walnuts.

## Winter Fruit Salad

1 16-ounce can pineapple chunks, drained
4 red Delicious apples, chopped
4 cups green seedless grapes
Sections of 2 Navel oranges
1 banana, sliced
2 cups plain low-fat yogurt

Combine pineapple, apples, grapes, oranges and banana in bowl; mix gently. Stir in yogurt gently. Chill until serving time. Yield: 10 servings.

**Approx Per Serving:** Cal 122; Prot 3 g; Carbo 27 g; Fiber 3 g; T Fat 1 g; Chol 3 mg; Sod 34 mg.
**Dietary Exchanges:** Milk 1/2; Fruit 1 1/2

"*Answering the Call of Those in Need*," Tennessee Chapter No. 21

## Colby Fiesta Salad

6 six-inch diameter flour tortillas
2 Tbsp. butter, melted
1 lb. ground chuck
1 1 1/4-oz. pkg. taco seasoning mix
3/4 cup water
2 cups iceberg lettuce, shredded
1 15 1/2-oz. can garbanzo beans, rinsed and drained
1 large tomato, chopped
1 medium onion, sliced into rings
1/2 cup pitted sliced ripe olives
1 cup evaporated milk
2 cups (8 oz.) shredded Colby cheese
chopped jalapeño peppers, if desired

Brush tortillas lightly with butter. Place tortillas, overlapping slightly in a round pie plate. Bake at 350 degrees for 10 minutes. Brown ground chuck in skillet until crumbly; drain off excess drippings. Add seasoning mix and water; simmer, uncovered, 10 minutes. Meanwhile, sprinkle lettuce over tortillas. Combine ground beef mixture, beans, tomatoes, onions, and olives. Spoon over lettuce. Heat evaporated milk in medium-sized saucepan until bubbles form around edges. Reduce heat to low. Stir in cheese until melted. Add peppers, if desired. Pour over ground meat mixture. Carefully, lift out tortillas and topping.

Ronnie Baxley, *Secret Recipes of Telephone Pioneers, Volume III*
South Carolina Chapter No. 61

## Taco Salad

1 lb. ground meat
1 medium onion, chopped
1 heaping tsp. chili powder
1 head lettuce
1 lb. Velveeta cheese
1 medium bell pepper, chopped
1 tsp. cumin seed
1 large tomato
1 medium bay Fritos
1 can Ro-Tel tomatoes

Brown meat, bell pepper, onion, chili powder and cumin seed. Drain and set aside. Chop tomato and lettuce, set aside. On low heat, melt cheese and Ro-Tel tomatoes. Crunch bag of Fritos. Mix all ingredients when ready to serve.

Billie Longkabel, *Pots, Pans & Pioneers II*, Louisiana Chapter No. 24

## Taco Salad

2 lb. hamburger meat
1 pkg. taco seasoning mix
2 cans red kidney beans
1 bottle white creamy Italian dressing
1 head lettuce, shredded
3–4 tomatoes, chopped
8 oz. Cheddar cheese, grated
1 bag taco flavored Doritos

Crumble and brown meat. Add taco mix and beans. Simmer 30 minutes and drain off grease. Make salad with remaining ingredients, reserving enough cheese and Doritos to cover dish. Mix salad and meat mixtures together. Put in serving dish and cover with remaining cheese and Doritos.

Kittie Mae Russell, *Dogwood Delights*, Dogwood Chapter No. 84

# *Cajun Chicken Salad*

1½ lbs. boneless, skinless, thinly sliced chicken breasts or chicken tenderloins

Spice Mixture:

1 tsp. garlic powder
1 tsp. onion powder
¼ tsp. cayenne pepper
1 tsp. chili powder
2½ tsp. dried thyme
2 tsp. dried oregano
¼ tsp. ground white pepper
½ tsp. freshly ground black pepper
½ tsp. ground cumin
½ tsp. paprika

Salad Mixture:

2 ripe fresh papayas
10 scallions, including 2 inches of the green, trimmed and sliced
½ c. finely chopped red bell pepper, seeds and ribs removed
¼ c. chopped fresh cilantro
6 tbsp. freshly squeezed lime juice

1. Cut the chicken breasts into strips ½ inch wide by 2 inches long. Set aside.

2. In a small bowl, combine the spice mixture.

3. Preheat oven to 350°. Place the spice mixture on a plate and roll the chicken strips in it to coat them evenly. Arrange the chicken strips in a single layer on a nonstick or lightly greased cookie sheet. Bake for 10–12 minutes. Remove from the oven and place strips in a mixing bowl.

4. While chicken is baking, peel and seed the papayas and cut into 1 inch cubes. Place the papayas in the mixing bowl. Add chicken strips, scallions, red bell pepper and cilantro. Drizzle with lime juice and toss to coat. Refrigerate until ready to serve. Yield: 6 servings. Calories: 24.

Jeanette Sutherland
*A Tablespoon of Pioneering and a Teaspoon of Horses and the Handicapped*
Florida Gold Coast Chapter No. 83

# California Chicken Salad

½ cup butter
2 cups mayonnaise
¼ cup minced parsley
½ teaspoon curry powder
¼ teaspoon minced garlic
Pinch of marjoram
Salt to taste
Pepper to taste
4 cups shredded cooked chicken breasts
2 cups sliced seedless green grapes
½ cup toasted slivered almonds
Lettuce leaves
Paprika to taste

Melt butter in saucepan. Remove from heat; cool to room temperature. Combine mayonnaise, parsley, curry powder, garlic, marjoram, salt and pepper in bowl; mix well. Stir in melted butter gently. Combine chicken, grapes and almonds in large bowl; toss well. Arrange on lettuce-lined salad plate. Spoon mayonnaise mixture over top; sprinkle with paprika. Yield: 4 servings.

Ladonna Darnell, *Kentucky Kitchens, Volume II*
Kentucky Chapter No. 32

# Chicken Salad Deluxe

2 c. chopped, cooked chicken
1 c. diced celery
1 c. pitted Bing cherries, cut in halves
½ c. blanched almonds, diced
3 hard-cooked eggs, chopped
½ c. pimiento-stuffed olives, sliced
1 c. mayonnaise

Combine all ingredients and mix gently. Chill. To serve, line a salad bowl with lettuce leaves and spoon salad into bowl. Sprinkle top with grated cheese. Yield: 10 servings.

Ham, lamb or pork may be substituted for the cooked chicken.

Mary C. Martin, *Calling All Cooks two*, Alabama Chapter No. 34

# Chicken Salad Hawaiian

**1 (8 oz.) Philadelphia cream cheese with pineapple**
**1/2 c. plain yogurt**
**2 c. diced, cooked chicken**
**1 c. red or green grapes, halved**
**1/2 c. chopped macadamia nuts**
**1/2 c. sliced celery**
**1/2 c. toasted coconut**

Mix cream cheese and yogurt until well blended. Stir in remaining ingredients. Serve in hollowed out pineapple halves. Makes 4 servings.

**Preparation time**: 15 minutes.

Claudia Burchfield, *Dogwood Delights Volume II*
Dogwood Chapter No. 84

# Old-Fashioned Chicken Salad

**1 large fryer**
**1/4 cup celery, chopped**
**1/4 cup onion, chopped**
**1/4 cup bell pepper, chopped**
**1 small jar pimentos**
**1 3 oz. package cream cheese with chives**
**1 tsp. salt**
**1 tsp. pepper**

Boil fryer until it pulls loose from bone. Remove all bones and skin. Chop with sharp knife until it is in very small pieces. Add all ingredients; then, add mayonnaise to reach the consistency you desire.

Delores Green, *Secret Recipes of Telephone Pioneers, Volume II*
South Carolina Chapter No. 61

# Mill St. Deli Chicken Salad

**2 c. diced, cooked chicken**
**2 c. chopped, boiled eggs**
**1/2 c. chopped celery**
**1/2 c. grapes, chopped**
**1/2 c. slivered almonds**
**1 tsp. lemon juice**
**1/2 tsp. salt**
**1/2 c. mayonnaise**
**1/2 c. sour cream**

Mix mayo, sour cream, and seasonings.

Dot Trinkner, *Bell's Best 3*, Mississippi Chapter No. 36

# Southwestern Chicken Salad

1 tablespoon fresh lime juice
1 teaspoon olive oil
1/4 teaspoon minced garlic
1 teaspoon chopped fresh thyme
Salt and freshly ground pepper to taste
1 pound chicken breast filets
3 tablespoons fresh lime juice
2 teaspoons honey
2 teaspoons olive oil
1/2 clove of garlic, crushed
6 cups torn lettuce
1 small red bell pepper, sliced into rings
1/2 cantaloupe, thinly sliced
2/3 cup fresh or frozen corn
1 small tomato, chopped
1 green onion, thinly sliced
2 tablespoons chopped fresh cilantro
2 teaspoons minced jalapeño pepper

Combine first 5 ingredients in 10-inch glass dish. Rinse chicken and pat dry. Add to marinade, turning to coat well. Let stand for 15 minutes. Microwave, loosely covered, on High for 4 to 4 1/2 minutes or until cooked through, turning once. Let stand for several minutes. Whisk 3 tablespoons lime juice, honey, 2 teaspoons olive oil, 1/2 clove of garlic, salt and pepper in small bowl. Slice chicken into 1/2-inch wide strips. Combine with 2 tablespoons honey mixture in bowl; mix well. Add lettuce, red pepper and cantaloupe; toss to coat well. Spoon onto serving platter. Mix remaining honey mixture with corn, tomato, green onion, cilantro and jalapeño pepper. Spoon over chicken mixture. Garnish with cilantro sprigs and lime wedges. Yield: 4 servings.

**Approx Per Serving:** Cal 275; Prot 30 g; Carbo 23 g; Fiber 4 g; T Fat 7 g; Chol 72 mg; Sod 191 mg.
**Dietary Exchanges:** Vegetable 1 1/2; Fruit 1/2; Bread/Starch 1/2; Meat 3; Fat 1

"*Answering the Call of Those in Need*," Tennessee Chapter No. 21

## A Helpful Hint

Salt salads at the table because salt tends to wilt and toughen salad greens.

## "Chip's" Caesar Salad

**½ c. olive oil**
**1 clove garlic, halved**
**1 egg**
**2 Tbsp. lemon juice**
**¼ tsp. black pepper**
**1½ c. herb croutons**
**1 large Romaine lettuce, torn into bite-sized pieces**
**½ tsp. salt**
**8 anchovy fillets, chopped**

Rub inside of salad bowl with cut side of garlic clove. In salad bowl beat egg; add lemon juice and salt. Add black pepper and fillets. Combine well. Add lettuce; toss lightly. Add croutons. Serves 6.

Chip Perot, *Pots, Pans and Pioneers, Volume I*, Louisiana Chapter No. 24

## Curried Crab Meat-Rice Salad

**8 ounces crab meat**
**2 cups cooked rice, chilled**
**¼ cup chopped green bell pepper**
**½ cup sliced green onions**
**1 6-ounce jar marinated artichokes, drained**
**½ teaspoon curry powder**
**¼ cup mayonnaise**

Combine crab meat, rice, green pepper, green onions and artichokes in bowl; toss to mix. Blend curry powder and mayonnaise in small bowl. Add to crab mixture; mix well. Garnish with hard-boiled egg and tomato wedges. Serve with croissants and white wine. Yield: 6 servings.

**Approx Per Serving:** Cal 210; Prot 10 g; Carbo 20 g; Fiber 2 g; T Fat 10 g; Chol 43 mg; Sod 308 mg.

Cheryl Griffin, *Carolina Cooking*, North Carolina Chapter No. 35

### Helpful Hints

For a nutritious meal, serve a salad bar as the main course with vegetables, pasta, kidney beans and chickpeas. Offer shredded cheese, whole grain bread and reduced-calorie and reduced-fat dressing.

For a summer deck party, offer crisp salad greens in a large bowl surrounded by "salad fixings" in small glass flowerpots.

## *Crab Salad Bowl*

(Bahamian Recipe)

**1 lb. cooked crab meat**
**3 hard-boiled eggs, diced**
**2 oz. green pepper, diced**
**4 oz. celery, diced**
**4 radishes, sliced**
**1/2 tsp. salt**
**2 oz. cucumber, diced**
**2 oz. green pepper strip**
**4 oz. mayonnaise**
**1 oz. lime juice**
**1/8 tsp. hot pepper**

Dice crab meat, blend mayonnaise, lime juice, cucumber, dice green pepper, hot pepper, salt, celery, eggs and crab meat and toss well. Using a large salad bowl, arrange lettuce around edge. Fill bowl with salad mix, garnish with green pepper strips, slice radishes, chill salad before serving.

Claire Quashie—TSPS, *Pioneers Pots and Pans—1985 Cookbook*
North Florida Chapter No. 39

## *Shrimp Salad*

**Origin:** Tennessee. **Country:** U.S.A. **City:** Johnson City. **Approximate year created:** 50 years old minimum. **Obtained from:** Friend. **Brief history:** It is tastier after refrigerated for at least 24 hours.

**Handful black pitted olives**
**1 (7 oz.) pkg. elbow macaroni, cooked**
**8 hard-boiled eggs, diced fine**
**1/3 to 1/2 green pepper, diced fine**
**1 small stalk (bunch) green onion (use stem and all), diced fine**
**1 bunch celery (minus 6 outside stalks), diced fine**
**2 regular cans shrimp or fresh steamed**
**Salt and pepper to taste**
**Mayonnaise (until smooth)**

Boil macaroni and eggs per normal; then, drain and peel. Dice eggs, pepper, green onion, and celery; add to macaroni. Slice olives; add to the preceding. Add shrimp (whole or cut, depending on size). Add salt and pepper. Mix all of the preceding with mayonnaise until smooth. Refrigerate.

Love the way this is written. I got it from a friend who got it from an old lady in Tennessee.

**Preparation time:** Approximately 1/2 hour.
**Cooking time:** Approximately 1/2 hour.
**No. of servings:** 6.

Lucy M. Platt, *A Taste of Pioneering*, Florida Gold Coast Chapter No. 83

# Shrimp and Pasta Salad

8 ounces rotini, cooked, drained
4 ounces snow peas, blanched
4 ounces fresh mushrooms, sliced
1 carrot, peeled, julienned
1/2 cup sliced green onions
Dressing
8 ounces tiny shrimp, cooked

Combine rotini, snow peas, mushrooms, carrot and green onions in large bowl; mix well. Add Dressing; mix well. Chill for several hours. Stir in shrimp just before serving. Yield: 10 servings.

## Dressing for Shrimp and Pasta Salad

1/3 cup olive oil
1/3 cup lemon juice
3 tablespoons soy sauce
4 teaspoons sugar
1 teaspoon dry mustard
1 teaspoon sesame seed, toasted

Combine olive oil, lemon juice, soy sauce, sugar, mustard and sesame seed in jar. Shake, tightly covered, until well mixed.

Approx Per Serving: Cal 203; Prot 9 g; Carbo 23 g; Fiber 2 g; T Fat 8 g; Chol 39 mg; Sod 352 mg.

Sheri Camp, *Carolina Cooking*, North Carolina Chapter No. 35

# Macaroni-Tuna Salad

7 oz. pkg. macaroni, cooked
1/2 c. mayonnaise
1/2 c. sour cream
1/2 tsp. celery seed
1/2 tsp. onion salt
1 (7 oz.) can tuna, drained
1 can green peas (very small peas)
3/4 c. diced mild Cheddar cheese
2 Tbsp. green pepper
1 Tbsp. pimento
1 Tbsp. diced onion
Salt and pepper to taste

Mix all ingredients; refrigerate. Best if mixed ahead to allow flavor to set.

Shirley Cates, *Kentucky Kitchens, Volume I*, Kentucky Chapter No. 32

# *Italian Macaroni Salad*

**3/4 c. salad oil**
**3/4 c. sugar**
**3/4 c. vinegar**
**2 medium onions, grated**
**1/2 tsp. salt**
**1 can tomato soup**
**1 lb. box shells**

Cook shells in salt water 8 minutes or until tender. Drain and cool. Mix other ingredients together and pour over shells, reserving 1 cup. Add 2 chopped peppers, small jar cut up pimentos, 2 or 3 tablespoons sweet relish. Add to reserve cup of mixture. Let shells refrigerate overnight, then add 1 cup of mixture and serve.

Shirley Dawson, *Pioneers Pots and Pans—1985 Cookbook*
North Florida Chapter No. 39

# *Pasta Salad*

**2 cups pasta**
**1/4 cup green onions**
**1 cup fresh mushrooms**
**1 cup shredded Cheddar cheese**
**2 hard-boiled eggs, chopped**
**1/4 cup green pepper, cut up**
**1/2 cup stuffed olives, chopped**
**1 small can of chicken/turkey/ tuna**
**1 medium fresh tomato, chopped**

Cook pasta and drain. Mix all ingredients, except tomato, with 1 cup of Italian dressing. Toss and chill. Just before serving, put tomato on salad.

Polly Jennings, *Secret Recipes of Telephone Pioneers, Volume III*
South Carolina Chapter No. 61

# *Broccoli Salad*

**2 bunches broccoli**
**1/4 to 1/2 c. raisins**
**1 medium red onion, sliced**
**10 to 12 slices bacon, cooked crisp and crumbled**

Dressing:

**1/2 c. mayonnaise**
**1/2 c. sugar (or less)**
**2 Tbsp. vinegar**

Clean broccoli and cut into bite-sized pieces. Cut stems diagonally. Mix all ingredients with dressing.

Carol Zarich, *Pots, Pans and Pioneers, Volume IV*
Louisiana Chapter No. 24

# Marinated Mixed Vegetables

1 16-ounce can French-style green beans, drained
1 16-ounce can sliced carrots, drained
1 16-ounce can bean sprouts, drained
1 8-ounce can sliced water chestnuts, drained
1 16-ounce can green peas, drained
1 16-ounce can whole kernel corn, drained
1 2-ounce jar chopped pimento, drained
1 2-ounce jar sliced green olives, drained
3 stalks celery, chopped
1 green bell pepper, chopped
1 onion, chopped
Dressing

Combine green beans, carrots, bean sprouts, water chestnuts, peas, corn, pimento, olives, celery, green pepper and onion in large bowl; toss to mix. Add marinade to vegetable mixture; mix well. Marinate, covered, in refrigerator overnight. Yield: 20 servings.

## Salad Dressing for Marinated Mixed Vegetables

1½ cups vinegar
1½ cups water
2 tablespoons oil
½ cup sugar
2 tablespoons (or less) salt
1 tablespoon pepper

Combine vinegar, water, oil, sugar, salt and pepper in small bowl; mix well.

**Approx Per Serving:** Cal 90; Prot 2 g; Carbo 18 g; Fiber 3 g; T Fat 2 g; Chol 0 mg; Sod 953 mg.

Mrs. Hugh L. McAulay, *Carolina Cooking*
North Carolina Chapter No. 35

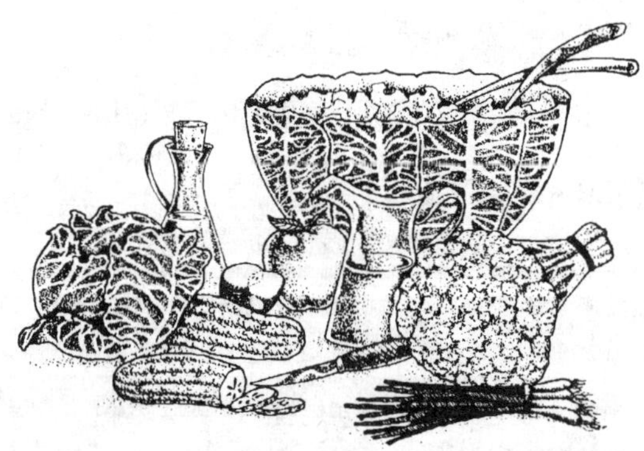

## Corn Bread Salad

1 8-ounce package Jiffy corn bread mix
1 egg
1/3 cup milk
4 medium tomatoes, peeled, chopped
1 green bell pepper, chopped
Chopped onion to taste
1/2 cup chopped sweet pickles
9 slices crisp-fried bacon, crumbled
1 1/4 cups mayonnaise
1/3 cup pickle juice

Combine corn bread mix, egg and milk in bowl; mix well. Pour into greased 8x8-inch baking pan. Bake at 400 degrees for 15 to 20 minutes or until brown. Cool slightly; crumble. Combine tomatoes, green pepper, onion, pickles and bacon in bowl; mix gently. Combine mayonnaise and pickle juice in bowl; mix well. Layer corn bread crumbs, vegetable mixture and mayonnaise mixture 1/2 at a time in glass serving dish. Chill, covered, for 2 hours or longer. Yield: 6 servings.

Carolyn W. Kennedy, *Lawfully Good Eating*, Dixie Chapter No. 23

## Mexican Corn Bread Salad

2 (6 oz.) pkg. Mexican corn bread mix
1 (15 oz.) can whole kernel corn (undrained)
1 onion, chopped
1 green pepper, chopped
1 1/2 c. fresh tomatoes, chopped
1/4 tsp. celery seed or leaves
1 c. grated Cheddar cheese
4 or 5 slices bacon, cooked (crispy) and crumbled
3 hard-boiled ebbs, chopped
1 tsp. Italian seasoning
Salt and pepper to taste
1 tsp. parsley flakes (optional)
1 c. mayonnaise or buttermilk salad dressing

Make corn bread by package directions; cool and crumble into large bowl. Mix other ingredients. Chill overnight. Serve cold. Makes 10 to 12 servings (approximately 219 calories).

I copied this from the Farmers and Consumers Market Bulletin, sent in by Roberta Cleapor, Lithia Springs, Georgia. I have made it many times. It tastes like corn bread dressing, except the veggies are not cooked.

Arlene Davis, *Dogwood Delights Volume II*, Dogwood Chapter No. 84

# Fire and Ice

6 large tomatoes, peeled, cut into quarters
1 green bell pepper, sliced into strips
1 medium onion, sliced into rings
3/4 cup white vinegar
1/4 cup water
1 tablespoon sugar
1 1/2 teaspoons cayenne pepper
1 1/2 teaspoons mustard seed
Salt and pepper to taste
1 cucumber, sliced

Combine tomatoes, green pepper and onion in bowl. Combine vinegar, water, sugar, cayenne pepper, mustard seed, salt and pepper in saucepan. Bring to a boil. Cook for 1 minute. Pour over vegetables in bowl. Chill in refrigerator. Add cucumber at serving time. Yield: 6 servings.

**Approx Per Serving:** Cal 50; Prot 2 g; Carbo 13 g; Fiber 3 g; T Fat <1 g; Chol 0 mg; Sod 12 mg.
**Dietary Exchanges:** Vegetable 1 1/2

"*Answering the Call of Those in Need*," Tennessee Chapter No. 21

# Waldo's Green Salad

*Place in layers in a large salad bowl:*
1 head lettuce, broken into small pieces
6–8 green onions, chopped (tops and all)
3/4–1 cucumber, sliced thin
10–15 radishes (or small pack), sliced thin
1 pkg. Swiss cheese, grated
3 boiled eggs, chopped

*Dressing (good only on preceding combination):*
1 Tbsp. French mustard
1 tsp. salt
1 tsp. M.S.G.
1 tsp. paprika
1/3 c. olive oil
2/3 c. red wine vinegar

Mix salt, MSG, mustard, and paprika into a paste; add oil and vinegar, in a blender beat into emulsion.

Add dressing to taste and toss just before serving. This makes about a pint of dressing, but it can be kept in the refrigerator if too much.

J. L. Alley, Jr., *Dining with Pioneers, Volume II*, Tennessee Chapter No. 21

## Kraut Salad

**2 cans chopped kraut**
**1 medium onion, chopped**
**1½ c. bell pepper, chopped**
**1 c. celery, chopped**
**1 small jar pimentos**
**2 large spoons grated carrots**
**¾ c. sugar**

Mix vegetables well. Sprinkle sugar over. Let stand overnight in refrigerator. Mix well before serving.

Brenda Hager, *Dogwood Delights Volume II*, Dogwood Chapter No. 84

## Kraut Salad

**1 large (No. 2½) can kraut**
**1 can bean sprouts**
**1¾ c. sugar**
**1 c. white vinegar**
**1 c. chopped onions**
**1 c. chopped celery**
**1 c. chopped bell pepper**
**1 c. stuffed olives, chopped**

Bring sugar and vinegar to boil and cool. Mix onion, celery, bell pepper and olives in Pyrex bowl with kraut and bean sprouts. Pour vinegar and sugar mixture over it and mix well. Keep refrigerated.

Polly Greenhill, *Calling All Cooks*, Alabama Chapter No. 34

## Marinated Mushrooms

**1 lb. fresh sliced mushrooms**
**1 onion, sliced**

*Mix together:*
**¾ c. oil**
**¾ c. red wine vinegar**
**¾ c. sugar**
**1 T. parsley**
**pepper**
**3 T. wine**
**1 garlic bud or garlic juice**

Place mushrooms and onions in a glass jar or bowl. Pour remaining ingredients over, mix. This may not cover but stir and after it sits mushrooms absorb liquid and pack down. Will keep several weeks. Eat as is or serve as a dressing for salads. If any juice is left, add more onions, and mushrooms. Keep covered in refrigerator.

Truman Cawthorne, *Taste of Dixie*, Dixie Chapter No. 23

## Oriental Salad

**1 pkg. cole slaw mix**
**1/2 c. sesame seeds or sunflower seeds**
**1 pkg. slivered almonds**
**2 pkg. Ramen noodles, discard seasoning packet, crumbled, not crushed**
**1/2 c. butter**
**1 c. sugar**
**1 c. salad oil**
**2 tsp. soy sauce**
**1/4 c. vinegar**

Brown seeds, almonds, and noodles in butter. Set aside to cool. Mix sugar, salad oil, soy sauce, and vinegar together. Mix everything together right before serving. May add 2 to 4 cups of chicken or turkey and serve as a main dish.

Dogwood Delights Volume II, Dogwood Chapter No. 84

## Old-Fashioned Potato Salad

**6 medium size boiled potatoes, chilled, peeled and cubed**
**4 hard-cooked eggs, chilled, peeled and diced**
**2 stalks celery, minced**
**1/4 c. sweet pickle relish**
**1/2 medium size sweet green pepper, cored, seeded and minced**
**1 medium size yellow onion, peeled and minced**
**1 c. mayonnaise**
**1 1/2 tsp. salt**
**1/8 tsp. pepper**

Stir all ingredients together to mix; cover and chill several hours before serving. Serve as is or in crisp lettuce cups.

Brenda Young, *Bell's Best* 2, Mississippi Chapter No. 36

## German Potato Salad

10 lbs. potatoes
1 lb. bacon
2 medium onions, chopped
5 stalks celery, chopped
1/4 c. flour
Salt to taste (about 2 Tbsp.)
1/4 tsp. pepper
2 c. sugar
2 c. vinegar
2 c. water
1 large green pepper, chopped

Boil potatoes, peel and slice. Add onions, celery, green pepper, salt and pepper; mix. Cut bacon into small pieces and fry. Remove bacon from fat and set aside. Add flour to fat; stir until smooth. Add sugar, vinegar and water to fat; bring to boil. Pour over potato mixture. Add bacon and mix well. Serve warm.

Dorothy Young, *Kentucky Kitchens, Volume I*, Kentucky Chapter No. 32

## Seven-Layer Salad

1 10-ounce package frozen green peas
1 head lettuce, chopped
1 cup chopped green bell pepper
1 cup chopped green onions or red onion
1 cup chopped celery
1 1/2 cups sour cream
1/2 cup mayonnaise
9 slices crisp-fried bacon, crumbled
4 ounces shredded Cheddar cheese or Parmesan cheese

Cook peas using package directions; drain. Cool. Layer lettuce, green pepper, green onions, celery and peas in 9x12-inch dish. Spread with mixture of sour cream and salad dressing. Top with crumbled bacon and cheese. Chill, covered, until serving time. May add water chestnuts with vegetables. May add sliced boiled eggs and croutons to top.
Yield: 6 to 8 servings.

*Kentucky Kitchens, Volume II*, Kentucky Chapter No. 32

# Another Cabbage Slaw

1 large head cabbage, shredded
2 large onions, chopped
1 cup sugar
1 cup vinegar
2/3 cup oil
2 tablespoons sugar
2 teaspoons prepared mustard
1 to 2 teaspoons celery seeds
1 teaspoon salt

Combine cabbage, onions and 1 cup sugar in large bowl; mix well. Bring vinegar, oil, 2 tablespoons sugar, mustard, celery seeds and salt to a boil in saucepan, stirring to mix well. Pour over cabbage mixture; mix well. Chill for several hours to several weeks. Yield: 12 servings.

**Approx Per Serving:** Cal 212; Prot 1 g; Carbo 26 g; Fiber 2 g; T Fat 12 g; 50% Calories from Fat; Chol 0 mg; Sod 203 mg.

Faye Husby, *Calling All Cooks three*, Alabama Chapter No. 34

# Apple Slaw

2 cups shredded cabbage
2 large red delicious apples, shredded
1/3 cup shredded carrot
1/4 cup currants
1/4 cup unsweetened applesauce
1/4 cup reduced-calorie mayonnaise
1/4 teaspoon celery seed
1/8 teaspoon pepper
1/4 cup oat bran

Combine cabbage, apples, carrot, currants, applesauce, mayonnaise, celery seed and pepper in salad bowl; mix well. Chill, covered, for 2 hours or longer. Sprinkle with oat bran at serving time. Yield: 6 servings.

Wellness Committee, *Kentucky Kitchens, Volume II*
Kentucky Chapter No. 32

## A Helpful Hint

For coleslaw to serve fifty people, use 8 pounds of cabbage, 1 cup of chopped pimentos, 3 cups of chopped pickles, 1 cup of chopped green pepper and 1 1/2 quarts of salad dressing.

## *Cheesy Cabbage and Apple Slaw*

**1 1-pound head cabbage, thinly sliced**
**1½ cups thinly sliced celery**
**½ cup sliced green onions**
**1 cup mayonnaise**
**½ cup sour cream**
**2 tablespoons lemon juice**
**1 teaspoon salt**
**¼ teaspoon white pepper**
**½ teaspoon fennel seed, crushed**
**4 medium apples, coarsely chopped**
**4 ounces Cheddar cheese, cubed**

Combine cabbage, celery and green onions in large bowl; mix well. Mix mayonnaise, sour cream, lemon juice, salt, white pepper and fennel seed in small bowl. Add to cabbage mixture; mix well. Chill, covered, for 2 to 3 hours. Add apples and cheese cubes; toss to mix.
Yield: 12 servings.

**Approx Per Serving:** Cal 229; Prot 4 g; Carbo 11 g; Fiber 2 g; T Fat 20 g; Chol 25 mg; Sod 366 mg.

Doris Kelly, *Carolina Cooking*, North Carolina Chapter No. 35

## *Marinated Slaw*

**1 head cabbage, shredded**
**1 small onion, sliced thin**
**1 c. sugar**
**1 c. vinegar**
**⅔ c. vegetable oil**
**1 tsp. salt**
**1 tsp. dry mustard**
**1 tsp. celery salt**
**1 tsp. mustard seed**

Shred cabbage. Slice onion on top. Pour cup of sugar over all and do not stir. Boil vinegar, oil and spices. Pour over cabbage and onion mixture. Do not stir. Let set overnight. Keep in refrigerator. Stir before serving. Good for 2 weeks or more.

Thanks to my sister, Mrs. Barney (Harriet) Hendricks, in Cochran, Georgia. She mixes it better than I, but it does make a great slaw (and so simple to make)!

Charlie Thorp, *Dogwood Delights Volume II*, Dogwood Chapter No. 84

## Marinated Slaw

1 head cabbage
1 large onion
1 large bell pepper
Shredded carrots (optional)
1/2 or 3/4 c. sugar

Pour sugar over cabbage mixture. Let stand; do not stir.

*Mix and bring to a boil:*
1 c. vinegar (apple)
3/4 c. oil
7 tsp. mustard seed
1 Tbsp. celery seed
1 Tbsp. salt

Pour over cabbage and stir.

Herman Scherer, *Calling All Cooks two*, Alabama Chapter No. 34

## Celery Seed Dressing (Low Sodium)

1/3 cup sugar
1 Tbsp. paprika
1/2 tsp. dry mustard
1/2 cup wine or cider vinegar
1/2 cup oil
1 onion, thinly sliced
1 Tbsp. celery seed

Place all ingredients in blender for 30 seconds. Store in refrigerator. Shake before serving. Yield: 1 1/2 cups.

Lenora Thomas, *Secret Recipes of Telephone Pioneers, Volume III*
South Carolina Chapter No. 61

## Sweet Celery Seed Dressing

1 14-ounce can sweetened condensed milk
1/3 cup oil
1/3 cup cider vinegar
1 teaspoon celery seed
3/4 teaspoon dry mustard
1/2 teaspoon salt
1/4 teaspoon pepper

Combine condensed milk, oil, vinegar, celery seed, dry mustard, salt and pepper in mixing bowl. Beat until well mixed. This dressing is especially good with cabbage slaw, lettuce salads and fruit salads. Yield: 2 1/2 cups.

Dollie D. Billiter, *Kentucky Kitchens, Volume II*
Kentucky Chapter No. 32

## Creamy Herb Dressing

1 egg
1 small onion, quartered
2 cloves garlic
3 tsp. Dijon mustard
1/2 tsp. salt
1/4 tsp. pepper
1 tsp. tarragon
1/2 tsp. basil
1/2 c. tarragon vinegar
1 1/2 c. vegetable oil
1/4 c. minced parsley

Process all ingredients except oil and parsley in a blender or food processor. With blender running slowly drizzle in 1 cup vegetable oil until the dressing is thick and creamy. Stir in 1 tablespoon minced parsley.

Makes 2 cups.

Jeanne Gray, *Pioneers Pots and Pans—1985 Cookbook*
North Florida Chapter No. 39

## French Dressing (Low Sodium)

1/2 cup oil
3 Tbsp. vinegar
2 Tbsp. lemon juice
1 tsp. dry mustard
1 1/2 tsp. paprika
1/4 tsp. pepper
1/8 tsp. garlic powder
1/8 tsp. onion powder
1/4 tsp. dried sweet basil

Combine all ingredients. Store in covered jar in refrigerator until ready to use. Shake well before using. Yield: 3/4 cup.

Lenora Thomas, *Secret Recipes of Telephone Pioneers, Volume III*
South Carolina Chapter No. 61

## Honey Mustard Dressing

1 cup plain low-fat yogurt
1/2 teaspoon honey
1 tablespoon mustard

Combine all ingredients in bowl; mix well. Store in refrigerator. Use as salad dressing or vegetable dip. Yield: 16 tablespoons.

**Approx Per Tablespoon:** Cal 11; Prot 1 g; Carbo 1 g; Fiber <1 g; T Fat <1 g; Chol <1 mg; Sod 22 mg.
**Dietary Exchanges:** Free

"*Answering the Call of Those in Need*," Tennessee Chapter No. 21

# Honey Mustard Salad Dressing

3/4 cup safflower oil
1/2 cup red wine vinegar
1/2 cup honey
1/4 cup Dijon Mustard
2 cloves garlic, minced, or 1/2 tsp. garlic powder
2 tsp. black pepper
2 tsp. salt

Mix well and chill. Makes enough for two salads. Keeps for 3 weeks.

David and Sandy Bradley
*Secret Recipes of Telephone Pioneers, Volume III*
South Carolina Chapter No. 61

# Spinach Salad Dressing

1 1/2 Tbsp. minced onion (can use dry onion)
3 Tbsp. yellow mustard
1 1/2 Tbsp. Accent
1 1/2 Tbsp. salt
2/3 c. warm water
1 tsp. Worcestershire
2/3 c. vinegar
2 1/2 c. salad oil
Dash of Tabasco

Mix well!

Joanne Cothern, *Pots, Pans and Pioneers, Volume IV*
Louisiana Chapter No. 24

# Thousand Island Dressing

1 8-ounce bottle of stuffed green olives
1 quart mayonnaise
2 tablespoons sugar
5 hard-boiled eggs
Juice of 1 lemon
1 8-ounce jar pickle relish
2 teaspoons chili powder
1 teaspoon paprika

Process olives in blender until chopped. Add mayonnaise, sugar, eggs, lemon juice, relish, chili powder and paprika, processing constantly until smooth. Yield: 112 (1-tablespoon) servings.

**Approx Per Serving:** Cal 66; Prot <1 g; Carbo 1 g; Fiber <1 g; T Fat 7 g; 90% Calories from Fat; Chol 14 mg; Sod 104 mg.

R. O. Whaley, *Calling All Cooks three*, Alabama Chapter No. 34

# Meats

1974-1994
TELEPHONE PIONEERS
OF AMERICA
DOGWOOD
CHAPTER NO. 84

# 7-Up Smoked Brisket

1 whole brisket
1 c. smoky BBQ sauce
1 c. 7-Up
1 pkg. onion soup mix
½ c. red wine
Liquid smoke to taste
Pepper to taste
Seasoned salt to taste

Marinate at least overnight in microwave of BBQ sauce, 7-Up, onion soup mix, and other seasonings. Put in covered roaster and bake 4 to 6 hours (according to size of brisket) in 325° oven, covering brisket with marinade.

Ina N. Porter, *Pots, Pans and Pioneers, Volume IV*
Louisiana Chapter No. 24

# Eye-of-Round Roast with Vegetables

1 2-pound eye-of-round roast, trimmed
3 medium carrots, cut into 2-inch pieces
8 ounces new potatoes, peeled, cut into eighths
1 medium onion, coarsely chopped
2 stalks celery, cut into 4-inch pieces
1 tablespoon low-sodium soy sauce
½ cup dry red wine
½ cup beef stock
½ teaspoon freshly ground pepper
1 tablespoon cornstarch
¼ cup cold water
½ cup chopped parsley

Place roast in oven-roasting bag. Add carrots, potatoes, onion, celery, soy sauce, wine, beef stock and pepper; secure bag. Place in baking pan; pierce several holes in top of bag. Roast at 325 degrees for 1 hour. Cool for 10 to 15 minutes. Remove roast to carving board; pour vegetables and drippings into saucepan. Remove vegetables to bowl with slotted spoon. Skim pan drippings. Spoon a small amount of drippings over roast, let roast stand for 10 minutes. Stir mixture of cornstarch and water into remaining drippings in saucepan. Cook until thickened, stirring constantly. Pour into gravy bowl. Slice roast cross grain; place on warm serving platter. Arrange vegetables around roast. sprinkle with chopped parsley. Serve with gravy. Yield: 8 servings.

**Approx Per Serving:** Cal 218; Prot 23 g; Carbo 13 g; Fiber 2 g; T Fat 7 g; Chol 64 mg; Sod 267 mg.

Phyllis Jones, *Carolina Cooking*, North Carolina Chapter No. 35

# *Beef and Broccoli Stir-Fry*

8 ounces boneless beef steak
1 tablespoon cornstarch
1 tablespoon soy sauce
1 teaspoon sugar
2 teaspoons minced gingerroot
1 clove of garlic, minced
1 tablespoon cornstarch
3 tablespoons soy sauce
1 cup water
3 tablespoons oil
Flowerets of 1 pound broccoli
1 onion, coarsely chopped
1 carrot, sliced

Cut beef cross grain into thin slices. Combine 1 tablespoon cornstarch, 1 tablespoon soy sauce, sugar, gingerroot and garlic in bowl. Add beef; mix to coat well. Let stand for 15 minutes. Combine 1 tablespoon cornstarch and 3 tablespoons soy sauce with water in bowl; set aside. Heat 1 tablespoon oil in wok. Add beef. Stir-fry for 1 minute; remove to bowl. Heat remaining 2 tablespoons oil in wok. Add broccoli, onion and carrot. Stir-fry for 4 minutes or until tender-crisp. Add beef and reserved cornstarch mixture. Cook until thickened, stirring constantly. Yield: 4 servings.

**Approx Per Serving:** Cal 237; Prot 16 g; Carbo 17 g; Fiber 5 g; T Fat 13 g; Chol 27 mg; Sod 1090 mg.
**Dietary Exchanges:** Vegetable 2; Bread/Starch 1/2; Meat 1 1/2; Fat 2

"*Answering the Call of Those in Need*," Tennessee Chapter No. 21

*Everyone helps with a Habitat for Humanity project.*
(Dogwood Chapter No. 84)

# *Beef Roll*

1 clove of garlic, finely sliced
1 teaspoon grated Parmesan cheese
1 hard-boiled egg, chopped
1/2 teaspoon chopped parsley
2 slices bacon, cut into 1-inch pieces
1/2 teaspoon salt
1/8 teaspoon pepper
1 1 1/2-pound round steak, 1/2 inch thick
1 small onion, sliced
1/4 cup olive oil
1 20-ounce can tomatoes, sieved
1 bay leaf
1/2 teaspoon salt
1/4 teaspoon pepper

Combine garlic, cheese, egg, parsley, bacon, 1/2 teaspoon salt and 1/8 teaspoon pepper in bowl; mix well. Spread on steak. Roll up steak to enclose filling; tie securely. Sauté onion in olive oil in skillet until tender. Add steak roll. Cook until brown on all sides. Combine tomatoes, bay leaf, 1/2 teaspoon salt and 1/4 teaspoon pepper in bowl; mix well. Spread over steak. Simmer, covered, for 1 1/2 hours or until done to taste. Discard bay leaf and string. Slice steak roll. Serve with sauce. Yield: 4 to 5 servings.

Margaret Casalino, *Lawfully Good Eating*, Dixie Chapter No. 23

# *Swiss Bliss*

1/2 Tbsp. butter or margarine
2 lbs. round steak, 1 inch thick
1 envelope onion soup mix
1/2 lb. mushrooms, sliced (may use canned)
1/2 green pepper, sliced
1 lb. canned tomatoes, drained and chopped (reserve juice)
1/4 tsp. salt
freshly ground pepper
1/2 c. juice from tomatoes
1 Tbsp. A-1 steak sauce
1 Tbsp. cornstarch
20 inch sheet heavy duty foil
1 Tbsp. chopped parsley
assorted garnishes

Spread center of foil with butter or margarine. Cut steak into serving portions. Arrange on foil, slightly overlapping each portion. Sprinkle with onion soup mix, mushrooms, green pepper, tomatoes. Season. Mix juice, A-1 sauce and cornstarch. Pour over meat and vegetables. Bring foil up over and fold tightly. Bake 2 hours at 375°. Roll back foil and sprinkle with parsley.

Makes 4 servings.

Linda F. Williams, *Pioneers Pots and Pans—1985 Cookbook*
North Florida Chapter No. 39

## *Hawaiian Pepper Steak*

1½ pounds beef sirloin steak
2 teaspoons MSG
¼ cup oil
1 can beef broth
½ teaspoon sugar
¼ teaspoon dry mustard
1½ tablespoons soy sauce
1 onion, finely chopped
1 green bell pepper, finely chopped
1 tablespoons cornstarch
2 tablespoons pineapple juice
1 small can pineapple chunks
4 servings cooked rice

Cut steak into thin strips; sprinkle with 1 teaspoon MSG. Brown in hot oil in large skillet. Add next 4 ingredients. Simmer for 15 to 20 minutes, stirring frequently. Add onion, green pepper and remaining 1 teaspoon MSG. Cook for 5 minutes. Blend cornstarch with pineapple juice in small bowl. Add to pepper steak gradually, stirring until thickened. Add pineapple. Simmer for 3 to 5 minutes or until heated through. Serve over rice. Yield: 4 servings.

Frank Fendley, *Kentucky Kitchens, Volume II*, Kentucky Chapter No. 32

## *Pepper Steak Quick and Easy*

1½ lb. sirloin (or round) steak (all fat removed)
½ tsp. salt
2 Tbsp. safflower or corn oil
2 medium onions, cut into rings
1 10½ oz. can of beef broth
3 Tbsp. soy sauce (or to taste)
1 clove garlic, minced
2 green peppers, cut into strips
¼ cup cold water
2 Tbsp. cornstarch
2 tomatoes, peeled and cut into eights

Trim fat from meat, cut meat into strips (one inch wide). Brown meat in oil in 12 inch skillet, seasoning with salt. Push meat to side of pan. Add onions, cook, and stir until tender. Drain well. Return to pan. Add broth, soy sauce and garlic. Cover, simmer 15 minutes or until meat is tender. Add green peppers and simmer 5 to 10 minutes longer. Blend cornstarch and water, stir gradually into meat mixture. Cook, stirring constantly, until mixture thickens and boils. Boil and stir one minute. Add tomatoes, heat through. Serve over rice. This takes about 30 minutes to prepare. Serves 4–6.

Maybelle Hawkinson, *Secret Recipes of Telephone Pioneers, Volume III*
South Carolina Chapter No. 61

## Aunt Eunice's Pepper Steak Stew

3 lbs. pepper steak
1 stick butter
3 cloves garlic
1/2 c. chopped onion
2 green peppers
1 can (1 lb.) tomatoes
1 beef bouillon
1 tbsp. cornstarch
1/4 c. water
3 tbsp. soy sauce
1 tsp. sugar
1 tsp. salt

In skillet melt butter. Add garlic, beef and sauté until browned. Remove meat. Add onions and green pepper, sauté 2 minutes. Return meat to skillet along with tomatoes and bouillon cube. Simmer 5 minutes.

Blend cornstarch, water, soy sauce, sugar and salt. Stir into meat mixture. Cook until thickened. Serve over noodles.

Moni (Ramona) Garceau
*A Tablespoon of Pioneering and a Teaspoon of Horses and the Handicapped*
Florida Gold Coast Chapter No. 83

## Marinated Shish Kabobs

1/2 cup oil
1 tablespoon cider vinegar
2 tablespoons fresh lemon juice
2 tablespoons finely chopped onion
1 small clove of garlic, minced
1 teaspoon chili powder
1/2 teaspoon poultry seasoning
1/2 teaspoon oregano
1/2 teaspoon ginger
2 teaspoons salt
1/4 teaspoon pepper
2 pounds sirloin steak cubes
12 cherry tomatoes
12 small onions
2 green bell peppers, cut into 1-inch pieces

Combine oil, vinegar, lemon juice, chopped onion, garlic, chili powder, poultry seasoning, oregano, ginger, salt and pepper in bowl. Add steak cubes; mix well. Marinate in refrigerator overnight or at room temperature for 3 to 4 hours. Thread steak cubes on skewers alternately with cherry tomatoes, small onions and green pepper pieces. Grill for 15 to 20 minutes or until done to taste, turning frequently. Serve with rice or baked potatoes for a complete meal. Yield: 6 servings.

**Approx Per Serving:** Cal 432; Prot 31 g; Carbo 16 g; Fiber 4 g; T Fat 28 g; Chol 85 mg; Sod 765 mg.
Nutritional information includes entire amount of marinade.

Wilma Burleson, *Carolina Cooking*, North Carolina Chapter No. 35

## Beef Stroganoff

**3 Tbsp. butter**
**1/2 lb. mushrooms**
**1 large onion, sliced**
**1 1/2–2 lb. flank steak**
**1 Tbsp. horseradish**
**1/2 c. water**
**1 tsp. A.1. Sauce**
**1 1/4 tsp. salt**
**1/8 tsp. pepper**
**1 c. sour cream**

Melt butter; sauté mushrooms and onions for 5 minutes; remove from fat. Trim fat from steak; mince fat and add to butter in skillet. Remove tough, fibrous skin from steak. Slice meat across grain into 1 inch strips; roll in flour; brown on all sides in butter. Place onion/mushroom mixture on top of meat. Add remaining ingredients except sour cream. Cover; cook over low heat for 2 or until meat is tender. Just before serving add sour cream. Thicken gravy if desired. Makes 6 servings.

Dianne Roberts, *Dining with Pioneers, Volume II*
Tennessee Chapter No. 21

## Beef Stroganoff

**1 1/2 lb. sirloin steak**
**Flour**
**1 1/2 tsp. salt**
**1/2 tsp. pepper**
**2 onions, finely chopped**
**1/2 lb. mushrooms, chopped**
**1 Tbsp. Worcestershire**
**1 clove garlic, crushed**
**6 Tbsp. butter**
**1 (10 oz.) can consommé**
**1 pt. sour cream**
**1 tsp. paprika**

Cut steak into strips and dredge with flour. Season with 1 teaspoon salt and 1/4 teaspoon pepper. Sauté onions, mushrooms and garlic in butter in skillet for 5 minutes. Add steak and cook over high heat 3 minutes, stirring constantly. Then remove steak and vegetables from skillet. Blend 2 tablespoons flour into 2 tablespoons drippings in the skillet; add consommé and cook, stirring until smooth and thickened. Stir in the sour cream and remaining salt and pepper; place over low heat. Add the paprika, Worcestershire sauce, beef and vegetables; heat thoroughly. Serve over noodles or rice. Serves 4.

Sandi Freeman, *Kentucky Kitchens, Volume I*, Kentucky Chapter No. 32

## Kentucky Burgoo

**2 lb. lean beef**
**1 medium size stewing chicken**
**1 lb. veal**
**4 qt. water**
**2 c. chopped okra**
**2 green peppers, chopped**
**1 small red pepper**
**1 qt. tomatoes**
**6 ears corn, cut off cobs**
**2 c. diced raw potatoes**
**2 c. onions, diced**
**3 large carrots, diced**
**1 garlic clove, mashed**
**1 c. minced fresh parsley**
**1 bunch celery, chopped (with leaves)**
**Salt and pepper to taste**
**3 c. dry sherry**

Boil beef, chicken and veal in water until tender. Remove meat from bones and replace meat in pot. Add other ingredients, except sherry, and cook over slow heat for 2 hours. The mixture should be very thick. Stir it up from the bottom occasionally. Before serving, add sherry and stir well. Serves 12.

Paula White, *Kentucky Kitchens, Volume I*, Kentucky Chapter No. 32

## Liver and Onions

**1½ lb. beef or calves liver, sliced ¼ inch thick**
**4 Tbsp. oleo**
**3 medium size onions, sliced**
**2–4 Tbsp. olive oil**
**2 Tbsp. cider or wine vinegar**
**1½ tsp. salt**
**¼ tsp. ground pepper**

Trim membrane from liver (if chilled it is easier to slice); rinse in cold water and dry on paper toweling. Cut into 1x2 inch strips. Heat butter in a large skillet. Add onions; sauté over medium heat until soft and light brown. Remove with slotted spoon to a plate; keep warm. Add 2 tablespoons oil to skillet; turn heat to high. Add liver; cook, stirring constantly, until liver loses its red color and starts to brown, about 3 to 4 minutes. Return onions to skillet; stir in vinegar, salt and pepper; toss with fork to blend. Cook 1 to 2 minutes.

This recipe is best if cooked quickly.

Mrs. Reg Lowery, *Kentucky Kitchens, Volume I*
Kentucky Chapter No. 32

## Burger Bundles

1 cup herb-seasoned stuffing mix
1 pound ground beef
1/2 cup evaporated milk
1 tablespoon catsup
1 can cream of mushroom soup
2 teaspoons Worcestershire sauce

Prepare stuffing mix using package directions. Combine ground beef with evaporated milk in bowl; mix well. Shape into five 6-inch patties on waxed paper. Spoon 1/4 cup stuffing into center of each patty. Fold edges of patties over to enclose filling; seal edges. Place in 1 1/2-quart baking dish. Combine catsup, soup and Worcestershire sauce in saucepan. Heat to boiling point. Pour over patties. Bake at 350 degrees for 45 to 50 minutes or until done to taste. Yield: 5 servings.

**Approx Per Serving:** Cal 445; Prot 25 g; Carbo 41 g; Fiber <1 g; T Fat 20 g; Chol 65 mg; Sod 1398 mg.

Nancy Riley, *Carolina Cooking*, North Carolina Chapter No. 35

## Cabbage Roll Casserole

1 to 3 lb. ground beef
1 Tbsp. oleo
1 chopped onion
1/2 Tbsp. salt
1/2 tsp. pepper
1 (10 oz.) can tomato soup
1 (14 oz.) can stewed tomatoes
5 Tbsp. raw rice
3 to 6 c. coarsely chopped cabbage

Brown meat in oleo. Pour off excess fat. Add onion, salt, pepper, rice, soup, and tomatoes; heat. Put raw cabbage in greased casserole. Pour meat mixture over. Do not stir. Bake, covered, for 90 minutes at 325° F.

Sara Davis, *Dogwood Delights Volume II*, Dogwood Chapter No. 84

### A Helpful Hint

One of the best ways to remove fat from ground beef or sausage is to microwave it in a colander. Place a bowl under the colander to collect the fat as it cooks out of the beef.

## Quick and Easy Unstuffed Cabbage

**small green cabbage**
**1 lb. ground chuck**
**1/4 c. chopped onions**
**1/4 c. chopped green pepper**
**1/4 c. chopped celery**
**1 can tomato sauce**

1. Coarsely chop cabbage and steam.

2. Brown meat and sauté onions, green pepper and celery and milk.

3. Heat tomato sauce.

To serve, on a bed of cabbage, spoon meat and vegetable mixture, then spoon tomato sauce over the top. Don't look like stuffed cabbage, but sure taste like it.

Timi Pratt, *Pioneers Pots and Pans—1985 Cookbook*
North Florida Chapter No. 39

## Stuffed Cabbage Rolls

**1 large head cabbage, cored**
**1/2 c. water**
**1 1/2 lb. ground beef**
**1/2 c. finely chopped onion**
**1/2 c. quick cooking rice**
**1 egg**
**1 tsp. Worcestershire sauce**
**1/2 tsp. leaf basil**
**1 tsp. salt**
**1/4 tsp. pepper**
**1 (8 oz.) can tomato sauce**

1. Place cabbage in 2 quart glass casserole dish. Pour water in bottom of dish. Cover with plastic wrap.

2. Microwave on high for 8–10 minutes or until cabbage is partly cooked; set aside. Crumble ground beef in medium mixing bowl. Stir in remaining ingredients, except tomato sauce. Remove 12 cabbage leaves from partly cooked cabbage. Place an equal amount of meat mixture in each leaf. Roll up and secure with toothpick. Place in 2 quart baking dish. Cover with plastic wrap. 3. Microwave on high for 13–15 minutes. Pour tomato sauce over cabbage rolls. Recover and continue cooking on high for 2–3 minutes or until hot. Let stand, covered, for 5 minutes before serving.

Nell Martin, *Bell's Best*, Mississippi Chapter No. 36

## Company Casserole

2 lbs. ground beef
1 pkg. (8 oz.) noodles
1/2 c. chopped onion
1/4 c. chopped green pepper
1 Tbsp. lard or drippings
1 1/2 tsp. salt
1/8 tsp. pepper
1 can (8 oz.) tomato sauce
1 can (4 oz.) mushroom stems and pieces
2 pkg. (3 oz. each) cream cheese
1/3 c. milk
1/4 tsp. garlic salt
2 tsp. lemon juice
1 tsp. Worcestershire sauce

Cook noodles according to direction on package. Brown ground beef, onions and green pepper in lard or drippings. Pour off drippings. Add salt, pepper, tomato sauce and mushrooms and liquid to meat mixture. Combine the cream cheese, milk, lemon juice, garlic salt and Worcestershire sauce and mix until smooth. Add the noodles to the cream cheese mixture. Alternate layers of noodles and meat mixture in a 2 1/2 quart casserole. Bake in a moderate oven (350° F.) 25 to 30 minutes.

Margaret Jones, *Pioneers Pots and Pans—1985 Cookbook*
North Florida Chapter No. 39

## Hamburger Casserole

1 1/2 lb. hamburger meat
1 small can tomato sauce
1 (12 oz.) can Mexicorn with red and green peppers
1 can Ro-Tel tomatoes
1 small onion
1 clove garlic
1 Tbsp. chili powder
1 (16 oz.) pkg. small macaroni shells
Salt and pepper to taste
1 medium size pkg. mild cheese, grated

Sauté onions and garlic in small amount of oil. Add hamburger; cook until browned well. Add chili powder, Mexicorn, tomatoes and tomato sauce. Cook in Dutch oven about 35 minutes with lid on. Cook shells until tender; drain. Add layer of shells, sauce, grated cheese and repeat until all is used. Good also with small can of mushrooms. Cook in 350° oven until cheese has melted well.

Tommie Willoughby, *Bell's Best 2*, Mississippi Chapter No. 36

# Mexican Casserole

Makes a lot!

**2 lb. ground beef**
**1 bell pepper**
**1 large onion**
**1 c. chopped mushrooms**
**1 can tomatoes**
**1 can tomato sauce**
**1 can white shoe peg corn**
**3 drops Tabasco or other hot sauce—or to taste**
**1 (8 oz.) bag egg noodles**
**grated cheddar cheese**
**seasoning salt to taste**

Brown beef, onions and bell peppers. Add mushrooms, tomatoes, tomato sauce, corn and Tabasco. Let simmer 20 minutes. Boil and drain noodles, add a small amount of oleo to keep from sticking together. Then add noodles to other ingredients. When ready to serve, add grated cheese and melt.

Delicious.

Mrs. Pyron, *Pioneers Pots and Pans—1985 Cookbook*
North Florida Chapter No. 39

# Mexicorn Casserole

**1 lb. ground chuck**
**1 onion**
**1 can Van Camp's Spanish rice**
**1 small or large can Mexicorn**
**1 can tomato sauce**
**Grated Cheddar cheese**
**Salt and pepper to taste**
**1/2 tsp. chili powder**

Brown onion and ground beef; salt and pepper to taste. Drain if desired. In large skillet (or electric skillet), combine onion, beef, Spanish rice, Mexicorn, tomato sauce, and chili powder. Mix together and cook over medium heat for 20 to 25 minutes, stirring occasionally. Spoon cheese over top of mixture and cook until cheese is melted.

Margie Sasser, *Bell's Best 3*, Mississippi Chapter No. 36

## A Helpful Hint

Use extra-lean ground round or ground beef in meat loaves and meatballs to reduce fat and cholesterol. Extra-lean ground beef contains about 11 percent fat.

## *Old English Casserole*

8 oz. pkg. noodles
$1\frac{1}{2}$ lb. ground beef
1 large onion, diced
1 Tbsp. flour
$\frac{1}{2}$ tsp. seasoned salt
$\frac{1}{4}$ tsp. lemon pepper
1 can (3 or 4 oz.) sliced mushrooms
1 can (1 lb.) French cut green beans
1 can (15 oz.) tomato sauce
1 c. grated cheddar cheese

Place cooked noodles in a lightly greased 8-cup baking dish. Brown beef in a large skillet; remove meat to a bowl and sauté onion in fat until tender; return beef. Blend in flour, seasoned salt and lemon pepper. Stir in mushrooms and liquid, green beans—drained and tomato sauce. Spoon mixture over noodles; sprinkle with cheese.

Tracy Wright, *Pioneers Pots and Pans—1985 Cookbook*
North Florida Chapter No. 39

## *Chili*

3 lb. lean diced beef
1 qt. water
3 tsp. salt
5 cloves garlic, finely chopped
1 tsp. marjoram
1 Tbsp. sugar
$\frac{1}{4}$ c. liquid shortening
8 chili pods, or 6 Tbsp. chili powder
1 tsp. ground cumin
1 tsp. red pepper
3 Tbsp. paprika
6 Tbsp. corn meal, 3 Tbsp. flour and 1 c. water for thickening

Heat oil in large pot, add meat and sear over high heat. Stir constantly until meat is gray, but not brown. Add water and cover, cook over low fire for $1\frac{1}{2}$–2 hours. Add remaining ingredients, except thickening, and cook at a bubbling simmer 30 minutes. Mix thickening ingredients together, add to chili mixture, cook about 5 minutes, stirring to prevent sticking. More water may be added for desired consistency. If meat is very fat, skim off before adding thickening. For milder flavor, cut chili powder and red pepper in half, but add 2 more tablespoons paprika for color.

Betty Harman, *Pots, Pans & Pioneers II*, Louisiana Chapter No. 24

# Alarm Chili

1 pound extra-lean ground beef
1 medium onion, finely chopped
3 cloves of garlic, finely chopped
1 large green bell pepper, cut into 1/2-inch pieces
2 28-ounce cans tomatoes, crushed
1 tablespoon oil
2 teaspoons oregano
2 teaspoons cumin
3 tablespoons chili powder
2 tablespoons baking cocoa
2 teaspoons sugar
1 teaspoon crushed hot pepper
1 teaspoon Tabasco sauce
1 15-ounce can kidney beans, rinsed, drained

Cook ground beef in 2 1/2-quart saucepan over medium heat for 6 to 8 minutes or until well done, stirring until crumbly. Remove ground beef with slotted spoon to paper towels to drain. Drain and wipe saucepan. Sauté onion, garlic and green pepper with 1/2 cup tomatoes in oil in saucepan for 3 minutes. Add oregano, cumin, chili powder, cocoa, sugar, hot pepper and Tabasco sauce. Cook for 3 minutes. Add beans, ground beef and remaining tomatoes. Simmer for 25 minutes.
Yield: 8 servings.

**Approx Per Serving:** Cal 255; Prot 18 g; Carbo 25 g; Fiber 8 g; T Fat 11 g; Chol 37 mg; Sod 360 mg.

Phyllis Jones, *Carolina Cooking*, North Carolina Chapter No. 35

# "Damn Good Chili"

2 lb. coarse ground round
1 large onion, chopped
1 green pepper, chopped
1 8-oz. can tomato sauce
1 8-oz. can water
1 Tbsp. chili powder
1/4 tsp. cayenne pepper
1/2 tsp. black pepper
1/2 tsp. oregano
1 tsp. ground cumin
2 cloves garlic, finely chopped
1 tsp. salt

Brown meat, onion and green pepper. Add remaining ingredients. Cook, covered, for 20 minutes on medium high heat. Reduce heat and cook for about 1 hour. Serve with kidney beans, or use for hot dogs or spaghetti.

Dorothy H. Roland, *Secret Recipes of Telephone Pioneers, Volume III*
South Carolina Chapter No. 61

# *South Florida Chili*

**Origin:** The Mind of the Beholder. **Year created:** 1982. **Brief history:** Produced from years of trying and trying and failing and failing, this finally erupted from the pot.

**1/4 c. vegetable oil**
**2 large cloves garlic, minced**
**2 large onions, chopped fine**
**1 lb. coarsely ground beef (lean)**
**1/2 lb. coarsely ground pork (lean)**
**1/2 lb. coarsely ground veal**
**4 slices diced lean bacon**
**2 (16 oz.) cans tomatoes (undrained)**
**1 c. water**
**1/2 c. chili powder or to taste**
**2 Tbsp. masa harina**
**1 Tbsp. sugar**
**2 tsp. ground cumin**
**2 tsp. salt**
**1 tsp. ground red pepper**
**1/8 tsp. freshly ground pepper**
**2 (16 or 17 oz.) can kidney beans, drained**
**2 to 3 jalapeño peppers, seeded and finely chopped**

Heat oil in Dutch oven or other heavy large pot over medium heat. Add onion, garlic and bacon and sauté until onions are softened, about 5 minutes. Increase heat; add beef, pork and veal and cook until onions are well browned. Spoon off any excess fat. Add remaining ingredients except beans and peppers and bring to boil over high heat. Reduce heat and simmer 2 hours, adding water if chili becomes too thick. Stir in beans during last 30 minutes of cooking time. Blend in peppers to taste just before serving or reserve for addition to taste.

You may want to grate some New York sharp Cheddar cheese to add on the top of this stuff.

**Preparation time:** 30 minutes.
**Cooking time:** 2 hours and 15 minutes.
**No. of servings:** 10 to 12.

Bill Wingender, *A Taste of Pioneering*
Florida Gold Coast Chapter No. 83

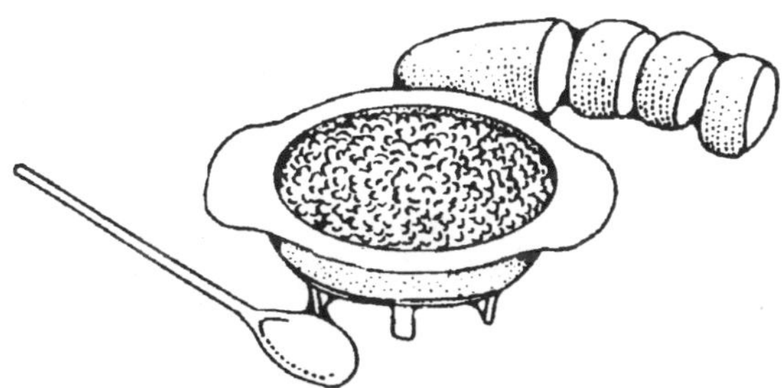

# Dirty Rice

2 or 2½ lb. ground beef
1 lb. ground pork
4 onions
1 head garlic
1 green bell pepper
3 stalks celery
1 bunch green onions
2 Tbsp. Kitchen Bouquet
1 Tbsp. smoke liquid
Salt and pepper to taste
2 to 3 Tbsp. parsley flakes
6 c. rice

Spray large pot with Pam. Fry down meat. Mix in seasonings, onions, garlic, bell pepper, and celery. Add Kitchen Bouquet, smoke liquid, salt, and pepper. Cook about 1 to 1½ hours. Add parsley flakes. Mix in *cooked* rice. Add green onions.

Wilma Reed, *Pots, Pans and Pioneers, Volume IV*
Louisiana Chapter No. 24

# Lasagna

½ lb. lasagna noodles
2 Tbsp. butter
½ c. finely chopped onion
1 clove garlic, finely chopped
1 lb. ground beef
¾ c. (6 oz. can) tomato paste
2½ c. (1 lb. 4 oz. can) tomatoes
1 tsp. salt
⅛ tsp. pepper
¼ tsp. dried basil
½ lb. Ricotta or cottage cheese
½ lb. Swiss cheese slices
½ c. grated Parmesan cheese
¼ Tbsp. dried oregano

Cook noodles in 4 quarts boiling salted water until tender. Stir occasionally while cooking. Drain and rinse with hot water. Separate noodles and hang over edge of colander. While noodles are cooking, melt butter in large skillet. Add onion and garlic, cook gently about 5 minutes. Add ground beef and cook slowly until browned. Stir in tomato paste, tomatoes, salt, pepper, basil, and oregano. Cook, stirring occasionally, for about 30 minutes.

Grease an 8-inch square baking dish; layer meat sauce, noodles, Ricotta, Swiss and Parmesan cheeses, using about ⅓ of each. Repeat layers twice to use all the ingredients. Top with Parmesan cheese. Bake in moderate oven (350°F.) until bubbly and cheese is lightly browned, about 35–40 minutes.

Scot Shaw, *Dining with Pioneers, Volume II*, Tennessee Chapter No. 21

# *Lasagna Pie*

1 pound ground beef
1 6-ounce can tomato paste
1 1/2 teaspoons basil
1 teaspoon oregano
1/2 cup shredded mozzarella cheese
1/2 cup cream-style cottage cheese
1/4 cup Parmesan cheese
Topping
1/2 cup shredded mozzarella cheese

Brown ground beef in skillet, stirring until crumbly; drain. Add tomato paste, basil, oregano and 1/2 cup mozzarella cheese; mix well. Layer cottage cheese, Parmesan cheese and ground beef mixture in greased 10-inch pie plate. Pour topping over layers. Bake at 400 degrees for 30 to 35 minutes or until knife inserted between center and edge comes out clean. Sprinkle with 1/2 cup mozzarella cheese. Yield: 6 servings.

## Topping for Lasagna Pie

2/3 cup baking mix
1 cup milk
2 eggs
1 teaspoon salt
1/4 teaspoon pepper

Combine all ingredients in blender container or bowl. Process or high speed for 15 seconds or beat for 1 minute with rotary beater.

**Approx Per Serving:** Cal 383; Prot 27 g; Carbo 19 g; Fiber 1 g; T Fat 22 g; Chol 146 mg; Sod 860 mg.

Eddie Haskin, *Carolina Cooking*, North Carolina Chapter No. 35

*Life Members donating flip tops for Ronald McDonald House.*
(Florida Gold Coast Chapter No. 83)

# Magnolia's Tallerine

2 lb. ground steak
1 medium sized onion, cut fine
2 Tbsp. butter
1 can tomato soup
2 c. (heaping) uncooked noodles
1 can corn
1 can ripe olives
1 c. grated cheese
Salt to taste

Melt butter and brown onion and meat in it. Add tomato soup and uncooked noodles to about 1 cup of water or more (enough to keep it moist). When noodles are tender, add corn and olives, which have been cut and seeded. Pour into buttered baking dish; spread grated cheese over top and bake at 350° for 45 minutes. Let stand in oven with heat off 15 minutes before servings.

*Pots, Pans and Pioneers III*, Louisiana Chapter No. 24

# Oven Porcupines

1 pound ground beef
1/2 cup uncooked rice
1/2 cup water
1/3 cup chopped onion
1/8 teaspoon garlic powder
1/2 teaspoon celery salt
1 teaspoon salt
1/8 teaspoon pepper
1 15-ounce can tomato sauce
1 cup water
2 teaspoons Worcestershire sauce

Combine ground beef, rice, 1/2 cup water, onion, garlic powder, celery salt, salt and pepper in bowl; mix well. Shape by rounded tablespoonfuls into balls; place in ungreased 8x8-inch baking dish. Combine tomato sauce, 1 cup water and Worcestershire sauce in bowl; mix well. Spoon over meatballs. Bake, covered with foil, at 350 degrees for 45 minutes. Bake, uncovered, for 15 minutes longer. Yield: 4 to 6 servings.

Kathy Bailey, *Lawfully Good Eating*, Dixie Chapter No. 23

## A Helpful Hint

Meat loaf will not stick to the pan if you place a slice of bacon in the bottom of the baking pan.

## *Easy Swedish Meatballs*

1 egg
1/2 c. evaporated milk
2 slices toast
1 medium onion, chopped
1 tsp. sugar
1 tsp. pepper
1 tsp. salt
1/2 tsp. nutmeg
1 large potato (or 1 c. instant mashed)
1 lb. ground beef
1/2 lb. ground pork

Beat eggs slightly, add milk and toast. Let stand. Mix remaining ingredients. Add milk mixture, mix well. Roll small balls in flour and brown in oil or oleo. Can be served in milk gravy.

Beverly Balue, *Pioneers Pots and Pans—1985 Cookbook*
North Florida Chapter No. 39

## *Ann Landers' Meat Loaf*

2 lb. ground round steak
1 tsp. monosodium glutamate
1 1/2 c. bread crumbs
1/4 c. warm water
3/4 c. ketchup
2 eggs
1 env. onion soup mix
1 (8 oz.) can tomato sauce

Combine all ingredients thoroughly. Place in large greased loaf pan. Cover with 2 strips of bacon, if you like the flavor. Pour over it all an 8 ounce can tomato sauce. Bake 1 hour in preheated 350° oven. Serves 6.

Dora Sills, *Bell's Best*, Mississippi Chapter No. 36

## *Microwave Meat Loaf*

*Combine:*
1 1/2 lb. ground beef
1 slightly beaten egg
1 c. soft bread crumbs
1/2 c. milk
3 Tbsp. Heinz 57 Sauce
1 1/4 tsp. salt
dash pepper

Shape into loaf pan (8x4x1 1/2 inch) lightly greased. Make it a shallow pan if possible. Brush top with additional 57 sauce. Microwave 20 minutes, uncovered, and let stand 10 minutes covered.

Connie Berryman, *Pioneers Pots and Pans—1985 Cookbook*
North Florida Chapter No. 39

# Old-Fashioned Meat Loaf

1 lb. ground chuck
1 can tomatoes (cheapest brand)
Dash of Worcestershire sauce
10 crackers (single)
1 egg
Salt and Pepper to taste
1 small bell pepper
1 medium onion, finely chopped

Lift tomatoes out of can with a fork. Combine tomatoes, crackers and well beaten egg; let stand for 5 minutes. Add meat, salt, pepper, and Worcestershire sauce. Grease black skillet; shape in 2 oval loaves. Pour tomato juice, that was left in can, in between loaves at end; put pepper wedges in juice. Start baking at 425° until juice starts bubbling; reduce heat down to 350°—about 45 minutes in all. Stir in small amount of flour in pan for gravy.

Kitty Logan, *Calling All Cooks two*, Alabama Chapter No. 34

# Pizza Meat Loaf

2 pounds ground beef
1 cup cracker crumbs
½ cup milk
½ cup chopped onion
2 eggs
½ cup grated Parmesan cheese
1 teaspoon oregano
1 8-ounce can pizza sauce
1 cup shredded mozzarella

Combine ground beef, cracker crumbs, milk, onion, eggs, Parmesan cheese and oregano in bowl; mix well. Shape into loaf in baking pan. Bake at 350 degrees for 30 minutes. Spread pizza sauce over top. Bake for 15 minutes. Sprinkle with mozzarella cheese. Bake just until cheese melts. Yield: 6 servings.

Linda Thompson, *Lawfully Good Eating*, Dixie Chapter No. 23

## Taco Meat Loaf

1½ lb. meat loaf
1 c. Italian bread crumbs
1 tsp. basil
1 tsp. parsley
1 c. milk
2 eggs
1 pkg. taco mix
½ c. onions
½ c. green peppers

Mix all ingredients and put in casserole. Add topping.

**Topping:**

6 Tbsp. brown sugar
2 tsp. dry mustard
½ c. catsup

Mix and pour over meat loaf. Bake at 350° for 1½ hours.

Helen Dickerson, *Dogwood Delights Volume II*, Dogwood Chapter No. 84

## Mexican Supper

1 lb. ground beef
1 large onion, chopped
1 8–10 oz. bottle mild taco sauce
1 pkg. taco seasoning mix
8–10 flour tortillas 8 inch

Cook ground beef in skillet until it turns grey. Add taco sauce, chopped onion and cook over low heat 8–10 minutes. Divide equally in center of flour tortillas. Fold envelope style and place in a large casserole dish or 2 small ones. Freezes well.

**Sauce:**

2 lb. Velveeta Cheese
1 can cream of chicken soup
1 small can or jar mild chili peppers, chopped

Cook in double boiler until smooth. Pour over tortillas and bake for 20 minutes at 300 degrees.

Edna Gray, *Secret Recipes of Telephone Pioneers, Volume III*
South Carolina Chapter No. 61

# Pirashke

1 cup milk
2 eggs, beaten
1 package dry yeast
1 tablespoon sugar
1 teaspoon salt
1/2 cup melted butter
Flour
1 1/2 pounds ground beef
1 onion, chopped
1 teaspoon cumin
2 hard-boiled eggs
Oil for deep frying

Combine milk, eggs, yeast, sugar, salt and butter in large bowl; mix well. Add enough flour to make a soft dough. Let rise. Roll to 1/4-inch thickness on floured surface. Cut into 3-inch triangles. Brown ground beef with onion and cumin in skillet, stirring until ground beef is crumbly; drain. Chop hard-boiled eggs; add to ground beef mixture; mix well. Spoon 1 tablespoon ground beef mixture onto each triangle of dough. Fold to enclose filling, pressing edges to seal. Deep-fry in hot oil until golden brown on all sides; drain.

Lloyd Hall, *Kentucky Kitchens, Volume II*, Kentucky Chapter No. 32

# Quick and Easy Hamburger-Macaroni

1 7-ounce package macaroni and cheese dinner
8 ounces lean ground beef
1 medium onion, chopped
Salt and pepper to taste
1 10-ounce can cream of chicken, mushroom or celery soup
Milk
Margarine

Cook macaroni using package directions; drain. Brown ground beef in saucepan, stirring until crumbly. Add onion, salt and pepper. Cook until onion is tender; drain. Stir in macaroni and soup. Add cheese packet from macaroni dinner, milk and margarine as directed on package. Cook until heated through, stirring until smooth.
Yield: 4 servings.

Regina Millirons, *Lawfully Good Eating*, Dixie Chapter No. 23

# *Salisbury Steak*

*For each pound of ground beef:*

**1 egg**
**1/4 c. cream**
**1 tsp. salt**
**1 tsp. pepper**
**2 Tbsp. cornstarch**
**1 tsp. parsley**
**1 slice bread in fine crumbs (1/4 c.)**
**1/2 tsp. Worcestershire sauce**
**1/2 tsp. prepared mustard**
**4 oz. can mushrooms**
**1 bouillon cube, dissolved in 1 c. water**

Mix egg, meat, cream, crumbs and seasoning. Form into patties and brown slowly in heavy skillet sprinkled with salt. Remove to warm plate. Mix cornstarch with a little mushroom liquid. Pour off accumulated fat from skillet and put in the mushroom liquid, cornstarch mixture and bouillon. Stir and cook until transparent and slightly reduced in volume. Pour over steaks. Sprinkle with parsley. Cook about 30 minutes.

Flo Gish, *Kentucky Kitchens, Volume I*, Kentucky Chapter No. 32

# *Shepherd's Pie*

**1 1/2 lb. ground beef**
**1 large onion, chopped**
**1 Tbsp. Worcestershire sauce**
**8 medium potatoes**
**1/2 stick margarine**
**1/2 c. milk**
**2 cans creamed corn**
**Salt and pepper to taste**

Boil and mash potatoes with butter, milk, salt, and pepper. In heavy skillet, combine beef, onion and Worcestershire. Cook until beef is browned and onions are transparent.

In deep casserole, layer ingredients, beginning with beef mixture. Add 1 1/2 cans corn, then potatoes. Pour remaining corn over potatoes. Dot corn with butter. Bake at 350° for 30 minutes. Serves 8 to 10.

Sara Davis, *Dogwood Delights Volume II*, Dogwood Chapter No. 84

# Baked Italian Spaghetti

1½ lbs. ground meat
1 medium onion
3 Tbsp. oil
3 (8 oz.) cans tomato sauce
¼ tsp. each: oregano, marjoram, sweet basil, rosemary, black pepper
½ tsp. salt
1 Tbsp. sugar
dash garlic salt
1 c. red cooking wine or beef broth
½ lb. spaghetti, broken into 2 inch pieces
1 c. grated cheddar or American cheese
1 pkg. sliced mozzarella cheese, optional

Brown onion and beef. Add tomato sauce, spices and wine or broth. Simmer, covered, 1 hour, stirring occasionally.

Meanwhile, cook spaghetti 7 to 8 minutes. Drain.

Add sauce with ½ cup of the cheese. Turn into 3 quart casserole and sprinkle with other ½ cup of cheese.

Cover and bake 45 minutes in 325° oven. Uncover and bake 30 minutes more.

If you love cheese, spread mozzarella slices on top and return to oven until melted.

Serves 6. Freezes well!

Sue Brigham, *Pioneers Pots and Pans—1985 Cookbook*
North Florida Chapter No. 39

# Summer Sausage

2 lb. hamburger or ground chuck
2 tsp. Morton's Tender-Quick salt
¼ tsp. mustard seed
1 c. water
1 tsp. liquid smoke
¼ tsp. garlic powder
¼ tsp. onion salt
¼ tsp. ground black pepper

Mix well and form into 3 rolls, about 1½x8 inches. Wrap in foil, shiny side in towards meat. Refrigerate for 24 hours. Poke holes in bottom of each roll with fork. Place in broiler pan on rack with ½ inch of water in bottom of pan. Bake for 90 minutes at 325°. Keeps in refrigerator like cold cuts.

June E. Nickels, *Pots, Pans & Pioneers II*, Louisiana Chapter No. 24

# Crepes Swinette

Crepes:

3 eggs
1 c. flour
2 c. milk
1/4 c. oil
1 tsp. salt
1 tsp. vanilla
1 Tbsp. sugar

Filling:

3 c. leftover ham, chopped
1/2 c. onions, chopped
1/2 c. mushrooms, chopped
1/4 c. white wine
Dash of salt and pepper
Dash of garlic powder

Sauce:

2 stalks celery
1/2 bell pepper
2 shallot cloves
1 medium can tomatoes
1/2 c. lard
1/2 c. flour
Dash of hot sauce

Crepes: Mix all ingredients in blender. Let stand overnight in refrigerator. Cook in traditional manner 10–20 minutes before serving. Yields 20.

Filling: Sauté all dry ingredients in butter; add wine and sauté very slowly until tender.

Sauce: In a large skillet or Dutch oven, make a dark brown roux of flour and lard. Add celery, bell pepper, and shallot cloves; sauté, uncovered, over medium heat until soft, about 30 minutes. Add tomatoes with liquid; simmer very slowly, partially covered, for 1 hour, stirring occasionally. Add hot sauce and remove from heat.

R. D. Erwin, *Dogwood Delights*, Dogwood Chapter No. 84

## A Helpful Hint

Buy a pre-cooked ham in a size suitable for your family. Plan quick meals for a busy week using ham in pasta dishes, omelets, casseroles, salads and sandwich spreads.

# Toasty Cheese Bake

8 slices white bread
Butter or margarine
1/2 lb. ground beef
1/4 c. chopped onion
2 Tbsp. chopped celery
1/2 tsp. salt
1 Tbsp. prepared mustard
1 c. shredded sharp cheese
1 egg, slightly beaten
3/4 c. milk
1/2 tsp. salt
Dash of pepper
1/8 tsp. dry mustard

Heat oven to 350°. Toast bread; butter both sides. Cook and stir meat, onion, celery, prepared mustard, and 1/2 teaspoon salt until meat is brown. Alternate layers of toast, meat mixture and cheese in greased baking pan, 9x9x2 inches. Mix remaining ingredients; pour over layers in pan. Bake uncovered 30–35 minutes.

Joan Cook, *Dogwood Delights*, Dogwood Chapter No. 84

# Hawaiian Ham

3 to 4 lb. boneless precooked ham
1/3 c. brown sugar
1/3 c. vinegar
3 Tbsp. butter
3 Tbsp. flour
1 (1 1/4 lb.) can sliced pineapple
2 Tbsp. Tomato sauce
3 Tbsp. prepared mustard

Have ham sliced into 1/2 inch thick slices. Drain pineapple, reserving syrup. Alternate ham and pineapple slices in large shallow casserole. Melt butter in pan; blend in flour until smooth. Combine reserved syrup, tomato sauce, brown sugar, vinegar, and mustard; gradually blend into flour mixture. Cook, stirring until slightly thickened. Pour sauce over ham and pineapple. Bake at 350° for 1 hour. Baste often. Serves 12.

Beverly Brodie, *Dogwood Delights Volume II*, Dogwood Chapter No. 84

# *Charlie's Bar-B-Q*

1 (5–8 lb.) fresh pork picnic shoulder (do not use smoked picnic)
4 Tbsp. salt (pickling salt is best)
Hickory smoke flavored salt
Hot Bar-B-Q Sauce

Preheat oven to 250°. Rub salt over picnic shoulder except skin. Place in 9x11 inch baking pan, skin up. Place on middle rack of oven for 8-9 hours. Skin should be hard and crusty. Remove from oven and place picnic shoulder on large cutting board. Remove skin and bone from meat. With a large knife, chop into small pieces. Season with smoked salt and Hot Bar-B-Q Sauce to the desired taste. Makes 3–5 pounds.

## Charlie's Hot Bar-B-Q Sauce:

2/3 c. vinegar (apple vinegar is better)
1/3 c. water
3 Tbsp. ground cayenne pepper
1 tsp. sugar
1 1/2 tsp. salt

Combine preceding ingredients in small saucepan. Place over low heat until it boils. Simmer for 5 minutes. Pour into small container with top. Can be stored for weeks in refrigerator.

Charlie Baldwin, *Dining with Pioneers, Volume II*
Tennessee Chapter No. 21

# *Rio Grande Pork Roast*

1 4 or 5-pound double boneless pork loin roast
1/2 teaspoon salt
1/2 teaspoon garlic salt
1/2 teaspoon chili powder
1 cup apple jelly
1 cup catsup
1 tablespoon vinegar
1 teaspoon chili powder
1/2 cup crushed corn chips

Rub roast on all sides with salt, garlic salt and 1/2 teaspoon chili powder. Place fat side up on rack in roasting pan. Insert meat thermometer into thickest section of roast but not touching fat. Bake at 325 degrees for 2 hours or to 165 degrees on meat thermometer. Combine jelly, catsup, vinegar and 1 teaspoon chili powder in saucepan; mix well. Bring to a boil; reduce heat. Simmer for 2 minutes, stirring constantly. Brush over roast. Sprinkle with corn chips. Bake for 10 to 15 minutes longer or to 170 degrees on meat thermometer. Serve with remaining sauce.
Yield: 6 to 8 servings.

Friend of the Pioneers, *Lawfully Good Eating*, Dixie Chapter No. 23

## Baked Pork Chops with Dressing

8 to 10 pork chops or boneless tenderloin
1/4 cup chopped celery
1/4 cup chopped onion
1 cup chicken broth
2 cups Pepperidge Farm Stuffing
Salt and pepper
1 tbsp. butter

Salt, pepper, and quickly brown pork chops on both sides and place in long Corning Ware or glass baking dish. Sauté celery and onion in small amount of butter or margarine. Sprinkle onion, celery, and stuffing over pork chops. Pour over all the chicken broth. Bake about 1 hour at 350°. Top should be brown and crusty. Bottom should be moist, pork chops tender. Serves 6 to 8. This is a good recipe for placing on timed bake Sunday morning while you go to church!

Etoile Crain, *Secret Recipes of Telephone Pioneers, Volume II*
South Carolina Chapter No. 61

## Easy Pork Chops

8 center-cut or butterflied pork chops
Salt and pepper to taste
1/2 cup flour
2 tablespoons oil
1 cup sour cream
1 10-ounce can cream of mushroom soup
1 envelope onion soup mix
1 cup white wine

Rinse pork chops and pat dry. Sprinkle with salt and pepper; coat with flour. Brown on both sides in oil in skillet; drain well. Arrange in single layer in rectangular baking dish. Combine sour cream, soup, soup mix and wine in bowl; mix well. Spoon over pork chops. Bake at 325 degrees for 45 minutes. Serve with wild rice and julienned carrots.
Yield: 8 servings.

**Approx Per Serving:** Cal 410; Prot 34 g; Carbo 11 g; Fiber <1 g; T Fat 23 g; 51% Calories from Fat; Chol 110 mg; Sod 482 mg.

Sue Diener, *Calling All Cooks three*, Alabama Chapter No. 34

### A Helpful Hint

Spices usually associated with desserts, such as cinnamon and cloves, are delicious additions to pork dishes.

# Pork Chops Jambalaya

4 Tbsp. shortening
4 lean pork chops, 1/4 to 1/2 inch thick
2 tsp. salt
1/2 tsp. pepper
1/8 tsp. cayenne pepper
1 onion, minced
1 clove garlic, minced
4 green onions, bottoms, minced
1 stalk celery, minced
1/2 green pepper, minced
1/4 c. water
3 bouillon cubes, dissolved in hot water
1/2 tsp. garlic, minced
1 Tbsp. minced parsley
4 green onion tops
1 1/2 c. uncooked rice

Melt shortening in 10 inch skillet over medium heat. Season chop with combined 1 teaspoon salt, 1/4 teaspoon pepper and cayenne. Brown on both sides in shortening about 10 minutes. Remove chops and stir in onion, garlic, green onion bottoms, celery, green pepper and 1/4 cup water. Continue cooking until seasonings are lightly browned, about 8 to 10 minutes. Slowly add bouillon, garlic and remaining 1 teaspoon salt and 1/4 teaspoon pepper. When water returns to boil, add parsley, onion tops and rice. Return chops to skillet, cover. Turn to low and continue cooking 30 minutes or until rice is done. Serves 4.

Jim Norris, *Pioneers Pots and Pans—1985 Cookbook*
North Florida Chapter No. 39

# Baked Lemon Pork Chops

6 (2 1/2–3 lb.) thick lean shoulder or loin pork chops
2 Tbsp. flour
1/2 tsp. salt
1/4 tsp. pepper
1 Tbsp. shortening
6 slices lemon
3/4 c. ketchup
3/4 c. water
3 Tbsp. brown sugar

Preheat oven to 350°F. Sprinkle chops with salt and pepper; dredge in flour. Melt shortening in large skillet; brown chops. Arrange in baking dish with a lemon slice on each. Mix ketchup, water and brown sugar. Pour over chops. Bake, uncovered, for 45 minutes. (You may need to add a little water in the latter part of baking if sauce cooks down too much.) Makes 6 servings, about 590 calories each.

Dorothy Bryant, *Dining with Pioneers, Volume II*
Tennessee Chapter No. 21

## Neapolitan Pork Chops

1 clove of garlic, minced
2 tablespoons olive oil
6 3/4- to 1-inch thick rib or loin pork chops
1 teaspoon salt
1/4 teaspoon pepper
1/2 teaspoon MSG
1 pound fresh mushrooms, sliced
2 green bell pepper, chopped
1/2 cup canned tomatoes, sieved
3 tablespoons dry white wine

Sauté garlic in olive oil in large skillet until light brown. Season pork chops with salt, pepper and MSG. Brown in skillet on both sides. Add mushrooms and peppers. Mix tomatoes with wine. Pour over pork chops gradually. Cook, covered, over low heat for 1 to 1 1/2 hours or until cooked through, adding water if necessary. Yield: 6 servings.

Margaret Casalino, *Lawfully Good Eating*, Dixie Chapter No. 23

## Pork Chop and Potato Bake

6 pork chops
Seasoned salt to taste
1 can cream of celery soup
1/2 cup milk
1/2 cup sour cream
1/4 teaspoon pepper
1/2 teaspoon seasoned salt
1 24-ounce package frozen hashed brown potatoes
1 cup shredded Cheddar cheese
1 3-ounce can French-fried onions

Brown pork chops in lightly greased skillet. Sprinkle with seasoned salt to taste. Combine soup, milk, sour cream, pepper and 1/2 teaspoon seasoned salt in large bowl; mix well. Add potatoes, half the cheese and half the onions; mix well. Spoon mixture into 9x13-inch baking dish. Arrange pork chops over potatoes. Bake, covered, at 350 degrees for 40 minutes or until pork chops are tender. Top with remaining cheese and onions. Bake, uncovered, for 5 minutes longer.
Yield: 6 servings.

Juyne Bushart, *Kentucky Kitchens, Volume II*, Kentucky Chapter No. 32

### A Helpful Hint

Rib, blade, arm and loin end pork chops are just as delicious and nutritious as center cuts and cost less.

## *Pork Chops and Potato Dinner*

**4 medium potatoes**
**2 medium onions, chopped**
**2 tablespoons butter**
**4 center-cut pork chops**
**Salt and pepper to taste**
**2 tablespoons vinegar**
**1/2 cup water**

Peel potatoes and cut into quarters. Cook in boiling water to cover in saucepan for 1 1/2 minutes; drain. Sauté onions in butter in large skillet; remove with slotted spoon. Sprinkle pork chops on both sides with salt and pepper. Brown on both sides in drippings in skillet. Add onions. Arrange potatoes around pork chops. Add vinegar and water. Simmer, covered, for 20 to 30 minutes or until pork chops are tender, turning potatoes once to brown evenly. Serve with crisp salad. May substitute white wine for water if preferred. Yield: 4 servings.

**Approx Per Serving:** Cal 527; Prot 37 g; Carbo 57 g; Fiber 6 g; T Fat 17 g; Chol 113 mg; Sod 143 mg.

Peggy C. Tchecheff, *Carolina Cooking*, North Carolina Chapter No. 35

## *Masas de Puerco—Pork Medallions*

**Country:** Cuba. **City:** Havana. **Relative obtained from:** Grandmother.

**3 lb. pork**
**1 tsp. salt**
**1/2 tsp. oregano**
**2 tsp. sour orange**
**3 cloves garlic**
**1 large onion**
**1/2 green pepper**
**1 tsp. olive oil**
**1 bay leaf**
**1 c. dry wine**

Cut the pork in 1 to 2 inch square pieces. Marinate pork with the crushed garlic, oregano, salt, orange, pepper, onion, bay leaf, and olive oil. Remove pork from marinade and place in frying pan (heated with 1 teaspoon oil and slices of onion). Brown pork for 10 minutes; add ingredients used to marinate and cook over low heat for approximately 20 minutes. Add wine if desired.

**Preparation time:** 20 minutes.
**Cooking time:** 20 minutes.
**No. of servings:** 4 to 6.

Mercedes Quintero, *A Taste of Pioneering*
Florida Gold Coast Chapter No. 83

# *Mushu Pork*

The Tiger Tiger Teahouse, Miami.

Pancakes:

2 c. unsifted all-purpose flour
3/4 c. cold water
Lard

Filling:

1 c. fungus (dried Chinese wood ears)
Water
1 c. dried lily flowers (golden needles)
1 pt. vegetable oil
1/2 lb. pork, shredded
4 eggs, lightly beaten
1/2 tsp. garlic, minced
4 c. American cabbage, thinly shredded
1/2 c. mushrooms, sliced
1/2 c. fresh snow peas
1/2 c. carrots
1/2 c. canned bamboo shoots
1/2 c. scallions (green and white parts)
1 tsp. MSG
2 tsp. sugar
1/2 tsp. salt
2 Tbsp. cooking sherry
4 Tbsp. dark soy sauce
2 Tbsp. sesame oil
2 Tbsp. oyster sauce
1/4 tsp. white pepper, ground

**Pancakes**: Place 2 cups unsifted all-purpose flour in a mixing bowl. Stir in approximately 3/4 cup cold water. Adjust the amounts of water and flour as necessary to make a dough that is not too sticky. Turn out on a lightly floured surface and knead until smooth. Place in a bowl; cover with a damp cloth, and let stand at room temperature for 1/2 hour. On a floured surface, with floured fingers, roll the dough into a long roll 1 1/2 inches in diameter. Cut into 1/2 inch slices, making 16 pieces. Roll each piece between your hands to make a smooth ball. In the palm of your hand, flatten 1 ball slightly. Spread 1 side of it with a teaspoon of lard. Flatten another ball and place it over the lard. Press to flatten slightly. On a floured surface, with a floured rolling pin, roll the double pancakes into a paper-thin circle about 6 to 7 inches in diameter.

In a hot, dry skillet, over low heat, fry 1 double pancake at a time for about 1/2 minute on each side (do not overcook); do not fry until pancake colors. While still hot, use your fingers to pull the pancakes apart into 2 pancakes. If they are to be served soon, place them on a towel and cover them with another towel. If they are to wait a long time, they must be wrapped airtight. (They may be stacked on top of each other, wrapped airtight, and frozen.) The pancakes must be steamed before serving. (If they have been frozen, they must be thawed first, unwrapped.)

**To steam:** Place a large strainer or colander over a large saucepan of shallow boiling water. Place a damp towel in the strainer. Cover them with a dry towel and then cover the saucepan with a pot cover. Steam over moderate heat for about 10 minutes.

**Filling:** The ingredients for the filling may be prepared for cooking even a day ahead, or shortly before serving. Soak fungus (dried Chinese wood ears) in boiling water to cover. Let stand for 15 minutes. Change the water twice. Rinse well; drain and dry. Prepare dried lily flowers (golden needles) in the same manner as the fungus. Cut off and discard any hard parts. Chop the remainder coarsely.

*A Taste of Pioneering*, Florida Gold Coast Chapter No. 83

## *Pea Pod Pork*

Mai Kai, Ft. Lauderdale.

**1/4 lb. pork tenderloin, sliced**
**4 Tbsp. peanut oil**
**1 tsp. salt**
**1 Tbsp. cooking sherry**
**1/2 c. chicken stock**
**1/4 c. celery, sliced**
**1/4 c. Bermuda onion, sliced**
**3 drops sesame oil**
**1/2 tsp. MSG**
**1 tsp. potato starch**
**1/2 lb. fresh Chinese pea pods**

Slice pork thinly; heat peanut oil over high heat. Add salt and pork and stir-fry for 2 minutes. Add sherry and stir-fry for 1 minute. Add chicken stock, celery, onion, sesame oil, and MSG and stir for 1/2 minute. Add 1 teaspoon starch or enough to slightly thicken the mixture. Add the pea pods and stir for 15 to 20 seconds. Remove and serve.
Serves 1 generously.

*A Taste of Pioneering*, Florida Gold Coast Chapter No. 83

### *A Helpful Hint*

Stir frying is a quick, nutritious way to prepare meats and vegetables. For uniform flavor and appearance, cut ingredients into uniform pieces. Spray skillet or wok with vegetable cooking spray to further reduce calories.

# Apricot Ribs

**1 17-ounce can apricot halves**
**1/3 cup packed brown sugar**
**3 tablespoons vinegar**
**1 clove of garlic, minced**
**4 teaspoons soy sauce**
**1/8 teaspoon ground ginger**
**6 pounds pork ribs, cut into 2-rib portions**

Drain apricots, reserving 1/3 cup syrup. Purée in blender with reserved syrup. Combine with brown sugar, vinegar, garlic, soy sauce and ginger in saucepan. Simmer over medium heat for 10 to 15 minutes, stirring occasionally. Grill ribs over medium-hot coals for 50 minutes, basting with apricot sauce during last 30 minutes. Yield: 6 servings.

Linda Kite, *Lawfully Good Eating*, Dixie Chapter No. 23

# Island Ribs with Rice

**4 lb. country style pork ribs**
**Salt and seasoned pepper**
**1 (7 3/4 oz.) jar junior peaches of 1 c. puréed canned peaches**
**1/2 c. chili sauce**
**1/2 c. cider vinegar**
**3 Tbsp. soy sauce**
**1/4 c. brown sugar, firmly packed**
**3 cloves garlic, crushed**
**1 Tbsp. ground ginger**
**3 c. hot cooked rice**

Rub ribs on all sides with salt and seasoned pepper. Place ribs, meaty side down, in a foil lined pan. Bake at 450° for 20 minutes. Spoon off excess fat. Blend remaining ingredients, except rice and pour over ribs. Cover; reduce the heat to 350° and bake 1 1/4 hours or until tender. Remove the cover 20 minutes before ribs are done so meat can brown. Baste with sauce several times while browning. Serve ribs and sauce with hot cooked rice.

**Cooking time**: 2 hours and 10 minutes.
**No. of servings**: 4 to 6.

Lenore Petretti, *A Taste of Pioneering*
Florida Gold Coast Chapter No. 83

# *Breakfast Pizza*

1 pound pork sausage
1 8-count package refrigerator crescent rolls
1 cup frozen hashed brown potatoes, thawed
1 cup shredded sharp Cheddar cheese
5 eggs
1/4 cup milk
1/2 teaspoon salt
1/4 teaspoon pepper
2 tablespoons Parmesan cheese

Brown sausage in skillet, stirring until crumbly; drain. Unroll crescent roll dough. Separate into 8 triangles. Arrange over bottom and up side of 12-inch pizza pan; seal edges. Spoon sausage over crust. Sprinkle with potatoes and cheese. Beat eggs, milk, salt and pepper in mixer bowl until smooth. Pour over top. Sprinkle with Parmesan cheese. Bake at 375 degrees for 25 to 30 minutes or until brown. Yield: 6 to 8 servings.

Patricia J. Tudor, *Kentucky Kitchens, Volume II*
Kentucky Chapter No. 32

# *Sausage and Egg Breakfast Casserole*

1 pound hot pork sausage
6 slices white bread, cut into cubes
6 eggs
2 cups milk
1 cup shredded sharp Cheddar cheese

Brown sausage in skillet, stirring until crumbly; drain. Layer bread cubes and sausage in 8x11-inch baking dish. Beat eggs with milk in bowl. Pour over layers. Top with cheese. Chill overnight. Bake at 350 degrees for 1 hour. Yield: 8 servings.

**Approx Per Serving:** Cal 321; Prot 15 g; Carbo 14 g; Fiber <1 g; T Fat 23 g; Chol 201 mg; Sod 451 mg.

Priscilla Wise, *Carolina Cooking*, North Carolina Chapter No. 35

## Sausage Fruit Bake

1 lb. pork sausage
1 medium can sweet potatoes, drained and sliced
1 medium can sliced peaches
3 tart cooking apples, cut into eighths
2 Tbsp. margarine or butter, melted
1/3 c. brown sugar

Pan fry crumbled sausage 15 to 20 minutes; drain off excess fat. In a buttered 2 quart casserole, alternate layers of sausage, sweet potatoes and fruit. Pour melted butter over top; sprinkle with brown sugar. Bake, covered, for 20 minutes at 375°. Remove cover and bake 15 minutes until apples are tender. Yield: 6 servings.

Mrs. Wavie Minke, *Dining with Pioneers, Volume I*
Tennessee Chapter No. 21

## Red Cabbage with Apples and German Sausage

2 tablespoons sugar
1/4 cup bacon drippings
1 small onion, chopped
4 cups shredded red cabbage
2 tart apples, sliced
2 tablespoons vinegar
1/2 teaspoon caraway seed
Salt and pepper to taste
6 links German sausage

Brown sugar in bacon drippings in large skillet, stirring constantly. Add onion; mix well. Cook over low heat until onions are slightly brown. Add cabbage, apples, vinegar, caraway seed, salt and pepper. Arrange sausage over top. Simmer for 45 minutes to 1 hour or until tender, adding enough water, stock or red wine to prevent sticking. May use white cabbage, 1/4 cup sugar and 1 tablespoon vinegar if preferred. Yield: 6 servings.

Lillian Muller, *Kentucky Kitchens, Volume II*, Kentucky Chapter No. 32

### A Helpful Hint

Sausage will shrink less and spatter less if rolled lightly in flour before frying.

## *Chris' Sausage Casserole*

1 pound milk pork sausage
1/4 cup chopped onion
1/4 cup chopped green bell pepper
6 eggs
1/2 cup sour cream
Salt and pepper to taste

Brown sausage with onion and green pepper in heavy skillet, stirring until sausage is crumbly; drain. Press 3/4 of the mixture into baking dish. Combine eggs and sour cream in bowl; mix well. Season with salt and pepper. Pour over sausage mixture. Bake at 350 degrees until eggs are partially set; stir eggs. Top with remaining sausage mixture. Bake until eggs are set. Yield: 6 servings.

**Approx Per Serving:** Cal 272; Prot 11 g; Carbo 2 g; Fiber <1 g; T Fat 24 g; Chol 246 mg; Sod 316 mg.

Chris Roberts, *Carolina Cooking*, North Carolina Chapter No. 35

## *Doc's Red Beans and Sausage*

1 lb. dry kidney beans
1 1/2–2 lb. smoked sausage (preferably Owens' spicy, packed by Owens Company, Richardson, Texas)
1 c. chopped celery
1 large bell pepper, chopped
2 medium onions, chopped
4 or 5 cloves garlic, chopped
1 tsp. chili powder
2 bay leaves
Pinch of oregano
Pinch of thyme

Soak beans overnight or 3–4 hours. Wash beans and place in large pot (4 quart) that can be covered. Add water, approximately 3 pints to 2 quarts. Cut sausage into 1 inch pieces (crosswise on tube) and add to beans. (If sausage is very fat, cook separately for about 5 minutes in boiling water and drain before adding to beans.) Bring beans and sausage to boil; add chopped vegetables and spices. Cook 3–4 hours, covered, over low heat until beans are tender. Add water as needed. Add salt and red pepper to taste. The amount needed will depend on spices in sausage and on your individual taste. Remove and crush 4 or 5 large serving spoons of beans and return to pot to thicken soup. Add water as necessary to provide for a soupy texture. Serve over fluffy rice with garlic bread and green salad.

Doc Braswell, *Bell's Best*, Mississippi Chapter No. 36

# Sausage and Wild Rice

1 lb. sausage
1 small onion, chopped
1/2 c. celery, chopped
1 box Uncle Ben's wild rice with seasonings
1 can chopped mushrooms
1 can water chestnuts, sliced

Brown sausage; crumble and drain. Reserve drippings. Sauté onion and celery in sausage drippings. Cook rice according to package directions; add sausage, onion and celery, then add mushrooms and water chestnuts. Turn into a casserole; bake at 350° for 15 minutes. This recipe may be prepared ahead and heated about 30 minutes at 300°.

Doris Binkley, *Dining with Pioneers, Volume I*, Tennessee Chapter No. 21

# Country Style Rabbit

2 to 2 1/2 lb. rabbit, cut into 8 pieces
1/4 lb. butter
1/2 c. flour
1 tsp. salt
1/2 tsp. black pepper
1/4 tsp. cayenne pepper
1/2 c. dry white wine or beer

Melt butter in heavy skillet over medium heat. Mix flour, salt, pepper, and cayenne together in a paper or plastic bag. Shake rabbit pieces in flour mixture to coat, then brown well in hot butter, turning to brown evenly on both sides. Remove rabbit to a heavy, covered casserole dish. Add 1/2 cup wine or beer. Cover and bake at 325° for 45 minutes to 1 hour until tender.

To the pan drippings left in the pan in which the rabbit was browned, add 2 tablespoons flour. Cook, stirring, over medium heat until the flour is cooked, but not browned. Add 1 cup milk and cook, stirring over medium heat until thickened.

When the rabbit is tender, remove to platter and pour any of the liquid remaining into the gravy. Cook to desired consistency. Serve with mashed potatoes, rice or noodles, and the gravy on the side.
Serves 4 to 6.

Debbie Giddens, *Dogwood Delights Volume II*
Dogwood Chapter No. 84

Florida Gold Coast Chapter 83

## Baked Chicken and Rice

1 large fryer, cut in pieces, salted and peppered
1 pkg. Lipton's onion soup mix
1 can cream of chicken soup
2 soup cans water
1/2 stick oleo
2 c. regular raw rice

Melt oleo in large deep dish or pan. Add chicken soup, onion soup mix and water. Simmer until smooth. Add rice. Place cut up chicken on top of mixture; cover with foil. Bake at 350° about 1 1/2 hours. Remove foil and cook 10 additional minutes.

Maxine Fletcher, *Pots, Pans & Pioneers II*, Louisiana Chapter No. 24

## Baked Chicken in Wine Gravy

1 2 1/2-pound chicken, cut up, skinned
1 can cream of chicken soup
1 soup can water
1 3-ounce can French-fried onions
3/4 cup Sauterne

Rinse chicken and pat dry. Place in 1 1/2-quart baking dish. Add mixture of soup and water; top with French-fried onions. Bake, covered, at 350 degrees for 1 hour. Add wine. Bake for 1 hour longer. Serve chicken with gravy over rice or noodles. Yield: 4 servings.

**Approx Per Serving:** Cal 413; Prot 40 g; Carbo 14 g; Fiber <1 g; T Fat 18 g; Chol 127 mg; Sod 745 mg.

Frances Fitch, *Carolina Cooking*, North Carolina Chapter No. 35

### A Helpful Hint

To save time, buy chicken breast filets or bone chicken breasts ahead of time and refrigerate or freeze them. They will cook in about half the usual time.

## Crusty Baked Chicken

1 cup oats
1/3 cup Parmesan cheese
1/2 teaspoon paprika
1/2 teaspoon salt
1/8 teaspoon pepper
1 3-pound chicken, cut up
1 egg
1/4 cup milk

Process oats in blender for 1 minute. Combine with cheese, paprika, salt and pepper in bowl. Rinse chicken and discard skin; pat dry. Dip into mixture of egg and milk; coat with oat mixture. Arrange in greased baking pan. Bake at 375 degrees for 1 hour. Oat mixture may also be used to coat fish. Yield: 6 servings.

**Approx Per Serving:** Cal 320; Prot 40 g; Carbo 10 g; Fiber 1 g; T Fat 13 g; Chol 147 mg; Sod 362 mg.
**Dietary Exchanges:** Bread/Starch 1/2; Meat 5; Fat 1/2

"*Answering the Call of Those in Need,*" Tennessee Chapter No. 21

## Casserole Barbecued Chicken

2 2 1/2 to 3-pound chickens, cut up
1 medium onion, sliced
Salt and pepper to taste
2 cups water
3 tablespoons catsup
1/2 cup vinegar
1 1/2 cups tomato juice
3 tablespoons butter
2 teaspoons lemon juice
3 tablespoons Worcestershire sauce
1 teaspoon prepared mustard
1 teaspoon sugar
2 tablespoons brown sugar
1/2 teaspoon thyme
2 teaspoons salt
2 teaspoons black pepper
1/2 teaspoon red pepper

Rinse chicken and pat dry. Layer chicken pieces and onion slices in large baking pan; sprinkle with salt and pepper to taste. Add water. Bake at 350 degrees for 1 hour, turning after 30 minutes. Combine remaining ingredients in saucepan; mix well. Bring to a boil. Pour over chicken. Bake, covered, until chicken is tender. Yield: 10 servings.

Doris Thornton, *Lawfully Good Eating*, Dixie Chapter No. 23

# Pa Pa's Barbecued Chicken

2 cups water
1/2 cup salt
3 cups vinegar
1/3 cup pepper
3 chickens, cut into halves

Combine water and salt in saucepan. Heat just until salt dissolves; do not boil. Stir in vinegar and pepper. Rinse chicken halves and pat dry. Place breast side up on grill over hot coals. Grill for 2 hours, basting every 15 to 20 minutes with sauce. Yield: 6 servings.

Butch Fitzgerald, *Lawfully Good Eating*, Dixie Chapter No. 23

# Chicken Cacciatore

1 tablespoon flour
1 oven cooking bag
1 3-pound chicken, cut up
1 teaspoon salt
1/4 teaspoon pepper
1 teaspoon paprika
1 cup thinly sliced onion
1 cup chopped green bell pepper
1 12-ounce can tomatoes
1/4 cup flour
1/4 teaspoon basil
1 teaspoon oregano
1/2 teaspoon garlic powder
1 tablespoon parsley flakes
1 bay leaf
1 1/2 teaspoons sugar
1/2 cup dry red wine

Sprinkle 1 tablespoon flour into oven cooking bag. Place bag in 9x13-inch baking dish. Wash chicken and pat dry. Season with salt and pepper; sprinkle with paprika. Place onion, green pepper, and chicken in prepared cooking bag. Drain tomatoes, reserving juice. Arrange tomatoes around chicken. Combine remaining 1/4 cup flour and reserved tomato juice in bowl; mix well. Stir in seasonings, bay leaf, sugar and wine. Pour into cooking bag. Seal bag. Cut six 1/2-inch slits in top of bag. Bake at 350 degrees for 1 hour and 20 minutes. Remove from bag. Discard bay leaf. Serve with hot fluffy rice. Yield: 4 to 6 servings.

Roy Dobbs, *Kentucky Kitchens, Volume II*, Kentucky Chapter No. 32

## A Helpful Hint

Baked or roasted chicken has fewer calories than stewed chicken. Remove skin to further reduce calories.

## *Chicken with Cauliflower and Peas*

**8 pieces chicken, skinned**
**1 clove of garlic, finely chopped**
**1/2 teaspoon basil**
**1/4 teaspoon paprika**
**1 teaspoon salt**
**1 medium onion, chopped**
**3 cups 1-inch caulifloweret s**
**1 10-ounce package frozen green peas**
**1/2 teaspoon salt**
**1/8 teaspoon pepper**

Wash chicken and pat dry. Arrange with thicker portions toward outside in 7x12-inch glass dish. Sprinkle with garlic, basil, paprika and 1 teaspoon salt. Add onion. Cover tightly with plastic wrap. Microwave on High for 10 minutes. Add cauliflower and peas; sprinkle with 1/2 teaspoon salt and pepper. Microwave, covered, on High for 10 to 15 minutes or until chicken and vegetables are tender. Let stand, uncovered, for 3 minutes. Yield: 8 servings.

**Approx Per Serving:** Cal 113; Prot 18 g; Carbo 8 g; Fiber 3 g; T Fat 1 g; Chol 37 mg; Sod 386 mg.

Connie Mangum, *Carolina Cooking*, North Carolina Chapter No. 35

## *Beer Battered Fried Chicken*

**1 3/4 c. sifted all-purpose flour**
**1 1/2 tsp. salt**
**1/2 tsp. pepper**
**1 (12 oz.) can beer**
**2 (2 1/2 lb.) broiler-fryers, cut up**
**Vegetable oil**

1. Combine flour, salt and pepper in a medium size bowl. Beat in beer with a wire whisk or rotary beater until smooth. Let stand 30 minutes.

2. Pour enough vegetable oil in a large skillet or saucepan to make 1-inch depth. Heat to 375° on a deep fry thermometer or until a cube of bread turns golden within 60 seconds.

3. Dip chicken pieces into beer batter a few at a time, allowing excess to drain back into bowl.

4. Fry chicken pieces, turning once, for 30 minutes, or until chicken tests done. Place on paper toweling to drain. Keep warm in a 250° oven until all chicken is browned. Garnish platter with parsley and serve with onion rings, if you wish.

Betty Lawson, *Dogwood Delights*, Dogwood Chapter No. 84

# Jambalaya (Ripper style)

5 chicken fryers, cut in small pieces
5 lb. sausage, country smoked, 3 hot and 2 mild
8 medium to large onions, chopped
8 c. rice (long grain)
Parsley (optional)
5 Bell peppers, chopped
1 stalk celery, chopped
1 pod garlic, minced (optional)
Salt to taste
15 c. water
3 Tbsp. cooking oil

Salt and pepper chicken pieces. Cut sausage in 1/2 inch pieces. Add small amount of cooking oil; add sausage and brown. Remove from pan. Brown chicken in sausage drippings, if needed add a small amount of oil. Remove chicken from pot. Brown onions, Bell peppers, celery and garlic. Stir periodically. When cooked down, add water, chicken, sausage, parsley and bring to boil. While still boiling, add rice; stir in and add salt as desired. Place lid on pot; reduce heat and simmer 20 minutes. If mixture is not dry, cook a little longer. Serves 20.

Ray Well, *Pots, Pans and Pioneers, Volume I*, Louisiana Chapter No. 24

# Chicken-in-the-Limelight

3 pounds chicken pieces
Juice of 1 lime
1/3 cup flour
1/2 teaspoon paprika
1 teaspoon salt
3 tablespoons oil
Grated rind of 1 lime
2 tablespoons brown sugar
1/2 cup chicken broth
1/2 cup white wine

Rinse chicken and pat dry. Drizzle with lime juice. Shake with mixture of flour, paprika and salt in bag, coating well. Brown on all sides in hot oil in skillet over medium-high heat. Arrange in single layer in 9x13-inch baking dish. Sprinkle with mixture of lime rind and brown sugar. Add chicken broth and wine. Bake, covered, at 375 degrees for 45 minutes. Yield: 6 servings.

**Approx Per Serving:** Cal 337; Prot 34 g; Carbo 11 g; Fiber <1 g; T Fat 15 g; Chol 101 mg; Sod 520 mg.

John E. Miles, *Carolina Cooking*, North Carolina Chapter No. 35

## Brunswick Stew

4 quarts water
1 tablespoon salt
1 large chicken, cut into pieces
1 onion, chopped
2 cups lima beans
6 ears of corn, cut
8 ounces salt pork
6 potatoes, cubed
1 teaspoon pepper
2 teaspoons sugar
4 cups chopped tomatoes
1 cup butter
Flour

Bring water and salt to a boil in large saucepan. Add chicken, onion, lima beans, corn, salt pork, potatoes and pepper; reduce heat. Simmer, covered, for 2 hours. Add sugar and tomatoes; mix well. Simmer for 50 minutes. Roll butter by teaspoonfuls in flour. Drop into stew mixture. Bring to a boil; remove from heat and serve.
Yield: 6 to 8 servings.

Rudy Jefferson, *Lawfully Good Eating*, Dixie Chapter No. 23

## Chicken Stew

1 (2 lb.) chicken, cut up and seasoned
1 c. onion, chopped
1/2 c. celery, chopped
1/4 c. chopped green onions
1/4 c. chopped parsley
6 cloves garlic, minced
1/2 c. flour
1/2 c. oil
2 c. water
2 tsp. salt
1/2 tsp. pepper

In large casserole dish, make roux with flour and oil. Brown chicken in iron pot on cooktop. Stir onions and celery in roux; sauté on high 3 minutes. Stir in green onions, parsley and garlic; sauté 2 minutes. Add water, seasoning and chicken; cook on high 5 minutes, then 30 minutes more on medium speed. Serve over rice.

Betty Stevens, *Pots, Pans and Pioneers III*, Louisiana Chapter No. 24

# Chicken and Cashews

1 cup bouillon
1 to 2 tablespoons cornstarch
2 tablespoons soy sauce
2 tablespoons peanut oil
1 clove of garlic
2 chicken breast filets
4 green onions, chopped
8 ounces pea pods
8 ounces mushrooms
1 8-ounce can bamboo shoots, drained
1/2 cup cashews

Cut chicken filets into slivers. Combine bouillon, cornstarch and soy sauce in bowl; mix well. Heat oil in wok. Add garlic. Cook until brown; discard garlic. Add chicken. Stir-fry for 1 to 2 minutes; push to side of wok. Add green onions. Stir-fry for 1 minute; push to side of wok. Repeat with pea pods, mushrooms and bamboo shoots. Add soy sauce mixture. Cook until thickened, stirring constantly. Mix all ingredients together; add cashews. Serve over hot cooked rice or chow mein noodles. Yield: 4 servings.

Joan Echsner, *Kentucky Kitchens, Volume II*, Kentucky Chapter No. 32

# Chicken, Broccoli and Rice Casserole

1/2 stick butter
1/3 c. onion, chopped
1/2 c. celery, chopped
1 c. cubed, cooked chicken
1 small jar Cheez Whiz
1/2 Tbsp. sugar
1 (10 oz.) pkg. frozen, chopped broccoli
1 (10 3/4 oz.) can cream of mushroom soup
1 c. raw instant rice
1 soup can of milk
1 Tbsp. chopped pimento

Melt butter; add onions and celery. Let simmer while preparing remaining ingredients. Drop broccoli in boiling salted water long enough to separate (do not cook); drain. Mix soup, rice, milk, sugar, Cheez Whiz, broccoli and chicken in a large bowl. Add celery and onions. Pour into a 6 1/2x9 inch buttered Pyrex dish. Cook 40 minutes, covered, at 350°. Uncover about 10–15 minutes until it is bubbly in the middle.

**Hint:** Serve as main dish, or omit chicken for a side dish. Can substitute shrimp or crab for chicken.

Teresa Sheilds, *Bell's Best 2*, Mississippi Chapter No. 36

## Company Chicken Casserole

1 6-ounce package long grain and wild rice
1 3-pound chicken, cooked, boned, chopped
2 16-ounce cans French-style green beans
1 10-ounce can cream of chicken soup
1 cup mayonnaise
1 onion, chopped
1 8-ounce can sliced water chestnuts
2 cups shredded Cheddar cheese

Prepare rice using package directions. Combine rice, chicken, green beans, soup, mayonnaise, onion, water chestnuts and cheese in bowl; mix well. Spoon into 3-quart baking dish. Cook, covered, at 350 degrees for 35 to 45 minutes or until bubbly; remove cover. Cook for 5 to 10 minutes or until brown. Yield: 8 servings.

Approx Per Serving: Cal 657; Prot 37 g; Carbo 31 g; Fiber 2 g; T Fat 43 g; 59% Calories from Fat; Chol 124 mg; Sod 1552 mg.

Betty McAnnally, *Calling All Cooks three*, Alabama Chapter No. 34

## Chicken and Green Bean Casserole

2 c. Pepperidge Farms stuffing
2 c. chicken
1 pkg. frozen French cut string beans
1 can cream of chicken soup
1/2 c. milk
1/4 c. almonds
1/4 c. hot water
2 Tbsp. butter

Boil chicken, cook beans according to directions on package. Butter a baking dish. Spread 1 1/2 cup stuffing in bottom of dish. Spread beans over dressing. Sprinkle almonds on top of beans, then add chicken.

Mix milk and cream of chicken soup and pour over chicken. Mix 1/2 cup dressing, hot water and melted butter and pour over top.

Bake at 300° for 25 minutes or longer.

Linda Hayden, *Pioneers Pots and Pans—1985 Cookbook*
North Florida Chapter No. 39

## Chicken Parmesan

4 to 6 chicken breasts
1 c. bread crumbs
1 c. Parmesan cheese
3 Tbsp. butter
2 eggs
1 c. milk

Skin the chicken breasts and wash in cold water. Dip the breasts in the egg and milk. Mix bread crumbs and Parmesan cheese together. Roll chicken in the bread crumb mixture.* Place in glass container. Microwave chicken about 15 minutes.

*I forgot to mention, place pats of butter on top of chicken before microwaving. Cook chicken until tender, then serve and eat.

Tingle Warner, *Pots, Pans and Pioneers, Volume IV*
Louisiana Chapter No. 24

## Party Chicken Casserole

4½ whole, cooked and deboned chicken breasts
1 small can sliced water chestnuts
2 cans cream of mushroom soup
1 c. mayonnaise
1 chopped pimiento
¾ c. celery, finely chopped
¾ c. onion, finely chopped
½ pkg. Pepperidge Farm stuffing mix
½ c. chicken broth
½ tsp. poultry seasoning
Salt and pepper to taste
Lemon pepper seasoning to taste

Mix all ingredients together and fill a 3 quart casserole and top with stuffing and moisten with broth. Can be fixed the day before the party. Bake at 350° uncovered for 40–50 minutes. Serves 8–10 people.

Mrs. John Levasseur, *Bell's Best*, Mississippi Chapter No. 36

### A Helpful Hint

Buy chicken in quantities and bake or stew it. Store meal-sized portions of chopped chicken in plastic bags in the freezer, ready for a busy-day meal.

# *Stuffed Chicken Breasts*

4 whole boneless chicken breasts, skinned and halved
1/2 c. all-purpose flour, divided
1 c. dry bread crumbs
1 c. dry white wine
1/2 tsp. salt
1 c. milk
4 slices boiled ham, halved
4 slices Swiss cheese, halved
1 egg, beaten
1/2 c. oleo, melted, divided
1/4 c. onion, finely chopped
1/2 tsp. pepper
1 c. half & half
Hot, cooked rice or noodles

Flatten chicken breasts with mallet or hammer. Place slice of ham and cheese on each chicken breast; secure with toothpicks. Dredge each roll in 1/4 cup flour; dip in egg. Coat with bread crumbs. Lightly brown on all sides in 1/4 of oleo. Add wine; cover and simmer for 20 minutes. Place chicken rolls in shallow pan, reserving dippings. Sauté onion in remaining butter until tender; blend in remaining flour, salt and pepper. Gradually add milks, stirring until smooth. Add drippings and stir until thickened. Pour sauce over rolls and bake, uncovered, at 325° for about 20 or 25 minutes. Serve over rice or noodles. Makes 8 servings.

Marilou Bridges, *Pots, Pans and Pioneers III*, Louisiana Chapter No. 24

# *Wild Rice-Chicken Casserole*

1 6-oz. pkg. long grain and wild rice mix
1/2 cup chopped onions
1/2 cup chopped celery
2 Tbsp. butter or margarine
1 can condensed cream of mushroom soup
1/2 cup sour cream
1/3 cup dry white wine
1/2 tsp. curry powder (optional)
2 cups cubed cooked chicken or turkey

Prepare rice mix according to package directions. Meanwhile, cook onion and celery in butter until tender. Stir in soup, sour cream, wine and curry. Stir in chicken and cooked rice; turn into a 2 quart casserole or a 12x7 1/2x2 baking dish. Bake, uncovered, at 350 degrees for 35 to 40 minutes. Stir before serving. Makes 4 to 6 servings.

Mildred Wieters, *Secret Recipes of Telephone Pioneers, Volume III*
South Carolina Chapter No. 61

# Chicken Chili

Vegetable cooking spray
2 tsp. vegetable oil
4 c. coarsely chopped onion
1 1/2 c. chopped green bell pepper
4 cloves garlic, thinly sliced
1 1/2 lbs. skinned, boned chicken breast, cut into 1/4 inch pieces
1/4 c. chili powder
1 tbsp. ground cumin
2 tsp. ground coriander
1/2 tsp. salt
1/2 tsp. ground red pepper
2 (14 1/2 oz.) cans no-salt-added whole tomatoes, undrained and chopped
1 (12 oz.) can beer
1 (10 1/2 oz.) can low-sodium chicken broth
1 (6 oz.) can tomato paste
1 bay leaf
2 (15 oz.) cans garbanzo beans, drained

Coat a large Dutch oven with cooking spray; add oil. Place over medium-high heat until hot. Add onion, bell pepper and garlic; sauté 5 minutes or until tender. Add chicken and cook 2 minutes or until browned, stirring constantly. Add chili powder, ground cumin and next 3 ingredients; cook 1 minute, stirring constantly. Add chopped tomatoes, beer and next 3 ingredients; bring to a boil. Cover, reduce heat, and simmer 40 minutes, stirring occasionally. Add beans, and cook, uncovered, an additional 20 minutes, stirring occasionally. Discard bay leaf. Yield: 12 servings (about 207 calories per 1 cup serving).

Gloria Sundy
*A Tablespoon of Pioneering and a Teaspoon of Horses and the Handicapped*
Florida Gold Coast Chapter No. 83

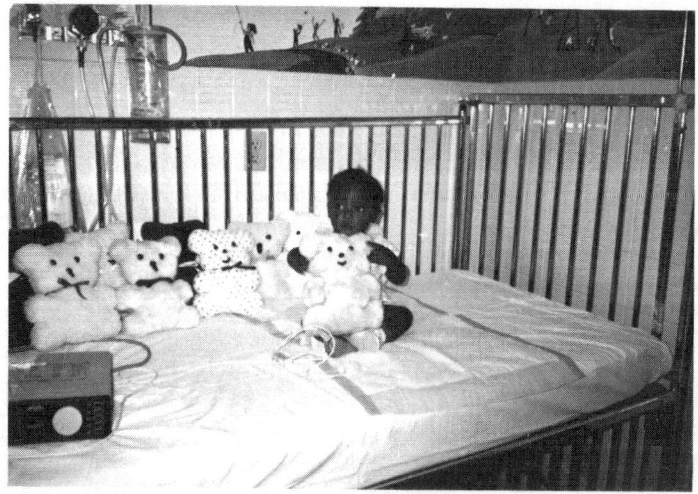

*Some of the hundreds of Hug-A-Bears annually donated to hospitals, police, EMTs and Coast Guard.* (Florida Gold Coast Chapter No. 83)

# Chicken Chow Mein

2 tbsp. butter
4 tbsp. minced onion
1 cup sliced mushrooms
1½ cups shredded cooked chicken
1 cup diced celery
1½ cups meat stock or water
2 tbsp. soy sauce
1 tbsp. sugar
1½ tbsp. cornstarch
3 tbsp. cold water

In hot butter, brown lightly minced onion and sliced mushrooms. Add chicken, diced celery, meat stock or water, soy sauce and sugar, simmer 15 minutes. Blend and stir into meat mixture, cornstarch and cold water. Cook until slightly thick and clear. Serve over hot rice with chow mein noodles. Serves 4.

Mrs. A. N. McAuley, *Secret Recipes of Telephone Pioneers, Volume II*
South Carolina Chapter No. 61

# Chicken Cordon Bleu

Chicken breasts, boned and beaten flat
Boiled ham slices
Swiss cheese slices

Pound chicken breasts between 2 sheets of waxed paper until very thin (twice the original size). Layer these with the ham and cheese slices and pound the edges of breasts together.

½ c. flour
½ tsp. salt
¼ tsp. pepper
¼ tsp. monosodium glutamate
¼ tsp. paprika
1 egg
2 tsp. milk
½ c. bread crumbs
3 tsp. margarine
½ c. chicken broth
2 tsp. dried parsley flakes
1 (10 oz.) can chicken soup
½ c. sour cream

Mix dry ingredients and coat each breast with mixture. Dip in beaten egg and milk; roll in crumbs. Brown slowly in margarine. Add chicken broth; sprinkle with parsley and simmer until chicken is tender, about 1 hour. Blend soup and pan drippings; stir in sour cream and heat gently. Serve over rice.

Addie Downs, *Dining with Pioneers, Volume I*, Tennessee Chapter No. 21

# Creamy Chicken Bake

4 to 6 chicken breasts (boneless and skinless)
8 oz. Swiss cheese
1 can cream of chicken soup
1/3 c. sauterne cooking wine
cornflake or bread crumbs
dots of butter

Slightly grease bottom of casserole dish. Add chicken. Lay Swiss cheese on chicken, mix together soup and wine and spread on top of chicken and cheese. Add crumbs and dot with butter. Bake 50 minutes at 375°. Serve with yellow rice or noodles.

Jan Alderman, *Pioneers Pots and Pans—1985 Cookbook*
North Florida Chapter No. 39

# Chicken Divan

1 layer broccoli, cooked
1 layer breast of chicken, cooked
1 can cream of celery soup
1 can cream of mushroom soup
1 c. mayonnaise
4 tsp, lemon juice
1/2 tsp. curry powder
Parmesan cheese, grated

Alternate broccoli and chicken layers twice in small individual Pyrex pie plates. Combine remaining ingredients, except cheese. Pour over chicken and broccoli. Sprinkle with cheese and brown under flame. The breasts of 2 hens will serve 5.

Beatrice McKnight, *Bell's Best*, Mississippi Chapter No. 36

*Taste of Atlanta, June, 1994.* (Dogwood Chapter No. 84)

# Chicken Divan

- 2 pkg. frozen broccoli
- 2 c. sliced, cooked chicken (or 3 chicken breasts)
- 2 cans cream of chicken soup
- 1 c. mayonnaise
- 1 tsp. lemon juice
- 1/2 tsp. curry powder
- 1/2 c. shredded sharp cheese
- 1/2 c. bread crumbs (soft) or Pepperidge Farm stuffing
- 1 Tbsp. melted butter

Cook broccoli in boiling salt water until tender; drain.

Arrange stalks in greased baking dish. Place chicken on top. Combine soup, lemon juice, mayonnaise, curry powder; pour over chicken. Sprinkle with cheese. Combine bread crumbs and butter; sprinkle over top. Bake at 350° for 25 to 30 minutes. Serves 4.

Sarah Baker, *Calling All Cooks*, Alabama Chapter No. 34

# Favorite Chicken Divan

- 2 cans cream of chicken soup
- 1/2 cup mayonnaise
- 1/2 cup sour cream
- 1/2 teaspoon curry powder
- 2 teaspoons lemon juice
- 6 chicken breasts, cooked
- 2 10-ounce packages frozen broccoli
- 3/4 cup bread crumbs
- 1 1/2 cups shredded Cheddar cheese
- 1 tablespoon melted butter
- Paprika to taste

Combine soup, mayonnaise, sour cream, curry powder and lemon juice in bowl; mix well. Bone chicken breasts; cut each into 2 strips. Layer broccoli and chicken in 9x11-inch baking dish. Spread soup mixture over top. Sprinkle with bread crumbs and cheese. Drizzle with butter. Sprinkle with paprika. Bake at 350 degrees for 30 to 45 minutes or until bubbly. Serve over rice. Yield: 6 servings.

**Approx Per Serving:** Cal 566; Prot 35 g; Carbo 24 g; Fiber 3 g; T Fat 38 g; Chol 112 mg; Sod 1274 mg.

Ruth Tucker, *Carolina Cooking*, North Carolina Chapter No. 35

## Chicken Dijon

2 8-ounce chicken breasts, skinned, trimmed
2 tablespoons lemon juice
2 teaspoons Dijon mustard
1/2 teaspoon basil
Paprika to taste
1/4 teaspoon garlic salt
1/8 teaspoon pepper

Wash chicken and pat dry; pierce with fork. Place in 9x9-inch glass dish. Sprinkle on both sides with lemon juice. Let stand for 20 to 30 minutes, turning once. Arrange chicken with thicker portions toward outside of dish. Spread with mustard; sprinkle with basil, paprika, garlic salt and pepper. Microwave, covered with waxed paper, on High for 3 minutes. Rotate dish 1/2 turn. Microwave on Medium for 6 to 7 minutes or until done to taste, rotating dish 1/2 turn after 3 minutes. Let stand, covered with foil, for 5 minutes. Garnish with celery leaves and tomato rose. Serve with peas. Yield: 2 servings.

**Approx Per Serving:** Cal 194; Prot 40 g; Carbo 2 g; Fiber <1 g; T Fat 2 g; Chol 98 mg; Sod 431 mg.

Barbara Clark, *Carolina Cooking*, North Carolina Chapter No. 35

## Dreamy Chicken

4 medium chicken breasts
1 can cream of mushroom soup
1 c. (8 oz.) sour cream
Crushed Ritz crackers
1 stick margarine, melted
Slivered almonds or sesame seeds (optional)

Cook chicken breasts until done. (Broth can be saved for later.) Break meat into bite-size pieces. In mixing bowl, combine chicken pieces, soup and sour cream. Mix together and pour in shallow baking dish. Smooth out evenly. Pour enough crushed Ritz crackers over chicken mixture to cover well. Pour melted margarine over cracker topping. Slivered almonds or sesame seeds may be sprinkled over crackers. Bake in 400° oven until bubbly. Serves 6 to 8 people.

Harriet Chambers, *Calling All Cooks two*, Alabama Chapter No. 34

### A Helpful Hint

Frozen chicken will defrost faster when immersed in a bowl of cold water.

# *Chicken and Dumplings*

**1 chicken**
**2 c. plain flour**
**6 Tbsp. cold water**
**1 egg, beaten**
**3 Tbsp. Crisco, melted**
**Salt and pepper to taste**

Boil chicken, salt and pepper in water until tender. Remove chicken; debone and save broth. Water should be added to make approximately 3 quarts of broth.

**Dumplings:** Combine egg, water and Crisco. Add flour, a little at a time, until dough is very stiff. Knead until all flour is used. Sprinkle some flour on a cloth or waxed paper and roll out dough. Wait for 20 minutes. Cut in squares. Bring broth to a boil again and drop dumplings, one at a time. Add chicken and remove from heat. Cover until ready to serve.

Leona Lathem, *Calling All Cooks two*, Alabama Chapter No. 34

# *Old Fashioned Chicken and Dumplings*

**3 to 4 lb. hen**
**2 to 3 ribs of celery (cut in chunks)**
**1 onion (whole)**
**salt and pepper**

Put the above ingredients in a heavy 6 to 8 quart pot with enough water to cover 3/4 of the chicken. Cook until the chicken falls off the bone. Cool and remove all bones and skin. (Chicken should be in all size pieces.)

**Dumplings:**

**3 to 4 cups of plain flour**
**1 tsp. pepper**
**1 tsp. salt**
**ice water**

Add flour, salt and pepper; then add enough ice water to make the dough. Place on a floured surface to roll out the dough. Separate into 4 or 5 balls and roll out very, very thin. (Add only enough flour to keep them from sticking.) Cut into narrow strips. As the strips are cut, drop them into the boiling chicken until all the dough has been cut. DO NOT COVER THE POT! Cook until tender (approximately 10 minutes after the last strips are dropped into the chicken). Serves 6 to 8. ENJOY! ENJOY!

Frances M. Fagan, *Secret Recipes of Telephone Pioneers, Volume II*
South Carolina Chapter No. 61

# Old Fashioned Chicken Pie

1 (2 lb.) chicken
4 Tbsp. butter
2 c. water
1 c. milk
1 tsp. celery seed
1 tsp. onion salt
1/4 tsp. thyme

Prepare chicken; cut into individual pieces; sprinkle with salt. Place in deep saucepan. Add 2 cups water, cover and simmer until tender. Add milk, butter and other seasonings. Bring back to simmer point. Do not boil. Add dumplings.

**Dumplings:**

2 c. flour
1 tsp. salt
5 Tbsp. fat
1/2 c. milk

Sift flour and salt together. Cut in fat. Add milk and stir to make soft dough. Divide dough in half. Roll 1 part to 1/4 inch thickness. Cut into strips. Drop dumplings, one at a time, into liquid. Keep dumplings pushed aside with a fork so that dumplings will be separate. Pour into baking dish. Roll remaining half of dough to fit baking dish. Place on top of chicken and crimp edges. Slash crust to allow for escape of steam. Brush crust with butter and bake.

Sandy Cook, *Dogwood Delights*, Dogwood Chapter No. 84

*Project FLAG, which stands for Freedom and Liberty for Americans in Georgia, provides flagpoles at rest areas on major interstate highways in Georgia.* (Dixie Chapter No. 23)

# Chicken Tetrazzini

1 large fryer
1 medium onion, chopped
½ c. chopped celery
½ c. chopped bell pepper
1 can cream of mushroom soup
1 small jar chopped pimiento
¾ lb. Velveeta cheese
8 oz. pkg. spaghetti or egg noodles
Salt and pepper to taste

Cut up and boil fryer until tender. Remove from broth and remove chicken from bone. Add celery, onion and bell pepper to broth, cook until tender. Then add soup, pimiento, cut up chicken, cheese and cooked spaghetti. Heat slowly until cheese is melted.

*Pots, Pans & Pioneers II*, Louisiana Chapter No. 24

# Chicken Little Fingers

6 whole chicken breasts, boned
1½ c. buttermilk
2 Tbsp. lemon juice
2 tsp. Worcestershire sauce
1 tsp. soy sauce
1 tsp. paprika
1 Tbsp. Greek seasoning
1 tsp. salt
1 tsp. pepper
2 cloves garlic, minced
4 c. soft bread crumbs (I use homemade biscuits)
½ c. sesame seed
¼ c. margarine, melted
¼ c. shortening, melted

Cut chicken into ½ inch strips. Combine next 9 ingredients; add chicken, mixing well. Cover and refrigerate overnight. Drain chicken. Combine bread crumbs and sesame seed, mixing well. Add chicken and toss to coat. Place chicken in 2 greased 13x9x2 inch baking dishes. Combine margarine and shortening; brush on chicken. Bake at 350° for 35 to 40 minutes. Serve with Plum Sauce. (Recipe follows.)

## Plum Sauce:

1½ c. red plum jam
1½ Tbsp. prepared mustard
1½ Tbsp. prepared horseradish
1½ tsp. lemon juice

Combine all ingredients in a small saucepan, mixing well. Place over low heat just until warm, stirring constantly. Dip chicken fingers into sauce.

Brownie-Lois Bruner, *Kentucky Kitchens, Volume I*
Kentucky Chapter No. 32

# Chicken-in-a-Garden

6 chicken breast filets
Marinade
2 tablespoons oil
3 green bell peppers, cut into 1-inch pieces
8 scallions, cut into 1/2-inch pieces
1 cup diagonally sliced 1-inch pieces celery
1 6-ounce package frozen snow peas, thawed, drained
1 teaspoon soy sauce
2 1/2 tablespoons cornstarch
3/4 cup water
3/4 teaspoon instant chicken bouillon
1/8 teaspoon ginger
3 medium tomatoes, peeled, chopped

Rinse chicken and pat dry. Cut into 1-inch pieces. Combine with marinade in bowl. Let stand for 20 minutes. Pour oil into preheated wok, coating well. Heat on medium-high (350 degrees) for 2 minutes. Add green peppers. Stir-fry for 4 minutes. Add scallions, celery and snow peas. Stir-fry for 2 minutes. Remove vegetables with slotted spoon. Add chicken. Stir-fry for 3 minutes. Combine soy sauce and cornstarch in bowl. Stir in water, instant bouillon and ginger. Add to wok with stir-fried vegetables and tomatoes. Cook over low heat (225 degrees) for 3 minutes or until thick and bubbly. Serve over hot cooked rice. Yield: 8 servings.

## Marinade for Chicken-in-a-Garden

1 tablespoon oil
1 teaspoon soy sauce
1 1/2 tablespoons cornstarch
1/2 teaspoon garlic powder
1/4 teaspoon pepper

Combine oil, soy sauce, cornstarch, garlic powder and pepper in bowl; mix well.

Approx Per Serving: Cal 172; Prot 17 g; Carbo 12 g; Fiber 3 g; T Fat 6 g; Chol 37 mg; Sod 365 mg.

Ann Neeley, *Carolina Cooking*, North Carolina Chapter No. 35

## Chicken Lasagna

5 cups chopped cooked chicken
2 cups chicken broth
1 10-ounce can cream of mushroom soup
1 8-ounce can sliced mushrooms
1 7-ounce can sliced water chestnuts
1 can evaporated milk
Poultry seasoning, salt and pepper to taste
8 lasagna noodles, cooked
3/4 cup shredded cheese

Combine chicken, chicken broth, soup, mushrooms, water chestnuts, evaporated milk, poultry seasoning, salt and pepper in saucepan; mix well. Cook over low heat for 10 minutes, stirring to mix well. Alternate layers of chicken mixture, noodles and cheese in baking dish until all ingredients are used, ending with cheese. Bake at 350 degrees for 45 minutes. Yield: 8 servings.

Debbi Palmer, *Lawfully Good Eating*, Dixie Chapter No. 23

## Chicken Breasts with Mushrooms

1/3 c. oil
1 small onion, finely chopped
1 clove garlic, finely chopped
2 large chicken breasts, cut in halves
1/2 lb. sliced mushrooms
1 c. dry white wine
Salt
Pepper

Heat oil; sauté onion and garlic until lightly browned. Add chicken and sauté until lightly browned on both sides. Turn heat to low and add remaining ingredients. Cover and simmer for 30 minutes or until chicken is tender. Serves 4.

Dianne Roberts, *Dining with Pioneers, Volume II*
Tennessee Chapter No. 21

## "Souper Chicken Patties"

1/4 cup chopped onion
2 tbsp. margarine
2 cans cream of chicken soup
2/3 cup milk
2 cups diced cooked chicken
2 hard boiled eggs, sliced
1/4 cup chopped pimiento
8 patty shells or slices of toast
1/4 cup slivered almonds

In saucepan, cook onion in margarine until tender. Blend in soup and milk. Add chicken, eggs and pimiento. Heat, stirring now and then. (If using frozen patty shells, bake according to instructions on package.) Serve in patty shells or on toast. Top with almonds. Serves 8.

It's easy—a main dish in minutes!

Myra Trevitz, *Secret Recipes of Telephone Pioneers, Volume II*
South Carolina Chapter No. 61

## Chicken Pie Delight

1 10-ounce can cream of mushroom soup
1 cup sour cream
1 3-pound chicken, cooked, boned, chopped
1 baked 9-inch pie shell
1/2 cup shredded Cheddar cheese
5 to 6 saltine crackers, crushed
1 tablespoon melted butter

Combine soup and sour cream in bowl; mix well. Stir in chicken. Spoon into pie shell. Sprinkle with cheese and cracker crumbs; drizzle with butter. Bake at 350 degrees for 10 to 15 minutes or until bubbly. Yield: 6 servings.

**Approx Per Serving:** Cal 576; Prot 39 g; Carbo 22 g; Fiber 1 g; T Fat 36 g; 57% Calories from Fat; Chol 133 mg; Sod 809 mg.

Faye Husby, *Calling All Cooks three*, Alabama Chapter No. 34

## *Martha's Chicken Pie*

**3 or 4 chicken breasts, cooked, boned, chopped**
**2 unbaked 9-inch deep-dish pie shells**
**1 cup sour cream**
**1/2 cup margarine**
**1 10-ounce can cream of chicken soup**
**1/2 cup chopped onion**
**1 9-ounce can mixed vegetables**

Arrange chicken in 1 pie shell. Spoon mixture of sour cream, margarine, soup, onion and mixed vegetables over chicken. Top with remaining pastry. Crimp edges to seal; cut vents. Bake at 350 degrees for 40 to 45 minutes or until brown. Yield: 6 servings.

**Approx Per Serving:** Cal 709; Prot 25 g; Carbo 39 g; Fiber 2 g; T Fat 50 g; 64% Calories from Fat; Chol 69 mg; Sod 1139 mg.

Martha M. Bolling, *Calling All Cooks three*, Alabama Chapter No. 34

## *Melt-in-Your-Mouth Chicken Pie*

**1 2 lb. chicken**
**1 10-oz. can cream of chicken soup**
**2 cups chicken broth**
**1 cup buttermilk**
**1 cup self-rising flour**
**1/2 tsp. salt**
**1/2 tsp. black pepper**
**1/2 cup margarine, melted**

Stew chicken and remove all bones. Cut into small pieces. Spread in 13x9x2 inch baking pan. Bring to boil chicken broth and chicken soup. Pour over chicken pieces. In separate bowl, mix melted margarine, buttermilk and flour with salt and pepper. Spoon this mixture over chicken and broth. Bake 25–30 minutes at 425 degrees. Serves 3–4.

Doris D. Morris, *Secret Recipes of Telephone Pioneers, Volume III*
South Carolina Chapter No. 61

## Chicken Pot Pie

**4 chicken breasts or 1 whole chicken, cooked**
**3/4 cup mayonnaise**
**1 cup Bisquick**
**1 cup milk**
**1 can Cream of Chicken soup**
**1 1/2 cup broth**
**1 can English peas, drained**
**1/2 onion, chopped**
**2 carrots or potatoes, chopped**
**1/2 cup celery**

Cook vegetables in broth. Do not cook peas. Add chicken. Mix soup with vegetables and chicken. Mix Bisquick with milk, getting all lumps out. Melt margarine in 9x13 inch pan. Pour chicken and vegetable mixture into pan. Pour Bisquick mixture over chicken and vegetables. Bake in a preheated 350° oven for 35 minutes or until the crust is done. Recipe serves 6.

Peggy Wyatt, *Secret Recipes of Telephone Pioneers, Volume II*
South Carolina Chapter No. 61

## Chicken Supreme

**Country:** U.S.A. **City:** Cape Cod. **Relative obtained from:** Mother-in-law. **Brief history:** Family favorite.

**2 boneless chicken breasts, cooked**
**1/4 c. chopped onion**
**3/4 c. chopped celery**
**2 Tbsp. melted butter**
**3/4 c. Hellmann's mayonnaise**
**1 can cream of chicken soup**
**1 1/2 c. cooked rice**
**2 tsp. Beau Monde seasoning**

**Topping:**

**6 Tbsp. butter**
**3 c. Special K cereal**
**1/4 c. slivered almonds**

Cut up chicken in bite-size pieces. Sauté onion and celery in 2 tablespoons butter for 5 minutes. Mix next 4 ingredients and add chicken and vegetables. Put in shallow casserole.

**Topping:** Lightly sauté almonds in remaining butter and add cereal and mix. Spread on top of chicken mixture and bake at 350° for 30 minutes.

**Preparation time:** 45 minutes.
**Cooking time:** 30 minutes.
**No. of servings:** 6 to 8.

Ruthann Woodbury, *A Taste of Pioneering*
Florida Gold Coast Chapter No. 83

# Hot Chicken Salad

1 chicken, cooked and chopped into small pieces
1 can cream of chicken soup
1 can cream of mushroom soup
3/4 c. finely chopped celery
2 Tbsp. chopped onion
1 c. water chestnuts, sliced
3/4 c. mayonnaise (mixed with soups)
1 boiled egg, grated
2 c. crushed corn flakes

Mix all ingredients with 1 cup corn flakes. Pour into buttered casserole dish. Mix the remaining cup of corn flakes with a little melted butter or margarine and sprinkle on top of casserole and bake at 300° for 45–60 minutes.

Edith Randolph, *Bell's Best*, Mississippi Chapter No. 36

# Hot Chicken Salad Casserole

(Serves 10–12)

4 c. diced, cooked chicken
2 cans cream of chicken soup
2 c. diced celery
4 Tbsp. minced onion
2 c. slivered almonds
1 c. mayonnaise
3/4 c. chicken stock
1 tsp. salt
1/2 tsp. black pepper
4 Tbsp. lemon juice
6 hard cooked eggs, chopped
1 c. cracker crumbs

Combine all ingredients, except cracker crumbs, and spoon into a 3–4 quart casserole dish. Cover top with cracker crumbs. Bake at 350° for 40 minutes.

Wilma Bugg, *Dogwood Delights*, Dogwood Chapter No. 84

## Helpful Hints

Canned chunk chicken is a quick source of chopped cooked chicken for salads, sandwich spreads and casseroles.

Chop leftover chicken and freeze in measured amounts for use in chicken salads.

# Chicken Spaghetti

1 large hen
1 large (24 oz.) pkg. spaghetti or noodles
1 c. chopped celery
1 c. chopped onions
1/4 c. butter or oil
1/2 lb. Velveeta cheese
1 large can chopped mushrooms
1 c. chopped bell peppers
1 can tomatoes, crushed
2 Tbsp. parsley
1 can cream of mushroom soup
1 large jar pimentos, crushed

Cook chicken until tender. Cook spaghetti in chicken broth. Cook butter, onion, celery, green peppers and mushrooms until tender; do not brown. Add pimentos, tomatoes and mushroom soup; mix all; add salt and pepper to taste. Pour into casserole dish. Cover; bake in slow oven at 350° for 45–50 minutes. If too dry, add broth. Just before serving, put cheese on top and let melt.

Mary M. Knight, *Bell's Best 2*, Mississippi Chapter No. 36

# Baked Chicken Sandwiches

2–3 cups boiled chicken, chopped
1 medium onion, finely chopped
2 eggs, boiled and chopped
1 small can sliced mushrooms—do not drain
1/2 cup mayonnaise
1/4 cup black olives, chopped
12 slices thin sliced bread (Pepperidge Farm or Arnold)

Mix first 6 ingredients (not bread). Cut crust from bread, butter one side of bread and line casserole dish, buttered side down. Top with chicken mixture. Then top with other slices of bread. Spread topping over top of bread. Sprinkle with paprika and sliced almonds.

**Topping:**

1 (8 oz.) cup sour cream
1 can cream of chicken soup
paprika
sliced almonds

Combine sour cream and chicken soup to make topping.

Bake at 350 degrees for 20 to 30 minutes until bubbly. May be made a day ahead and placed in refrigerator. Remove and bake. Freezes well after baked. Then just microwave and serve.

Sylvia Mitchum, *Secret Recipes of Telephone Pioneers, Volume III*
South Carolina Chapter No. 61

# *Chicken Livers Chablis*

2 Tbsp. butter or margarine
Salt and pepper
3/4 c. chablis (or other dry wine)
2 Tbsp. catsup
16 to 20 chicken livers
2 1/2 Tbsp. all-purpose flour
1/4 c. minced onion

Melt butter in 10 inch ceramic skillet in radar oven for 1 minute. Season livers with salt and pepper. Dredge livers in flour; arrange in butter. Cook in radar oven, uncovered, for 7 minutes. Turn livers over halfway through cooking time. Remove and stir in wine, onion and catsup. Cook 3 minutes more. Serve with hot rice.

Phyllis Whaley, *Dining with Pioneers, Volume I*
Tennessee Chapter No. 21

# *Barbecued Cornish Game Hens*

1 env. *Good Seasons* Italian salad dressing mix
1/4 c. red or white wine vinegar
2 Tbsp. water
2/3 c. oil
2 Tbsp. Dijon-style mustard
4 Cornish game hens, split and skinned

Prepare salad dressing mix with vinegar, water, and oil as directed on envelope. Add mustard and shake well. Place hens in shallow dish. Pour on the marinade. Cover and refrigerate for 1 to 2 hours, turning hens at least once. Place on grill, turning and brushing frequently with marinade, until hens are tender and done.

**Broiler:** Place hens on broiler rack. Broil 6 inches from heat, turning and brushing frequently with marinade, until hens are tender and done, approximately 25 to 35 minutes.

**Note:** Two and one-half to three pounds chicken pieces may be used.

Ann McCoy, *Bell's Best 3*, Mississippi Chapter No. 36

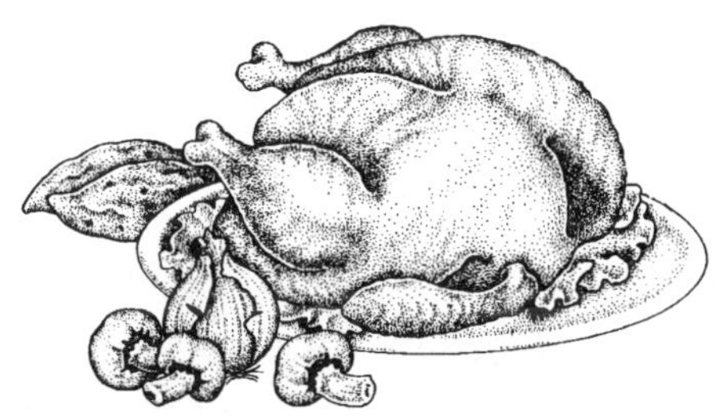

# Hot Brown

*This recipe has been changed and duplicated for years in Louisville, but this is the one that is now served at the Brown Hotel.*

**1/2 cup melted butter**
**1/2 cup flour**
**3/4 cup half and half**
**3/4 cup heavy cream**
**1/3 cup grated Romano cheese**
**1/4 cup grated Parmesan cheese**
**1/2 cup Sherry**
**2 egg yolks, well beaten**
**4 toast points**
**2 slices cooked turkey breast**
**4 slices crisp-fried bacon**

Blend butter and flour in saucepan. Cook until mixture is dry and golden brown, stirring constantly. Stir in half and half and cream. Cook until thickened, stirring constantly. Add Romano and Parmesan cheeses. Cook until cheeses melt, stirring constantly. Bring Sherry to a boil in small saucepan for 30 seconds. Add to sauce. Cook until smooth, stirring constantly. Remove from heat. Strain sauce into bowl. Stir a small amount of hot mixture into egg yolks; stir egg yolks into hot mixture. Place 2 toast points in each of 2 ovenproof dishes. Top with turkey slices and hot brown sauce. Broil until sauce is lightly browned. Top with 2 crossed slices bacon. Garnish with additional Parmesan cheese. Yield: 2 servings.

*Kentucky Kitchens, Volume II*, Kentucky Chapter No. 32

# Hot Turkey Salad

**2 cups chopped cooked turkey**
**1 medium onion, chopped**
**2 cups chopped celery**
**3 hard-boiled eggs, chopped**
**1 7-ounce can sliced water chestnuts, drained**
**1 10-ounce can cream of chicken soup**
**1/2 cup mayonnaise**
**1/4 cup lemon juice**
**Salt and pepper to taste**
**3/4 cup shredded cheese**
**3/4 cup crushed potato chips**

Combine turkey, onion, celery, eggs, water chestnuts, soup, mayonnaise, lemon juice, salt and pepper in bowl; mix well. Spoon into greased 3-quart baking dish. Top with mixture of cheese and potato chips. Bake at 350 degrees for 30 to 35 minutes or until bubbly. May add 1/4 cup pimento strips and/or one 4-ounce jar mushroom pieces if desired. May substitute chicken for turkey. Yield: 8 servings.

Bibb County Sheriff's Department, *Lawfully Good Eating*
Dixie Chapter No. 23

## Smoked Turkey

2 quarts apple juice
2 cups dry white wine
1 small red onion, chopped
3 large cloves of garlic, chopped
10 whole peppercorns
1/4 cup sugar
1 tablespoon rosemary
1 tablespoon thyme
1 small bay leaf
Noniodized salt to taste
1 12-pound turkey

Combine apple juice, wine, onion, garlic, peppercorns, sugar, rosemary, thyme, bay leaf and salt in large stockpot. Bring to a boil, stirring to dissolve sugar. Cool completely. Combine with turkey in large plastic bag; seal tightly. Marinate in refrigerator for 8 hours or longer. Drain and rinse turkey; pat dry inside and out. Place in smoker. Smoke for 2 1/2 to 3 hours; pat dry inside. Place in roasting pan. Roast using directions on turkey wrapper, decreasing roasting time by 10% for each hour of smoking time. Yield: 10 servings.

**Approx Per Serving:** Cal 611; Prot 80 g; Carbo 29 g; Fiber <1 g; T Fat 14 g; Chol 208 mg; Sod 228 mg.
Nutritional information includes entire amount of marinade.
**Dietary Exchanges:** Fruit 1 1/2; Meat 9 1/2

"*Answering the Call of Those in Need*," Tennessee Chapter No. 21

## Hot Shot Turkey Chili

2 pounds ground turkey
1 large onion, chopped
1 tablespoon olive oil
2 cloves of garlic
1/4 cup sugar
2 bay leaves
2 cups water
1/4 teaspoon cayenne pepper
2 tablespoons chili powder
1 28-ounce can tomatoes
1 16-ounce can tomatoes
3 16-ounce cans pinto beans
1 8-ounce can tomatoes and green chilies
2 4-ounce cans chopped green chilies

Brown turkey and onion in olive oil in 5-quart saucepan, stirring frequently. Add remaining ingredients. Simmer for 45 minutes, stirring occasionally. Remove bay leaves. Yield: 10 to 12 servings.

Gene Hodge, *Lawfully Good Eating*, Dixie Chapter No. 23

# Turkey Lasagne

1 lb. ground turkey
1 med. onion, diced
2 cloves garlic, minced
1 bay leaf
1 tsp. oregano
1/2 tsp. basil
1/2 tsp. salt
1 (12 oz.) can tomato paste
1 (28 oz.) can tomatoes
1/2 med. green pepper, chopped
1 tbsp. oil
1/2 c. carrots, chopped (optional)
1/2 c. broccoli, chopped (optional)
1/2 c. zucchini, chopped (optional)
1 lb. Mozzarella cheese
1 lb. lasagne noodles, cooked

In a large pot heat oil and cook over medium heat, onions, pepper and garlic. Add turkey and continue cooking until turkey has lost its redness. Add the rest of the ingredients (except cheese and noodles). Bring to a boil, reduce to simmer and cook for 1 hour.

(While sauce is cooking, make noodles.)

When sauce is ready, begin to layer in a 13x9x2 pan with a little sauce, pasta and cheese. Continue until pan is about full ending with a nice layer of cheese. Bake at 325 degrees for about 25 to 30 minutes.

Sarah Lawson
*A Tablespoon of Pioneering and a Teaspoon of Horses and the Handicapped*
Florida Gold Coast Chapter No. 83

# Mexican Meatloaf

1 lb. ground turkey
1 (15 oz.) tomato sauce
1/3 c. crushed tortilla chips
1/4 c. chopped onions
2 Tbsp. chopped green pepper
1 (1 1/4 oz.) pkg. taco seasoning mix

Reserve 1 cup tomato sauce. Mix all ingredients. Spoon mixture into 9x5 inch loaf pan. Add sauce to top. Bake in a 350° oven for 45 to 50 minutes.

Helen Dickerson, *Dogwood Delights Volume II*, Dogwood Chapter No. 84

## A Helpful Hint

Roast a larger turkey than you need and freeze the leftovers in meal-sized portions for future use.

# Turkey Spaghetti Sauce

**8 ounces ground turkey**
**1 small onion, chopped**
**1/4 green bell pepper, chopped**
**1 teaspoon oil**
**1 beef bouillon cube**
**1 16-ounce jar spaghetti sauce**
**1 4-ounce can sliced mushrooms, drained**
**1/2 teaspoon garlic salt**
**1/2 teaspoon salt 'n spices seasoning**

Brown turkey with onion and green pepper in oil in skillet, stirring until ground turkey is crumbly; drain. Dissolve bouillon cube in a small amount of water. Add bouillon, spaghetti sauce, mushrooms and seasonings to turkey; mix well. Simmer for 20 minutes. Serve over spaghetti. Yield: 4 servings.

**Approx Per Serving:** Cal 227; Prot 16 g; Carbo 22 g; Fiber 1 g; T Fat 9 g; Chol 33 mg; Sod 1066 mg.
**Dietary Exchanges:** Vegetable 3 1/2; Meat 1 1/2; Fat 1 1/2

"*Answering the Call of Those in Need*," Tennessee Chapter No. 21

# Oven-Fried Bluefish

Country: U.S.A. City: Port St. Lucie. **Approximate year created:** 1985.

**2 lb. fish fillets (fresh or frozen)**
**1 tsp. salt**
**1/4 tsp. pepper**
**1 c. instant mashed potato flakes**
**1 (7 or 10 oz.) pkg. cheese garlic salad dressing**
**1 egg, beaten**
**1/4 c. butter**
**Paprika**
**Parmesan cheese (optional)**

Season fish with salt and pepper. Combine potato flakes and salad dressing mix. Dip fish in beaten egg, then roll in potato mixture. Place fish in a single layer on a well greased bake and serving platter. Pour melted butter over fish. Sprinkle with paprika. Bake in hot oven at 500° for 10 to 12 minutes or till fish flakes easily.

**Preparation time:** 8 minutes.
**Cooking time:** 12 minutes.
**No. of servings:** 6.

Doris B. Reick, *A Taste of Pioneering*
Florida Gold Coast Chapter No. 83

# Deviled Bluegill

1 cup milk
4 thick slices white bread, trimmed
1/2 cup butter
3 tablespoons chopped parsley
4 1/2 teaspoons finely chopped onion
3/4 teaspoon salt
Dash of pepper
Dash of Tabasco sauce
3 tablespoons Worcestershire sauce
1 teaspoon dry mustard
1 green bell pepper, chopped
1 pimento, finely chopped
4 cups flaked cooked Bluegill
Crushed cornflakes

Combine first 12 ingredients in large saucepan; mix well. Cook for 10 minutes, stirring constantly. Add fish. Cook for 5 minutes longer, stirring constantly. Spoon into shallow casserole; sprinkle with crushed cornflakes. Bake at 350 degrees for 10 to 15 minutes or until brown. Yield: 6 servings.

Henry Bennett, *Kentucky Kitchens, Volume II*, Kentucky Chapter No. 32

# Fried Catfish

2 lb. catfish
1 tsp. salt
1/2 tsp. pepper
1 c. corn meal
1 egg, well beaten with 1 Tbsp. water
1 c. fat
Lemon wedges

Skin catfish and filet (remove backbone). Cut into portions. Season with salt and pepper. Dip into corn meal, into beaten eggs, then into corn meal again. Sauté in hot fat for about 12 minutes until golden brown, turning once. Garnish with lemon. Serve hot. Makes 4 servings.

Martha Minyard, *Bell's Best*, Mississippi Chapter No. 36

## A Helpful Hint

Cook fish for 10 minutes for each inch of thickness. This time applies to steaks, filets or whole fish and to all cooking methods.

# Fish Courtbouillon

3 lb. redfish, bass or red snapper (or any firm fish)
2 stalks celery, chopped
1 c. butter or oleo
1 can tomato paste
1 Tbsp. sugar
Garlic powder
Season all salt
Hot sauce
1 large onion, chopped
1 c. green onions, chopped
1 Bell pepper, chopped
1 can tomato paste
Lemon juice
Salt and pepper
Paprika
Parsley flakes
3 c. water

Sprinkle fish with lemon juice and season with hot sauce, pepper and salt. Do this overnight or several hours before cooking. Cook onions, Bell pepper, celery in butter until wilted. Add tomato paste and stir constantly. Cook until practically brown. Add tomato sauce and cook for 1 hour. Add water and cook for 30 minutes. Add sugar and remainder of seasonings. Stir well and pour over fish and garnish with parsley flakes. Bake in oven at 375° for 1 hour and 15 minutes.
8 servings.

Mary Ann Migues, *Pots, Pans and Pioneers, Volume I*
Louisiana Chapter No. 24

# Grilled Salmon

1 lb. fresh salmon fillet
1/4 c. orange juice
3 tbsp. soy sauce
2 tbsp. snipped parsley
2 tbsp. water
2 tbsp. cooking oil (Puritan or peanut oil)
1 clove garlic, minced
1/2 tsp. basil (dried, crushed)

Rinse and pat dry salmon fillet. Mix rest of ingredients in small non-reactive bowl. Place salmon in a glass or non-reactive casserole pan and pour marinade over fillet. Marinate 20 to 40 minutes, turn once.

Put salmon fillet in well greased grilling basket. Cook over medium hot fire on Bar-B-Q grill. Turn once until cooked. Fish easily flakes but still moist and should be light pink. Baste frequently with marinade.

Glen Moegenburg
*A Tablespoon of Pioneering and a Teaspoon of Horses and the Handicapped*
Florida Gold Coast Chapter No. 83

## Best Ever Salmon Patties

1 (16 oz.) can pink salmon
1 egg
1/3 c. chopped onion
2 Tbsp. salmon juice
1 1/2 tsp. baking powder
1/2 c. flour
1 1/2 c. shortening or oil

Drain salmon. In a medium mixing bowl, mix salmon, egg and onion until sticky. Stir in flour. Add baking powder to salmon juice; stir into salmon mixture. Form into small patties and fry until golden brown.

Mary S. Shoemake, *Bell's Best* 2, Mississippi Chapter No. 36

## Salmon Loaf with Creamy Dijon Sauce

1 7-ounce can salmon, drained
2 cups chopped cooked potatoes
1/4 cup chopped celery
1/4 cup milk
1 egg, beaten
1/4 cup minced green onions
1/2 teaspoon grated lemon rind
Pepper to taste
2 tablespoons minced onion
1 tablespoon oil
1 tablespoon butter
1 tablespoon flour
1 cup milk
2 tablespoons Dijon mustard

Flake salmon in bowl. Add potatoes, celery, 1/4 cup milk, egg, green onions, lemon rind and pepper; mix well. Press into lightly greased loaf pan. Bake at 350 degrees for 25 minutes or until set. Sauté onion in mixture of oil and butter in skillet until tender. Blend in flour. Stir in 1 cup milk gradually. Cook until thickened, stirring constantly. Blend in mustard. Serve sauce with Salmon Loaf. Yield: 4 servings.

**Approx Per Serving:** Cal 266; Prot 16 g; Carbo 19 g; Fiber 1 g; T Fat 13 g; Chol 86 mg; Sod 466 mg.
**Dietary Exchanges:** Milk 1/2; Bread/Starch 1; Meat 1 1/2; Fat 2

"*Answering the Call of Those in Need*," Tennessee Chapter No. 21

# Virginia's Prize Winning Fiesta Salmon

4 hard cooked eggs
2 Tbsp. mayonnaise
1/4 tsp. salt
1/4 tsp. dry mustard
Dash of bottled hot pepper sauce
1 (1 lb.) can salmon
1 tsp. lemon juice
1/4 c. butter or margarine
1/4 c. flour
1/2 tsp. salt
2 c. milk
3/4 c. shredded process cheese
12 ripe olives, sliced
1 c. crushed sour cream and onion potato chips

Make deviled eggs of the first 4 ingredients. Break fish into chunks and place in a 10x6x1 1/4 inch dish; sprinkle fish with lemon juice. Melt margarine; blend in flour and salt and slowly stir in milk. Cook and stir till thick. Stir in process cheese; pour 1/4 cheese sauce over fish. Arrange deviled eggs and olives on top. Cover with remaining sauce. Sprinkle with crushed potato chips. Bake at 375° for 25 minutes.
Serves 5–6.

Zoerita Proctor, *Dining with Pioneers, Volume II*
Tennessee Chapter No. 21

# Oven-Fried Trout

1 pound trout filets
1 tablespoon olive oil
1/4 teaspoon salt substitute
1/8 teaspoon garlic powder
1/8 teaspoon pepper
1/3 cup cornflake crumbs

Rinse trout; pat dry. Brush with olive oil; sprinkle with salt substitute, garlic powder and pepper. Coat with cornflake crumbs. Arrange in baking pan sprayed with nonstick cooking spray. Bake, uncovered, at 500 degrees for 10 minutes or until fish flakes easily. Remove carefully to serving platter. Garnish with lemon slices and parsley.
Yield: 4 servings.

**Approx Per Serving:** Cal 190; Prot 24 g; Carbo 5 g; Fiber <1 g; T Fat 7 g; Chol 66 mg; Sod 101 mg.
**Dietary Exchanges:** Bread/Starch 1/2; Meat 3; Fat 1/2

"*Answering the Call of Those in Need*," Tennessee Chapter No. 21

## Trout Amandine

**3 lb. trout fillets**
**½ c. margarine**
**¼ c. sliced blanched almonds**
**2 Tbsp. lemon juice**
**1 tsp. chopped parsley**

Rinse fish; pat dry with paper towels. Heat ¼ cup margarine in large skillet until very hot. Add fillets; brown on each side for about 3 minutes per side. Remove to warm platter and keep warm. Add remaining margarine to skillet; heat. Add almonds. Sauté until well browned. Stir in lemon juice. Pour over fish. Sprinkle with parsley. Serves 4.

Catfish fillets may be used.

Helen Graham, *Bell's Best 3*, Mississippi Chapter No. 36

## Tuna Delight

**1 cup small peas**
**2 6-ounce cans tuna, drained, flaked**
**1 cup chopped celery**
**1 to 2 tablespoons mayonnaise**
**1 tablespoon lemon juice**
**1 teaspoon soy sauce**
**1 onion, chopped**
**⅛ teaspoon garlic salt**
**⅛ teaspoon curry powder**
**1 cup chow mein noodles**
**Lettuce wedges**

Combine peas, tuna, celery, mayonnaise, lemon juice, soy sauce, onion, garlic salt and curry powder in bowl; mix well. Chill in refrigerator until serving time. Stir in noodles. Serve on lettuce wedges. Yield: 4 servings.

Joyce Litt, *Lawfully Good Eating*, Dixie Chapter No. 23

## Low-Fat Barbecued Tuna

**1 7-ounce can tuna, drained**
**⅓ cup hickory-smoke barbecue sauce**
**1 or 2 tablespoons vinegar**

Combine tuna, barbecue sauce and vinegar in saucepan; mix well. Simmer for 5 to 15 minutes or until heated through. Yield: 2 servings.

**Approx Per Serving:** Cal 148; Prot 26 g; Carbo 6 g; Fiber <1 g; T Fat 2 g; 10% Calories from Fat; Chol 30 mg; Sod 675 mg.

Donna Nix, *Calling All Cooks three*, Alabama Chapter No. 34

# Frog Legs in Mushroom Sauce

6 large frog legs
2 thin slices lemon
1/2 tsp. salt
1/8 tsp. pepper
2 Tbsp. onion, diced
2 Tbsp. parsley, chopped
2 Tbsp. celery, diced
3 Tbsp. butter
1 c. sliced mushrooms
1 1/2 Tbsp. flour
1 1/2 c. chicken stock or stock substitute
Salt
Paprika
3 egg yolks, beaten
3 Tbsp. rich cream
1 1/2 tsp. lemon juice

Clean and skin frog legs and cut each leg into 3 or 4 pieces. Put them in a saucepan and cover with boiling water and add 2 thin slices of lemon, 1/2 teaspoon salt, 1/8 teaspoon pepper, onion, parsley and celery. Simmer until frog legs are tender; drain them well. Melt butter; add 1 cup sliced mushrooms and sauté until light brown. Stir in 1 1/2 tablespoons flour; stir in slowly chicken stock. Season with salt and paprika. When the sauce reaches the boiling point, add the frog legs and reduce heat to simmer for a few minutes. Mix beaten egg yolks and rich cream and slowly pour into mixture, stirring constantly. Add 1 1/2 teaspoons lemon juice slowly and stir. Serve immediately.

Peggy Kessinger, *Kentucky Kitchens, Volume I*, Kentucky Chapter No. 32

# Scorch Conch

Hot sauce
2 pieces conch meat, chopped in sm. strips
1 chopped hard ripe tomato
1/4 c. chopped onion
1/4 c. chopped celery
1/4 c. chopped red pepper
1/4 c. chopped green pepper
Juice from freshly squeezed lime

In a bowl combine and mix chopped conch, tomatoes, onions, peppers and celery. Mix in lime juice and add hot (scorch) sauce. Season to taste.

Eat within 24 hours. Any longer and the lime juice will cook the conch. Use the whitest conch meat you can find. Makes about 2–3 servings depending on how much conch is used.

Cathy Downs
*A Tablespoon of Pioneering and a Teaspoon of Horses and the Handicapped*
Florida Gold Coast Chapter No. 83

## Stewed Conch

1 lb. linguini
2 lbs. conch (1/2 inch pieces)
16 oz. spaghetti sauce
2 stalks celery, chopped
1 lg. onion, chopped
1 lg. bell pepper, chopped
2 tbsp. butter
2 tbsp. lemon juice

Stir fry onion, celery, bell pepper in butter.

In separate bowl pour lemon juice over conch pieces.

Heat spaghetti sauce in large pot along with onion, celery, bell pepper mixture. Once spaghetti sauce is heated almost to boiling, add conch meat and turn off burner.

Cook linguini as directed on box.

**To serve:** Place pasta in a large platter and pour conch over. Toss slightly.

Gloria James
*A Tablespoon of Pioneering and a Teaspoon of Horses and the Handicapped*
Florida Gold Coast Chapter No. 83

## Eva's Crab Cakes

**Origin:** Eva N. Godard. **Country:** U.S.A. **City:** Miami. **Approximate year created:** 1985. **Relative obtained from:** Herself. **Brief history:** Published by *Gourmet Magazine*, March, 1985.

8 scallions, chopped
8 large mushroom caps, minced
1/2 green bell pepper, chopped
1 1/2 sticks unsalted butter
1 lb. lump crabmeat, picked over
2 c. fresh bread crumbs
8 dashes Tabasco
2 Tbsp. dry sherry
1/2 to 1 tsp. cayenne or to taste
White pepper to taste

In a skillet, cook scallions, mushrooms, and bell pepper in moderate heat with butter, stirring for 3 minutes, or until soft. In a bowl, combine scallion mixture with crabmeat, 1/2 cup of bread crumbs, Tabasco, sherry, cayenne, white pepper, and salt and chill the mixture, covered, for at least 30 minutes or up to 6 hours. Form mixture into 6 (2 inch) round cakes and coat cakes with remaining 1 1/2 cups bread crumbs. In a skillet, cook cakes in batches in remaining 1/2 stick butter over moderately high heat for 2 minutes on each side or until golden, transferring to heated dish when done.

**Cooking time:** 45 minutes total.
**No. of servings:** 6 to 8.

Eva N. Godard, *A Taste of Pioneering*, Florida Gold Coast Chapter No. 83

# Miss Chris' Deviled Crab

1 green bell pepper, chopped
1 large onion, chopped
4 stalks celery, chopped
1/2 cup margarine
1 pound crab meat
2 eggs, beaten
Salt and pepper to taste
1 1/2 teaspoons seafood seasoning
Tabasco sauce to taste
1 cup bread crumbs
Cracker crumbs

Sauté vegetables in margarine in skillet until tender. Combine with crab meat in bowl; mix well. Stir in next 6 ingredients. Spoon into aluminum shells sprayed with nonstick cooking spray. Sprinkle with cracker crumbs. Bake at 400 degrees for 20 to 25 minutes or until golden brown. Yield: 4 to 6 servings.

Chris Echols, *Lawfully Good Eating*, Dixie Chapter No. 23

# Crab Imperial

1/4 cup margarine
2 Tbsp. flour
1 cup milk
1 tsp. dry mustard
1/2 tsp. salt
1/8 tsp. pepper
1 tsp. worcestershire sauce
1/2 cup green peppers, chopped fine
1 lb. crab meat
1/4 cup bread crumbs, fine
2 tsp. butter
sprinkle of paprika

Melt margarine and stir in flour. Add milk and stir until bubbly. Stir in dry mustard, salt, pepper, worcestershire and green pepper. Fold in crab meat. Spoon into shells or casserole. Mix bread crumbs and butter, sprinkle over crab and garnish with sprinkle of paprika. Bake 15–20 minutes at 425 degrees. Makes a quick—great meal—served with tossed salad and French bread. Serves 6.

Catherine Guible, *Secret Recipes of Telephone Pioneers, Volume III*
South Carolina Chapter No. 61

## A Helpful Hint

For best results, thaw frozen seafood in the refrigerator. It will lose moisture and flavor at room temperature or in warm water. Never refreeze thawed seafood.

## *Crab Rangoon*

1/2 lb. crabmeat
4 oz. Gruyere cheese, shredded
4 oz. cream cheese, softened
1/2 tsp. A-1 sauce
1/4 tsp. garlic powder
Wonton noodle squares
1 egg yolk, beaten

Chop crabmeat and blend with cheeses, A-1 sauce and garlic powder. Put 1/2 teaspoon of mixture in center of wonton square. Fold square over cornerwise. Moisten edges slightly with beaten egg and twist together. Fry in deep fat until brown and serve hot. Makes 190 to 195.

Donna Wheeler
*A Tablespoon of Pioneering and a Teaspoon of Horses and the Handicapped*
Florida Gold Coast Chapter No. 83

## *Crawfish Macque Chaux*

1 medium onion, chopped
1/2 medium bell pepper, chopped
1/2 celery rib, chopped
1 tsp. minced garlic
1 stick margarine
1 can diced Ro-Tel
2 cans whole kernel corn, drained
1 can cream corn
1 lb. crawfish
2 Tbsp. cornstarch
1/2 c. water
1/2 lb. shredded Cheddar cheese

Sauté first 4 ingredients in margarine. Add Ro-Tel. Cook 30 minutes. Add corn. Cook 30 minutes. Add crawfish, salt, black pepper, and red pepper. Cook 15 minutes. Thicken with cornstarch and water. Cook 5 minutes. Pour into a casserole dish. Top with Cheddar cheese. Bake 15 minutes in 350° oven.

Mickie Soileau, *Pots, Pans and Pioneers, Volume IV*
Louisiana Chapter No. 24

# *Lobster Enchilada*

**Origin:** Key West, Florida. **Brief history:** Famous Key West Specialty. Enjoyed by all islanders.

**10 raw crawfish tails, peeled, cleaned**
**3 (10¾ oz.) cans tomato purée**
**3 large onions**
**3 large green peppers**
**1 large clove garlic**
**¼ pt. olive oil**
**1 bay leaf**
**⅛ tsp. oregano**
**½ tsp. salt**

Chop onions, peppers and garlic. Brown in olive oil, then add purée, bay leaf, oregano, and salt. Cook about 20 minutes, then add lobsters that have been cut in quarters. Cook slowly for 1 hour. Serve over rice with French bread.

**Preparation time:** 30 minutes.
**Cooking time:** 1 hour.
**No. of servings:** 8.

Addie Kyker, *A Taste of Pioneering*, Florida Gold Coast Chapter No. 83

# *Jiffy Lobster Newburg*

**1 can frozen condensed cream of shrimp soup**
**¾ c. evaporated milk or cream**
**2 egg yolks, beaten**
**5 oz. canned or frozen lobster, flaked**
**1 (4 oz.) can sliced mushrooms, drained**
**2 Tbsp. sherry**

Place all ingredients in crock pot. Cook on high; stir occasionally until soup is melted. Cover and cook on low 4 to 6 hours. Serve over hot rice, chow mein noodles or in puff pastry shells.

Linda Crawford, *Pots, Pans and Pioneers III*, Louisiana Chapter No. 24

## Artichoke Oyster Casserole

1 large can artichoke hearts, cut in pieces
4 Tbsp. minced shallots
1 (7 oz.) can mushroom slices, undrained
Bread crumbs
5 Tbsp. flour
1 stick butter or oleo
2 1/2 dozen oysters and liquid, cut in pieces
Salt and pepper to taste

Stir flour in heated skillet over low heat until lightly browned. Set aside. Melt butter; add shallots and sauté about 7 minutes. Add flour to butter mixture and stir until smooth. Mix in remaining ingredients except artichoke hearts and bread crumbs. Cook over low heat until it thickens. Alternate oyster mixture and artichoke hearts in casserole and top with bread crumbs. Dot with butter. Bake in 350° oven for 15 minutes. Serve warm on small crackers.

Jim McCarthy, *Pots, Pans and Pioneers, Volume I*
Louisiana Chapter No. 24

## Oysters Dunbar

1 stick oleo
1 medium white onion, finely minced
1/4 cup flour (plain)
2 pods garlic, pressed
1/2 teaspoon fresh thyme, or pinch dried thyme
1/2 teaspoon parsley, chopped
1 teaspoon kitchen bouquet
1/2 pint oysters, with juice to make 1/4 cup liquid
1 small can artichoke hearts
4 slices lemon
Paprika
Salt to taste

Melt oleo and add flour. Add onions, garlic, salt and simmer until they are soft and transparent. Add thyme and kitchen bouquet. Add oysters and liquid. Cook slowly. Add parsley. Pour into ramekins over chunks of artichoke hearts. Cover with buttered bread crumbs. Top with slice of lemon and dust with paprika. Put in oven until bubbly. Serve with artichoke leaves. Serves 4.

Mrs. Janie Harrison, *Secret Recipes of Telephone Pioneers, Volume I*
South Carolina Chapter No. 61

## *Mama Ott's Fried Oysters*

**1 pint of oysters**
**2 or 3 eggs**
**Salt**
**Pepper**
**Flour**

Drain oysters. Remove any shell particles. Salt and pepper as desired, add eggs in bowl and stir until mixed good. Coat with self-rising flour. Fry on medium heat until brown. Remove and drain on paper towels. Serves 4 to 6.

Barbara Ott, *Secret Recipes of Telephone Pioneers, Volume II*
South Carolina Chapter No. 61

## *Oyster Pie*

*Place in a casserole dish:*
**1 layer of saltine crackers**
**1 layer of oysters**
**1 layer of hard-cooked eggs**

Add salt and pepper and butter. Build this up as big a pie as you wish, with a pint or quart of oysters. Then pour in sweet milk to the top layer. Cook until oysters are done and don't let it be too dry.

Mrs. Mabel Holcombe, *Secret Recipes of Telephone Pioneers, Volume I*
South Carolina Chapter No. 61

## *Oyster Puppies*

**1 pt. fresh oysters**
**1 c. flour (self-rising)**
**2 c. corn meal (self-rising)**
**1 c. chopped onions**
**2 large eggs**
**Milk (enough to make batter with consistency of pancake batter)**

Mix flour, corn meal, eggs and onions using water off oysters and milk. Add oysters to mix. Spoon one oyster and mix into deep fryer. Cook until golden brown.

Hugh Stephens, *Dogwood Delights*, Dogwood Chapter No. 84

## *Newfee Oyster Stew American-Style*

10 slices bacon
1 large onion, chopped
3 tablespoons flour
1 12-ounce can beer
3 cups milk
2 12-ounce cans evaporated milk
3 8-ounce cans salt and water-pack whole oysters, chopped
1 tablespoon pepper
1 teaspoon salt

Fry bacon in large saucepan until crispy. Drain on paper towels, reserving 3 to 4 tablespoons pan drippings. Sauté onion in pan drippings until tender. Stir in flour. Cook until golden, stirring constantly. Stir in beer and milk. Cook until bubbly but do not boil, stirring constantly. Remove from heat. Add oysters, pepper and salt; mix well. Cook until heated through. Ladle into soup tureen; sprinkle with crumbled bacon. Yield: 8 to 10 servings.

Dianne Fitzgerald, *Lawfully Good Eating*, Dixie Chapter No. 23

## *Stuffed Oysters*

1 stick butter or margarine
6 dozen oysters
1 c. onion, chopped fine
1 c. celery, chopped fine
5 slices day old bread
2 eggs
Worcestershire sauce (1 serving spoonful)
Salt and pepper to taste
1/2 c. each parsley and onion tops

Mrs. Charles Eschete, *Pots, Pans and Pioneers, Volume I*
Louisiana Chapter No. 24

## *Judy's Boiled Shrimp in Beer*

3 c. beer
3 c. water
1 Tbsp. salt
2 Tbsp. dried minced onions
1 tsp. garlic powder
1 bay leaf
dash of hot pepper sauce
2 lbs. shrimp

Bring all ingredients to a boil. Add 2 pounds shrimp and boil 3 to 5 minutes. For more than 2 pounds of shrimp, cook in 2 pound batches using the same liquid for all.

Judy McClure, *Pioneers Pots and Pans—1985 Cookbook*
North Florida Chapter No. 39

# Shrimp Creole

- 1½ c. chopped onion
- 1 c. finely chopped celery
- 2 cloves garlic, minced
- ¼ c. butter or margarine
- 1 (15 oz.) can tomato sauce
- 1 c. water
- 2 tsp. snipped parsley
- ⅛ tsp. cayenne red pepper
- 2 bay leaves, crushed
- 14–16 oz. fresh or frozen cleaned, raw shrimp
- 3 c. hot cooked rice

Cook and stir onion, celery, green pepper and garlic in butter until onion is tender. Remove from heat. Stir in tomato sauce, water and seasonings. Simmer uncovered 10 minutes. Add water, if needed. Stir in shrimp. Heat to boiling. Cover and cook over medium heat 10–20 minutes or until shrimp are pink and tender. Serve over rice. Makes 6 servings. Rinse frozen shrimp under running cold water to remove the ice glaze before putting them into sauce.

Brenda Young, *Bell's Best*, Mississippi Chapter No. 36

# Shrimp Eggplant Casserole

- 1 large onion, chopped
- 2 Tbsp. cooking oil
- 1 pt. cleaned shrimp
- 1 can crabmeat
- 2 pods garlic
- 2 medium size eggplant
- Salt and pepper to taste
- ½ c. plus 3 Tbsp. cracker meal

Cook onion in oil until clear. Add shrimp and garlic. When shrimp turns pink, add crabmeat and eggplant. Season to taste. Cook over medium heat until eggplant breaks up. Stir in 2 tablespoons cracker meal. Turn into buttered casserole dish. Sprinkle with remaining cracker meal and bake at 350° for 30 minutes.

Lee Anna Beaugh, *Pots, Pans and Pioneers, Volume IV*
Louisiana Chapter No. 24

## Big Jim's Shrimp or Crawfish Etouffe

½ stick butter or margarine per lb. of crawfish
4 lb. crawfish or shrimp
2 sticks butter or margarine
2 cans Ro-Tel tomatoes
2 cans regular tomatoes
4 large onions
Worcestershire sauce (dash)
Tabasco sauce (dash)
4 cans golden mushroom soup
4 c. rice

Melt butter in 10 quart Magnalite pot. Add chopped onion. Sauté until wilted. Blend tomatoes in blender. Add tomatoes. Cook approximately 15 minutes. Preheat 4 cans golden mushroom soup. Add soup and cook approximately 30 minutes. Stir often. Add crawfish and cook until tender. Serve over cooked rice. Serves approximately 14.

Jim Tunnard, *Pots, Pans and Pioneers, Volume IV*
Louisiana Chapter No. 24

## Seafood Lasagna

1 cup chopped onion
2 tablespoons margarine
8 ounces cream cheese, softened
1½ cups cream-style cottage cheese
1 egg, beaten
2 teaspoons basil
Salt and pepper to taste
⅓ cup dry white wine
2 10-ounce cans cream of mushroom soup
1 soup can milk
1 pound peeled shrimp, cooked
1 7-ounce can crab meat, drained, flaked
8 lasagna noodles, cooked
¼ cup Parmesan cheese
½ cup shredded Cheddar cheese

Sauté onion in margarine in skillet; remove from heat. Add cream cheese; stir until melted. Add cottage cheese, egg and seasonings; mix well. Blend wine, soup and milk in bowl. Add shrimp and crab meat; mix well. Layer noodles, cottage cheese mixture and seafood mixture ½ at a time in greased 9x13-inch baking dish. Sprinkle Parmesan cheese over top. Bake at 350 degrees for 45 minutes. Top with Cheddar cheese. Bake for 3 minutes longer. Let stand for 15 minutes. Yield: 12 servings.

**Approx Per Serving:** Cal 338; Prot 21 g; Carbo 21 g; Fiber <1 g; T Fat 18 g; Chol 134 mg; Sod 818 mg.
**Dietary Exchanges:** Bread/Starch 2; Meat 2; Fat 4½

"*Answering the Call of Those in Need*," Tennessee Chapter No. 21

# Shrimp in Lobster Sauce

- 2 Tbsp. peanut oil
- 2 cloves garlic, crushed
- 1/4 lb. ground pork
- 1 lb. fresh uncooked shrimp, shelled and deveined
- 1 1/2 c. water
- 1 Tbsp. cornstarch dissolved in 1 Tbsp. water
- 1 Tbsp. soy sauce (1 or 2 Tbsp.)
- 1/2 tsp. sugar
- 1/2 tsp. salt
- 2 scallions, washed and cut in 2 inch pieces
- 2 eggs, slightly beaten

Heat oil in skillet over a high flame. Add the garlic and stir a few times. Add pork and continue stirring until the pork turns white, about 3 minutes. Add shrimp and stir until they turn pink. Add soy sauce, salt, sugar and scallions. Mix well.

Serve over rice immediately.

Marie S. Taylor, *Pioneers Pots and Pans—1985 Cookbook*
North Florida Chapter No. 39

# Shrimp with Mushrooms and Celery

- 1 lb. shrimp, cleaned and peeled
- 3 Tbsp. white wine
- 1 slice fresh ginger root
- 2 c. celery, sliced diagonally into 1/2-inch slices
- 1 Tbsp. cornstarch
- 1 tsp. salt
- 2 Tbsp. vegetable oil
- 1/4 lb. mushrooms, sliced into "T" shapes
- 1 scallion, sliced in 1/2-inch slices
- 1/2 c. cold chicken broth

Combine shrimp, salt and white wine. Marinate in refrigerator for 30 minutes. Heat oil in wok or pan and brown ginger to flavor the oil. Remove and discard ginger. Stir-fry mushrooms 1–2 minutes; set aside. Stir-fry celery and scallions 1-2 minutes until color brightens; set aside. Stir-fry shrimp and marinade 2 minutes or until shrimp turn pink. Return vegetables to shrimp. Combine cornstarch and broth and add to mixture. Heat until sauce boils. Serve at once with rice.

Connie Younker, *Pots, Pans & Pioneers II*, Louisiana Chapter No. 24

## Shrimp Pie

6 thin slices bread, toasted
1/4 lb. butter
1 cup tomatoes or tomato juice
2 tsp. Worcestershire sauce
2 tbsp. sherry
1 slice bell pepper, chopped
Salt, red and black pepper to taste
1/4 tsp. dry mustard
2 lbs. small shrimp, cooked and peeled
Bread crumbs or crumbled saltines

Place toast in bowl. Pour tomatoes over toast and knead. Add Worcestershire sauce, sherry, bell pepper, salt, red pepper, black pepper and mustard. Melt 6 tbsp. butter and pour over mixture. Add shrimp and mix well. Pour into greased 8x11x2 inch glass dish. Sprinkle bread crumbs on top. Melt remaining butter and pour over crumbs. Bake 30 minutes at 400°. Recipe serves 6. Delicious!

Julia Boykin, *Secret Recipes of Telephone Pioneers, Volume II*
South Carolina Chapter No. 61

## Shrimp Pilau

1 c. rice
1/2 t. salt
4 T. butter
1 lb. cooked shrimp
2 c. water
1 large onion, finely cut
1 large green pepper, finely chopped
1 #2 can tomatoes (if desired)

Cook rice in boiling, salted water until tender—about 30 min. Cook onion and pepper in butter until tender. (Add tomatoes if desired.) Turn mixture into rice. Add shrimp. Simmer for 10 min. Serves 4–6 people.

John L. Clendenin, *Taste of Dixie*, Dixie Chapter No. 23

### A Helpful Hint

After peeling shrimp, rub your hands with fresh parsley to remove the odor.

# Scampi

**1 lb. shrimp, deveined and cleaned**
**1 tsp. vinegar**
**2 recipes Garlic Butter**
**2 Tbsp. Parmesan cheese**
**4 lemon slices**

Cook shrimp in boiling water with 1 teaspoon vinegar for 3 minutes. Combine Garlic Butter Sauce and Parmesan cheese in saucepan. Heat until cheese melts. Pour over shrimp in a baking dish and bake at 300° for 5 minutes.

**Garlic Butter:**

**1/4 c. melted butter**
**2 cloves garlic, put through garlic crusher**
**Krazy Salt or Season Salt to taste**
**1/8 tsp. minced chives**
**Dash of red pepper (optional)**

Combine together in saucepan and cook for 1 minute and serve hot.

Beth Harbour, *Bell's Best*, Mississippi Chapter No. 36

# Shrimp Scampi

**2 lbs. large shrimp**
**3 cloves garlic, finely chopped**
**2 Tbsp. shallots, finely chopped**
**2 Tbsp. fresh parsley, chopped or 1/2 tsp. dried parsley**
**1 Tbsp. fresh basil, chopped or 1/4 tsp. dried basil**
**1/2 tsp. dried oregano**
**1/2 tsp. salt**
**1/8 tsp. freshly grated pepper**
**1/2 c. olive oil**
**2 Tbsp. lemon juice**
**1/4 c. white wine (vermouth)**
**bay leaf**

Remove shells of raw shrimp, leaving only the tails. Run knife along the vein to remove and open the bottom part of the shrimp like a butterfly. Put shrimp and all the ingredients in a bowl and marinate for around an hour. Stand the shrimp in a serving dish that will go into the oven with all the ingredients and bake for approximately 8 to 12 minutes, according to the size of the shrimp. Bake 400°. When finished, the shrimp should be opaque and pink. Do not overcook.

Jeanne Gray, *Pioneers Pots and Pans—1985 Cookbook*
North Florida Chapter No. 39

# Seafood Casserole

- 2 cans shrimp
- 3 eggs, beaten
- 1/2 c. melted butter
- 1 t. mustard
- 1 T. Worcestershire
- dash of Tabasco
- 1 can white crab meat
- 1 can evaporated milk
- 1/2 c. mayonnaise
- 1/4 c. diced bell pepper
- 1/2 c. celery
- 1/4 c. onion
- 1 t. lemon juice
- Grated cheese or crushed crackers

Drain seafood well. Combine in bowl, adding eggs and butter, dash of salt and pepper to taste. Grease casserole. Top with grated cheese. Bake at 325° for 30 min.

Patsy Mullinax, *Taste of Dixie*, Dixie Chapter No. 23

# Creole Filé Gumbo

- 1 c. crabmeat
- 2 doz. oysters and water
- 3 c. shrimp, cleaned
- 1 lb. smoked sausage, sliced
- 1 lb. hot sausage, sliced
- 1 lb. boneless stew meat, cooked
- 1/2 lb. seasoning ham, diced
- Microwave roux
- 1 1/2 qt. hot water
- 1 tsp. thyme
- Gumbo filé to taste
- Salt and pepper to taste
- 1 c. diced cooked chicken

To microwave roux, add 1 1/2 quarts water. Render smoked sausage, ham, and hot sausage; drain. Add all other ingredients. Stir. Microwave on MEDIUM for 30 minutes. Add oysters last 7 minutes. Add filé to taste. Serve over rice.

## Roux

- 1 c. oil
- 1 c. flour
- 5 cloves chopped garlic
- 2 medium onions, chopped fine
- 1/2 c. chopped parsley
- 1/4 c. chopped bell pepper
- 1 tsp. crushed red pepper

Combine oil and flour. Microwave 6 minutes (every 2 minutes stir until medium brown). Slowly add onions, garlic, and bell pepper. Cook on HIGH for 2 minutes. Stir well. Roux should be dark brown. Add parsley and red pepper. Stir. Microwave 3 minutes and you're done.

Good for gumbo, stews, and brown gravies.

Eva G. Harleaux, *Pots, Pans and Pioneers, Volume IV*
Louisiana Chapter No. 24

# Jambalaya

½ lb. chaurice (hot link sausage) or ½ lb. smoked sausage (but then increase bacon grease to 4 Tbsp., do not sauté smoked sausage)
3 Tbsp. bacon grease
½ lb. ham, minced
1 c. chopped yellow onions
1 c. chopped green onions
1 c. chopped green pepper
3 garlic cloves, minced
1 bay leaf
½ tsp. thyme
2 c. long grain rice, washed and drained (but uncooked)
2 Tbsp. tomato paste
2 c. chopped tomatoes, drained (reserve liquid)
½ c. chopped celery
¼ c. chopped parsley
2 tsp. salt
½ tsp. black pepper
Cayenne to taste (optional)
3 c. liquid from tomatoes and oysters
3 lb. cleaned, raw shrimp
1 qt. oysters, drained (reserve liquor)

In a 4-quart heavy pot, sauté sausage until firm, and remove with slotted spoon. Add bacon grease to drippings and sauté ham for 3 minutes. Add onions, green onions, green pepper, garlic, bay leaf, thyme, and sauté 5 minutes. Add rice, and sauté 3 minutes, stirring constantly; add tomato paste and cook 3 minutes. Add sausage, tomatoes, celery, parsley, salt, pepper and liquid. Bring to a boil, reduce heat, and cook slowly, covered, stirring occasionally until rice is done, about 12–15 minutes.

Transfer to a shallow 4-quart baking dish and stir in seafood. Place uncovered in a preheated 350° oven and cook until seafood is done, 20–30 minutes. Stir twice while baking using a large fork to fluff the rice and ensure the seafood cooking evenly.

R. D. Erwin, *Dogwood Delights*, Dogwood Chapter No. 84

## A Helpful Hint

Wrapping seafood in paper is a good way to cook and serve it, as it retains its moisture and the wrapping paper adds a dramatic touch. Cooking parchment is recommended, however, because much paper now contains recycled material which may be toxic when heated.

# Sue's Seafood Tarts

**Filling:**

**1 c. mayonnaise**
**1/3 c. grated Parmesan**
**1/3 c. shredded Swiss cheese**
**1/3 c. chopped onion**
**1/4 tsp. Worcestershire**
**2 drops Tabasco**
**1/2 lb. chopped seafood (crabmeat, shrimp or mushrooms)**

**Tart:**

**1 loaf thin bread**
**Melted butter**

Preheat oven to 400 degrees.

In a bowl mix all ingredients for filling. Set aside.

To make tarts flatten each slice of bread with a rolling pin. Cut rounds using a 2 1/2 inch cutter. Dip rounds into melted butter and press into 1 1/2 inch mini muffin pans. Bake 10 minutes or until brown. Remove and cool.

To prepare Sue's Tarts, fill each tart with seafood mixture and sprinkle with paprika. Place under hot broiler until bubbly. You can freeze tarts and reheat for 10 minutes at 400 degrees.

Sue Maas
*A Tablespoon of Pioneering and a Teaspoon of Horses and the Handicapped*
Florida Gold Coast Chapter No. 83

## Market Terms for Buying Fish

**Drawn:**
Fish is scaled and only the insides removed.

**Dressed:**
Fish is scaled and the head, tail and fins are removed.

**Pan-dressed:**
This term is usually applied to small fish that are cooked whole. The insides, head, tail and fins are removed and fish is sometimes split and the backbone removed.

**Steaks:**
These are crosswise sections of large fish, such as salmon, swordfish or cod. The steaks are cut no less than 1 inch thick and contain a piece of backbone and sometimes a few larger bones.

**Filets:**
These are the sides of small- to medium-sized fish cut lengthwise away from the backbone. There is one filet to each side. They are usually boneless.

# Vegetables & Side Dishes

# Elva's Artichoke Casserole

3 cans artichoke hearts
1 c. Italian cheese, grated
1½ c. bread crumbs
2 Tbsp. garlic purée
3 eggs
1 c. olive oil

Drain artichoke hearts and mash. Add all ingredients; blend well. Bake 1 hour at 350°.

Elva Driscoll, *Pots, Pans and Pioneers III*, Louisiana Chapter No. 24

# Asparagus Casserole

½ c. chopped onion, sautéed in oil
½ c. chopped celery, sautéed in oil
1 c. raw rice, cooked in 2 c. water
1 pkg. cooked asparagus

*Add:*

1 can cream of chicken soup
1 can cream of mushroom soup
18 oz. Cheez Whiz
Cracker crumbs

Bake at 400° for 12 minutes. Leave a little Cheez Whiz to put on top and cracker crumbs on top of Cheez Whiz.

Dorothy Bryant, *Dining with Pioneers, Volume I*, Tennessee Chapter No. 21

*One of 40 homes patched, painted or revamped for the poor and disabled in Jefferson County.* (Kentucky Chapter No. 32)

# Asparagus Parmigiana

1 1/2 lb. fresh asparagus, cooked
1 onion, chopped
1 garlic clove, chopped
3 Tbsp. oil
1/2 tsp. salt
1/4 tsp. Tabasco
1 (1 lb.) can tomatoes
1/4 tsp. thyme
1 (8 oz.) can tomato sauce
8 oz. Mozzarella, sliced
2 Tbsp. Parmesan cheese

Drain asparagus. Arrange in shallow baking dish. Sauté onion and garlic in oil until golden brown. Add salt, Tabasco sauce and tomatoes. Simmer, uncovered, for 10 minutes. Add thyme and tomato sauce. Simmer 20 minutes. Pour sauce over asparagus; place Mozzarella cheese over top. Sprinkle with Parmesan cheese. Bake at 350° for 30 minutes.

J. W. Borden, Jr., *Kentucky Kitchens, Volume I*, Kentucky Chapter No. 32

# Calico Beans

1/2 lb. bacon, sliced
1/2 lb. ground beef
1 (16 oz.) can lima beans
1 (16 oz.) can kidney beans
1 (16 oz.) can pork and beans
1 (16 oz.) can vegetarian beans
1/2 chopped green pepper
1 med. onion, chopped
1 tsp. vinegar
2 tbsp. mustard
1/2 c. brown sugar
1/4 c. sugar
1/3 c. ketchup

*Drain all beans.

Brown the meat and bacon. Salt and pepper to taste. Add onion and green pepper. Sauté until tender. Add other ingredients and stir.

Place in baking dish and cook in oven 350 degrees for 45 minutes, or cook 3 hours in crock pot on low.

Carole Schmoll
*A Tablespoon of Pioneering and a Teaspoon of Horses and the Handicapped*
Florida Gold Coast Chapter No. 83

## A Helpful Hint

To keep vegetables fresh longer, line the refrigerator food crisper with 2 layers of paper towels to absorb the moisture.

## Hot Bean Salad

- 1 1/3 c. fine cracker crumbs, buttered, divided
- 1 (16 oz.) can kidney beans, drained
- 3 green onions, chopped
- 1 c. (4 oz.) shredded Cheddar cheese
- 1/2 c. mayonnaise
- 1/3 c. chopped sweet pickle

Combine all ingredients except 1/3 cup cracker crumbs. Toss lightly and spoon into a greased 1 quart casserole dish. Sprinkle with crumbs and bake at 450° for 10 minutes. Makes 4 servings.

Flo Thompson, *Calling All Cooks*, Alabama Chapter No. 34

## Old Settlers' Baked Beans

- 8 ounces bacon
- 1 pound ground beef
- 1/3 cup packed brown sugar
- 1/3 cup sugar
- 1/4 cup catsup
- 2 tablespoons mustard
- 2 tablespoons molasses
- 1/2 teaspoon chili powder
- 1 teaspoon salt
- 1 onion, chopped
- 1 16-ounce can red kidney beans
- 1 16-ounce can pork and beans
- 1 16-ounce can baby butter beans

Fry bacon in skillet until crisp; drain and crumble. Brown ground beef in skillet, stirring until crumbly; drain. Combine brown sugar, sugar, catsup, mustard, molasses, chili powder and salt in large bowl; mix well. Add onion, ground beef and bacon. Stir in beans. Pour into baking dish. Bake at 350 degrees for 1 hour. May simmer in slow cooker overnight. Yield: 6 to 8 servings.

Denise Jackson, *Lawfully Good Eating*, Dixie Chapter No. 23

### A Helpful Hint

One cup of dried beans equals three cups of cooked beans; one pound of dried beans yields six cups of cooked beans.

# *Harvard Beets*

**1/3 c. sugar**
**1/2 c. vinegar**
**2 T. butter**
**1 T. cornstarch**
**onion, diced**
**3 c. beets, cooked and cubed**

Combine sugar, vinegar and cornstarch in saucepan. Heat and stir continuously until thickened. Add butter. Stir in onions and beets. Let stand to absorb flavor. Serve hot or cold.

Bettye Williford, *Taste of Dixie*, Dixie Chapter No. 23

# *Orange Beets*

**1 1/2 c. brown sugar**
**1 (6 oz.) can frozen orange juice**
**3/4 c. water**
**2 Tbsp. cornstarch**
**3/4 c. cider vinegar**
**1 can small beets**

Mix sugar and cornstarch together. Add orange juice, vinegar and water. Boil until thick. Pour over beets.

Mrs. Rex Primeaux, *Pots, Pans and Pioneers, Volume I*
Louisiana Chapter No. 24

*Pioneers preparing to clean a stretch of highway, a small part of 80 miles of adopted highways in the state.* (Mississippi Chapter No. 36)

# Hopping John

**2 c. dried black-eyed peas, soaked overnight and drained**
**1 piece fatback**
**2 medium onions**
**1 pod okra**
**1 c. uncooked rice**
**4 Tbsp. meat drippings**
**Salt and pepper (to taste)**

Place the peas in a large pot and cover with water; add 3 cups more water. Add fatback, onion, okra, salt, and pepper; bring to a boil. Cover, reduce the heat and simmer until the peas are tender. Add more water if needed. Remove peas and save 3 cups liquid in the pot to cook rice. Add rice and drippings; bring to a boil. Cover, reduce heat and simmer until rice is tender. Return the peas and mix well. Cook for a few more minutes. Serves 6 to 8.

Debbie Giddens (Network), *Dogwood Delights Volume II*
Dogwood Chapter No. 84

# Hoppin' John

**1 lb. black-eyed peas**
**1/2 lb. smoked ham, cut up**
**1 onion, diced**
**1/4 tsp. cayenne pepper**
**3/4 c. uncooked rice**
**Salt to taste**
**Pepper to taste**

Put peas and ham cut in pieces in kettle and cover with water; bring to a boil and then turn down to simmer. If necessary, add boiling water as needed. Cook until tender. Add all other ingredients and simmer until rice is tender, about 20 to 25 minutes. If necessary, add more boiling water to cook rice.

Sharon Duke, *Kentucky Kitchens, Volume I*, Kentucky Chapter No. 32

## Baked Broccoli

**1 medium bunch broccoli, cooked**
**2/3 c. sliced stewed tomatoes**
**2 Tbsp. grated Parmesan cheese**
**1 scant Tbsp. chopped parsley**

Break up broccoli into flowerettes or chop coarsely. Mix with tomatoes and pour into baking dish. Cover with cheese and parsley. Bake, uncovered, at 350° F. for 35 to 40 minutes.

Yields: 4 servings.

Dot Heraty, *Pioneers Pots and Pans—1985 Cookbook*
North Florida Chapter No. 39

## Broccoli-Cheese Casserole

**2 medium onions, chopped**
**1 c. melted butter or margarine, divided**
**2 (10 oz.) cans cream of mushroom soup, undiluted**
**2 (4 oz.) cans chopped mushrooms, drained**
**2 (6 oz.) rolls pasteurized process cheese with garlic, chopped**
**2 tsp. chopped parsley**
**Salt and pepper to taste**
**1/2 c. slivered almonds**
**4 (10 oz.) pkg. frozen chopped broccoli, partially cooked and drained**
**4 c. herb seasoned stuffing mix**

Sauté onions in 1/2 cup butter until tender. Combine onion, soup, mushrooms, cheese, parsley, salt, pepper, almonds and broccoli; mix well. Spoon into two lightly greased 2 quart casseroles. Combine stuffing mix and 1/2 cup butter; spoon over broccoli mixture. Bake at 350° for 20–30 minutes. Yields 12 to 14 servings.

Sudie Sredonja, *Dining with Pioneers, Volume I*
Tennessee Chapter No. 21

# Broccoli-Corn Casserole

**1 10-ounce package frozen chopped broccoli, cooked**
**1 egg, beaten**
**1 17-ounce can cream-style corn**
**1 tablespoon minced onion**
**Salt and pepper to taste**
**3/4 cup cracker crumbs**
**Shredded cheese**
**Butter to taste**

Combine broccoli, egg, corn, salt, pepper and half the cracker crumbs in bowl; mix well. Spoon into greased baking dish. Top with remaining cracker crumbs. Sprinkle with cheese; dot with butter. Bake at 350 degrees for 20 minutes. Yield: 4 servings.

Linda M. Brown, *Lawfully Good Eating*, Dixie Chapter No. 23

# Broccoli, Onion Deluxe Dish

**Country:** U.S.A. **City:** Port St. Lucie, Florida. **Approximate year created:** 1979.

**1 lb. fresh broccoli or 1 (10 oz.) pkg. frozen**
**1 c. frozen whole small onions or 2 medium onions, quartered**
**4 tsp. butter or margarine**
**2 Tbsp. all-purpose flour**
**1 c. milk**
**1 (3 oz.) pkg. cream cheese**
**2 oz. sharp process Cheddar cheese, shredded**
**1/2 c. soft bread crumbs**

Slit fresh broccoli spears lengthwise, cut into 1 inch pieces. Cook in boiling salted water till tender (or cook frozen broccoli according to package directions). Drain; cook onions in boiling, salted water till tender. Drain. Melt 2 tablespoons butter in saucepan. Blend in flour, 1/4 teaspoon salt, and dash of pepper. Add milk; cook and stir until bubbly and thick; reduce heat. Blend in cream cheese till smooth. Place vegetables in 1 1/2 quart casserole. Pour sauce over; mix lightly. Top with process cheese; cover and chill. Melt remaining butter; toss with crumbs. Cover. Chill. Before serving, bake casserole, covered, at 350° for 30 minutes. Remove from oven. Sprinkle crumbs around edge. Return to oven and bake, uncovered, till heated through, about 30 minutes.

**Preparation time:** 30 minutes.
**Cooking time:** 1 hour.
**No. of servings:** 6.

Doris B. Reick, *A Taste of Pioneering*
Florida Gold Coast Chapter No. 83

## Mary's Broccoli Casserole

2 pkg. broccoli, cooked by pkg. directions
1 medium onion, chopped
1 can mushroom soup
1/2 c. milk
1/2 c. rice, cooked by pkg. directions
3/4 stick oleo
Salt and pepper to taste
Sharp cheese, grated

Mix soup and milk. Cook onion in oleo. In casserole dish, put broccoli, onion mixture, soup mixture, then rice and sprinkle grated cheese on top; cook for 30 minutes at 350°.

Emma Rousseau, *Calling All Cooks*, Alabama Chapter No. 34

## Broccoli and Rice Casserole

1 cup uncooked minute rice
1 10-ounce package frozen broccoli
1 small onion, chopped
2 tablespoons butter
1 cup cream of chicken soup
1/2 cup Cheez Whiz
1/2 cup milk
1 cup bread crumbs
1 tablespoon melted butter
1 cup shredded Cheddar cheese

Cook rice using package directions. Cook broccoli using package directions; drain. Sauté onion in 2 tablespoons butter in large saucepan until tender. Add soup, Cheez Whiz and milk; mix well. Cook until cheese melts, stirring constantly. Add onion, broccoli and rice; mix well. Pour into 3-quart casserole. Sprinkle with mixture of bread crumbs, 1 tablespoon melted butter and cheese. Bake at 350 degrees for 30 minutes. Yield: 8 servings.

**Approx Per Serving:** Cal 245; Prot 9 g; Carbo 22 g; Fiber 2 g; T Fat 14 g; Chol 37 mg; Sod 559 mg.

Debra Swilling, *Carolina Cooking*, North Carolina Chapter No. 35

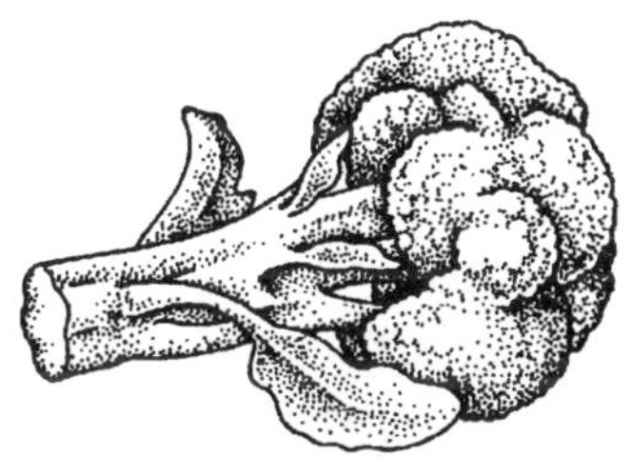

# *Broccoli Rice Casserole*

2 c. cooked (not instant) rice
3 Tbsp. butter
1 box frozen chopped broccoli
1 can cream of chicken soup
1 soup can milk
1 small jar Cheez-Whiz
1 c. chopped onion
1 c. chopped celery
Salt and pepper
1/2 teaspoon red pepper.

Thaw broccoli in 1 cup boiling water; drain; sauté onions and celery in butter. Add soup and milk to onions and celery, then add Cheez-Whiz; simmer. Then add broccoli, rice and seasonings. Bake 30 to 40 minutes at 350°. Makes 10 generous servings and can be made ahead of time.

*Pots, Pans and Pioneers, Volume I*, Louisiana Chapter No. 24

# *Broccoli Rice Casserole*

1 stick butter or oleo
1 large onion, chopped fine
1 rib celery ( inside piece), chopped fine
1 can cream of chicken soup
1 (8 oz.) jar jalapeño Cheez Whiz
1 soup can milk
1 1/2 c. rice (uncooked, but cooked before adding to mixture)
2 pkg. frozen chopped broccoli

Sauté onion and celery in butter until limp. Add soup, milk, and Cheez Whiz. After Cheez Whiz is melted, add cooked rice and broccoli to mixture. Pour into casserole and bake in oven about 20 minutes at 325°. *Enjoy!*

Rose Schmidt, *Pots, Pans and Pioneers, Volume IV*
Louisiana Chapter No. 24

# Broccoli-Squash Casserole

1 bunch fresh broccoli
5 or 6 small fresh squash
1 medium onion
2 or 3 oz. mushrooms, optional
8 oz. sharp cheddar cheese or cheese of your choice
1 (8 to 10 oz.) can cream of mushroom soup
1/2 c. milk
2 Tbsp. butter or margarine
1 c. toasted bread crumbs

Preheat oven to 350°. Sauté broccoli, onion, squash and mushrooms (optional) in butter or margarine until tender (not done). Set aside. Prepare soup using directions on label, but using 1/2 water and 1/2 milk. Slice cheese. In a casserole dish layer first vegetable mixture, then soup, then cheese slices; vegetable mixture, soup, cheese slices. Top with bread crumbs. Bake for 30 minutes or until bubbling.

Serves 6.

Carolyn W. Bell, *Pioneers Pots and Pans—1985 Cookbook*
North Florida Chapter No. 39

# Broccoli Stir-Fry

1/2 lb. broccoli
2 Tbsp. margarine
1 c. mushroom slices
1 c. bean sprouts, optional
1/2 c. (1 oz.) grated Parmesan cheese

Cut tops from broccoli; cut stems into thin pieces, 1/2 inch long. Stir fry in margarine over medium-high heat 5 to 7 minutes or until crisp-tender, stirring constantly. Stir in mushrooms and bean sprouts. Continue stir frying 2 minutes. Remove from heat. Sprinkle with cheese. Mix lightly. Serve immediately.

Yield: 4 servings.

Margaret Stalling, *Pioneers Pots and Pans—1985 Cookbook*
North Florida Chapter No. 39

## Cabbage Supreme

1 cabbage, cut in wedges
1/4 cup finely chopped green bell pepper
1/2 cup finely chopped onion
1/4 cup margarine
1/4 cup flour
1/2 teaspoon salt
1/8 teaspoon pepper
2 cups milk
1/2 cup mayonnaise
1/2 cup shredded Cheddar cheese
3 tablespoons chili sauce

Cook cabbage in small amount of salted water in covered skillet until tender; drain. Spread in 9x13-inch baking dish. Sauté green pepper and onion in margarine in saucepan until tender. Stir in flour, salt, and pepper. Add milk gradually. Cook over medium heat until bubbly, stirring constantly. Pour over cabbage. Bake at 375 degrees for 20 minutes. Mix mayonnaise, cheese and chili sauce in bowl. Spoon over cabbage. Bake for 5 minutes longer. Yield: 4 to 6 servings.

Linda Helms, *Lawfully Good Eating*, Dixie Chapter No. 23

## Hot and Zesty Cabbage

1 small cabbage, chopped
1 medium onion, sliced
4 strips bacon, browned and broken
1/2 tsp. salt
2 Tbsp. sugar
2 green tomatoes, quartered
1 hot green pepper or 2 Tbsp. hot pepper sauce, finely chop pepper

In medium fry pan, brown bacon, remove place on paper towel. In grease lightly cook onion 1 minute. Add cabbage, salt, sugar, stir well and cook, uncovered, 3 minutes. Add tomatoes and hot pepper or sauce. Cover and simmer 5 minutes. Remove from heat. Top with broken bacon strips.

Barbara Stewart, *Pioneers Pots and Pans 1985 Cookbook*
North Florida Chapter No. 39

# Cabbage and Celery Casserole

- 4 Tbsp. butter
- 1 onion, sliced
- 1 small stalk celery, sliced
- 1/2 small head cabbage, shredded
- 2 Tbsp. butter
- 3 Tbsp. flour
- 1 1/4 c. milk
- Salt
- Pepper
- 1/2 c. fresh white bread crumbs
- 2 Tbsp. butter

Melt butter; add onion and celery; cook gently for 5 minutes; stir occasionally. Add cabbage and allow to simmer on gentle heat for another 5 minutes. Melt the butter in a saucepan and add the flour to make a roux. Add milk gradually; stir until a smooth sauce is formed. Season well. Put the vegetables into a casserole and season. Pour sauce over vegetables and sprinkle with bread crumbs dotted with butter. Cook in 350° oven for 20 minutes until the crumb topping is golden brown.

Brenda Chitty, *Kentucky Kitchens, Volume I*, Kentucky Chapter No. 32

# Candied Carrots

- 8 medium carrots
- 1 tsp. salt
- 6 Tbsp. brown sugar
- 2 Tbsp. margarine

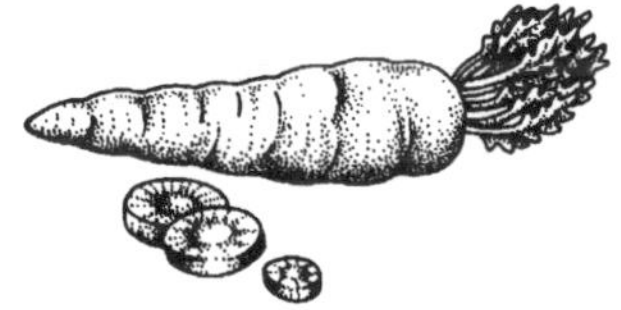

Pare and scrape carrots and cut in quarters, then lengthwise. Cook until tender. Melt margarine and brown sugar in heavy skillet. Add the drained carrots and simmer over low heat. Turn over occasionally until the carrots are coated with margarine and sugar. Remove from heat and serve.

Stella Moore, *Kentucky Kitchens, Volume I*, Kentucky Chapter No. 32

# I Can't Believe It's Carrots Casserole

2 c. mashed cooked carrots
1 stick oleo
1 tsp. baking powder
1/4 tsp. cinnamon
3 Tbsp. flour
1 c. sugar
3 eggs, well beaten

Melt oleo in warm mashed carrots. Mix dry ingredients together and add to carrots, mixing well. Beat eggs and add to other ingredients. Pour into Pyrex baking dish and bake at 400° for 15 minutes. Reduce heat to 350° and bake for an additional 45 minutes.

This is a great way to get children to eat carrots because most people would never know that is what is in it unless you told them.

Beverly Knight, *Dining with Pioneers, Volume II*
Tennessee Chapter No. 21

# Marinated Carrots

2 lb. fresh carrots, peeled and sliced. Cook until tender and drain.
Dressing:
1 c. sugar
1/2 c. salad oil
1/4 c. vinegar
1 t. salt
1 can tomato soup
1 t. prepared mustard
1 t. Worcestershire sauce

Combine ingredients and heat to boiling, pour over carrots. Add a chopped med. onion and 1 chopped green pepper, if desired, after mixture has cooled. Will keep in covered container in 'frig' for a long time. Use as a vegetable or salad on lettuce.

Jean Flemister, *Taste of Dixie*, Dixie Chapter No. 23

## A Helpful Hint

Some foods are particularly rich in the carotene which protects against stroke, heart attack and oral and stomach cancer. Nutritionists recommend dark green leafy vegetables such as kale and spinach; and orange-red vegetables such as carrots, sweet potatoes and pumpkin.

# Marinated Carrots

5 c. sliced carrots
1 medium sweet onion (purple)
1 small green pepper
1 can tomato soup
1 tsp. prepared mustard
1 tsp. Worcestershire sauce
1 tsp. black pepper
1/2 c. cooking oil
1 c. sugar
3/4 c. vinegar
1 tsp. salt

Cook carrots (do not overcook). Drain and cool. Cut onions, green pepper in round slices, then mix with carrots. Mix all other ingredients together, then pour over vegetables. Cover and marinate 12 hours.

Jane Watts, *Bell's Best*, Mississippi Chapter No. 36

# Favorite Corn Casserole

8 oz. cream cheese
1/4 c. milk
2 Tbsp. butter
1/4 tsp. garlic salt
2 (16 oz.) cans whole kernel corn, drained
2 (4 oz.) cans chopped green chilies

Melt cream cheese, milk, butter, and garlic salt over low heat. Add corn and chilies. Put in casserole and bake, uncovered, at 350° for 20 to 25 minutes. Serve 6.

Cissy Cothern, *Pots, Pans and Pioneers, Volume IV*
Louisiana Chapter No. 24

*The visually impaired playing checkers, thanks to Telephone Pioneer Life Members who make braille checkerboards.* (Alabama Chapter No. 34)

## Beaumont Inn's Corn Pudding

**Origin:** Beaumont Inn (in Harrodsburg, Kentucky), old Kentucky Inn. **Brief history:** This corn pudding recipe was originated by the family that owns the inn—years ago. Was handed down from one generation to the next.

**2 c. white whole kernel corn, or fresh corn, cut off the cob**
**4 eggs**
**8 level Tbsp. flour**
**1 qt. milk**
**4 rounded tsp. sugar**
**4 Tbsp. butter, melted**
**1 tsp. salt**

Stir into the corn, the flour, salt, sugar, and butter. Beat up the eggs well; put them into the milk, then stir into the corn and put into a pan or Pyrex dish. Bake inside of oven at 450° for about 40 to 45 minutes.

Stir vigorously with long prong fork 3 times, approximately 10 minutes apart, while baking, disturbing the top as little as possible.

Sharlis Wheeler, *A Taste of Pioneering*
Florida Gold Coast Chapter No. 83

## Fresh Corn Pudding

**2 cups fresh corn**
**2 tablespoons melted butter**
**1 cup milk**
**2 tablespoons flour**
**1 teaspoon salt**
**1 tablespoon sugar**
**Pepper to taste**
**3 eggs, beaten**

Combine corn with butter, milk, flour, salt and sugar in bowl. Add eggs; mix well. Pour into greased 1-quart baking dish. Place dish in baking pan half filled with boiling water. Bake at 350 degrees for 1¼ hours or until pudding is set. Yield: 6 servings.

**Approx Per Serving:** Cal 152; Prot 6 g; Carbo 14 g; Fiber 2 g; T Fat 9 g; Chol 122 mg; Sod 1513 mg.

Barbara D. Scott, *Carolina Cooking*, North Carolina Chapter No. 35

## Sam's Corn (Ahem, Vegetable—That Is!)

*Select absolutely fresh corn. (If possible, snatch it out of your neighbor's garden while the early morning dew is still on it, and run lickety-split to your kitchen with it!)*

Remove husks, all silk and bad spots. Rinse (if your wife is looking). With a very sharp, thin knife, begin to cut corn off cob. Begin at broad end and cut to tip. Do not cut deep. Slice about halfway through kernels.

When all kernels are removed, scrape juice of cob into bowl with corn. Add just enough water to keep corn from sticking or scorching. Stir frequently, adding water in small amounts if needed. Meanwhile fry out 2 or 3 pieces of streak-o-lean. When corn is almost done (10 or 15 minutes, depending on tenderness of corn), add meat and drippings to corn. Salt and pepper to taste. Continue cooking until corn is done. Not more than 5 minutes.

Some folks like to cut off a fresh, hot pepper and dab at the corn with it—at the table.

S. A, Hunt, Jr., *Secret Recipes of Telephone Pioneers, Volume I*
South Carolina Chapter No. 61

## Stuffed Cucumbers

**2 cucumbers**
**1 lb. Monterey Jack or Cheddar cheese**
**1 onion**
**1 egg**
**1 tsp. garlic salt**
**1 Tbsp. Worcestershire sauce**
**Bread, toasted or dried (enough to absorb juices)**
**1/4 c. butter or margarine**
**Parmesan cheese**

Cut cucumbers in half lengthwise. Scrape out insides; shred cheese. Chop onion. Add egg, garlic salt, Worcestershire, butter, and bread mix together. Put stuffing in cucumber shells. Sprinkle top with Parmesan. Bake at 400° for 20 minutes.

*Dogwood Delights Volume II*, Dogwood Chapter No. 84

# Delmonico Baked Creole Eggplant

2 eggplant, peeled and diced
1 medium onion, chopped
2 stalks celery, chopped
1 tomato, chopped
1 c. small shrimp
1/4 c. seasoned bread crumbs

Parboil eggplant. Sauté onion, celery, and shrimp in butter or oil. Add tomato and cook. Add seasoning (a dash of Tabasco, a dash of Lea & Perrins, and 1 bay leaf). When all are melted and blended together, fold in eggplant. Place in baking dish. Top with seasoned bread crumbs and bake in oven set at 350° for approximately 20 minutes.

Betty Byrd, *Bell's Best* 3, Mississippi Chapter No. 36

# Stuffed Eggplant—Old Stone Inn

1 large eggplant
1/2 c. water
1/2 tsp. salt
1 (10 1/2-oz.) can condensed cream of mushroom soup
1 tsp. Worcestershire sauce
1 c. Ritz cracker crumbs, rolled fine (about 24 crackers)
1 c. chopped onion
1 Tbsp. butter
1 Tbsp. chopped parsley
1 Tbsp. butter, melted
1 1/2 c. cold water

Slice off one side of eggplant. Remove pulp to 1/2 inch of skin. Heat water and salt until boiling. Cook eggplant in water until tender, about 10 minutes. Drain thoroughly. Cook onion in butter until tender. Add eggplant, parsley, soup, sauce and all but 2 tablespoons of crackers. Fill eggplant shell with mixture. Place in a 10x6x1 1/2 inch baking dish. Pour melted butter over eggplant and sprinkle with reserved crumbs. Carefully pour 1 1/2 cups of water in bottom of dish. Bake at 375° for 1 hour or heated through. Serves 4 to 6.

Dorothy O'Neal, *Kentucky Kitchens, Volume I*, Kentucky Chapter No. 32

## Green Bean Casserole

- 2 cans green beans (any style)
- 1 can cream of mushroom soup
- 1 small can sliced mushrooms
- 1 c. liquid from beans
- 1/2 c. mild Cheddar cheese, grated
- 1/4 c. bacon bits
- 1 can French fried onion rings
- 1 can slivered water chestnuts, if desired

Drain beans. Place in long casserole dish. In small saucepan, heat mushroom soup, liquid from beans and cheese, stirring until cheese melts. Sprinkle drained mushrooms and bacon bits over beans. Cover with cheese sauce. Cook in 350° oven for 30 minutes. Crush onion rings and sprinkle on top. Heat in oven for 5 minutes.

Doris B. Cole, *Bell's Best*, Mississippi Chapter No. 36

## Green Beans with Garlic

- 1 1/2 pounds young tender green beans
- 2 tablespoons dry bread crumbs
- 2 tablespoons chopped leaf parsley
- 6 cloves of garlic, minced
- Salt and freshly ground pepper to taste
- 2 tablespoons extra-virgin olive oil
- 2 tablespoons margarine

Steam green beans in saucepan for 6 to 8 minutes or until tender-crisp; drain. Rinse with ice water. Sauté bread crumbs, parsley, garlic, salt and pepper in olive oil in skillet over low heat for 1 minute. Add margarine and green beans. Cook until heated through. Serve immediately. Yield: 6 servings.

**Approx Per Serving:** Cal 126; Prot 3 g; Carbo 12 g; Fiber 2 g; T Fat 9 g; Chol 0 mg; Sod 65 mg.
**Dietary Exchanges:** Vegetable 2; Fat 2

"*Answering the Call of Those in Need*," Tennessee Chapter No. 21

## Vicki's Southern Collard Greens

Fresh collard greens, washed
Any of the following meats:
  Salt pork, ham hocks, smoked pigtails or smoked neckbones (pork)
3 tbsp. bacon drippings
Salt and pepper to taste
2 tsp sugar
Hot peppers to taste
Optional: Okra, green bell peppers

Parboil meats. Chop greens fine. Fry bacon to get 3 tablespoons of drippings. Remove bacon. Add greens and cover with water (but not too much). Add sugar and seasonings. Add parboiled meats. Simmer for 1 hour.

**Note:** You can crumble bacon and add it back into greens or make a BLT. Don't use too much water — you're not making soup.

Don't forget to reduce the liquid remaining and pour it over the greens. The "pot likker" can and should, be soaked up with cornbread.

Vicki Deal
*A Tablespoon of Pioneering and a Teaspoon of Horses and the Handicapped*
Florida Gold Coast Chapter No. 83

## Mushroom Turnovers

9 oz. cream cheese, room temperature
1 stick butter, room temperature
1 1/2 c. flour
1 large onion, chopped
1 large can mushrooms, chopped, drained
3 Tbsp. butter
1/4 tsp. thyme
1/2 tsp. salt
2 Tbsp. flour
1/4 c. milk

**Dough:** Combine cream cheese, butter and flour; chill 1/2 hour. Roll 1/8 inch thick. Cut with 3 inch diameter circle. Put filling in center. Fold dough over and press edges together with a fork. Place on greased cookie sheet and bake at 375° for 15 minutes.

**Filling:** Sauté onion and mushrooms in butter. Add rest of ingredients; heat until smooth. Yield: 2 dozen.

Janis G. Black, *Dining with Pioneers, Volume I*
Tennessee Chapter No. 21

## Baked Onions

**4 large onions, cut into halves**
**2 tablespoons brown sugar**
**Salt to taste**
**3 tablespoons butter**
**1 teaspoon lemon juice**
**1/4 teaspoon paprika**
**Chopped parsley to taste**

Arrange onions in buttered shallow baking dish. Top with brown sugar and salt; dot with butter. Bake at 350 degrees until tender. Sprinkle with lemon juice, paprika and parsley. Yield: 8 servings.

**Approx Per Serving:** Cal 76; Prot 1 g; Carbo 9 g; Fiber 1 g; T Fat 4 g; 51% Calories from Fat; Chol 12 mg; Sod 47 mg.

Fran Rhodis, *Calling All Cooks three*, Alabama Chapter No. 34

## Easy Vidalia Onion Casserole

**2 Vidalia onions, thinly sliced**
**1 10-ounce can cream of mushroom soup**
**1 cup crushed potato chips**
**1/2 cup shredded Cheddar cheese**

Layer onions, soup, chips and cheese in baking dish. Bake at 350 degrees for 45 minutes. Yield: 4 servings.

**Approx Per Serving:** Cal 232; Prot 6 g; Carbo 18 g; Fiber 2 g; T Fat 15 g; 59% Calories from Fat; Chol 16 mg; Sod 791 mg.

Shirley Waldrop, *Calling All Cooks three*, Alabama Chapter No. 34

## Onion Pie

**Crust:** Crush crackers (Ritz or saltines). Mix with 1/2 stick melted margarine. Press in bottom of casserole dish.

Chop 3 or 4 medium to large onions. Sauté in butter till tender.

*Mix with:*
**1 pt. sour cream**
**2 eggs, beaten**
**Salt to taste**

Pour mixture over crust. Top with 2 cups grated Cheddar cheese. Bake for approximately 4 minutes in microwave on HIGH or 10 minutes in a 375° oven (or until cheese melts completely).

Frances McFate, *Dogwood Delights Volume II*
Dogwood Chapter No. 84

## *Dakota Potatoes*

4 slices bacon
4 cups pared sliced raw potatoes
1 onion, sliced
2 cups cooked tomatoes
2 teaspoons salt
1/4 teaspoon pepper
1 teaspoon prepared mustard
1 teaspoon sugar
1/4 teaspoon celery salt

Pan fry bacon until done. Remove bacon and place on absorbent paper to drain. Add the potatoes and onion to the bacon fat and sauté for 10 minutes. Turn gently to distribute the fat. Add remaining ingredients and simmer until potatoes are tender and tomato juice is slightly thickened, about 20 minutes. Break the crisp bacon into small pieces and sprinkle over top when ready to serve. Makes 4 to 6 servings.

Mrs. Juanita Cook, *Secret Recipes of Telephone Pioneers, Volume I*
South Carolina Chapter No. 61

## *Easy Potato Casserole*

1 (32 oz.) pkg. frozen shredded hash brown potatoes, thawed
1 medium onion, chopped
1/2 c. chopped green pepper
1 (10 3/4 oz.) can cream of potato soup, undiluted
1 (10 3/4 oz.) can cream of celery soup, undiluted
1 (8 oz.) ctn. commercial sour cream
1/2 tsp. salt
1/8 tsp. pepper
1 c. (4 oz.) shredded Monterey Jack cheese

Combine all ingredients, except cheese; stir well. Spoon potato mixture into a greased shallow 2 quart casserole. Bake at 325° for 1 hour and 15 minutes. Sprinkle with cheese and bake an additional 15 minutes. Makes 8 servings.

Billie Fleming, *Dining with Pioneers, Volume I*
Tennessee Chapter No. 21

# Golden Potato Casserole

2 c. shredded cheddar cheese
1/4 c. butter or margarine
1 (16 oz.) carton sour cream
1/3 c. chopped green onions
1 tsp. salt
1/4 tsp. pepper
6 medium potatoes
1 Tbsp. butter or margarine

Cook potatoes and peel and shred. (I cook mine the night before.)

Combine cheese and butter in a saucepan; stir over low heat until cheese is melted.

Remove from heat; stir in sour cream, onion, salt and pepper.

Add potatoes, mixing gently. Pour into a buttered 2 quart casserole. Dot with 2 tablespoons butter.

Bake 350° for 30 minutes.

Yield: 8 to 10 servings.

Dorothy Rayfield, *Pioneers Pots and Pans—1985 Cookbook*
North Florida Chapter No. 39

# Potato Casserole

1 pkg. frozen shoestring fries
1 medium onion, chopped
1 small pkg. cream cheese
1 can cream of chicken soup
3/4 can water
3/4 c. grated cheese

Sauté onion in small amount of margarine; add cream of chicken soup, water; stir till smooth. Chip in cream cheese and stir; cook about 5 minutes or till cheese has melted. Lightly butter 9x9 inch casserole; add layer of potatoes, sauce. Lightly sprinkle cheese, then potatoes, sauce and cheese. Bake at 350° for 45 minutes.

Hazel Campbell, *Calling All Cooks*, Alabama Chapter No. 34

### *A Helpful Hint*

To keep boiled potatoes white, add a small amount of milk to the cooking water. The potatoes will taste better, too.

## Potato Casserole

6 medium potatoes, boiled
1 can cream of celery soup
1 can cream of mushroom soup
1 small can mushrooms
1 tsp. celery salt
8 oz. sharp cheese
8 oz. jalapeño cheese

Slice boiled potatoes and layer in long pan. Heat both soups, sharp cheese and jalapeño cheese and celery salt until cheese melts. Add mushrooms; pour sauce over potatoes. Cook for 20–25 minutes at 350°.

Donna Finn, *Bell's Best*, Mississippi Chapter No. 36

## Italian Potatoes

2 cloves garlic, minced
3 c. thinly sliced onions
2 Tbsp. olive oil
2 (16 oz.) cans tomatoes (undrained), chopped
2 Tbsp. dried parsley
2 tsp. dried basil
2 tsp. dried oregano
1/2 tsp. pepper
2 1/2 lb. potatoes
1/4 tsp. salt, divided
1 c. (4 oz.) shredded Swiss cheese
3 Tbsp. grated Parmesan cheese

Sauté onion and garlic in oil till crisp tender. Add chopped tomatoes, parsley, basil, oregano, and pepper; stir well. Peel potatoes and slice 1/8 inch thick. Spoon 1/3 of tomato mixture into a lightly greased 13x9x2 inch baking dish. Top with 1/2 of the potatoes; sprinkle with 1/8 teaspoon salt and 1/2 Swiss cheese. Spoon half of remaining sauce over cheese. Repeat layers to use remaining potatoes, salt, Swiss cheese, and sauce. Cover and bake for 45 minutes at 375° F. Uncover and sprinkle with Parmesan cheese. Bake for 35 minutes more or until potatoes are tender.

Tony Kubiak, *Dogwood Delights Volume II*, Dogwood Chapter No. 84

## Onion-Roasted Potatoes

2 pounds potatoes, peeled, cubed
1 envelope onion soup mix
1/3 cup olive oil

Combine potatoes, onion soup mix and olive oil in large plastic bag. Shake well to coat potatoes. Pour into baking dish. Bake at 450 degrees for 40 minutes, stirring occasionally. Yield: 6 servings.

Pauline Newman, *Lawfully Good Eating*, Dixie Chapter No. 23

# Portuguese Potatoes

**8 potatoes**
**1 pound Velveeta cheese, cut into cubes**
**1 onion, chopped**
**1 2-ounce jar chopped pimento, drained**
**1 tablespoon parsley flakes**
**Paprika and garlic salt to taste**
**2 slices bread, cut into small cubes**
**1 cup melted margarine**

Cut potatoes into cubes. Cook in water to cover in saucepan until just tender; drain. Layer potatoes and next 7 ingredients in 9x13-inch casserole. Pour margarine over top. Bake at 350 degrees for 15 minutes or until brown and bubbly. Yield: 8 servings.

**Approx Per Serving:** Cal 663; Prot 18 g; Carbo 58 g; Fiber 5 g; T Fat 41 g; Chol 54 mg; Sod 1131 mg.

Marty Ursery, *Carolina Cooking*, North Carolina Chapter No. 35

# Twice-Baked Potatoes

**4 large baking potatoes**
**1/2 cup milk**
**1/4 cup margarine**
**1/2 teaspoon salt**
**Pepper to taste**
**1 cup shredded sharp Cheddar cheese**
**2 tablespoons chopped green onions**
**4 slices bacon, crisp-fried, crumbled**
**1/2 cup shredded sharp Cheddar cheese**

Pierce potatoes with fork. Bake at 425 degrees until tender. Slice potatoes into halves lengthwise. Scoop pulp into mixer bowl, reserving shells. Add milk, margarine, salt, pepper and 1 cup cheese to pulp; beat until smooth. Stir in half the green onions and bacon. Spoon into reserved shells; place on baking sheet. Bake at 350 degrees for 20 minutes; increase oven temperature to 400 degrees. Toss remaining green onions and bacon with 1/2 cup cheese in bowl. Sprinkle over potatoes. Bake for 15 minutes longer or until cheese melts.
Yield: 8 servings.

**Approx Per Serving:** Cal 264; Prot 9 g; Carbo 24 g; Fiber 2 g; T Fat 15 g; 50% Calories from Fat; Chol 27 mg; Sod 397 mg.

Virginia H. Greene, *Calling All Cooks three*, Alabama Chapter No. 34

# Nacho Potato Wedges

3 potatoes, baked in skins
1 tablespoon melted margarine
Pepper to taste
Chili powder to taste
3 ounces Monterey Jack cheese, shredded
3 tablespoons thinly sliced scallions

Cool potatoes completely. Cut into wedges lengthwise. Place cut side up in single layer on baking sheet. Brush with melted margarine; sprinkle with pepper. Broil for 10 minutes or until light brown. Sprinkle with chili powder, cheese and scallions. Broil for 1 to 2 minutes or until cheese is melted. Yield: 6 servings.

**Approx Per Serving:** Cal 132; Prot 6 g; Carbo 18 g; Fiber 2 g; T Fat 5 g; Chol 8 mg; Sod 87 mg.
**Dietary Exchanges:** Bread/Starch 1; Meat 1/2; Fat 1/2

"*Answering the Call of Those in Need*," Tennessee Chapter No. 21

# Potato Wedges

4 large potatoes
1/2 cup self-rising flour
1/2 cup Parmesan cheese
1 teaspoon salt
1 teaspoon pepper
1/2 teaspoon chili powder
1/2 teaspoon onion salt
1 tablespoon parsley flakes
1/2 cup melted butter

Scrub potatoes; do not peel. Cut each into 4 wedges. Soak in cold water to cover for several minutes; dry. Mix flour, cheese, salt, pepper, chili powder, onion salt and parsley flakes in shallow bowl. Dip potato wedges in melted butter; coat with flour mixture. Place in 9x13-inch baking dish. Bake at 350 degrees for 45 minutes or until tender and brown. May microwave, covered, for 7 minutes, stirring once.
Yield: 8 servings.

**Approx Per Serving:** Cal 286; Prot 6 g; Carbo 36 g; Fiber 5 g; T Fat 15 g; Chol 35 mg; Sod 759 mg.

Joyce Campbell, *Carolina Cooking*, North Carolina Chapter No. 35

## A Helpful Hint

Scoop a small portion out of a potato and insert a baby onion in the cavity before baking for a taste surprise.

## Sour Cream Potatoes

About 3 lbs. new potatoes
1 c. sour cream
1/4 c. fresh parsley or flakes
1 1/2 c. mayonnaise
2 med. onions, chopped
1 t. celery salt
1 1/2 t. horseradish
1 1/2 t. salt

Boil potatoes, cool and slice thin. Mix other ingredients. Alternate layers of potatoes and sauce. Optional: Sprinkle top with paprika. This can be made day before, covered and kept chilled.

Sybil A. Mills, *Taste of Dixie*, Dixie Chapter No. 23

## Spinach Casserole

2 pkg. frozen spinach or 1 lrg. can
3 eggs
8 oz. carton cottage cheese
1 stick margarine
1/2 c. grated cheddar cheese
2 T. flour
1/8 t. salt

Cook spinach according to directions. Canned spinach is fully cooked. Drain spinach and sit aside. Beat eggs, add cottage cheese, cheddar cheese, flour and salt. Melt margarine, add spinach, then cheese mixture. Mix thoroughly. Place in greased 2 qt. baking dish. Bake at 400° for 45 minutes. Let set 15 min. before serving.

Sybil A. Mills, *Taste of Dixie*, Dixie Chapter No. 23

## Spinach Jeremy

3 packs frozen spinach
1 medium onion, chopped
1 stick butter
1 (8 oz.) pack cream cheese
3/4 c. bread crumbs
1/2 c. Cheddar cheese
1/4 c. Parmesan cheese
1 (8 oz.) jar marinated artichoke hearts

Cook spinach and drain thoroughly. While spinach is draining, sauté onion in butter until clear. Reduce heat and add cream cheese and Cheddar cheese. Cook just until mixture is melted. Drain and chop artichoke hearts. Mix spinach, artichokes, and cream cheese mixture together. Place in 9x11x13 inch pan. Sprinkle Parmesan cheese and bread crumbs on top. Bake at 350° for 30 minutes.

LeAnne Berard, *Pots, Pans and Pioneers, Volume IV*
Louisiana Chapter No. 24

# Squash Casserole

**1½ lb. squash**
**1 stick oleo**
**1 pkg. Pepperidge Farm corn bread crumbs**
**½ pt. sour cream**
**½ c. chopped onion**
**1 can cream of chicken soup**

Cook squash in small amount of salted water until tender; drain. Melt oleo in 2 quart casserole. Stir in crumbs until oleo is absorbed. Remove about half of the crumbs. Pour squash into casserole; sprinkle with chopped onion. Mix soup with sour cream and spread over vegetables. Sprinkle the remaining crumbs on top. Bake at 350° for about 20 minutes or until bubbly.

Mrs. R. T. Alliston, *Bell's Best 2*, Mississippi Chapter No. 36

# Special Squash Casserole

**2 cups mashed cooked yellow squash**
**1 can cream of mushroom soup**
**1 can cream of chicken soup**
**1 medium onion, chopped**
**1 carrot, shredded**
**1 cup sour cream**
**1 6-ounce package corn bread stuffing mix**
**½ cup melted butter**

Combine squash, mushroom soup, chicken soup, onion, carrot and sour cream in bowl; mix well. Layer half the stuffing mix, squash mixture and remaining stuffing mix in 9x13-inch casserole. Drizzle with butter. Bake at 350 degrees for 30 to 40 minutes or until brown. Yield: 10 servings.

**Approx Per Serving:** Cal 267; Prot 5 g; Carbo 21 g; Fiber 1 g; T Fat 19 g; Chol 38 mg; Sod 806 mg.

Gladys Hinson, *Carolina Cooking*, North Carolina Chapter No. 35

# Squash Croquettes

2 cups grated squash
1 cup finely chopped onion
1 egg, beaten
1 teaspoon salt
1 teaspoon pepper
1½ tablespoons flour
Oil for deep frying

Combine squash, onion, egg, salt, pepper and flour in bowl; mix well. Drop by teaspoonfuls into hot oil. Deep-fry until brown; drain. Serve hot. Yield: 32 servings.

**Approx Per Serving:** Cal 7; Prot <1 g; Carbo 1 g; Fiber <1 g; T Fat <1 g; Chol 7 mg; Sod 69 mg.
Nutritional information does not include oil for deep frying.

Carolyn Hord, *Carolina Cooking*, North Carolina Chapter No. 35

# Scalloped Tomatoes—Cheese

1 c. herb bread stuffing
½ tsp. garlic salt
¼ tsp. oregano
2 tsp. sugar
1 (13 oz.) can tomatoes
1 c. grated Cheddar cheese
1 large onion, thinly sliced
2 Tbsp. butter

Combine stuffing, garlic salt, oregano and sugar. Arrange half of tomatoes in 10x16x1½ inch pan. Top with layer of bread stuffing; sprinkle with ½ cup of the cheese and onion. Spread with remaining tomatoes; sprinkle with remaining cheese. Dot with butter. Bake in 350° preheated oven for 30 minutes. Makes 6 to 8 servings.

Ella M. Crockett, *Dining with Pioneers, Volume I*
Tennessee Chapter No. 21

## Tomato-Potato Pie

**2 medium tomatoes, cut in 1/4 inch thick slices**
**1 1/2 c. cold mashed potatoes**
**1 c. flour**
**1/4 tsp. crushed thyme**
**1/4 tsp. salt**
**1/8 tsp. pepper**
**1 1/2 c. shredded Mozzarella cheese**
**1/2 c. seasoned dry bread crumbs**
**Vegetable oil**

Combine potatoes, flour, thyme, salt and pepper. Shape mixture into a ball; place on counter and knead lightly to thoroughly combine ingredients. Press onto bottom and sides of a greased 9-inch pie pan, prick bottom and sides with fork tines. Bake at 400° until almost firm, about 15 minutes. Remove from oven; reduce heat to 350°. Combine cheese, bread crumbs and oil; sprinkle half in potato crust. Arrange half of tomato slices on top. Repeat with remaining cheese-crumb mixture and tomato slices. Sprinkle with remaining cheese. Brush tomatoes with oil lightly. Bake until tomatoes are cooked and potato crust is firm, about 20 minutes. Serves 6.

Nancy Johnson, *Dogwood Delights*, Dogwood Chapter No. 84

## Creamy Green Vegetable Casserole

**2 10-ounce packages chopped frozen broccoli**
**2 beef bouillon cubes**
**Salt and pepper to taste**
**1 10-ounce package frozen baby lima beans**
**1 beef bouillon cube**
**1 8-ounce can water chestnuts, drained, chopped**
**1 cup sour cream**
**1 10-ounce can cream of mushroom soup**
**3 cups crisp rice cereal**
**1/2 cup melted margarine**

Cook broccoli using package directions, adding 2 beef bouillon cubes, salt and pepper to cooking water; drain. Cook lima beans using package directions, adding 1 beef bouillon cube to cooking water; drain. Combine broccoli, lima beans, water chestnuts, sour cream and mushroom soup in bowl; mix well. Spoon into baking dish. Top with mixture of cereal and melted margarine. Bake at 325 to 350 degrees for 30 to 35 minutes or until bubbly and browned. Yield: 8 servings.

C. Nasworthy, *Lawfully Good Eating*, Dixie Chapter No. 23

# Frozen Vegetable Casserole

10 oz. pkg. frozen broccoli
10 oz. pkg. frozen cauliflower
1 jar onions
10 oz. pkg. frozen Brussels sprouts

Cook and drain vegetables. Mix with 1 cup medium white sauce and 1 cup shredded sharp cheese. Pour into 9x13 inch pan. Sprinkle with 1/2 cup buttered bread crumbs. Bake at 350° for 30 to 35 minutes or until browned.

Serves 8.

Bonnie Eidenberger, *Pioneers Pots and Pans—1985 Cookbook*
North Florida Chapter No. 39

# Vegetable Casserole

1 can English peas
1 4-ounce can whole button mushrooms
2 or 3 chopped pimientos
1 cup Irish potato balls
2 cups creamed sauce
Salt and pepper to taste

Cook potato balls in salted water until just tender—do not overcook. (Use small end of melon baller to cut potato balls.) Drain potatoes and set aside.

**Make a cream sauce as follows:** 4 tablespoons margarine, melted slowly, stir in 4 tablespoons flour until smooth. Add 2 cups of liquid consisting of 1 cup undiluted evaporated milk, 1 cup of liquid, using liquid from mushrooms, and enough liquid from peas to make cupful. Stir slowly into flour mixture until thickened. Mixture should not come to a boiling point. Add salt and pepper to suit taste. Remove from heat and add peas, mushrooms and chopped pimientos. Add potato balls; mix. Put in 8 1/2x8 1/2x2-inch casserole, or 10x6 1/2x2-inch casserole. Grate aged Wisconsin cheese over top, at least 1/2-inch deep. Bake in oven at 400° until cheese melts through other ingredients, approximately 25 minutes. Serve hot.

Mrs. Agnes Kelly, *Secret Recipes of Telephone Pioneers, Volume I*
South Carolina Chapter No. 61

## Vegetable Casserole

2 cans Veg-All, drained
1 c. chopped onion
1 c. chopped water chestnuts
1 c. grated Cheddar cheese
3/4 c. mayonnaise
1 roll Ritz crackers, crushed
1 stick oleo, melted

Mix first 5 ingredients. Pour into casserole. Then top with the crackers, mixed with melted oleo. Bake at 350° for 30 minutes.

Mary C. Martin, *Calling All Cooks*, Alabama Chapter No. 34

## Coconut-Topped Sweet Potato Casserole

3 cups cooked sweet potatoes
1 cup sugar
1/4 cup margarine
1/2 cup evaporated milk
2 eggs
1/2 teaspoon butter flavoring
1 cup packed brown sugar
1/3 cup flour
1/4 cup margarine
1 cup coconut
1 cup chopped pecans

Mash potatoes in mixer bowl. Add sugar, 1/4 cup margarine, evaporated milk, eggs and butter flavoring; mix well. Spoon into baking dish. Combine brown sugar, flour, 1/4 cup margarine, coconut and pecans in bowl; mix until crumbly. Sprinkle over casserole. Bake at 350 degrees for 35 minutes. Yield: 8 servings.

Shirley Carmichael, *Carolina Cooking*, North Carolina Chapter No. 35

## Sweet Potato Soufflé

2 tsp. vanilla extract
1 stick oleo
1 c. sugar
3 c. sweet potatoes, mashed
1 tsp. salt
2 eggs
1/2 c. milk

Topping:

1 c. nuts, chopped
1 stick oleo
1 c. brown sugar
1 c. flour (plain)

Mix soufflé ingredients. Pour into buttered dish.

Topping: Mix these 4 ingredients together and sprinkle over sweet potato mixture. Bake at 350° for 40 to 45 minutes.

Murlene McKnight, *Pots, Pans and Pioneers, Volume IV*
*Louisiana Chapter No. 24*

# Sunday Sweet Potatoes

3 cups mashed sweet potatoes
1 cup sugar
1/2 cup milk
1/3 cup butter or margarine, softened
2 eggs, beaten
1 teaspoon vanilla extract
1/4 teaspoon cinnamon
1/4 teaspoon nutmeg
1 cup chopped pecans
1 cup packed brown sugar
1/3 cup flour
1/3 cup butter or margarine, softened

Combine sweet potatoes, sugar, milk, 1/3 cup margarine, eggs, vanilla, cinnamon and nutmeg in large bowl; mix well. Spoon into greased baking dish. Mix pecans, brown sugar, flour and 1/3 cup margarine in small bowl. Sprinkle over sweet potato mixture. Bake at 375 degrees for 20 minutes or until browned. Yield: 4 to 6 servings.

Linda Helms, *Lawfully Good Eating*, Dixie Chapter No. 23

# Apple Yambake

2 apples, sliced
1/3 c. chopped pecans
1/2 c. brown sugar, packed
1/2 tsp. cinnamon
2 (17 oz.) cans yams, drained
1/4 c. margarine
2 c. miniature marshmallows

Toss apples and nuts with combined brown sugar and cinnamon. Alternate layers of apples and yams in 1 1/2 quart casserole. Dot with margarine. Cover. Bake at 350° for 35 to 40 minutes. Sprinkle marshmallows over yams and apples. Broil until lightly browned.
Makes 6 to 8 servings.

Marsha Golden, *Kentucky Kitchens, Volume I*, Kentucky Chapter No. 32

## A Helpful Hint

Cook vegetables with the least amount of water possible to preserve both nutrients and flavor.

# Zucchini Squares

3 c. thin sliced zucchini
1 c. Bisquick mix
1/2 c. Parmesan cheese
1/2 tsp. salt
1/2 tsp. seasoned salt
1/2 c. Wesson or Crisco oil
1 c. grated Swiss cheese
4 beaten eggs
1/2 c. chopped onion
2 tsp. parsley
Dash of pepper
Clove garlic, minced

Combine all ingredients. Bake in 13x9x2 inch greased and floured pan for 25 to 30 minutes in 350° oven.

I also sprinkle Parmesan on top.

Sonia Hunt, *Pots, Pans and Pioneers, Volume IV*
Louisiana Chapter No. 24

# Cashew Chili

1 onion, chopped
1 green bell pepper, chopped
2 stalks celery, chopped
3 tablespoons butter
2 cups cooked kidney beans, drained
2 8-ounce cans tomato sauce
2 cups cooked corn
1 18-ounce can whole tomatoes
2 to 3 teaspoons chili powder
3 drops of hot pepper sauce
1 teaspoon ground cumin
2 cloves of garlic, minced
1 teaspoon basil
1 teaspoon oregano
1 bay leaf
1/2 teaspoon pepper
1 cup raisins
1 cup raw whole cashews
Shredded Monterey Jack or Cheddar cheese

Sauté onion, green pepper and celery in melted butter in large saucepan until tender-crisp. Add kidney beans, tomato sauce, corn, tomatoes, chili powder, pepper sauce, cumin, garlic, basil, oregano, bay leaf and pepper; mix well. Bring to a boil; reduce heat. Simmer for 30 minutes, stirring occasionally. Add raisins and cashews. Simmer for 20 minutes or until raisins are plumped and cashews are tender. Remove bay leaf before serving. Serve with shredded cheese on top. Yield: 4 to 6 servings.

Georgia Sheriffs Youth Homes, *Lawfully Good Eating*
Dixie Chapter No. 23

# *Dan's 6-Alarm Chili*

2 tbsp. Puritan oil
1 onion, chopped—Spanish onion
1½ stalks celery, chopped
2 carrots, chopped
3 cloves garlic, chopped
½ green pepper, chopped
½ red pepper, chopped
4 jalapeño peppers, seeded and deveined, chopped
2 Cubanello peppers, chopped
2 long hot peppers, seeded and chopped
Lots of black pepper, freshly ground
1 (28 oz.) can tomato purée or crushed tomatoes
1 lg. can whole tomatoes or 4 tomatoes, chopped coarsely
2 tbsp. chili powder
1 tbsp. cumin seed
2 tsp. crushed oregano
½ tsp. marjoram
½ tsp. sage
2 cans red kidney beans, drained or ½ bag dried, soaked and precooked
1 lg. eggplant, diced, salted and briefly sautéed
1 tbsp. cocoa

In a large pot, heat oil over medium fire. Add onions, sauté until softens and starts to become translucent then add celery and carrots. Cook 5 minutes. Add garlic, cook 2 minutes stirring frequently. Add next 6 ingredients. Cook 5 to 7 minutes, stirring occasionally, don't burn the garlic.

Add tomato purée and tomatoes. Stir. Add water if necessary. Add spices and herbs. Stir. Add beans and eggplant. Cover; reduce heat to low. Simmer at least 1 hour. Adjust seasonings. Add cocoa. Cook another 15 minutes.

Dan Spera
*A Tablespoon of Pioneering and a Teaspoon of Horses and the Handicapped*
Florida Gold Coast Chapter No. 83

## Brenda's Breakfast Pie

1 lb. turkey sausage
1 carton (8 oz.) egg substitute, Healthy Choice or Egg Beaters
1/4 c. chopped scallions
1/4 c. chopped green pepper
1/4 c. chopped red pepper
1/2 c. light cream
1 1/2 c. Colby or Jack cheese, shredded
2 deep dish Ritz pie shells
1/4 tsp. coarse ground black pepper

Preheat oven to 375 degrees.

Cook sausage in skillet. When almost done add peppers and onions. Cook until onions are soft and sausage is cooked through. Remove from heat and drain liquid. Mix in cheese with sausage mixture. Crumble sausage and put in pie shell.

In medium bowl lightly beat egg substitute. Add cream and beat until frothy. Pour in pie shell over sausage mixture. Bake at 375 degrees for 45 minutes (until set). Cool 10 minutes.

Brenda Lee James
*A Tablespoon of Pioneering and a Teaspoon of Horses and the Handicapped*
Florida Gold Coast Chapter No. 83

## The Bridle Path Breakfast Casserole

4 cups thinly sliced potatoes
1 pound spicy sausage, cooked, crumbled, drained
1 cup shredded Swiss cheese
2 cups cubed ham
6 eggs
1/4 teaspoon dry mustard
Salt and pepper to taste
1 cup milk
1 cup shredded Swiss cheese

Layer potatoes in buttered baking dish. Top with sausage, 1 cup cheese, and ham. Beat eggs with mustard, salt, pepper and milk in bowl. Pour over top layer. Sprinkle with remaining cheese. Bake at 350 degrees for 45 minutes. Serve with toast or banana bread. Yield: 6 to 8 servings.

Karen J. Taylor, *Lawfully Good Eating*, Dixie Chapter No. 23

### A Helpful Hint

Freeze unused egg whites in ice cube trays. Store in plastic bags in the freezer for up to one year.

## *Cheese-Egg Breakfast Casserole*

10 slices white bread, remove crust and cut into cubes
1/4 lb. margarine, melted
3/4 lb. sharp cheese, grated
4 eggs
1 t. salt
1 t. dry mustard
1/2 t. pepper
2 1/4 c. milk
1 small onion, grated
1 small jar chopped pimento or 1 small green pepper, sliced

Place cubes of bread in a buttered 9x13-inch pan or casserole. Pour melted butter over bread. Spread grated cheese over bread and margarine mixture. Beat eggs, add remaining ingredients and pour over all. Refrigerate overnight. Bake at 350° about 45 min. Diced ham may be added. Place ham on bread cubes before adding grated cheese.

"Pete" McQuaig, *Taste of Dixie*, Dixie Chapter No. 23

## *Cheese-Ham Casserole*

12 slices white bread
1 10 oz. package frozen broccoli (or spinach or favorite vegetable)
1/4 cup chopped onion
2 cups cooked ham cubes
2 1/2 cups milk
1 10 oz. package sharp cheddar cheese
4 eggs
1/2 tsp. salt
1/2 tsp. dry mustard
1/8 tsp. pepper
1 tsp. Maggi seasoning (optional)

Cut circles out of bread. Fit leftover scraps on bottom of 2 qt. baking dish. Arrange vegetable over bread, sprinkle with onion and ham cubes. Place bread rounds on top, overlapping slightly. In saucepan, combine 2 cups of milk and cheese. Heat, stirring constantly until mixture is smooth. Beat eggs slightly. Add eggs and other ingredients to cheese mixture. Pour over bread rounds. Refrigerate, covered, 6 hours. Preheat oven to 325°, bake, uncovered, 55–60 minutes. May be prepared in advance and frozen. When ready to use, thaw partially and proceed with baking. Serves 6.

This recipe is from a book called "Colonial Kitchen of Amherst, N.H." and is excellent. Can be served as a side dish or main course with salad. Wonderful for a party or covered dish supper. I have made it with asparagus and it is good. Favorite dish of the men in the family.

Helen Rober, *Secret Recipes of Telephone Pioneers, Volume II*
South Carolina Chapter No. 61

# *Egg and Sausage Casserole*

**1½ lb. sausage**
**9 eggs, slightly beaten**
**3 cups milk**
**1½ tsp. dry mustard**
**1 tsp. salt**
**3 slices white bread, cut in cubes**
**1½ cups grated cheese**

Brown and crumble sausage. Drain Well. Mix eggs, milk, mustard and salt. Stir in bread, sausage and cheese. Pour in greased 13x10 pan. Refrigerate overnight. Bake 1 hour at 350°, uncovered.

Jean Moore, *Secret Recipes of Telephone Pioneers, Volume II*
South Carolina Chapter No. 61

# *Real Men Don't Eat Quiche*

**4 eggs**
**1 can cream of celery soup**
**½ cup light cream**
**1 cup shredded Cheddar cheese**
**6 slices crisp-fried bacon, crumbled**
**½ cup chopped cooked spinach**
**1 unbaked 9-inch pie shell**
**Nutmeg to taste**

Beat eggs in mixer bowl until foamy. Add soup and cream gradually, mixing well. Layer cheese, bacon and spinach in pie shell. Pour soup mixture over top; sprinkle with nutmeg. Bake at 350 degrees for 50 minutes or until center is set. Let stand for 10 minutes before serving. Yield: 6 servings.

Frank Fendley, *Kentucky Kitchens, Volume II*, Kentucky Chapter No. 32

## *A Helpful Hint*

When making quiche, seal the crust and prevent it from soaking up the custard mixture and becoming soggy by brushing the bottom with egg whites, eggs or Dijon mustard.

## *Sausage Quiche (K)*

**Country:** America. **City:** Perry, Florida. **Approximate year created:** 1930's. **Relative obtained from:** Mother. **Brief history:** Used as part of Sunday brunch on late night (lite) meal.

**6 eggs**
**2 c. milk**
**1 c. grated Cheddar cheese**
**2 tsp. ground mustard**
**1 small onion, chopped fine**
**1 small green pepper, chopped**
**1 (2 to 3 oz.) small jar mushrooms, chopped small**
**6 slices bread, diced**
**1 lb. ground sausage**

Chop sausage into small pieces and brown with green pepper and onion. Drain on paper towel and cool. In separate bowl, beat eggs and milk together. Add all other ingredients. Pour in a 9x13 inch pan and refrigerate overnight. Bake at 350° for 45 minutes. Serve hot with Bloody Mary's or whatever you want.

**Preparation time:** 30 minutes.
**Cooking time:** 45 minutes.
**No. of servings:** 6.

Ethel Standish, *A Taste of Pioneering*
Florida Gold Coast Chapter No. 83

## *Spinach Quiche*

**1 small onion, chopped**
**1/2 tsp. butter for sautéing**
**1 (10 oz.) pkg. frozen spinach, chopped**
**5 eggs**
**3/4 lb. cheese, grated**
**salt and pepper to taste**

Sauté chopped onion in butter. Thaw spinach and squeeze excess water out. Beat eggs and stir in grated cheese. Salt and pepper to taste. Bake in a 10 inch greased pie plate at 350° for 45 minutes. Do not cut until 5 minutes after removing.

June Evans, *Pioneers Pots and Pans—1985 Cookbook*
North Florida Chapter No. 39

## Apple Cheese Casserole

*Mix with hands:*

**1 pkg. Velveeta cheese**

**1 stick of butter (room temp., do not substitute.)**

*Then add:*

**1 c. sugar and 3/4 c. all purpose flour**

Mix well and sit aside. Drain 1 can unsweetened apples (sliced) and spread in a greased glass baking dish. Spread cheese mixture on the top to cover. Start in cold oven and bake at 350° for approx. 15 min. or until browned. May be served as a side dish or as a dessert. For a dessert it may be served chilled or for a special treat, serve warm with ice cream.

Sybil Cuthbertson, *Taste of Dixie*, Dixie Chapter No. 23

## Pineapple Casserole

**1 20-ounce can pineapple chunks**
**1/2 cup sugar**
**3 tablespoons flour**
**1 cup shredded Cheddar cheese**
**1/4 cup melted margarine**
**1/2 cup crushed butter crackers**

Drain pineapple, reserving 3 tablespoons juice. Combine sugar and flour in bowl; mix well. Stir in reserved pineapple juice, pineapple chunks and cheese; toss to mix well. Spoon into greased 1-quart casserole. Combine melted margarine and cracker crumbs in bowl; mix well. Sprinkle over pineapple mixture. Bake at 350 degrees for 20 to 30 minutes or until light brown. Yield: 6 servings.

Lois Byers, *Lawfully Good Eating*, Dixie Chapter No. 23

## Corn Bread Dressing

- 2 cake pans corn bread (use buttermilk in the mix)
- 10 canned buttermilk biscuits, baked as usual
- 1 heart of celery with leaves
- 6 eggs, beaten
- 3 or more c. turkey broth
- 1 big onion, chopped fine
- 2 pieces wheat toast, crumbled
- 1/2 tsp. poultry seasoning or to taste
- 1/2 tsp. salt
- 1/2 tsp. pepper
- 1/2 tsp. sage or to taste

Mix all ingredients together; add about 3 cups turkey broth or more if needed to make dressing thin and moist. Put in ungreased 13x9 inch pan and bake at 325° for approximately 30 minutes or until lightly browned.

Deborah Rigdon, *Kentucky Kitchens, Volume I*, Kentucky Chapter No. 32

## Elaine's Corn Bread Dressing

- 1 cornbread (see recipe below)
- 1 package herb dressing mix
- 2 cups chopped onion
- 2 cups chopped celery
- 1 stick oleo
- 2 eggs
- salt and pepper to taste
- chicken broth

Cornbread

- 2 cups self-rising meal
- 1 cup self-rising flour
- 1 egg
- 1 stick oleo melted in pan in which bread will be cooked
- milk

Mix together and bake in large pan at 450°. Sauté onion and celery in oleo. Crumble cornbread and add rest of ingredients. Add enough broth to get desired consistency. Put in baking dish and bake in 425° until browned. This makes a large amount. I usually use several pans and freeze part for another time. Recipe serves 10–12.

Janie Peach, *Secret Recipes of Telephone Pioneers, Volume II*
South Carolina Chapter No. 61

# Squash Dressing

1 pone corn bread made with 2 eggs (set aside to cool)
1 large onion, chopped
1 bell pepper, chopped
3 eggs
1 can cream of chicken soup
1 can cream of celery soup
1 can water
1 stick margarine
3 ribs celery, chopped
2 pieces toasted bread
Salt
Pepper
Garlic powder (amount you would desire)
Sage or poultry seasoning
2 c. cooked yellow squash drained and mashed

Sauté onions, peppers, and celery in stick of butter. Add both cans soup and water; stir well and simmer. In large mixing bowl, crumble corn bread and toast; add squash, seasoning, and 3 eggs (beaten). Mix well. Add soup and onion mixture to this; mix. Pour into baking dish. Bake at about 300° for 30 minutes.

Linda Clark, *Bell's Best 3*, Mississippi Chapter No. 36

# Gnocchi

(Italian dumplings)

4 lb. potatoes
5 c. flour
salt and pepper

Boil and rice potatoes. Gradually add 5 cups of flour. Knead until smooth and dough is manageable. Add a little more flour if necessary.

Roll dough into long rope strips about 3/4 of an inch thick. Cut into 3/4 inch pieces, dip in flour.

Make dented design in dumplings with side of fork tine.

Boil in 8 quarts of rapidly boiling, salted water 10 minutes. Drain. Place on warmed platter or individual plates.

Serve with Italian meat sauce or tomato sauce with grated Parmesan cheese.

Serve 6 to 8.

Loretta Williams, *Pioneers Pots and Pans—1985 Cookbook*
North Florida Chapter No. 39

# *Cheese Grits*

6–8 servings grits, cooked

**1 stick (1/2 c.) butter or margarine**
**1 (6 oz.) roll Kraft garlic cheese spread**
**2 eggs**
**Milk (approx. 1 c.)**

Cook grits per directions on package. Add butter or margarine and garlic cheese; let melt. Blend thoroughly. Break eggs into measuring cup; beat slightly. Add milk to make 1 cup. Add milk-egg mixture to grits mixture. Stir until smooth and well mixed. Pour into 9x13 inch casserole dish. Bake at 350° for 35–40 minutes or until golden brown crust forms.

Mrs. Kendall Clark, *Dining with Pioneers, Volume I*
Tennessee Chapter No. 21

# *Deluxe Cheese Grits Soufflé*

**Butter, softened**
**Parmesan cheese**
**1 cup grits**
**4 cups boiling salted water**
**3 tablespoons butter**
**3 tablespoons flour**
**1 cup milk**
**1 cup cream**
**1 cup shredded Cheddar cheese**
**1/2 cup Parmesan cheese**
**6 egg yolks**
**6 egg whites**
**Pinch of cream of tartar**

Butter 3-quart soufflé dish. Fit with buttered foil collar. Dust dish and collar with Parmesan cheese. Stir grits into boiling salted water in saucepan. Bring to a boil; reduce heat. Cook over medium-high heat until grits are of the consistency of mashed potatoes. Melt 3 tablespoons butter in large saucepan. Stir in flour. Cook over medium-high heat for 2 minutes, whisking constantly. Heat milk and cream in saucepan. Stir into flour gradually. Cook until thickened, whisking constantly. Stir in grits, Cheddar cheese and 1/2 cup Parmesan cheese; remove from heat. Beat egg yolks in bowl until lemon-colored. Add to grits; mix well. Beat eggs at high speed in mixer bowl until foamy. Add cream of tartar. Beat until medium-soft peaks form. Fold gently into grits; do not overmix. Spoon into prepared dish. Place in 400-degree oven; reduce temperature to 375 degrees. Bake for 30 minutes or until brown on top. Serve immediately. May bake for 20 minutes in two 1 1/2-quart soufflé dishes or shallow baking dish. Yield: 10 servings.

Shirley Smith, *Kentucky Kitchens, Volume II*, Kentucky Chapter No. 32

# Garlic Grits

**1 c. grits, cooked and salted**
**1 roll garlic cheese**
**1 stick oleo**
**1 egg, beaten, add milk to make 1 c. liquid**

Add cheese and butter to cooked grits. Stir until cheese melts. Add egg mixture; mix well. Bake 1 hour at 325°, until brown.

Hershal Grady, *Bell's Best*, Mississippi Chapter No. 36

# Nassau Grits

(Good with fish)

**2 medium bell peppers, chopped**
**2 medium onions, chopped**
**4 slices bacon (or bacon drippings)**
**1 can tomato paste (small)**
**1 can tomatoes**
**Grits**

Sauté onion and pepper with bacon. (I cut bacon into small pieces.) Add tomato paste, 2 cans water and tomatoes. Cook on medium heat about 15 minutes. Stir in grits and cook until done. Amount of grits depends upon consistency desired. Salt and pepper to taste.

I usually add onion salt and garlic powder. Use judgement.

Nancy Hughes, *Pioneers Pots and Pans—1985 Cookbook*
North Florida Chapter No. 39

# Fettucini Alfredo

**1 pkg. fettucini**
**1/2 c. grated Parmesan cheese**
**1 c. sour cream**
**1/4 lb. butter**
**1 egg yolk**

Cook noodles. While noodles are cooking, beat egg yolk lightly with fork and add to cream. Melt butter. Place drained hot noodles in warm serving bowl or platter. Pour over the noodles egg and cream mixture, melted butter and about half of the grated cheese. Toss noodles with fork and spoon until well blended, adding a balance of cheese a little at a time. Top with additional grated cheese and serve.

Kathy Kearney
*A Tablespoon of Pioneering and a Teaspoon of Horses and the Handicapped*
Florida Gold Coast Chapter No. 83

# Fettucini Alfredo

**8 ounces uncooked linguine**
**6 tablespoons butter**
**1½ cups whipping cream**
**1 cup Parmesan cheese**
**Salt, pepper and nutmeg to taste**

Cook linguine using package directions until just tender; drain. Brown butter in large skillet over high heat, stirring frequently. Add ½ cup whipping cream. Boil rapidly until slightly thickened, stirring constantly. Reduce heat to medium. Add linguine; mix gently. Add ½ cup cream and ½ cup Parmesan cheese; toss gently. Add remaining cream and Parmesan cheese; mix gently. Season with salt, pepper and nutmeg. Serve immediately. Yield: 4 servings.

**Approx Per Serving:** Cal 762; Prot 18 g; Carbo 46 g; Fiber 2 g; T Fat 57 g; Chol 185 mg; Sod 557 mg.

Diane Grace, *Carolina Cooking*, North Carolina Chapter No. 35

# Macaroni and Cheese Surprise

**1 8-ounce package elbow macaroni**
**1 10-ounce can cream of mushroom soup**
**¼ cup chopped green bell pepper**
**¼ cup chopped onion**
**¼ cup chopped pimento**
**1 cup mayonnaise**
**8 ounces sharp Cheddar cheese, shredded**

Cook macaroni using package directions; drain. Heat soup in saucepan over medium heat. Add green pepper, onion and pimento. Cook for 5 to 10 minutes over low heat, stirring constantly. Stir in mayonnaise gradually. Layer macaroni, soup mixture and cheese ½ at a time in 2-quart casserole. Bake at 350 degrees for 30 minutes. Yield: 4 servings.

Bob Carter, *Lawfully Good Eating*, Dixie Chapter No. 23

## A Helpful Hint

Shaped pasta usually costs more than plain, but it still is an economical way to liven up a meal.

# My Mom's Red Rice

**1/8 cup Wesson oil**
**1 medium sized onion, chopped**
**a pinch of rosemary**
**a pinch of thyme**
**1/8 tsp. oregano**
**3 shots worcestershire sauce**
**ham (diced) or smoked sausage**
**1 can whole tomatoes (or Hunts special sauce)**

Put everything into a pan, except tomatoes, fry until onions are clear and ham is brown. Add tomatoes, salt and pepper. Add rest of ingredients. Add one cup of rice. Bring to a boil, stir until rice absorbs majority of juice. Transfer to rice steamer. Steam, checking every 15 minutes to fluff. Leave cover off last 15 minutes to dry out.

Betsy DeVault, *Secret Recipes of Telephone Pioneers, Volume III*
South Carolina Chapter No. 61

# Portuguese Rice

**2 med. onions**
**1 jar pepper salad (Progresso in oil), 10 oz.**
**16 oz. pepperoni**
**2 (15 oz.) cans tomato sauce**
**1 c. uncooked white rice**

Dice onions and cut pepperoni into bite size chunks. Sauté onions and pepperoni together with the pepper salad until onions are golden. Drain off oil.

Pour in tomato sauce and bring to a boil. Pour in rice and simmer for 1 hour covered, stirring occasionally. Check for doneness. When rice is tender, fluff and enjoy.

Jacqueline Gonzalez and Hugo Cardoso
*A Tablespoon of Pioneering and a Teaspoon of Horses and the Handicapped*
Florida Gold Coast Chapter No. 83

## A Helpful Hint

Rice bran has a cholesterol-reducing action similar to that of oatbran. The result is attributed to an oil that occurs naturally in the bran and inhibits the body's absorption of cholesterol. It may also decrease the liver's production of cholesterol.

## *Tempura*

**3 eggs**
**1 2/3 c. flour**
**1 tsp. salt**
**2 1/2 tsp. soy sauce**
**2 Tbsp. sugar**
**1 1/4 c. water**

Make batter just before using. Beat eggs with mixer; add soy sauce and water. Gradually add flour, sugar and salt, beating until smooth. Dip meat or vegetables into batter to coat lightly. Deep-fry a few pieces at a time.

Ruth Ackerman, *Kentucky Kitchens, Volume I*, Kentucky Chapter No. 32

## *Apple Butter*

**1 bushel apples, peeled, cored and quartered**
**8 lb. sugar**
**4 Tbsp. cinnamon**
**1/4 tsp. allspice**
**1 tsp. salt**
**1/2 c. red hots**

Cook apples in saucepan until tender, then add to roaster. Mix with sauce the sugar, cinnamon, allspice, salt and red hots (will give color and also add to the flavor). Bake at 325° until thick.

Maxine Welch, *Kentucky Kitchens, Volume I*, Kentucky Chapter No. 32

## *Paula's Apple Butter*

**4 cups cooked apple purée**
**3 cups sugar**
**2 tablespoons vinegar**
**1 teaspoon cinnamon**
**2 tablespoons lemon juice**
**1/4 teaspoon cloves**

Combine apple purée, sugar, vinegar, cinnamon, lemon juice and cloves in saucepan. Cook until smooth and thick, stirring frequently. Ladle into hot sterilized jars, leaving 1/2-inch headspace; seal with 2-piece lids. Process in boiling water bath for 10 minutes. Yield: 60 servings.

**Approx Per Serving:** Cal 54; Prot <1 g; Carbo 14 g; Fiber 1 g; T Fat <1 g; Chol 0 mg; Sod 4 mg.

Paula Mills, *Carolina Cooking*, North Carolina Chapter No. 35

## Orange Butter

5 pounds of sugar
1 can of crushed pineapple (about 2 cups)
1/4 pound of butter (1 stick)
8 nice oranges

Grind oranges in food grinder (include peeling). Mix all ingredients. Cook until thick, about 2 minutes. Seal in jars.

Mrs. Fern S. Hall, *Secret Recipes of Telephone Pioneers, Volume I*
South Carolina Chapter No. 61

## Pepper Jelly

3/4 c. ground green peppers
1/4 c. ground hot pepper
6 c. sugar
1 1/2 c. vinegar
2 (3 oz.) pkg. liquid fruit pectin

Combine pepper, sugar and vinegar in a large saucepan. Place over high heat and stir until mixture comes to a hard boil. Boil hard 1 minute, stirring constantly. Remove from heat; stir in pectin. Let set 5 minutes. Skim off foam with a metal spoon and pour quickly into hot sterilized jelly glasses, leaving 1/2 inch headspace. Seal at once with 1/8 inch layer of hot paraffin or metal lids.

Yield: 6 cups.

Kathy Thornton, *Pioneers Pots and Pans—1985 Cookbook*
North Florida Chapter No. 39

## Frozen Strawberry Preserves

2 cups mashed strawberries
4 cups sugar
1 box Sure-Jel
3/4 cup water

Mix strawberries and sugar in bowl. Boil Sure-Jel and water for 1 minute in saucepan. Pour over strawberries. Stir for 3 minutes. Pour into sterilized jars, leaving 1/2-inch headspace; add lids. Let stand at room temperature for 24 hours. Freeze until firm. May substitute peaches, blueberries or other fruit for strawberries. Yield: 16 servings.

**Approx Per Serving:** Cal 201 ; Prot <1 g; Carbo 52 g; Fiber 1 g; T Fat <1 g; Chol 0 mg; Sod 2 mg.
Nutritional information does not include Sure-Jel.

Karen Stallings, *Carolina Cooking*, North Carolina Chapter No. 35

# *Bread and Butter Pickles*

8 c. sliced cucumbers
2 c. sliced onions
2 c. vinegar (white)
2 c. sugar
1½ tsp. salt
2 tsp. mustard seed
1 tsp. celery seed
½ tsp. turmeric powder

Put all in an enamel or stainless steel container. Cook 20 minutes from time put on stove. Do not boil hard. Jar and seal.

Makes 4 pints.

Blanch Rawls, *Pioneers Pots and Pans—1985 Cookbook*
North Florida Chapter No. 39

# *Never Fail Cucumber Pickles (11 Days)*

Wash cucumbers; fill a 3 gallon churn. Add 6 cups salt (not iodized). Fill or cover with tap water. Let stand 7 days. Drain off brine and cover with cold water (add some ice). Let stand 1 day (24 hours). Drain off cold water and cover with alum water (2 tablespoons alum to 1 gallon water). Let stand 2 days (48 hours). Drain off alum water and cover with vinegar that has been slightly boiled with your favorite spices. (I use 1 box of mixed pickling spices, 3 sticks cinnamon and 2 tablespoons mustard seed tied in a bag.) Let stand 1 day (24 hours). Drain off vinegar and wash churn well. Slice cucumbers thin. Place a layer of cucumbers and a layer of sugar, ending with sugar. Let stand until syrup rises over cucumbers. Place in jars; cover with syrup and seal with jar tops that have been boiled.

Becky Richardson, *Bell's Best 2*, Mississippi Chapter No. 36

# *Refrigerator Pickles*

7 c. sliced cucumbers
1 c. sliced onions
1 c. sliced sweet pepper
2 c. sugar
1 c. white vinegar
1 Tbsp. salt
1 Tbsp. celery seed

Combine all ingredients. Put in covered container. Refrigerate 1 week. Then eat and enjoy.

Polly Kirby, *Dining with Pioneers, Volume II*, Tennessee Chapter No. 21

# Watermelon Pickles

**Preparation time:** 40 minutes.
**Cooking time:** 1½ to 2 hours.
**Standing time:** 1 hour.

Perhaps the most novel of preserves is watermelon pickles. Made from the discarded portion of the melon, watermelon pickles are sweet and pungent, crisp and mouth-watering, and delicious served with a variety of dishes.

*For 6 pints pickles, you will need:*

**2 lb. watermelon rind**
**1 qt. cold water**
**½ Tbsp. slake lime**
**2 c. cider vinegar**
**2 c. water**
**1¾ lb. sugar**
**1 Tbsp. whole allspice**
**1 Tbsp. whole cloves**
**3 (3 inch) pieces stick cinnamon**
**½ lemon, thinly sliced (optional)**
**Green food coloring (optional)**

1. Use firm, not overripe, watermelon with thick rind. Trim off green skin and all pink pulp. Cut into 1 inch cubes.

2. Combine 1 quart cold water and slake lime. Pour over rind in enamel pan. Let stand for 1 hour. Drain. Cover with fresh water.

3. In enamel pan, place rind and fresh water to cover. Bring to a boil. Reduce heat. Simmer for 30 to 40 minutes or until rind is tender when pierced with a fork. Drain.

4. Make a syrup of the vinegar, the 2 cups water and sugar by bringing to a boil. Cook until sugar is dissolved.

5. Add spices (tied in a cheesecloth bag for easy removal) and the rind. Simmer, uncovered, over low heat for 1 to 1½ hours or until rind looks clear. Remove spices. Add lemon slices and food coloring if used.

6. Pack pickles into hot sterile jars. Fill with hot syrup, leaving ½ inch head space. Seal and store in a cool place. *Money-saving!*

**Tips:** Drained watermelon pickles can be an interesting addition to fruit cakes. Slaked lime can be purchased from a hardware store.

*Dogwood Delights Volume II*, Dogwood Chapter No. 84

# *Uncooked Cucumber Pickles*

**1 gallon apple cider vinegar**
**1 pint salt**
**1 pint sugar**
**1 1/2 ounce box mustard**
**Cucumber strips to fill 6 quart jars**

Combine the apple cider vinegar, salt, sugar and dry mustard. Blend thoroughly. DO NOT heat. Wash cucumbers and split in long strips—finger size. DO NOT peel. Soak cucumbers in ice water overnight in refrigerator. Drain on towel. Place in 6 quart jars, packing tightly. Pour vinegar mixture to fill jars and seal—and keep for two weeks or months before using.

Mrs. Audrey Hunt, *Secret Recipes of Telephone Pioneers, Volume I*
South Carolina Chapter No. 61

# *Pickled Okra*

**garlic (1 clove for each jar)**
**hot peppers (1 for each jar)**
**okra**
**dill seeds (1 tsp. for each jar)**
**1 quart white vinegar**
**1 c. water**
**1/2 c. salt**

Place garlic and hot pepper in hot, sterilized pint jars. Pack firmly with clean, young okra pods from which only part of the stem has been removed. Add dill seeds.

Bring vinegar, water and salt to a boil; simmer about 5 minutes. Pour boiling hot vinegar mixture over okra. Seal jars immediately. This amount of pickling solution will fill 5 to 7 pint jars.

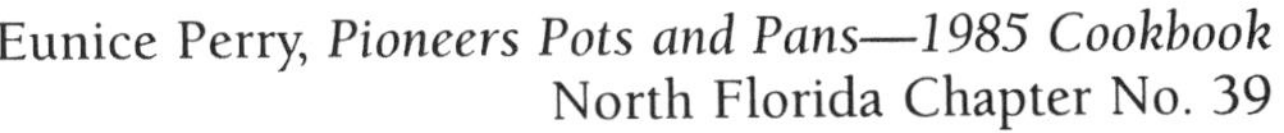

Eunice Perry, *Pioneers Pots and Pans—1985 Cookbook*
North Florida Chapter No. 39

# Cucumber Relish

3 cups sugar
2 cups vinegar
2 teaspoons celery seed
1 teaspoon cinnamon
1 teaspoon turmeric
8 cups chopped cucumbers
3 green bell peppers, chopped
4 medium onions, chopped

Combine sugar, vinegar, celery seed, cinnamon and turmeric in saucepan, stirring to dissolve sugar. Add cucumbers, peppers and onions. Bring to a boil. Cook for 20 minutes. Spoon into hot sterilized jars, leaving 1/2-inch headspace; seal with 2-piece lids. May substitute 1 red bell pepper for 1 green bell pepper. Yield: 8 to 10 pints.

Betty Schweinhart, *Kentucky Kitchens, Volume II*
Kentucky Chapter No. 32

# Green Tomato Relish

24 medium green tomatoes
12 medium onions
1 cabbage
6 bell peppers
12 hot red peppers
1 cucumber, peeled
1/2 c. salt
6 c. sugar
2 Tbsp. mustard seed
2 Tbsp. turmeric

Chop vegetables; add salt and let stand overnight. Wash and drain in colander. Heat sugar, mustard seed and turmeric to a boil; pour over mixture and simmer 10 minutes. Put in jar and seal.

Jean Wharton, *Calling All Cooks*, Alabama Chapter No. 34

# Pear Relish

1 gallon cored pears
3 medium onions
3 sweet red peppers
2 cups sugar
1 1/2 teaspoons salt
1 1/2 teaspoons allspice
1 1/2 teaspoons turmeric
2 1/2 cups vinegar

Run pears, onions and peppers through food chopper (not too fine). Add other ingredients. Cook for 3 minutes after it begins to boil. Seal in jars immediately. This is delicious with vegetables and meats. Makes approximately 8 pints.

Miss Ruth Evans, *Secret Recipes of Telephone Pioneers, Volume I*
South Carolina Chapter No. 61

# *Squash Relish*

**8 large squash, chopped**
**5 medium onions, chopped**
**2 cups chopped red bell peppers**
**2 cups chopped green bell peppers**
**2 tablespoons salt**
**2 cups sugar**
**2 teaspoons celery seed**
**2 teaspoons mustard seed**
**1/2 teaspoon turmeric**
**2 cups cider vinegar**

Combine squash, onions, red peppers and green peppers in large bowl. Add salt; mix well. Let stand for 1 hour. Drain and rinse. Combine sugar, celery seed, mustard seed, turmeric and vinegar in large saucepan. Bring to a boil. Add vegetable mixture; mix well. Bring to a boil. Cook for 1 minute, stirring frequently. Ladle into hot sterilized jars, leaving 1/2-inch headspace; seal with 2-piece lids. Process in boiling water bath for 10 minutes. Yield: 60 servings.

**Approx Per Serving:** Cal 35; Prot <1 g; Carbo 9 g; Fiber 1 g; T Fat <1 g; Chol 0 mg; Sod 214 mg.

Shirley Carmichael, *Carolina Cooking*, North Carolina Chapter No. 35

# *Barbecue Sauce*

**1 stick butter**
**Juice of 1 lemon**
**2/3 to 1 c. vinegar**
**2 Tbsp. Worcestershire sauce**
**1 chopped onion, optional**
**2–3 dashes Tabasco sauce**

Combine all ingredients. Bring to a boil. Good over chicken or pork.

Ruth Mims, *Pioneers Pots and Pans—1985 Cookbook*
North Florida Chapter No. 39

# *Raisin Sauce*

**1/2 c. brown sugar**
**1 tsp. dry mustard**
**1 Tbsp. flour**
**2 Tbsp. sugar**
**2 Tbsp. lemon juice**
**1/4 tsp. grated lemon peel**
**1 1/2 c. water**
**1/3–2/3 c. seedless raisins**

Mix first 3 ingredients, slowly add 2 tablespoons sugar. Add rest of ingredients. Cook over low heat until thick; stir constantly.

**Note:** Good over ham.

Renee Wallace, *Kentucky Kitchens, Volume I*, Kentucky Chapter No. 32

# Rotisserie's Kum-Back Sauce

1 c. mayonnaise
1/4 c. chili sauce
1/4 c. catsup
1 tsp. French's mustard
1/2 c. Wesson oil
1 tsp. Lea & Perrins sauce
1 tsp. paprika
1 tsp. black pepper
1 medium onion, grated fine
3 cloves garlic, grated fine
Juice of 1 lemon
Dash of Tabasco sauce
Salt to taste

Do not substitute any of the ingredients.

Pat Denham, *Bell's Best*, Mississippi Chapter No. 36

# "Pioneer Shrimp Boil" Shrimp Sauce

Ten Gallons:

6 gal. mayonnaise
12 (6 oz.) bottles mustard
2 boxes salt
2 large bottles Lea & Perrins sauce
7 stalks celery
8 bell peppers
16 onions
6 boxes garlic
10 pt. lemon juice
2 bottles Tabasco sauce
2 large boxes black pepper
2 boxes paprika
6 jars horseradish
10 (14 oz.) bottles catsup
1 1/2 gal. Wesson oil
20 bottles chili sauce

Five Gallons:

3 gal. mayonnaise
6 (6 oz.) bottles mustard
1 box salt
1 large bottle Lea & Perrins sauce
4 stalks celery
4 bell peppers
8 onions
3 boxes garlic
5 pt. lemon juice
1 bottle Tabasco sauce
1 large box black pepper
1 box paprika
3 jars horseradish
9 (14 oz.) bottles catsup
3 qt. Wesson oil
10 bottles chili sauce

Two and One-Half Gallons:

1 1/4 gal. mayonnaise
3 (6 oz.) bottles mustard
1/2 box salt
1/2 large bottle Lea & Perrins sauce
2 stalks celery
2 bell peppers
4 onions
1 1/2 boxes garlic
2 1/2 pt. lemon juice
1/2 bottle Tabasco sauce
1/2 large box black pepper
1/2 box paprika
1 1/2 jars horseradish
4 1/2 (14 oz.) bottles catsup
3 pt. Wesson oil
5 bottles chili sauce

One Gallon:

1/2 gal. mayonnaise
1 1/2 (6 oz.) bottles mustard
1/4 box salt
1/4 large bottle Lea & Perrins sauce
1 stalk celery
1 bell pepper
2 onions
1 box garlic
1 1/4 pt. lemon juice
1/4 bottle Tabasco sauce
1/4 large box black pepper
1/4 box paprika
1 jar horseradish
2 1/4 (14 oz.) bottles catsup
1 1/2 pt. Wesson oil
3 bottles chili sauce

One-Half Gallon:

1/4 gal. mayonnaise
3/4 (6 oz.) bottle mustard
1/8 box salt
1/8 large bottle Lea & Perrins sauce
1/2 stalk celery
1/2 bell pepper
1 onion
1/2 box garlic
3/4 pt. lemon juice
1/8 bottle Tabasco sauce
1/8 large box black pepper
1/8 box paprika
1/2 jar horseradish
1 1/8 (14 oz.) bottles catsup
3/4 pt. Wesson oil
1 1/2 bottles chili sauce

Wash and cut in small pieces the celery, bell pepper, onions and garlic; pour in all other ingredients and mix well. Put all mixture through blender. This is the best shrimp sauce in the world and believe it or not, we have to increase the 10 gallon amount for our shrimp boil every year.

This is submitted in loving memory of Pat Jones, who, ever since I can remember, has cooked our shrimp. How we are going to miss him this year.

Lou Sparks, *Bell's Best*, Mississippi Chapter No. 36

# *Spicy Dunk Sauce for Seafood*

1/2 c. chili sauce
1/4 c. well-drained bottled horseradish
1 tsp. Worcestershire
1 tsp. minced onion
1/4 tsp. garlic salt
1/2 tsp. salt
1/8 tsp. pepper
1 Tbsp. vinegar
2 dashes Tabasco
1/4 tsp. bottled meat sauce
1 tsp. celery seeds
2 Tbsp. granulated sugar
1 tsp. celery salt

Combine all ingredients. Keep in covered jar in refrigerator 2 or 3 days before using to thoroughly blend flavors.

Makes about 3/4 cup.

Barbara Patty, *Pioneers Pots and Pans—1985 Cookbook*
North Florida Chapter No. 39

# *Taco Hot Sauce*

6 jalapeño peppers (or more if needed for hotness)
3 bell peppers
6 banana peppers
12 oz. can tomato paste
1 Tbsp. ginger
1/2 c. sugar
1/2 c. vinegar
1 onion
1 Tbsp. salt
1 tsp. pepper
as many fresh tomatoes as you think you need

Peel tomatoes, chop very fine and simmer 10 minutes. Remove seed from peppers. Combine all ingredients in food processor and chop very fine. Then add all ingredients to tomatoes and simmer for 1 hour. Put in jars under 5 pounds pressure for 10 minutes.

(This is very good, can be served with crackers.)

Helen L. Rodgers, *Pioneers Pots and Pans—1985 Cookbook*
North Florida Chapter No. 39

## *A Helpful Hint*

Place pasta in a strainer in the saucepan to cook. It will drain automatically when you lift it from the saucepan.

## Richard's Tartar Sauce

1 cup mayonnaise-type salad dressing
1 tablespoon minced dill pickle
2 tablespoons grated onion
1 teaspoon minced parsley
1 teaspoon chopped pimento

Combine salad dressing, pickle, onion, parsley and pimento in bowl; mix well. Chill until serving time. Serve with seafood.
Yield: 15 servings.

**Approx Per Serving:** Cal 62; Prot <1 g; Carbo 4 g; Fiber <1 g; T Fat 5 g; 74% Calories from Fat; Chol 4 mg; Sod 122 mg.

Jane Green, *Calling All Cooks three*, Alabama Chapter No. 34

## Zesty Sauce

$1/4$ c. cider vinegar
$1/2$ tsp. dry mustard
$1/2$ c. chili sauce
$1/2$ c. brown sugar
$1/4$ c. catsup
1 tsp. salt
1 tsp. Accent
$1/4$ tsp. black pepper
2 Tbsp. chopped onions
4 drops hot sauce
3 drops bitter (name-brand Angosture)

Mix all ingredients well in saucepan or boiler. Bring to boil under medium heat, simmer 10 minutes. Pour over meat balls or any other desired cooked meat. (If desire, let meat simmer in sauce 10 minutes to penetrate.)

Mary Ellen Gulley, *Pioneers Pots and Pans—1985 Cookbook*
North Florida Chapter No. 39

## Microwave Maple Syrup

1 c. white sugar
1 c. brown sugar
1 c. white corn syrup
1 c. water
1 tsp. maple flavoring

Combine all ingredients in 2 quart glass container. Microwave on HIGH until mixture boils. Boil 5 to 7 minutes, stirring twice. Store in clean syrup bottle and reheat in microwave (removing metal cap).

Paddie Anderson, *Pots, Pans and Pioneers, Volume IV*
Louisiana Chapter No. 24

## Scalloped Pineapple

**1 (20 oz.) can crushed or chunk pineapple, drained (save juice)**
**1/4 c. flour**
**1/2 c. sugar**
**1/4 lb. Cheddar cheese, grated**

Mix flour and sugar in boiler. Add 1/2 cup pineapple juice. Cook until thick, stirring constantly. Place pineapple and grated cheese in buttered casserole. Pour cooked mixture over this and blend well. Dot with butter. Bake 30 minutes at 325°. Serves 8.

JoAnn M. Russell, *Pots, Pans and Pioneers, Volume IV*
Louisiana Chapter No. 24

## Easy Low-Fat Pineapple Casserole

**4 cups fresh 1-inch bread cubes**
**1 20-ounce can crushed pineapple**
**3 eggs, beaten**
**2 cups sugar**
**1/4 cup butter, sliced**

Toss bread cubes and pineapple in bowl; spoon into greased 2-quart baking dish. Beat eggs with sugar; pour over pineapple mixture. Dot with butter. Bake at 350 degrees for 30 minutes. Yield: 8 servings.

**Approx Per Serving:** Cal 368; Prot 4 g; Carbo 72 g; Fiber 1 g; T Fat 8 g; 20% Calories from Fat; Chol 96 mg; Sod 159 mg.

Donna Nix, *Calling All Cooks three*, Alabama Chapter No. 34

## Homemade Yogurt

**1 qt. whole milk (you can use skim or lowfat milk)**
**1/4 c. nonfat dry milk (gives yogurt body)**
**3 Tbsp. plain yogurt with active culture**

In a heavy 2 quart saucepan over low heat, heat milk until tiny bubbles appear around the side of pan, about 180°. Stir in nonfat dry milk. Let milk mixture cool to 100° to 110°. Remove scum from surface and discard. Stir in yogurt until well mixed. Pour the milk mixture into the cups of an electric yogurt maker or a clean warmed thermos. Set aside undisturbed for about 5 hours where the temperature is about 90° to 120°. The electric yogurt maker automatically maintains a proper temperature. Refrigerate yogurt until cold before serving. Makes about 4 cups.

Janice Davis, *Dogwood Delights Volume II*, Dogwood Chapter No. 84

# Breads

LOUISIANA PIONEERS
Making The World a Better Place
24
TELEPHONE PIONEERS OF AMERICA
174465
1875
1911

## *Angel Biscuits*

5 cups unsifted flour (plain)
1/4 cup sugar
3 teaspoons baking powder
1 teaspoon soda
1 teaspoon salt
1 cup shortening
1 package yeast
2 tablespoons warm water
2 cups buttermilk

Sift dry ingredients and cut in shortening. Dissolve yeast in warm water. While cutting, add buttermilk and yeast to dry mixture, and mix well; let stand a few hours or overnight if you like. Turn out on floured board. Add more flour as needed. Roll to 1/2 inch thickness. Cut. Dip in butter. Fold to pocket-book rolls. Bake at 400° for 15 minutes or less if done. Let stand to rise for 15 to 20 minutes before baking. Melt butter, just tip biscuit to make them stick; then pat or brush on top when you get them cut and in pan.

Miss Joan Southerlin, *Secret Recipes of Telephone Pioneers, Volume I*
South Carolina Chapter No. 61

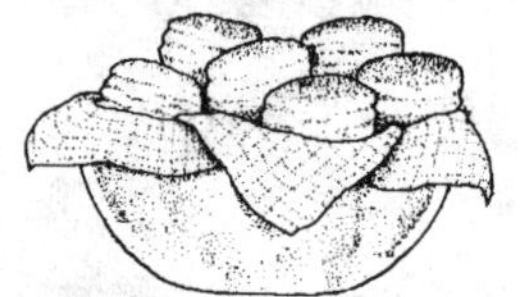

## *Angel Biscuits*

5 c. all-purpose flour
3/4 c. shortening
1 tsp. baking soda
1 tsp. salt
3 tsp. baking powder
3 Tbsp. sugar
1 cake yeast, dissolved in 1/2 c. lukewarm water
2 c. buttermilk

Sift dry ingredients together. Cut in shortening until mixed thoroughly. Add buttermilk and dissolved yeast. Mix all ingredients thoroughly. Cover bowl and put in refrigerator until ready to use as needed. Roll out on floured board to 1/2 inch thickness and cut. Bake at 400° in a shallow pan until brown or about 12 minutes.

Dough will keep in refrigerator for about 2 weeks.

Bessie Litchford, *Kentucky Kitchens, Volume I*, Kentucky Chapter No. 32

## Buttermilk Biscuits

**1 cup self-rising flour**
**1 teaspoon sugar**
**1/4 cup shortening**
**1/2 cup buttermilk**
**1 to 2 tablespoons margarine, softened**

Sift flour into bowl. Add sugar. Cut in shortening until crumbly. Add buttermilk; mix well. Roll or pat to 1/2-inch thickness on floured surface. Cut with biscuit cutter. Arrange on greased baking sheet. Brush with margarine. Let stand for 5 to 10 minutes. Bake at 450 degrees for 10 minutes or until golden brown. Serve hot. Yield: 7 servings.

**Cheese Biscuits**
Add 1/3 cup shredded sharp cheese. Drop by spoonfuls onto baking sheet. Brush with butter; sprinkle with garlic powder and bake.

**Yeast Biscuits**
Increase sugar to 2 teaspoons; add 1/2 envelope dry yeast to flour mixture. Heat buttermilk to slightly warmer than room temperature before adding. Let stand for 10 to 20 minutes before baking.

**Approx Per Serving:** Cal 167; Prot 2 g; Carbo 15 g; Fiber <1 g; T Fat 11 g; 59% Calories from Fat; Chol 1 mg; Sod 283 mg. Nutritional information is for basic biscuits only.

Maxine Pinckard (Mrs. Ken Pinckard), *Calling All Cooks three*
Alabama Chapter No. 34

## Buttery Biscuits

**1 c. all-purpose flour**
**2 tsp. baking powder**
**1 tsp. sugar**
**1/4 tsp. cream of tartar**
**1/4 tsp. salt**
**1/4 c. butter or margarine**
**1/3 c. milk**

Combine dry ingredients; cut in butter until mixture resembles coarse meal. Add milk, mixing well. (Dough will be soft.) Turn dough out onto floured surface; knead 10 times. Roll dough to 1/2 inch thickness; cut with a 2 1/2 inch biscuit cutter. Place biscuits on a lightly greased baking sheet. Bake at 450° for 10–12 minutes or until golden brown. Yield: About 6 biscuits.

Eurcle Culipher, *Bell's Best* 2, Mississippi Chapter No. 36

## Cheese Biscuits

**2 cups margarine, softened**
**1 pound sharp Cheddar cheese, shredded**
**5 cups flour**
**1/2 teaspoon cayenne pepper**
**Sesame seed to taste**

Cream margarine and cheese in large bowl until smooth. Mix flour and cayenne pepper together. Add to cheese mixture gradually, mixing well after each addition. Knead on floured surface until elastic. Shape into 1-inch balls. Place 1 inch apart on baking sheet. Sprinkle with sesame seed. Bake at 400 degrees for 9 to 12 minutes or until brown. May be frozen before baking. Yield: 250 servings.

**Approx Per Serving:** Cal 30; Prot 1 g; Carbo 2 g; Fiber <1 g; T Fat 2 g; Chol 2 mg; Sod 28 mg.

Wilma Burleson, *Carolina Cooking*, North Carolina Chapter No. 35

## Mayonnaise Biscuits

**1 cup self-rising flour**
**2 tbsp. Duke's mayonnaise**
**1/2 cup milk**
**1 egg (optional)**

Combine all ingredients and drop by spoonfuls onto cookie sheet. Makes approximately 12 biscuits. Bake for 15 to 20 minutes at 450°.

W. D. (Bill) Hagins, *Secret Recipes of Telephone Pioneers, Volume II*
South Carolina Chapter No. 61

## Sweet Potato Biscuits

**2 c. sifted all-purpose flour**
**2 tsp. baking powder**
**1 tsp. salt**
**1/4 tsp. baking soda**
**1 tsp. sugar**
**2–3 Tbsp. vegetable shortening**
**1 1/2 c. mashed sweet potatoes**
**3/4 c. buttermilk**

Sift together the dry ingredients. With fork, work in shortening and mashed sweet potatoes. Add liquid slowly, mixing to make as soft a dough as can be handled. Use more or less liquid as required. Knead gently. Roll to about 1/2 inch thick. Cut. Bake in preheated 425° F. oven for 15–20 minutes.

Mary Jane Gordon, *Dogwood Delights*, Dogwood Chapter No. 84

# Scotch Scones

**2 cups flour**
**1 teaspoon salt**
**5 teaspoons baking powder**
**1/3 cup milk**
**2 tablespoons sugar**
**4 tablespoons shortening**
**2 eggs**

Mix and sift flour, salt, baking powder and 1 tablespoon sugar. Cut in shortening with a knife or rub in with the finger tips. Add the beaten eggs (reserving 1 egg white for the tops). Add milk and mix to a soft dough. Roll out on a slightly floured board to 1/2-inch thickness into a round piece and cut into quarters. Brush with white of egg and sprinkle with the remaining tablespoon of sugar. Bake in a quick oven (425°) 10 to 15 minutes. This recipe makes 10 to 12 scones. Cinnamon may be sprinkled on scones before baking.

Miss Patsy McEntire, *Secret Recipes of Telephone Pioneers, Volume I*
South Carolina Chapter No. 61

# Caramel Pecan Ring

**1 can buttermilk biscuits**
**1/4 c. packed brown sugar**
**2 Tbsp. light corn syrup**
**1/2 can pineapple chunks**
**1/2 c. pecan halves**
**10–20 cherries, halved**

Mix brown sugar and corn syrup in pie plate. Place glass upside down in middle of plate. Arrange pineapple chunks, pecans and cherries around glass. Arrange biscuits on top. Bake at 400° for 10–12 minutes. Invert pie plate on plate letting syrup drizzle down before removing. Serve warm.

Lucy Barnett, *Dogwood Delights*, Dogwood Chapter No. 84

## A Helpful Hint

Dress up refrigerator biscuits by dipping them in melted butter and then in crumbled bleu cheese or a mixture of Parmesan cheese and dillweed. Bake according to package directions.

## Monkey Bread

**1 cup sugar**
**1¼ tablespoons cinnamon**
**4 10-count cans biscuits**
**½ cup pecans**
**½ cup raisins**
**½ cup coconut (optional)**
**½ cup margarine**
**1 cup packed brown sugar**

Mix sugar and cinnamon in plastic bag. Cut each biscuit into 4 pieces. Add to sugar mixture; shake to coat well. Layer in greased tube pan, sprinkling with pecans, raisins and coconut. Bring margarine and brown sugar to a boil in saucepan, stirring to mix well. Spoon over biscuits. Bake at 350 degrees for 45 minutes. Cool in pan for 15 minutes. Remove to serving plate. Pull apart to serve. Yield: 16 servings.

*Lawfully Good Eating*, Dixie Chapter No. 23

## Peachy Bran Coffee Cake

**1 16-ounce can juice-pack sliced peaches**
**1 cup wheat bran cereal**
**1 egg**
**¼ cup corn oil margarine, softened**
**1 cup unbleached flour**
**3¾ teaspoons low-sodium baking powder**
**¼ teaspoon cinnamon**
**3 tablespoons maple syrup**
**½ teaspoon cinnamon**

Drain peaches, reserving ⅔ cup juice. Combine cereal and reserved peach juice in large bowl; mix well. Let stand until juice is absorbed. Add egg and margarine; mix well. Sift flour, baking powder and ¼ teaspoon cinnamon together. Add to cereal mixture; mix just until moistened. Spread batter evenly in greased 9x9-inch baking pan. Mark diagonal grooves 1½ inches apart in lattice pattern using floured spoon. Toss peach slices with maple syrup in bowl. Arrange peach slices in grooves; sprinkle with remaining ½ teaspoon cinnamon. Bake at 400 degrees for 30 minutes. Serve warm. May substitute an equal amount of thawed frozen apple juice concentrate for maple syrup.
Yield: 9 servings.

**Approx Per Serving:** Cal 174; Prot 4 g; Carbo 30 g; Fiber 4 g; T Fat 6 g; 31% Calories from Fat; Chol 24 mg; Sod 179 mg.

Bonnie Golden, *Calling All Cooks three*, Alabama Chapter No. 34

# Broccoli Cornbread

1 (10 oz.) pkg. frozen chopped broccoli, thawed
1 (8 1/2 oz.) pkg. cornbread mix
3 eggs, beaten
1 med. onion, chopped
1 c. (4 oz.) shredded Cheddar cheese
1/2 c. butter or margarine
1/2 tsp. salt
1/4 to 1/2 tsp. garlic powder
1/4 tsp. ground red pepper

Press broccoli between paper towels to remove excess moisture. Combine cornbread mix, eggs, chopped onion, cheese, butter, and seasonings; stir well. Stir in broccoli (batter will be thick).

Pour mixture into a greased 8 inch square pan. Bake at 375 degrees for 25 to 30 minutes or until golden. Cool slightly, and cut into squares. Yield: 9 servings.

Jan Bancroft
*A Tablespoon of Pioneering and a Teaspoon of Horses and the Handicapped*
Florida Gold Coast Chapter No. 83

# Clyde's Broccoli Corn Bread

2 7-ounce packages corn bread mix
1/4 cup butter, softened
4 eggs, lightly beaten
12 ounces small curd cottage cheese
1 10-ounce package frozen chopped broccoli, thawed

Combine corn bread mix, butter, eggs and cottage cheese in bowl; mix well. Drain broccoli; stir into batter. Spoon into lightly greased 9x13-inch baking pan. Bake at 350 degrees for 30 minutes or until golden brown. Cool slightly before cutting. Serve warm or cool. Store leftovers in refrigerator. Yield: 15 servings.

**Approx Per Serving:** Cal 186; Prot 7 g; Carbo 20 g; Fiber 2 g; T Fat 9 g; 42% Calories from Fat; Chol 68 mg; Sod 438 mg.

Helen Shirley, *Calling All Cooks three*, Alabama Chapter No. 34

## Low-Fat Buttermilk Corn Bread

**2 cups self-rising cornmeal**
**2 tablespoons vegetable oil**
**1½ cups buttermilk**
**1 egg**

Combine cornmeal, oil, buttermilk and egg in bowl; mix well. Pour a small amount of additional oil into cast-iron skillet. Preheat skillet in 450-degree oven. Sprinkle a small amount of cornmeal over bottom of skillet. Pour in cornmeal batter. Bake at 450 to 500 degrees for 15 to 20 minutes or until golden brown. Yield: 8 servings.

**Approx Per Serving:** Cal 136; Prot 5 g; Carbo 28 g; Fiber 2 g; T Fat 5 g; 25% Calories from Fat; Chol 28 mg; Sod 521 mg.

Clara T. Sharpe, *Calling All Cooks three*, Alabama Chapter No. 34

## Corn Spoon Bread

**Brief history:** I can't remember where this recipe came from but it has been a smash hit at many a covered dish lunch.

**2 eggs, slightly beaten**
**1 (8½ oz.) pkg. corn muffin mix**
**1 (8 oz.) can cream style corn**
**½ c. butter or margarine**
**1 (8 oz.) can whole kernel corn, drained**
**1 c. sour cream**
**1 c. shredded Cheddar cheese**

Combine eggs, muffin mix, cream and whole corn, sour cream, and butter. Spread in an 11x7x1¾ inch baking dish. Bake at 350° for 35 minutes. Sprinkle cheese on top; bake 10 to 15 minutes more or till knife comes out clean.

**Preparation time:** 10 minutes, tops.
**Cooking time:** 45 minutes.
**No. of servings:** 6 to 8.

Sandy Bealle, *A Taste of Pioneering*, Florida Gold Coast Chapter No. 83

### *A Helpful Hint*

Add chopped celery and onion to your favorite corn bread recipe and bake it in advance. It will be ready for your holiday corn bread dressing with the addition of eggs, turkey broth and seasonings. Add pecans for a special treat.

## *Corn Bread*

1 c. corn meal
½ c. flour
1 tsp. salt
1 egg
1½ tsp. baking powder
2 tsp. sugar
1 c. sweet milk

Sift dry ingredients; add milk and stir. Add egg and stir thoroughly. Pour in pan which has 1½ tablespoons melted shortening in it. Bake in preheated 450° oven for about 20 minutes.

Jane Watts, *Bell's Best*, Mississippi Chapter No. 36

## *Hot! Cornbread*

1 c. cream style corn
1 c. self-rising flour
1 c. sharp Cheddar cheese (grated)
½ c. oil
3 beaten eggs
6 jalapeño peppers, chopped

Preheat oven to 400 degrees.

Mix all ingredients in a large bowl until blended.

Lightly grease an iron skillet and pour corn batter into skillet. Bake at 400 degrees for about 1 hour. Serve warm with butter.

Jo Hartmeyer
*A Tablespoon of Pioneering and a Teaspoon of Horses and the Handicapped*
Florida Gold Coast Chapter No. 83

## *Jalapeño Hot Corn Bread*

3 c. self-rising meal
1 small can hot El Paso chili peppers
2 c. milk
3 eggs, beaten
½ tsp. salt
½ tsp. baking powder
2 Tbsp. sugar
½ c. Wesson oil
1½ c. grated Cheddar cheese
1 bunch green onions, chopped
1 small can cream corn

In mixing bowl, whip eggs and milk together; add all liquid ingredients. Add meal, to which baking powder, salt and sugar have been added; mix well. Stir in grated cheese. Pour into oiled pan. Bake at 350° for about 45 minutes. This bread freezes well. Cut into squares; wrap in foil to freeze.

Mrs. George Price, *Dining with Pioneers, Volume I*
Tennessee Chapter No. 21

## Mexican Corn Bread

$^2/_3$ c. cooking oil
1 c. sour cream
1 c. creamed corn
1$^1/_2$ c. self-rising corn meal
1 tsp. baking powder
1 tsp. salt
2 eggs
2 or 3 jalapeño peppers, chopped
2 c. grated Cheddar cheese (1 c. cheese in batter, sprinkle other on top)

Put in greased large iron skillet or rectangular pan. Bake at 350° for 45 minutes.

Ludie Wells, *Bell's Best*, Mississippi Chapter No. 36

## Old Southern Corn Bread

2 cups self-rising cornmeal
1 cup self-rising flour
$^1/_2$ cup sugar
3 tablespoons bacon drippings
2 eggs, beaten
2 cups buttermilk
2 tablespoons bacon drippings

Combine cornmeal, flour and sugar in medium bowl; mix well. Add 3 tablespoons bacon drippings, eggs and buttermilk; mix well. Heat remaining 2 tablespoons bacon drippings in 10-inch cast-iron skillet until sizzling hot. Pour batter into skillet. Cook over medium heat until batter is bubbly. Bake at 400 degrees for 35 to 45 minutes or until brown. Yield: 10 servings.

**Approx Per Serving:** Cal 281; Prot 6 g; Carbo 43 g; Fiber 2 g; T Fat 9 g; Chol 86 mg; Sod 271 mg.

Audrey Brock, *Carolina Cooking*, North Carolina Chapter No. 35

## Sour Cream Corn Bread

2 c. self-rising corn meal
2 eggs, well beaten
1 (8 oz.) ctn. sour cream
1 small (8$^1/_4$ oz.) can kernel corn
$^1/_2$ c. Wesson oil or cooking oil

Mix well. Bake in greased pan, stick pan or muffin rings. Bake at 400° for 20 minutes or till brown.

Pattie Carpenter, *Dining with Pioneers, Volume I*
Tennessee Chapter No. 21

## Texas Corn Bread

**1½ cups self-rising cornmeal**
**⅔ cup oil**
**2 eggs**
**1 cup sour cream**
**1 8-ounce can cream-style corn**
**½ cup chopped onion**
**¼ cup chopped green bell pepper**
**1 cup (or more) shredded cheese**

Combine cornmeal, oil, eggs, sour cream and corn in bowl; mix well. Stir in onion and green pepper. Layer half the batter, cheese and remaining batter in greased baking pan. Bake at 350 degrees for 45 minutes. Yield: 8 servings.

Friend of the Pioneers, *Lawfully Good Eating*, Dixie Chapter No. 23

## Grits Spoon Bread

**Origin:** Southern Living. **Brief history:** I have used this recipe for over 10 years and think it is delicious.

**2 c. milk**
**⅓ c. quick grits**
**1 tsp. sugar**
**½ tsp. salt**
**3 eggs, separated**
**3 Tbsp. melted butter or margarine**

Scald milk in heavy 2 quart saucepan. Combine grits, sugar and salt; stir in milk. Bring to a boil; reduce heat and cook, stirring constantly, 4 to 5 minutes or until thick. Let cool. Beat egg yolks and stir into grits. Beat egg whites until stiff peaks form. Fold into mixture. Place butter in a 1½ quart casserole and spoon in grits mixture.

**Cooking time:** 35 to 40 minutes at 375°. Serve hot.
**No. of servings:** 6 to 8.

Regina Godard (Mrs. J. D.), *A Taste of Pioneering*
Florida Gold Coast Chapter No. 83

# Spiced Applesauce Bread

1¼ cups applesauce
1 cup sugar
½ cup oil
2 eggs
3 tablespoons milk
2 cups sifted flour
1 teaspoon soda
½ teaspoon baking powder
¼ teaspoon cinnamon
¼ teaspoon salt
¼ teaspoon nutmeg
¼ teaspoon allspice
½ cup chopped pecans
¼ cup packed brown sugar
½ teaspoon cinnamon
¼ cup chopped pecans

Combine first 5 ingredients in mixer bowl; beat until well blended. Sift flour, soda, baking powder, ½ teaspoon cinnamon, salt, nutmeg and allspice into medium bowl. Add to applesauce mixture; mix well. Fold in ½ cup pecans. Spoon into well-greased 5x9-inch loaf pan. Combine brown sugar, remaining ½ teaspoon cinnamon and ¼ cup pecans in bowl. Sprinkle over batter. Bake at 350 degrees for 1 hour or until loaf tests done. Remove to wire rack to cool. Yield: 12 servings.

**Approx Per Serving:** Cal 317; Prot 4 g; Carbo 43 g; Fiber 1 g; T Fat 15 g; Chol 36 mg; Sod 143 mg.

Sally Vinton, *Carolina Cooking*, North Carolina Chapter No. 35

*A hunters' safety class.* (Louisana Chapter No. 24)

# Banana Bread

3 c. sifted flour
3/4 tsp. salt
1/2 tsp. baking soda
4 tsp. baking powder
2/3 c. butter
4 eggs
2 c. mashed bananas
1 1/4 c. sugar

Sift together the flour, salt, baking soda and baking powder. Cream together the butter and sugar and the eggs, one at a time. Beat until fluffy and smooth. Beat in the flour alternately with the bananas until smooth. Pour into 2 (9 inch) buttered loaf pans. Bake 1 hour at 350°. Cool in pan on cake rack for 15 minutes, then carefully turn out.

Makes 2 loaves.

Freezes well. Cool for 4 hours before freezing. Remove from freezer 1 1/2 hours before serving.

Priscilla Young, *Pioneers Pots and Pans—1985 Cookbook*
North Florida Chapter No. 39

# Moist Banana-Nut Bread

1 cup margarine, softened
2 1/2 cups sugar
4 eggs
3 cups flour
1 teaspoon baking soda
1/2 cup buttermilk
2 teaspoons vanilla extract
4 or 5 bananas, chopped
Confectioners' sugar
1 teaspoon vanilla extract

Cream margarine and sugar in mixer bowl until light and fluffy. Beat in eggs. Add flour, baking soda, buttermilk, 2 teaspoons vanilla and bananas; mix well. Spoon into 2 greased and floured baking pans. Bake at 350 degrees for 1 hour or until loaves test done. Remove to wire rack. Combine confectioners' sugar and 1 teaspoon vanilla with enough water to make a thin icing in bowl; mix well. Spread over warm loaves. Yield: 24 servings.

Sara Tadlock, *Lawfully Good Eating*, Dixie Chapter No. 23

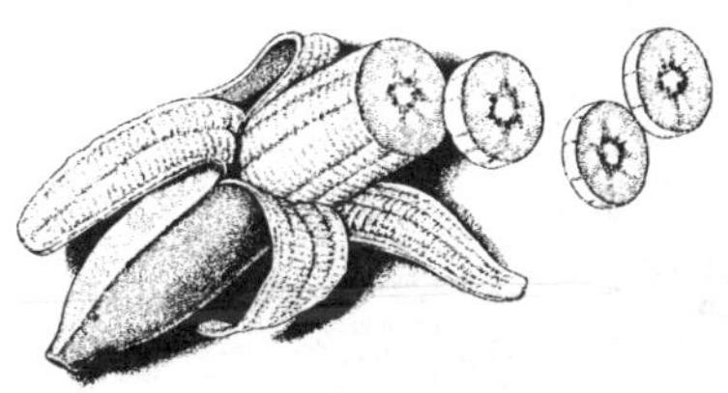

## Orange-Banana Bread

1 cup sugar
1/4 cup butter, softened
1 egg, beaten
1 cup mashed banana
2 tablespoons grated orange rind
1/2 cup milk
2 1/2 cups flour
1 tablespoon baking powder
1 cup coarsely chopped walnuts

Combine sugar, butter and egg in bowl; beat until smooth. Add banana, orange rind and milk; mix well. Sift in dry ingredients; beat just until smooth. Stir in walnuts. Pour into greased 5x9-inch loaf pan. Bake at 350 degrees for 1 hour or until loaf tests done. Cool in pan for 15 minutes. Remove to wire rack to cool completely. Serve in thin slices. Yield: 12 servings.

**Approx Per Serving:** Cal 289; Prot 5 g; Carbo 44 g; Fiber 2 g; T Fat 11 g; 34% Calories from Fat; Chol 29 mg; Sod 133 mg.

Ruth Kelly, *Calling All Cooks three*, Alabama Chapter No. 34

## Beer Bread

*Mix until thoroughly moist:*
3 c. self-rising flour
3 Tbsp. sugar
12 oz. can beer

Bake in greased loaf pan at 375° for 35 to 40 minutes. Yields: 1 loaf.

Karen Haltiwanger, *Pioneers Pots and Pans—1985 Cookbook*
North Florida Chapter No. 39

# Fresh Blueberry Banana Bread

1 cup fresh blueberries
1 3/4 cups flour, sifted
2 tsp. baking powder
1/4 tsp. baking soda
1/2 tsp. salt
1/3 cup butter or margarine
2/3 cup sugar
1 cup mashed bananas
2 eggs

Wash and thoroughly drain blueberries; toss berries with 2 Tbsp. flour, sift together remaining flour, baking powder, soda and salt. Cream butter, gradually beat in sugar until light and fluffy. Beat in eggs one at a time. Add flour mixture and bananas alternately in 3 parts. Stir in blueberries. Spoon into greased loaf pan (9x5x3 inch). Bake in 350 degree oven 50 minutes or until done. Makes 1 loaf.

Elizabeth Scott-Gregory, *Secret Recipes of Telephone Pioneers, Volume III*
South Carolina Chapter No. 61

# Blueberry Tea Loaf

**Origin:** Family Cookbook. **Country:** U.S.A. **City:** Vero Beach. **Approximate year created:** 1950–1986. **Relative obtained from:** All.

2 1/2 c. flour
1 1/2 tsp. baking powder
1/2 tsp. baking soda
1 tsp. salt
1/2 c. butter or margarine, softened
1 c. sugar
2 eggs
1 c. sour cream
2 Tbsp. grated lemon peel
1 tsp. vanilla
1/4 tsp. nutmeg
1 c. chopped walnuts
1 c. fresh blueberries*

Preheat oven to 350°. Grease 9x5 inch loaf pan; set aside. Sift together flour, baking powder, baking soda, and salt. Beat butter and sugar until light and fluffy. Add eggs, sour cream, lemon peel, vanilla, and nutmeg, beating until smooth. Gradually beat in dry ingredients until thoroughly blended. Stir in walnuts. Gently fold in blueberries. Using spatula, gently spread the batter into the pan. Bake 1 hour and 30 minutes or until cake tester inserted in center comes out clean. (If top is getting too brown, cover with foil.) Cool in pan on wire rack 15 minutes. Remove from pan; cool completely.

*If using frozen blueberries, toss in 1 tablespoon flour before adding to batter. Do not thaw.

**No. of servings:** 10.

R. W. Rhodes, *A Taste of Pioneering*, Florida Gold Coast Chapter No. 83

# Cherry Pecan Bread

2 cups flour
1/2 teaspoon soda
1 teaspoon salt
1/2 cup butter, softened
3/4 cup sugar
2 eggs
1/2 teaspoon vanilla extract
1 cup buttermilk
1 10-ounce jar maraschino cherries, drained, chopped
1 cup chopped pecans

Combine flour, soda and salt in bowl. Cream butter, sugar and eggs in bowl until light and fluffy. Add mixture of vanilla and buttermilk alternately with flour mixture, mixing well after each addition. Fold in cherries and pecans. Pour into greased loaf pans or small tube pan. Bake at 325 degrees for 30 minutes or until slightly brown. Remove to wire rack to cool. Yield: 8 servings.

Francele Black, *Kentucky Kitchens, Volume II*, Kentucky Chapter No. 32

# Cinnamon Bread

1/4 c. shortening
3/4 c. sugar
2 eggs, beaten
2 c. flour
3/4 tsp. salt
1 Tbsp. baking powder
1 1/2 tsp. cinnamon
1 c. milk

Cream sugar and shortening; add eggs and beat until light and fluffy. Sift flour, salt, baking powder and cinnamon. Add alternately with milk to creamed mixture. Pour into greased 9x9x1 1/2 inch pan. Sprinkle with topping mixture. Bake 375° for 40 minutes. Cool 10 minutes before slicing.

**Topping:** Mix 1 1/2 teaspoons cinnamon, 1/2 cup sugar and 2 teaspoons melted butter.

Renee Dearen, *Pioneers Pots and Pans—1985 Cookbook*
North Florida Chapter No. 39

## A Helpful Hint

Most sweet breads freeze well. Be sure that they are completely cool and well wrapped before freezing.

# *Gift of the Magi Bread*

Christmas. **Origin:** Unknown, but sooo good.

**1/2 c. butter or margarine**
**1 c. granulated sugar**
**2 eggs**
**1 tsp. vanilla**
**2 c. flour**
**1 tsp. baking soda**
**Pinch of salt**
**1 c. mashed bananas**
**1 (11 oz.) can mandarin orange segments, drained**
**1 (6 oz.) pkg. chocolate chips**
**1 c. shredded coconut**
**2/3 c. sliced almonds**
**1/2 c. chopped maraschino cherries**
**1/2 c. chopped dried figs**

Preheat oven to 350°. Cream butter or margarine with granulated sugar. Add eggs and vanilla. Sift flour with baking soda and salt. Add alternately with bananas. Stir in mandarin oranges, chocolate chips, coconut, 1/2 cup sliced almonds, cherries, and figs. Pour into 2 greased 7 1/2x3 3/4 inch loaf pans. Sprinkle remaining sliced almonds over tops. Bake 1 to 1 1/4 hours at 350°. When cool, sieve confectioners' sugar over tops.

**Preparation time:** 35 minutes.
**Cooking time:** 1 hour to 1 1/4 hours.
**No. of servings:** 2 loaves.

Helen S. Moody, *A Taste of Pioneering*
Florida Gold Coast Chapter No. 83

*Working on a Habitat for Humanity house in Columbia.*
(South Carolina Chapter No. 61)

# Ginny's Mango Bread

1 c. (solid) Crisco
1 1/2 c. sugar
4 eggs
4 c. sifted flour
2 tsp. baking soda
1/2 tsp. salt
1 tsp. cinnamon
1/2 tsp. cloves
1/2 tsp. nutmeg
2 3/4 c. raw mango (chopped in blender)
2 tbsp. lime juice
1 c. chopped nuts
3/4 c. raisins

Cream shortening and sugar. Add eggs. Stir in dry ingredients, mango and lime juice. Mix all together. Add nuts and raisins.

Grease and flour baking loaf pans. Bake at 375 F. for one hour or until done (this depends on pan size). Cool on racks 15 minutes before releasing from pans.

Do not cut until the second day.

Makes 3 large loaves; 4 medium loaves or 6 tiny loaves.

Baked bread freezes good.

Gary and Ginny Carroll
*A Tablespoon of Pioneering and a Teaspoon of Horses and the Handicapped*
Florida Gold Coast Chapter No. 83

# Spicy Peach Nut Bread

2 c. flour
2/3 c. sugar
2 tsp. baking powder
1/2 tsp. salt
1/2 tsp. soda
1/2 tsp. ground cloves
2 Tbsp. melted margarine
2 eggs
2 c. (16 oz. can) chopped peaches
1 c. chopped nuts
1 c. raisins (optional)
1/2 c. peach syrup

Grease and flour bottom of loaf pan. In large bowl, combine flour, sugar, baking powder, salt, soda, ground cloves, margarine, eggs, peaches, and syrup. Beat 2 minutes at medium speed. Stir in nuts and raisins. Pour into prepared pans. Bake at 350° F. for 60 minutes. Remove from pans. Cool completely.

Martha Hooper, *Kentucky Kitchens, Volume I*, Kentucky Chapter No. 32

## Pumpkin Bread

3½ c. sugar
1 c. oil
2 c. pumpkin
4 eggs
3½ c. flour
2 tsp. soda
1½ tsp. salt
1 tsp. each nutmeg, allspice, cinnamon and vanilla
1 c. pecans

Blend the sugar and oil in mixer; add pumpkin and the eggs, 1 at a time. Mix flour, soda, salt, nutmeg, cinnamon, allspice and vanilla. Slowly add to other ingredients and continue beating until well mixed. Slow mixer and add the pecans. Fill 4 greased 1 pound coffee cans half full. Bake at 350° for 1½ hours. Makes nice gifts and is good.

Laura McClelland, *Bell's Best 2*, Mississippi Chapter No. 36

## Pumpkin Cheese Bread

2½ c. sugar
1 (8 oz.) pkg. Philadelphia cream cheese
½ c. Parkay margarine
4 eggs
1 (16 oz.) can pumpkin
3½ c. flour
2 tsp. baking soda
1 c. chopped nuts
1 tsp. salt
1 tsp. cinnamon
½ tsp. baking powder
¼ tsp. ground cloves

Combine sugar, softened cream cheese and margarine, mixing until well blended. Add eggs, one at a time, mixing well after each addition. Blend in pumpkin. Add combined dry ingredients, mixing just until moistened. Fold in nuts. Pour into 2 greased and floured 9x5 inch loaf pans. Bake at 350° for 1 hour and 10 minutes or until wooden pick inserted in center comes out clean. Cool 10 minutes; remove from pans. Yields 2 loaves.

Debbie Wilson, *Dining with Pioneers, Volume II*
Tennessee Chapter No. 21

# *Zucchini Bread*

**3 eggs, beaten**
**2 c. sugar**
**1 c. oil**
**1 tsp. vanilla**
**2 c. grated zucchini (raw—don't peel it)**
**1 small can crushed pineapple**
**1/2 c. raisins**
**1/2 c. walnuts, chopped**
**3 c. flour**
**1 tsp. baking powder**
**1 tsp. baking soda**
**1/2 tsp. salt**
**3 tsp. cinnamon**

Mix eggs, sugar, oil, and vanilla. Add zucchini, pineapple, raisins, and nuts. Mix well, then mix dry ingredients. Grease 2 regular bread pans. Bake at 325° for 1 hour or until done.

I have enjoyed this recipe given me by Phyllis Healey.

Loraine Elmerick, *Bell's Best 3*, Mississippi Chapter No. 36

# *Onion Bread*

**1 egg**
**3/4 cup sour cream**
**1 tablespoon melted butter**
**1 teaspoon salt**
**1/2 teaspoon pepper**
**2 onions, sliced**
**1 pound frozen bread dough, thawed**

Combine egg and sour cream in bowl; mix with wooden spoon. Stir in butter, salt and pepper. Add onions; mix well. Divide bread dough into 6 portions. Pat into 5-inch circles on lightly floured surface. Place 2 inches apart on ungreased baking sheet. Top with onion mixture. Bake at 425 degrees for 20 minutes or until golden brown. Yield: 6 servings.

Hart County Sheriff's Department, *Lawfully Good Eating*
Dixie Chapter No. 23

## *A Helpful Hint*

Use your slow cooker as a bread warmer. Place a damp cloth
ker and heat on Low for 30 minutes. Remove
large napkins. Place bread inside. Bread will
to 2 hours.

## Italian Sausage Bread

2 loaves frozen bread dough
1 pound ground beef
1 pound Italian sausage, skinned, crumbled
1 onion, chopped
1 green bell pepper, chopped
3 cups shredded Cheddar cheese

Place frozen bread dough on well-greased baking sheets. Grease top of each loaf. Let stand, covered, for 2 hours or until thawed. Do not let rise. Brown ground beef and sausage with onion and green pepper in skillet, stirring frequently; drain. Cool. Press dough with greased hands over surface of baking sheets. Layer with ground beef mixture and cheese. Roll as for jelly roll. Place seamside down on baking sheets. Bake at 350 degrees for 20 minutes or until golden brown.
Yield: 24 servings.

**Approx Per Serving:** Cal 275; Prot 15 g; Carbo 19 g; Fiber 1 g; T Fat 15 g; Chol 46 mg; Sod 469 mg.

Lee Davis, *Carolina Cooking*, North Carolina Chapter No. 35

## Applesauce Muffins

1/4 c. Crisco
1 1/2 c. sugar
1 egg
1 tsp. soda
1 tsp. cinnamon
2 c. flour
1 c. applesauce
1/2 c. raisins

Mix well and bake 375° for 20 to 25 minutes for muffin tins. 350° for 50 to 60 minutes for loaf pan.

Dottie Leswell, *Pioneers Pots and Pans—1985 Cookbook*
North Florida Chapter No. 39

## Bacon Bran Muffins

1 c. all-purpose flour
3 tsp. baking powder
2 Tbsp. sugar
3/4 c. milk
1 1/4 c. bran flake cereal
1/2 tsp. salt
1/3 c. shortening
1 egg, well beaten
1/3 c. crisp bacon, crumbled

Combine flour, baking powder, sugar and salt, cutting in shortening. Combine egg and milk; add to mixture, stirring only enough to moisten. Add cereal and bacon. Spoon into greased muffin pans about 2/3 full. Bake at 400° for 20 minutes or until done. Makes 8–10 muffins.

Marilou Bridges, *Pots, Pans and Pioneers III*, Louisiana Chapter No. 24

## Icebox Bran Muffins

2 c. boiling water
2 c. 100% Nabisco Bran
1 c. Crisco (not oil)
2 c. sugar (or 1 c. honey and 1 c. sugar)
4 beaten eggs
1 qt. buttermilk
5 c. flour
5 tsp. soda
1 tsp. salt
5 c. Kellogg's All-Bran

Mix water with 100% Bran. Let stand. Cream Crisco and sugar, then add eggs, buttermilk, and soaked bran. Add sifted flour, soda, and salt. Fold in All-Bran. Store in glass jars (Tupperware is too tight). Bake in greased muffin pans. Bake at 400° for 15 minutes.

You may add dates, nuts, or bananas before cooking.

This recipe makes a lot, but can be kept in the refrigerator for several weeks and used as you desire.

Corky Hall, *Pots, Pans and Pioneers, Volume IV*
Louisiana Chapter No. 24

## Sweet Potato Muffins

2 cups sugar
$1^1/_2$ cups oil
4 eggs
1 teaspoon cinnamon
3 cups self-rising flour
1 cup mashed sweet potatoes
1 cup chopped walnuts
1 cup raisins

Combine sugar and oil in bowl until light. Stir in eggs until well blended. Add cinnamon, flour, sweet potatoes, walnuts and raisins; stir just until moistened. Fill greased muffin cups $^1/_2$ full. Bake at 350 degrees for 15 to 20 minutes or until brown. Cool for 5 minutes. Remove to wire rack to cool completely. Yield: 36 servings.

Approx Per Serving: Cal 211; Prot 2 g; Carbo 25 g; Fiber 1 g; T Fat 12 g; Chol 24 mg; Sod 126 mg.

Lib Sandlin, *Carolina Cooking*, North Carolina Chapter No. 35

## Yogurt Whole Wheat Muffins

1 cup whole wheat flour
$^1/_2$ cup all-purpose flour
1 teaspoon baking powder
1 teaspoon soda
$^1/_3$ cup sugar
$^1/_3$ cup chopped pecans
1 egg, slightly beaten
8 ounces plain low-fat yogurt
5 tablespoons melted reduced-calorie margarine

Combine whole wheat flour, all-purpose flour, baking powder, soda, sugar and pecans in large bowl. Make a well in center of mixture. Mix egg with yogurt and margarine in bowl. Add to dry ingredients; stir just until moistened. Fill greased muffin cups $^3/_4$ full. Bake at 350 degrees for 18 to 20 minutes or until lightly browned. Yield: 12 muffins.

Robbie Lowery, *Kentucky Kitchens, Volume II*, Kentucky Chapter No. 32

### A Helpful Hint

Muffins can be easily removed from the pan if it is first placed on a damp towel.

## Crêpes

**1 cup flour**
**1½ cups milk**
**½ teaspoon salt**
**3 eggs**
**1 tablespoon melted butter**

Combine flour, milk, salt, eggs and melted butter in blender container. Process until smooth. Pour scant ¼ cup batter into hot lightly greased crêpe pan. Tilt pan to spread batter evenly. Bake until light brown on both sides; stack between waxed paper. May sprinkle with sugar or confectioners' sugar or fill with jam, fresh fruit or preserves.
Yield: 12 servings.

**Approx Per Serving:** Cal 85; Prot 4 g; Carbo 10 g; Fiber <1 g; T Fat 3 g; Chol 60 mg; Sod 127 mg.

Candace W. Joehrendt, *Carolina Cooking*
North Carolina Chapter No. 35

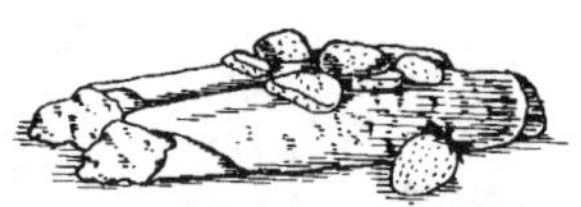

## Baked Doughnuts

**1 c. mashed potatoes**
**1 (¼ oz.) pkg. yeast**
**¼ c. warm potato water**
**1 c. milk, scalded**
**¾ c. shortening**
**½ c. sugar**
**1 tsp. salt**
**2 eggs, beaten**
**4½ c. flour (regular)**
**Butter**
**Sugar**

Add shortening, sugar and salt to hot milk; cool to lukewarm. Add potatoes and yeast, dissolved in warm potato water. Blend in eggs; work flour in gradually. Cover; let rise until light, about 1 hour. Knead dough lightly on floured board (dough may be frozen for later use). Roll out ½ inch thick and cut with doughnut cutter. Set on buttered cookie sheets and let rise about 1 hour. Bake at 425° until delicately browned. While still warm, brush with butter on all sides; roll in sugar.
Makes 3 dozen.

Paddie Anderson, *Pots, Pans and Pioneers III*, Louisiana Chapter No. 24

## Funnel Cakes

1 1/4 c. all-purpose flour, sifted
2 Tbsp. sugar
1 tsp. soda
3/4 tsp. salt
1 egg
3/4 c. milk

Combine dry ingredients; add egg and milk, beating until smooth. Heat 1 inch oil to 375° in a deep pan or skillet. Cover bottom opening of a funnel with finger. Pour 1/4 cup of batter in funnel. Hold funnel over center of pan; remove finger from end to release batter into hot oil. Move funnel in a slow circular motion to form a spiral, beginning at center and move outward. Fry for 2 minutes or until golden brown, turning once. Drain on paper towel; sprinkle with powdered sugar. Serve hot with honey.

Janice Davis, *Dogwood Delights Volume II*, Dogwood Chapter No. 84

## Hush Puppies

1 c. plain flour
4 tsp. baking powder
1 egg
1/2 c. milk
1 c. corn meal
1/2 tsp. salt
1 small onion, grated
3 Tbsp. cooking oil

Mix all ingredients well. Dip clean tablespoon in hot oil first, then in mix and drop in hot oil to cook. These are better if deep fried.

Mrs. Tony Corcoran, *Pots, Pans & Pioneers II*, Louisiana Chapter No. 24

## Johnny Cakes

1 egg
3/4 c. corn meal
1/8 lb. butter, melted
1 tsp. salt
1 c. flour
1 c. sour milk
1 tsp. baking soda
1/3 c. sugar

Mix sugar, egg, and about a third of the melted butter. Use rest of butter to grease griddle. Add sour milk, baking soda, corn meal, salt, and flour. Let stand in a cool place for 1/2 hour. Heat griddle and test to see if butter spits. Rub griddle with melted butter. Spoon out batter onto griddle by tablespoonfuls. Brown on one side; turn and brown on the other. Serve hot with maple syrup, jam or honey.

*Dogwood Delights Volume II*, Dogwood Chapter No. 84

# Basic Pancakes

1 egg, slightly beaten
2 tablespoons margarine
1 1/4 cups milk
1 1/2 cups self-rising flour

Beat egg with margarine and milk. Add flour. Mix just until moistened; do not beat. Ladle desired amount of batter onto hot greased griddle. Bake until brown on both sides, turning once. Yield: 6 servings.

**Approx Per Serving:** Cal 187; Prot 6 g; Carbo 26 g; Fiber 1 g; T Fat 7 g; 32% Calories from Fat; Chol 45 mg; Sod 458 mg.

Camille Meggs, *Calling All Cooks three*, Alabama Chapter No. 34

# Banana Pancakes

1 c. flour
1 1/2 tsp. baking powder
1/2 tsp. salt
1 egg, beaten
2 Tbsp. melted butter
3 Tbsp. sugar
1/4 tsp. nutmeg
4 or 5 over-ripe bananas (fruit very soft, skins dark brown)
Butter or vegetable oil for frying

Sift together flour, baking powder, and salt. Add egg, butter, sugar, and nutmeg. Mix well. Mash bananas; add to batter. Heat pan over moderate heat; grease lightly with butter. Drop batter by tablespoonful into pan. Brown lightly on both sides. Serve hot with butter, confectioners' sugar, honey or syrup. Serves 4 to 6.

Paula White, *Kentucky Kitchens, Volume I*, Kentucky Chapter No. 32

## A Helpful Hint

Replace the liquid in your pancake recipe with club soda for the lightest pancakes ever. This batter must be used at once, however, since the soda goes flat.

# Potato Pancakes

**1/4 c. milk**
**1/4 onion, sliced**
**1/4 c. flour**
**2 eggs**
**1/2 tsp. salt**
**1/4 tsp. baking powder**
**2 1/2 c. raw potatoes, diced**

In a blender, blend milk, onion, flour, eggs, salt, and baking powder; blend until smooth. While blender is running, add potatoes. Blend 2 seconds. Cook on hot griddle and serve with sour cream.

*Dogwood Delights Volume II*, Dogwood Chapter No. 84

# Plättar—Swedish Pancakes

**Origin:** Lost in the course of many centuries of Vikings! **Country:** Sweden. **Approximate year created:** 1050. **Relative obtained from:** Grandmother Bengtson.

**3 eggs**
**2 c. milk or 1 c. milk and 1 c. light cream**
**1 c. flour**
**6 Tbsp. unsalted butter, melted**
**1/2 tsp. salt**

Beat the eggs together with 1/2 cup of milk for 2 or 3 minutes with a rotary beater or whisk. Add the flour all at once and beat to a heavy, smooth consistency. Beat in the remaining milk and then the melted butter and salt. Because of the large amount of butter in the batter, the skillet will require little, if any, additional buttering.

Use, if you happen to have one, a Swedish 5 or 7 section pancake pan, or you can use a plain heavy skillet. Butter lightly and when good and hot pour batter into pan, a bit at a time. Pancakes should be small. Serve with lingonberries and whipped cream for dessert, if you wish.

**Preparation time:** Approximately 1/2 hour.
**Cooking time:** Approximately 4 minutes for each set of pancakes.

Helen B. Pickel, *A Taste of Pioneering*
Florida Gold Coast Chapter No. 83

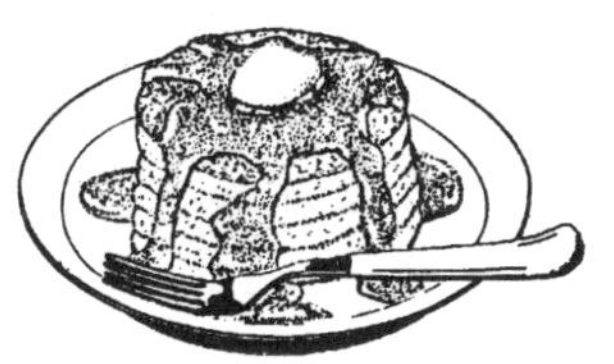

# *Bless-Your-Heart Bread*

2 envelopes dry yeast
1/2 cup warm water
1/4 cup margarine
2 cups skim milk, scalded
1/2 cup molasses
1/4 cup honey
2 tablespoons brown sugar
1 cup whole wheat flour
1 cup oats
1/4 cup bran cereal
1/3 cup rye flour
4 to 5 cups unbleached flour
2 teaspoons salt
1 teaspoon ginger

Dissolve yeast in warm water. Combine margarine and hot milk in bowl; stir until margarine melts. Add molasses, honey and brown sugar. Let stand until lukewarm. Add yeast; mix well. Combine whole wheat flour, oats, cereal and rye flour in bowl; mix well. Add milk mixture gradually, mixing well after each addition. Add enough unbleached flour to make medium dough. Knead on floured surface for 4 to 5 minutes. Place in greased bowl, turning to coat surface. Let rise, covered with damp cloth, until doubled in bulk. Shape into 2 loaves; place in 2 greased 5x9-inch loaf pans. Let rise for 1 to 1 1/2 hours or until doubled in bulk. Bake at 325 degrees for 40 minutes or until loaves test done. Yield: 28 servings.

"*Answering the Call of Those in Need*," Tennessee Chapter No. 21

*The Dixie Chapter and Georgia Sheriffs' Youth Homes have joined hands between 1992 and 1995 to support the Youth Home Pineland Campus in LaGrange, Georgia, by establishing Camp Pioneer. Almost $200,000 and many hours of work have already been committed to this ongoing project.* (Dixie Chapter No. 23)

# Old Fashioned Potato Loaves

1 med. potato
Water
Hot tap water
2 pkgs. Fleischmann's active dry yeast
2 tbsp. Blue Bonnet margarine, softened
2 tbsp. sugar
1 tbsp. salt
1 c. warm milk (105–115 degrees F.)
6½ to 7½ c. all-purpose flour
Flour

Pare and dice potato; boil in water to cover until tender, about 20 minutes. Drain; reserving liquid. Add hot tap water to potato liquid to make 1 cup; cool to warm (105–115 degrees F. ). Mash potato; set aside.

Pour warm potato water into large warm bowl. Sprinkle in yeast; stir until dissolved. Add margarine, sugar and salt. Stir in mashed potato, warm milk and 3 cups flour; beat until smooth. Stir in enough additional flour to make a stiff dough. Turn out onto lightly floured board; knead until smooth and elastic, about 8 to 10 minutes. Place in greased bowl, turning to grease top. Cover; let rise in warm place, free from draft, until doubled in bulk, about 35 minutes.

Punch dough down; turn over in bowl. Cover and let rise again about 20 minutes.

Punch dough down. Turn out onto lightly floured board; divide in half. Roll each half to 14x9 inch rectangle. Shape into loaves. Place in 2 greased 9x5x3 inch loaf pans. Cover; let rise in warm place, free from draft, until doubled in bulk, about 50 minutes.

Dust loaves with flour. Bake at 375 degrees F. 35 to 40 minutes, or until done. Remove from pans and cool on wire racks.

Dottie McLaughlin
*A Tablespoon of Pioneering and a Teaspoon of Horses and the Handicapped*
Florida Gold Coast Chapter No. 83

## Helpful Hints

To knead bread dough, fold the dough toward you, then push it away with the heels of your hands in a rocking motion. Rotate it a quarter turn and repeat until dough is springy and blistered with tiny bubbles under the surface and smooth on top.

Shape yeast dough as desired and freeze before allowing to rise. Store in plastic freezer storage bags in freezer for up to 4 weeks. Allow dough to thaw, then rise as recipe directs before baking.

# Sourdough Bread

Starter:

1¾ c. unsifted flour
1 Tbsp. sugar
1 Tbsp. salt
1 pkg. active dry yeast
2½ c. water

Dough:

5–6 c. unsifted flour
3 Tbsp. sugar
1 tsp. salt
1 pkg. active dry yeast
1 c. milk
2 Tbsp. oleo
1½ c. starter

To make starter, combine flour, salt and undissolved yeast in a large bowl. Gradually add warm water to dry ingredients and beat 2 minutes at medium speed of electric mixer, scraping bowl occasionally. Cover; let stand at room temperature (78°–80°F.) for 4 days. Stir down daily.

To make dough, combine 1 cup flour, sugar, salt and undissolved yeast in a large bowl. Combine milk and oleo in a saucepan. Heat over low heat until liquid is warm; oleo does not need to melt. Gradually add to dry ingredients and beat 2 minutes at medium speed of electric mixer, scraping bowl occasionally. Add 1½ cups starter and 1 cup flour, or enough flour to make a thick batter. Beat at high speed 2 minutes, scraping bowl occasionally. Stir in enough additional flour to make a soft dough. Turn out onto lightly floured board; knead until smooth and elastic, about 8–10 minutes. Place in greased bowl, turning to grease top. Cover; let rise in warm place, free from draft, until doubled in bulk, about 1 hour. Punch dough down; turn out onto lightly floured board. Let rest 15 minutes. Divide dough in half. Shape each half into loaf and place in greased 9x5x3 inch loaf pan. Cover; let rise in warm place, free from draft, until doubled in bulk, about 1 hour. Bake in hot oven at 400°F. about 30 minutes, or until done. Remove from pans and cool on wire racks.

**To Reuse Starter**: Add 1½ cups lukewarm water, ¾ cup unsifted flour and 1½ teaspoons sugar to unused starter. Beat for 1 minute at medium speed. Cover and let stand until ready to make bread again. Stir down daily.

Linda Crane, *Bell's Best*, Mississippi Chapter No. 36

## Monkey Bread

1 pkg. dry yeast
1/2 c. lukewarm water
1/2 c. shortening
3/8 c. sugar
3/4 tsp. salt
1/2 c. boiling water
1 egg, beaten
3 c. plain flour
1 stick melted butter

Dissolve yeast in lukewarm water and set aside. Mix shortening, sugar and salt together. Add boiling water and mix well. Add egg to this mixture and stir. Add flour and yeast mixture alternately to shortening mixture until all is well mixed. Let rise until dough doubles in size. Punch down. Roll dough out on floured board until 1/2 to 1/4 inch thick. Cut dough into various shapes and dip each piece in melted butter. Lay pieces in tube pan layer on layer. Let rise about 2 hours. Bake at 350° about 45 minutes, until top is real brown.

This bread is easier to pull apart than slice.

Hazel Walker, *Kentucky Kitchens, Volume I*, Kentucky Chapter No. 32

## Potato Rolls

1 qt. milk, warm till skim on top
1 c. mashed potatoes (no salt)
1 c. potato water (used to cook potatoes)
2 Tbsp. salt
1 c. Crisco
1 c. sugar
1 tsp. soda
2 tsp. baking powder
1 yeast cake
Approx. 10 c. plain flour

Mix Crisco, sugar, potatoes and yeast dissolved in lukewarm potato water. Add milk and flour with soda, salt and baking powder sifted in a little at a time (about 4–5 cups flour). Put in container large enough to let rise double; then work in enough flour to make stiff dough (about 4–5 cups). This dough will keep up to a week in the refrigerator. Cut out and dab in melted butter or Crisco and let rise about double before cooking.

B. Short, *Dining with Pioneers, Volume II*, Tennessee Chapter No. 21

## *Prize Rolls*

**2 packages dry yeast**
**2 1/2 cups warm water**
**7 teaspoons sugar**
**4 teaspoons salt**
**7 1/2 cups sifted flour**
**1/2 cup melted shortening**

Dissolve yeast in warm water in large bowl. Add sugar and salt; mix well. Combine flour and shortening in bowl; mix well. Add flour mixture to yeast mixture gradually to form soft dough. Place in greased bowl, turning to coat surface. Let rise, covered, until doubled in bulk. Punch dough down. Let stand for 5 minutes. Shape into rolls. Place on greased baking sheet. Let rise, covered, until doubled in bulk. Bake at 400 degrees for 12 to 15 minutes or until lightly browned.
Yield: 40 servings.

**Approx Per Serving:** Cal 105; Prot 2 g; Carbo 17 g; Fiber 1 g; T Fat 3 g; Chol 0 mg; Sod 214 mg.

Wilhelmenia Cofield, *Carolina Cooking*, North Carolina Chapter No. 35

## *Rice Rolls*

**1 envelope dry yeast**
**1/2 cup warm water**
**1 cup milk**
**1/4 cup shortening**
**1/3 cup sugar**
**1 cup cooked rice**
**2 teaspoons salt**
**2 eggs, beaten**
**Flour**

Dissolve yeast in warm water. Scald milk in saucepan. Add to shortening, sugar, rice and salt in bowl; mix well. Add eggs and yeast; mix well. Stir in enough flour to form dough. Knead lightly on floured surface. Place in greased bowl, turning to coat surface. Let stand, covered, overnight. Knead lightly. Roll on floured surface; cut as desired. Place in baking pan. Let rise for 1 1/2 hours or until doubled in bulk. Bake at 425 degrees for 15 to 20 minutes or until golden brown.
Yield: 4 dozen.

Mrs. Jack T. Bell, *Lawfully Good Eating*, Dixie Chapter No. 23

# Desserts

Mississippi Chapter 36

# Apple Mystery Delight

1 can crushed pineapple (20 oz., undrained)
3 c. apples, sliced and peeled
1/2 c. sugar
2 T. lemon juice
1 box yellow cake mix (18 1/4 oz.)
1/2 c. melted butter or margarine
1 c. chopped pecans

Preheat oven to 350°. Lightly grease 8x12-inch baking dish. Pour canned pineapple into dish. Layer apples, 1/4 c. sugar and lemon juice on top of pineapple. Sprinkle fruit layers with cake mix. Top with layers of melted butter, 1/4 c. sugar and chopped pecans. Bake 20 min., then cut with a knife to allow juice to rise over top. Bake 30 min. longer. Serve warm with ice cream or whipped cream. Serves 12.

*Taste of Dixie*, Dixie Chapter No. 23

# Arlene's Apple Pastry

8 to 10 Granny Smith apples
1 1/2 c. sugar
1 1/4 tsp. cinnamon
2 1/2 c. flour
1 tbsp. sugar
1 tsp. salt
1 c. shortening
2 egg yolks
2/3 c. milk
1 c. corn flakes or rice krispies
1 egg white, lightly beaten
1 c. powdered sugar frosting

Preheat oven to 350 degrees.

Peel apples, core and slice. Add sugar and cinnamon. Toss together, coating apples well. Let stand while making the rest.

Mix flour, sugar and salt. Cut in shortening. Mix egg yolks and milk together and add to flour mixture. Work into dough. Roll out 1/2 of dough and fit in jelly roll pan.

Sprinkle 1 cup corn flakes over dough then cover with apples. Roll out rest of dough for top crust. Use egg white to brush on top of crust. Bake 350 degrees for 1 hour. Frost with 1 cup of powdered sugar frosting.

Arlene Zimmer
*A Tablespoon of Pioneering and a Teaspoon of Horses and the Handicapped*
Florida Gold Coast Chapter No. 83

## English Apple Dessert

1 cup self-rising flour
1 teaspoon cinnamon
3 or 4 large tart apples, chopped
1 cup sugar
1 teaspoon cinnamon
1/2 cup butter, softened
1/2 cup packed light brown sugar
2 1/2 tablespoons hot water
3/4 cup chopped pecans

Sift flour and 1 teaspoon cinnamon together. Arrange apples in well-buttered 2-quart baking dish. Sprinkle with mixture of sugar and 1 teaspoon cinnamon. Cream butter and brown sugar in mixer bowl until light and fluffy. Add flour mixture and hot water alternately to creamed mixture, beating well after each addition. Stir in pecans; mixture will be stiff. Spread over apples. Bake at 350 degrees for 1 hour or until top is browned. Yield: 4 to 6 servings.

Lieutenant Dennis L. Tanner, *Lawfully Good Eating*
Dixie Chapter No. 23

## Baklava (Greek Pastry)

3 lbs. walnuts in shell
1 cup. sugar
1 1/2 tsp. cinnamon
1 lb. butter, melted
1 lb. phyllo pastry sheets (from frozen food section of grocery store)

Syrup:

3 c. sugar
2 1/2 c. water

Bring to a boil and simmer for 15 minutes.

Shell walnuts and finely chop the meat. Add sugar and cinnamon. Mix well. Butter a large oblong baking pan. Line pan with 5 sheets of phyllo pastry, buttering each sheet evenly. Spread some of the nut mixture over entire surface, covering evenly. Add 2 buttered pastry sheets and spread with some nut mixture. Continue alternating pastry and nut mixture until only 5 sheets of phyllo pastry are left. Cover the top with the 5 sheets. Be careful to butter each sheet of pastry with the melted butter. With a sharp knife cut baklava into diamond shaped pieces. Bake in 325° oven for 30 minutes on middle shelf of oven. Move to the top shelf for an additional 30 minutes. Remove from oven. Pour the syrup over the hot baklava. Cool and serve. 30 to 36 servings.

Marlene Oestricher, *Pioneers Pots and Pans—1985 Cookbook*
North Florida Chapter No. 39

# Banana Split Dessert Casserole

1 20-ounce can crushed pineapple
3 large bananas, sliced
1/2 cup melted margarine
2 cups graham cracker crumbs
2 cups confectioners' sugar
1 cup margarine, softened
2 eggs
16 ounces whipped topping
1/2 cup chopped pecans
1/2 cup chopped maraschino cherries

Drain pineapple, reserving juice. Pour pineapple juice over banana slices in small bowl; set aside. Spread mixture of melted margarine and graham cracker crumbs in 9x13-inch baking dish. Cream confectioners' sugar, softened margarine and eggs in mixer bowl for 15 minutes or until light and fluffy. Spread into prepared dish. Layer banana slices, pineapple and whipped topping over creamed mixture. Sprinkle with pecans and cherries. Chill until serving time. Yield: 15 servings.

**Approx Per Serving:** Cal 486; Prot 3 g; Carbo 51 g; Fiber 2 g; T Fat 31 g; Chol 28 mg; Sod 330 mg.

Jo Ann Goins, *Carolina Cooking*, North Carolina Chapter No. 35

*Pioneer clowns cheer the day for those less fortunate.*
(Mississippi Chapter No. 36)

## Caramel Fondue

2 (14 oz.) bags caramels
1 (5 oz.) can Carnation evaporated milk
1 (10.5 oz.) bag miniature marshmallows
Assorted cut fruit for dipping — ex. apples, pineapple, cherries, bananas, etc.

Melt caramels in a large double boiler, stir frequently. Stir in milk and marshmallows slowly until completely blended together.

Transfer to fondue pot and serve with cut fruit for dipping. (Toss apples in lemon juice to keep from browning. —Edit.)

Kathy Zane
*A Tablespoon of Pioneering and a Teaspoon of Horses and the Handicapped*
Florida Gold Coast Chapter No. 83

## Charlotte Russe

2 packages ladyfingers
1 envelope unflavored gelatin
$1/4$ cup cold water
$1/2$ cup boiling water
$1/2$ to $3/4$ cup sugar
2 eggs, beaten
1 cup scalded milk
2 ounces bourbon
2 cups whipping cream, whipped

Line springform pan with ladyfingers. Soften gelatin in cold water. Add boiling water; stir until dissolved. Add sugar to eggs gradually, beating constantly. Add milk and gelatin mixture; mix well. Chill until partially set. Fold bourbon into whipped cream in bowl. Fold into gelatin mixture. Pour into prepared pan. Chill until set. Yield: 10 servings.

Friend of the Pioneers, *Lawfully Good Eating*, Dixie Chapter No. 23

### Helpful Hints

Whipped cream will be fluffier and less likely to separate if sweetened with confectioners' sugar instead of granulated sugar.

Flavor whipped cream with cocoa or tint with food coloring for garnishes.

## Chocolate Cheesecake

1¾ cups graham cracker crumbs
½ cup melted butter
½ teaspoon cinnamon
1 cup sour cream
24 ounces cream cheese, softened
¼ cup baking cocoa
1 cup sugar
4 eggs

Combine first 3 ingredients in bowl; mix well. Pack firmly in springform pan. Combine sour cream, cream cheese, baking cocoa and eggs in mixer bowl; mix well. Pour into prepared pan. Bake at 325 degrees for 1¼ hours or until set. Cool in pan. Chill until serving time. Yield: 12 servings.

**Approx Per Serving:** Cal 488; Prot 9 g; Carbo 33 g; Fiber 2 g; T Fat 37 g; Chol 160 mg; Sod 370 mg.

Sue Rivenbark, *Carolina Cooking*, North Carolina Chapter No. 35

## Chocolate Chip Cheesecake

½ c. finely crushed creme filled chocolate sandwich cookies (about 18)
2 to 3 Tbsp. butter or margarine, melted
3 (8 oz.) pkg. cream cheese, softened
1 (14 oz.) can sweetened condensed milk
3 eggs
2 tsp. vanilla
1 c. mini chocolate chips
1 tsp. flour

Combine cookie crumbs and butter. Press firmly on bottom of 9 inch greased springform pan. Beat cheese until fluffy; gradually beat in condensed milk until smooth. Add eggs and vanilla; mix well. Toss ½ cup chips with flour to coat; stir into cheese mixture. Pour into pan; sprinkle remaining ½ cup chips evenly over top. Bake in 350° preheated oven for 1 hour. Cool. Chill thoroughly. Serves 8.

Nella Duckworth, *Bell's Best 3*, Mississippi Chapter No. 36

### A Helpful Hint

Milk chocolate is the best known kind of eating chocolate. It is made by combining the chocolate liquid, extra cocoa butter, milk or cream, sweetening and flavorings.

## Diet Cheesecake

28 ounces low-fat cottage cheese
2 tablespoons lemon juice
3 tablespoons flour
3 eggs
3/4 cup sugar
1/2 cup confectioners' sugar
1/8 teaspoon vanilla extract

Combine cottage cheese, lemon juice, flour, eggs, sugar, confectioners' sugar and vanilla in blender container. Process until smooth. Pour into 9-inch springform pan sprayed with nonstick cooking spray. Bake at 325 degrees for 35 to 40 minutes or until set. Cool to room temperature. Store in refrigerator. Place on serving plate; remove side of pan. Yield: 12 servings.

**Approx Per Serving:** Cal 151; Prot 11 g; Carbo 21 g; Fiber <1 g; T Fat 3 g; Chol 74 mg; Sod 286 mg.
**Dietary Exchanges:** Meat 1 1/2

"*Answering the Call of Those in Need*," Tennessee Chapter No. 21

## Kay Paul's Cheesecake

**Country:** U.S.A. **City:** Linwood, New Jersey. **Relative obtained from:** Sister-in-law. **Brief history:** My sister-in-law and husband served this delicious dessert in their restaurant and it was their customer's favorite.

1 lb. cream cheese
1 c. sugar
4 eggs, beaten
2 tsp. vanilla
3 c. sour cream
2 c. graham crackers
1/4 c. sugar
1 tsp. vanilla
3/4 stick margarine

1. Make crust by mixing graham crackers, 1/4 cup sugar, 1 teaspoon vanilla, and margarine together. Press into 9 inch springform pan and bake 10 minutes at 350°. Cool.

2. Combine cream cheese and 1 cup sugar and beat 10 to 15 minutes; then add beaten eggs, vanilla and sour cream until well blended. Pour into baked crust and bake 40 minutes at 375°.

**Preparation time:** 1/2 hour.
**Cooking time:** 40 minutes.
**No. of servings:** 12.

Ethel M. Paul, *A Taste of Pioneering*
Florida Gold Coast Chapter No. 83

# Freezer Lemon Cheesecake

1 9x13x2-inch graham cracker crust made from graham cracker crumbs and margarine
1 large can evaporated milk, place in freezer until it begins to freeze around edges
1 pkg. lemon jello reg.
1 c. hot water, mix jello and water, let cool but not set
1 large pkg. cream cheese, softened
1 c. sugar
1 t. vanilla

Mix cheese, sugar and vanilla—set aside.

Whip milk like whipped cream, add the cool jello, then add the cheese mixture. Beat all well. Pour over crust and freeze. Eat frozen or thaw 20–30 min.

Ruth Fuller, *Taste of Dixie*, Dixie Chapter No. 23

# Glazed Cheesecake Puffs

24 vanilla wafers
3/4 cup sugar
16 ounces cream cheese, softened
2 eggs
1 teaspoon vanilla extract
1 21-ounce can cherry pie filling

Place vanilla wafers in paper-lined muffin cups. Cream sugar, cream cheese, eggs and vanilla in mixer bowl until light and fluffy. Fill prepared muffin cups 3/4 full. Bake at 375 degrees for 10 to 15 minutes or until set. Cool. Spread pie filling on cooled cheesecakes. Chill until serving time. Yield: 24 servings.

**Approx Per Serving:** Cal 139; Prot 2 g; Carbo 16 g; Fiber <1 g; T Fat 8 g; Chol 41 mg; Sod 84 mg.

Becky Adams, *Carolina Cooking*, North Carolina Chapter No. 35

# *Italian Cheesecake*

1/3 c. dried apricots
1 pkg. Jell-O cheesecake
1 c. cold milk
1 1/2 tsp. grated lemon peel
1/4 c. toasted slivered or sliced almonds
2 Tbsp. chopped maraschino cherries
1 sq. Baker's semi-sweet chocolate, chopped
1 to 2 Tbsp. rum
1/3 c. oleo or butter, melted
3/4 c. Ricotta cheese

Soak apricots in rum; set aside. Mix contents of cheesecake crumb pouch and margarine in 8 inch pie plate or springform pan. Press firmly on bottom and sides.

Combine milk and cheese in medium bowl, mixing until smooth. Add cheesecake filling mixture. Beat on medium speed 3 minutes. Stir in lemon peel, almonds, cherries, chopped chocolate, and apricots with rum. Spoon into crust. Refrigerate until firm, at least 1 hour. Garnish with additional apricots if desired. Makes 8 servings.

Donny Palliser, *Pots, Pans and Pioneers, Volume IV*
Louisiana Chapter No. 24

*Volunteering for Habitat for Humanity in Louisiana.*
(Louisiana Chapter No. 24)

# Praline Cheesecake

1 c. graham cracker crumbs
3 Tbsp. granulated sugar
3 Tbsp. melted butter
3 (8 oz.) pkg. cream cheese, softened
1 1/4 c. dark brown sugar
2 Tbsp. flour
3 eggs
1 1/2 tsp. vanilla
1/2 c. chopped pecans
Maple syrup
Pecan halves

Combine crumbs, 3 tablespoons sugar and butter; press onto bottom of 9 inch springform pan. Bake at 350° for 10 minutes. Blend cream cheese, brown sugar and flour at medium speed with a mixer. Add eggs. Stir in vanilla and nuts. Pour over crumbs. Bake at 350° for 50 to 55 minutes or until set. Cool before removing from pan. Brush with maple syrup and garnish with pecan halves.

Sandi Spears, *Dogwood Delights Volume II*, Dogwood Chapter No. 84

# Easy Cherry Puffs

1 c. butter
1 1/2 c. sugar
4 eggs, beaten
2 c. sifted all-purpose flour
1 tsp. vanilla or almond extract
1 tsp. lemon or orange extract
1 (1 lb. 5 oz.) cherry pie filling

In large mixing bowl, cream together butter and sugar. Add eggs and flour. Mix in extracts; blend well. Spread batter into greased 15 1/2x10 1/2x1 inch pan. Cut surface of batter into 28 squares.

Spoon pie filling in center of each square. (During baking batter puffs around filling.)

Bake at 350° about 25 minutes or until golden brown. Sprinkle with confectioners' sugar. Cool and remove from pan.

Elaine Watley, *Pioneers Pots and Pans—1985 Cookbook*
North Florida Chapter No. 39

## A Helpful Hint

For a delicious topping for cobblers and puddings, mix 1 cup sour cream and 1/2 cup brown sugar. Chill for 1 hour or longer and mix well before serving.

# Chocolate Delight

12 Oreo cookies, crushed
1 lb. cut up pitted dates
3/4 cup water
1 cup heavy cream
1/4 tsp. salt
2 cups small marshmallows
1/2 cup nuts
1/2 tsp. vanilla

Combine dates, water and salt; boil and then simmer 3 minutes. Remove from heat, add marshmallows. Cool. Stir in nuts. Spread over crushed Oreos (reserve 1/4 cup Oreo crumbs for topping), then whipped cream, vanilla, and the 1/4 cup crushed crumbs on top. Cut into squares. Chill and serve.

Evelyn Ratteree, *Secret Recipes of Telephone Pioneers, Volume III*
South Carolina Chapter No. 61

# Blackberry Cobbler

2 pounds blackberries
2/3 cup packed brown sugar
1 teaspoon cinnamon
1 16-ounce package nut bread mix
2 egg whites

Spread blackberries in 9x11-inch baking dish sprayed with nonstick cooking spray. Sprinkle with brown sugar and cinnamon. Prepare nut bread mix using package directions, substituting egg whites for whole egg and omitting oil. Pour over berries. Bake at 400 degrees for 1 hour and 5 minutes or until toothpick inserted in center comes out clean. May substitute other berries for blackberries.
Yield: 12 servings.

**Approx Per Serving:** Cal 87; Prot 1 g; Carbo 21 g; Fiber 5 g; T Fat <1 g; Chol 0 mg; Sod 12 mg.
Nutritional information does not include bread mix.
**Dietary Exchanges:** Fruit 1

"*Answering the Call of Those in Need*," Tennessee Chapter No. 21

# Blackberry-Dewberry Cobbler

5 c. fresh berries
3/4 c. sugar
1 heaping Tbsp. cornstarch
1/8 tsp. salt
2 Tbsp. butter
1 box Pillsbury All-Ready pie crusts
1 Tbsp. lemon juice (optional)
1 Tbsp. milk
1 Tbsp. sugar
Vanilla ice cream

Wash berries thoroughly and drain well. Spread 1 teaspoon flour on one side of pie crust, spreading evenly to all edges of crust; place floured-side down in a 9 inch square baking dish. Press crust evenly to top of baking dish on all sides. Place berries in dish. Combine 3/4 cup sugar, cornstarch, and salt; sprinkle mix over berries. Add lemon juice and dot with butter.

Place second crust over berries, sealing to edge of dish. Brush crust with 1 tablespoon milk and sprinkle with 1 tablespoon sugar. Cut 3 or 4 slits in top of crust. Bake at 425° for 30 to 35 minutes or until crust is golden brown. Serve with ice cream. Yield: 6 servings.

Betty Parks, *Pots, Pans and Pioneers, Volume IV*
Louisiana Chapter No. 24

*Installing a bluebird house in honor of the state's Camp Bluebird.*
(Tennessee Chapter No. 21)

## Fresh Blueberry Cobbler

½ c. sugar
1 Tbsp. cornstarch
4 c. blueberries
1 tsp. lemon juice
1 c. Gold Metal Flour*
1 Tbsp. sugar
1½ tsp. baking powder
½ tsp. salt
3 Tbsp. shortening
½ c. milk

Heat oven to 400°. Blend ½ cup sugar and the cornstarch in medium saucepan. Stir in blueberries and lemon juice. Cook, stirring constantly, until mixture thickens and boils. Boil and stir 1 minute. Pour into ungreased 2 quart casserole; place in oven while preparing biscuit topping. Measure flour, 1 tablespoon sugar, the baking powder and salt into bowl. Add shortening and milk. Cut through shortening 6 times; mix until dough forms a ball. Drop dough by 6 spoonfuls onto hot fruit. Bake, uncovered, 25 to 30 minutes or until biscuit topping is golden brown. Serve warm.

Makes 6 servings.

*If using self-rising flour, omit baking powder and salt.

Suzanne Lord, *Pioneers Pots and Pans—1985 Cookbook*
North Florida Chapter No. 39

## Prize Peach Cobbler

¾ c. flour
⅛ tsp. salt
2 tsp. baking powder
1 c. sugar
¾ c. milk
½ c. margarine
2 c. fresh, sliced peaches
1 c. sugar

Sift flour, salt and baking powder; mix with 1 cup sugar. Slowly stir in milk to make batter. Melt margarine in 8x8x2 inch pan. Pour batter over melted oleo. Do not stir. Carefully spoon over this the peaches and sugar, which have been mixed thoroughly. Bake 1 hour at 325°. Serves 6. Delicious hot or cold. Serve with cream, if desired.

Annie O. Edwards, *Bell's Best 2*, Mississippi Chapter No. 36

# Sweet Potato Cobbler

(Serves 6–8)

**Biscuit dough**
**3 lb. sweet potatoes, sliced**
**1 2/3 c. sugar**
**1 1/2 sticks butter**
**2 c. water**
**1 tsp. vanilla**
**1/4 tsp. nutmeg**
**1/4 tsp. cinnamon**

Grease sides only of round deep pan. Roll out enough dough to line sides of pan. Add half of the potatoes and sprinkle with cinnamon and nutmeg. Sprinkle 1 cup of sugar over this. Roll out some of the dough and cut into small pieces and add for dumplings. Add rest of potatoes, sprinkle with nutmeg and cinnamon. Add a few dumplings. Cut up 1 stick butter and add to mixture. Sprinkle with remaining sugar. Pour in water. Roll out remaining dough for crust and fit loosely over the top. Dot with 1/2 stick of butter and a little sugar. Bake at 300° for 1 1/2 hours.

Lucy Smith, *Dogwood Delights*, Dogwood Chapter No. 84

# Egg Custard

**5 eggs, well beaten**
**1 c. sugar, beat a little more**
**2 c. milk**
**1 tsp. vanilla flavoring**

Pour into unbaked pie crust and sprinkle with nutmeg, bake 1 hour at 300°.

Cynthia Gailey, *Pioneers Pots and Pans—1985 Cookbook*
North Florida Chapter No. 39

## A Helpful Hint

Prevent a "skin" from forming on custards and puddings by placing a piece of plastic wrap directly on the surface after removing from the heat.

## Blender Egg Custard

**3 eggs**
**1 (13 oz.) can milk**
**1 c. sugar**
**3 Tbsp. flour**
**3 Tbsp. melted butter or margarine**
**1/4 tsp. nutmeg**
**1/4 tsp. vanilla**

Blend all ingredients well. Bake in a greased and floured glass pie plate at 350° till light brown.

Lois Moman, *Calling All Cooks two*, Alabama Chapter No. 34

## No-Crust Egg Custard

**1 1/2 cups sugar**
**3 tbsp. flour**
**3 tbsp. butter or margarine (cut in small pieces)**
**3 large whole eggs**
**1 tsp. butter-nut flavoring**

Put all ingredients in mixing bowl and stir with spoon until well mixed. Spray deep pie dish with Pam or Joy and fill with batter. Bake 35 minutes at 350°.

**Variations:** Use vanilla or coconut flavoring with 1/2 to 1 cup coconut. 1/2 cup ground nuts, pecans, walnuts, or almonds.

Good served hot or cold. Whipped cream or Cool Whip may be added but not really needed. Recipe serves 8.

Donna Pettit, *Secret Recipes of Telephone Pioneers, Volume II*
South Carolina Chapter No. 61

## Dump Cake

**1 large can crushed pineapple**
**1 can apple pie filling**
**1 yellow cake mix**
**2 sticks butter**

Mix pineapple and apple pie filling in pan you cook it in. Sprinkle cake mix on top. Cut butter and layer on top of mix. Cook at 350° until light brown. Sprinkle nuts on top. Return to oven until golden brown.

Geraldine Buice, *Dogwood Delights*, Dogwood Chapter No. 84

# Eclair Dessert

**2 4-ounce packages instant French vanilla pudding mix**
**2 1/2 cups milk**
**8 ounces whipped topping**
**12 ounces graham crackers**
**1/4 cup margarine**
**1 cup confectioners' sugar**
**1 tablespoon (heaping) baking cocoa**
**1 to 2 teaspoons milk**
**1 teaspoon vanilla extract**

Beat pudding mix and 2 1/2 cups milk in mixer bowl. Add whipped topping; beat well. Alternate layers of graham crackers and pudding mixture in square dish, beginning and ending with graham crackers. Combine margarine, confectioners' sugar, cocoa, remaining milk and vanilla in microwave-proof bowl. Microwave for 1 minute or until of pouring consistency. Pour over graham crackers. Spread with spoon to cover all. Chill until serving time. Yield: 15 servings.

Dale Reems, *Lawfully Good Eating*, Dixie Chapter No. 23

# Ice Cream

**6 eggs, beaten stiff**
**1 can condensed milk**
**2 small cans evaporated milk**
**1 c. sugar**
**1 tsp. vanilla extract**
**1 tsp. lemon extract**

Combine eggs, sugar, condensed milk and evaporated milk and put in a boiler over medium heat. Cook just until it coats a wooden spoon. Do not cook until it is custard. Add vanilla and lemon extract and pour into hand freezer. Finish filling freezer to 3/4 full with sweet milk. Freeze until hard. It's delicious!

Lou Sparks, *Bell's Best 2*, Mississippi Chapter No. 36

## A Helpful Hint

Dress up homemade or store-bought ice cream with the addition of interesting ingredients. For almond toffee ice cream, add 1/4 cup crushed toffee candy and 1/4 cup chopped toasted almonds to 1 quart of vanilla ice cream. For apple ice cream, add 1 cup apple pie filling to 1 quart of vanilla ice cream or frozen yogurt. For cantaloupe ice cream, add 1 puréed ripe cantaloupe and 1/3 cup sugar to 1 quart of vanilla ice cream.

## *Bits o' Brickle Ice Cream and Sauce*

**2 c., graham cracker crumbs**
**1 stick melted butter or oleo**
**1/2 (7.8 oz.) bag bits o' brickle**
**1/2 gal. vanilla ice cream, softened to spoon easily, but not melted**

Mix Graham cracker crumbs and oleo. Pat in bottom of 9x13 inch pan. Spoon 1/2 of softened ice cream over graham cracker crumbs. Spoon 1/2 bag of bits o' brickle on top. Heap on remaining ice cream; freeze.

Sauce:

**1 1/2 c. sugar**
**1 c. evaporated milk**
**Remaining 1/2 bag bits o' brickle**
**1/4 c. butter or oleo**
**1/4 c. light corn syrup**
**Dash of salt**

Combine sugar, milk, butter, syrup and dash of salt. Bring to boil over low heat; boil 1 minute. Remove from heat and add remaining bits o' brickle. Cool, stirring occasionally; chill. To serve: Stir sauce well and spoon over cut-out squares.

Jan Morrow, *Dining with Pioneers, Volume I*, Tennessee Chapter No. 21

## *Italian Ice Cream Dessert*

**Origin:** Original recipe. **Approximate year created:** 1986. **Brief history:** Could not locate a recipe for spumoni or tortoni and needed to do something in a hurry.

**1/2 gal. vanilla ice cream**
**1 small jar maraschino cherries**
**1 small pkg. slivered almonds**
**1/2 c. coconut**
**1/3 c. Amaretto**

Toast slivered almonds and coconut in a little butter or margarine in small skillet and let it cool. Cut cherries in halves. Mix together and place in container to freeze.

Be innovative: Could add any drained canned fruit, crushed pineapple or chocolate chips. I've crumbled up soft macaroons with great results. You could substitute almond flavoring for Amaretto. Ice cream will be soft.

**Preparation time:** 15 minutes.
**No. of servings:** 8.

Janet Boyd, *A Taste of Pioneering*, Florida Gold Coast Chapter No. 83

## Vanilla Ice Cream Custard Base

2 c. milk
1 c. sugar
1/4 tsp. salt
2 tsp. vanilla
2 eggs, beaten
1 Tbsp. flour
2 c. light cream

Scald milk. Combine 2 beaten eggs, 1 tablespoon flour and the salt. Add the milk and cook over low heat until slightly thickened. Cool and add the cream and vanilla. Yield: 1 1/2 quarts.

**Variation:** For chocolate ice cream, add 2 ounces of unsweetened chocolate to the cold milk and allow to melt as the milk is scalded.

Dee Caillouet, *Pots, Pans and Pioneers, Volume I*
Louisiana Chapter No. 24

## Party Jello

1 c. boiling water
1 pkg. Jello (lime or any flavor)
1 c. vodka (90 proof or less)

Empty 1 package of Jello into mixing bowl. Add 1 cup of boiling water. Stir until dissolved. Add 1 cup vodka. Pour into mold or leave in bowl and refrigerate until it wiggles (sets). Serve when the Washington Redskins play.

Belinda Baker
*A Tablespoon of Pioneering and a Teaspoon of Horses and the Handicapped*
Florida Gold Coast Chapter No. 83

## Low-Fat Popsicles

1 envelope cherry instant drink mix
1 3-ounce package cherry gelatin
3/4 cup sugar
2 cups hot water
2 cups cold water

Combine drink mix, gelatin, sugar, hot water and cold water in bowl, stirring until dry ingredients are dissolved. Pour into desired freezer containers. Freeze until set. Yield: 4 servings.

**Approx Per Serving:** Cal 230; Prot 2 g; Carbo 58 g; Fiber 0 g; T Fat <1 g; <1% Calories from Fat; Chol 0 mg; Sod 56 mg.

Maxine Pinckard, *Calling All Cooks three*, Alabama Chapter No. 34

## *Lemon Lush*

**1½ c. flour—plain**
**¾ c. margarine**

Blend the above ingredients and press into 9x13 inch pan. Bake at 350° for 15 minutes or until brown.

**1 (8 oz.) cream cheese**
**1 c. powdered sugar**
**1 c. Cool Whip**

Blend cream cheese and sugar together. Blend in Cool Whip. Spread over cooled crust.

Put 3 cups milk in mixing bowl and add 2 (3 ounce) packages or 1 (6 ounce) instant lemon pudding mix. Beat 1 minute and spread over cheese mixture, then spread the rest of large carton of Cool Whip over top. Sprinkle with coconut. Refrigerate 1 hour before serving.

Patti Mackesy, *Pioneers Pots and Pans—1985 Cookbook*
North Florida Chapter No. 39

## *Quick Peach Pie*

**2 c. fresh peaches (sweetened and mashed)**
**½ c. sugar**
**½ c. flour**
**½ c. milk**
**1 rounded tsp. baking powder (if plain flour is used)**
**⅔ stick butter**

Cut butter into small casserole. Mix sugar, flour, baking powder and milk to make a running batter. Pour batter over butter. Pour peaches over batter; bake at 350° until brown. Makes about 4 servings.

Florence Toney, *Calling All Cooks*, Alabama Chapter No. 34

### *A Helpful Hint*

Make a party sundae by arranging scoops of different flavors of ice cream in a large bowl. Serve with toppings such as crushed pineapple, coconut, nuts, mandarin oranges, chocolate syrup or strawberry preserves.

# *Pears Amaretto*

**Origin:** My own. **Country:** U.S.A. **City:** North Lauderdale. **Approximate year created:** 1982. **Brief history:** The pears were too hard to eat raw—so I concocted this.

**4 Anjou pears, peeled, sprinkled with lemon juice and kept covered, sliced 1/4 inch thin**
**1/3 c. honey**
**1/3 c. Amaretto**
**1/2 c. dark raisins**
**About 1 c. water**
**Cinnamon**
**Ginger**
**2 Tbsp. cornstarch**
**1/4 c. water**

In deep stainless steel skillet (with cover) put pears, honey, Amaretto, and raisins. Put enough water in so it just peeks through top of pears. Stir around pan gently. Sprinkle (from can) cinnamon and ginger lightly on top of pears. Cover; bring to boil. Reduce heat and simmer 5 to 10 minutes, only till just tender. Stir together cornstarch; add to juice in pan and cook til thickened. (Push aside pears in pan, then spoon thickened juice over pears.) Serve warm or cold.

**Preparation time:** 1/2 hour.
**Cooking time:** 5 to 10 minutes.
**No. of servings:** 5 to 6.

Marita T. Krikorian, *A Taste of Pioneering*
Florida Gold Coast Chapter No. 83

# *Pineapple Cream Cheesecake*

**1 yellow cake mix**
**1 stick oleo**
**1 (15 1/2 oz.) can crushed pineapple**
**1 (8 oz.) pkg. cream cheese**
**1 c. chopped pecans**
**3 eggs, divided**
**1 lb. powdered sugar**

Combine cake mix, oleo, 1 egg and pecans. Press in bottom of greased 13x9 inch pan. Drain pineapple; spread evenly over cake mixture. Mix cream cheese, 2 eggs and powdered sugar; pour over pineapple. Bake in preheated 350° oven for 45 minutes or until golden brown. Cool; cut into small squares to serve as it is very rich. Tastes good, too!

Donald F. Newman, *Pots, Pans and Pioneers III*
Louisiana Chapter No. 24

## Fruit Pizza

1 yellow cake mix
2 eggs
1/2 c. Crisco oil
1/4 c. cold water
1/4 c. brown sugar
1/4 c. granulated sugar
1 tsp. vanilla, butter and nut flavoring
1 c. chopped pecans

Mix all ingredients well with a large spoon, adding pecans last. Spread in 2 (12 inch) pizza pans that have been lined with wax paper. Bake in 200° to 225° oven about 1 1/2 to 2 hours or until golden brown and crust is set well.

Remove from oven and when cool remove wax paper and turn upside in same pizza pan and spread with Cool Whip whipped topping and decorate with fruit of your choice. Fruit may be fresh or frozen. Sprinkle with 1 1/2 cups chopped pecans and coconut.

Cherries, peaches, orange slices, apples, grapes, bananas, etc. Slice like pizza and serve.

Carolyn Voight, *Pioneers Pots and Pans—1985 Cookbook*
North Florida Chapter No. 39

## Apple Pudding

1/2 c. margarine
1 c. sugar
1 c. sifted flour
2 tsp. baking powder
1/4 tsp. salt
1/4 tsp. cinnamon
1 c. milk
2 c. cooked or canned apples, drained

Melt butter in 2 quart casserole. Combine next 6 ingredients to make batter. Pour on butter. Drain apples; pile in center of batter. Bake 375° until batter covers fruit and crust browns, 30 to 40 minutes.

Makes 4 to 6 servings.

Delicious with ice cream or whipped cream. Easy to make.

Lorraine Pinkerton, *Pioneers Pots and Pans—1985 Cookbook*
North Florida Chapter No. 39

# Apricot Pudding

2 c. powdered sugar
1 c. butter
4 eggs, well beaten
1 lb. box vanilla wafers, crushed
2 c. whipping cream
2 c. chopped nuts
2 (No. 2½) cans peeled apricots

Cream butter and sugar; add eggs; beat well. Cook in double boiler till thick. Butter 13x9 inch baking dish; spread ⅔ crumbs over bottom of dish. Pour cooled custard over crumbs and sprinkle 1 cup nuts over custard. Whip cream and spread ½ over nuts. Mash apricots and pour on top of cream. Add remaining cream; sprinkle with nuts and cover with remaining crumbs. Refrigerate for 24 hours. Cut and serve.

Mrs. George Baker, *Dining with Pioneers, Volume II*
*Tennessee Chapter No. 21*

# Banana Pudding

8 oz. pkg. cream cheese
1 can sweetened condensed milk
1 large box instant vanilla pudding
3 c. milk
1 large container Cool Whip
6 or 7 bananas
1 pkg. vanilla wafers

With electric mixer, beat softened cream cheese. Add condensed milk and beat again. (Beat into soft consistency.) Mix pudding and milk. Fold in Cool Whip. (If too thick after mixing, add a little more milk. Mixture needs to soak down into layers.) Layer vanilla wafers, then bananas and pour pudding mix over each layer.

Irene Foster, *Pioneers Pots and Pans—1985 Cookbook*
North Florida Chapter No. 39

## A Helpful Hint

Sprinkle bananas lightly with sugar to keep them from darkening on the top of desserts.

## Bread Pudding

**3 c. bread crumbs**
**2 eggs**
**1/4 tsp. salt**
**1 tsp. vanilla**
**4 c. scalded milk**
**1/2 c. sugar**
**3/4 tsp. nutmeg**
**1/2 c. raisins (optional)**

Soak bread crumbs in milk. Beat eggs until light, add sugar, salt, nutmeg and vanilla. Mix thoroughly with bread crumbs. Pour into baking dish and cook in 350° oven for 1 hour. Serve hot or cold.

Cher White, *Pots, Pans & Pioneers II*, Louisiana Chapter No. 24

## Low-Fat Chocolate Pudding

**2 cups sugar**
**3 tablespoons baking cocoa**
**1/4 cup cornstarch**
**2 cups warm water**
**2 cups milk**
**2 tablespoons butter**
**1 tablespoon vanilla extract**

Combine sugar, baking cocoa and cornstarch in saucepan; mix well. Add 1 cup warm water, stirring until smooth. Stir in 1 cup warm water and milk. Cook over low heat until thickened, stirring constantly. Stir in butter and vanilla. Yield: 6 servings.

**Approx Per Serving:** Cal 375; Prot 3 g; Carbo 77 g; Fiber 1 g; T Fat 7 g; 16% Calories from Fat; Chol 21 mg; Sod 81 mg.

Lyn Jordan, *Calling All Cooks three*, Alabama Chapter No. 34

## Primo's Donut Pudding

**9 donuts**
**1/2 c. sugar**
**2 1/2 c. milk**
**1 Tbsp. lemon flavoring**
**Custard Sauce Topping:**
**3 c. milk**
**2 1/2 c. sugar**
**3 Tbsp. flour**
**Oleo**
**1 Tbsp. lemon flavoring**

Dice donuts in 2 1/2 inch deep pan; sprinkle with sugar. Pour in milk and lemon flavoring. Stir. Bake until golden brown.

**Custard Sauce Topping:** Heat milk and mix sugar with flour and enough melted oleo to dissolve. Add lemon flavoring. Pour topping over pudding and serve.

Chet Wells, *Bell's Best*, Mississippi Chapter No. 36

## *Persimmon Pudding*

**Origin:** North Carolina. **Country:** U.S.A., Alamance County. **Approximate year created:** Around 1900. **Relative obtained from:** Mother (Elsie Ritchie). **Brief history:** Old North Carolina country recipe passed down from mother to daughter.

**2 c. persimmon pulp**
**3 eggs**
**1¼ c. sugar**
**1½ c. flour**
**1 tsp. baking powder**
**1 tsp. soda**
**½ tsp. salt**
**½ c. butter**
**2½ c. canned milk**
**2 tsp. cinnamon**
**1 tsp. ginger**
**½ tsp. nutmeg**
**Pecans or raisins or coconut (optional)**

Peel 5 persimmon (large) and strain pulp. Mix all ingredients together. Bake in greased 13x9x2 inch dish. Bake at 325° for about 1 hour or until firm. Slice when cool.

**Preparation time:** 30 minutes.
**Cooking time:** 60 minutes.
**No. of servings:** 15.

Shirley Tillman, *A Taste of Pioneering*
Florida Gold Coast Chapter No. 83

## *Strawberry Pudding*

**¾ c. sugar**
**3 Tbsp. flour**
**2 c. milk**
**2 eggs, separated**
**40 or more vanilla wafers**
**1½ pt. strawberries**

Wash, stem and slice in halves the strawberries. Mix sugar and flour in saucepan. Add part of the milk and blend until smooth. Add beaten egg yolks and rest of milk. Cook over low heat, stirring constantly, until custard starts to thicken.

Line bottom and sides of baking dish with vanilla wafers. Add a layer of half of the strawberries, then half of the boiled custard. Repeat layer of wafers, rest of strawberries and rest of custard. Beat egg whites until stiff. Add 4 tablespoons sugar and beat well. Spread on top of pudding. Brown in preheated 375° F. oven. Makes 6 to 8 servings.

Pat Gulley, *Dogwood Delights Volume II*, Dogwood Chapter No. 84

# Strawberry Pretzel Dessert

- 3 Tbsp. granulated sugar
- 1/2 c. powdered sugar
- 2 c. crushed pretzels
- 3/4 c. oleo, melted
- 1 (9 oz.) carton Cool Whip
- 1 (8 oz.) pkg. cream cheese
- 2 c. miniature marshmallows
- 1 (6 oz.) pkg. strawberry jello
- 2 1/2 c. boiling water
- 1 (10 oz.) pkg. frozen strawberries

Mix granulated sugar, pretzels and oleo in a 9x13 inch pan; bake 15 minutes in 350° oven. Set aside to cool. Cream softened cheese; add powdered sugar. Fold in Cool Whip; fold in marshmallows. Spread over baked layer. Dissolve gelatin; stir in berries and chill until thick. Spread over cream cheese layer and chill. Serves 16–20 people.

Louise Simpson Maze, *Calling All Cooks*, Alabama Chapter No. 34

# Sweet Potato Pudding

- 2 cups raw sweet potatoes, peeled and grated, or chopped fine in blender
- 1/4 cup melted margarine
- 1/2 teaspoon nutmeg
- 1/2 teaspoon cinnamon
- 1 cup white sugar, (brown sugar may be used)
- 2 eggs, well beaten
- 1/2 cup milk
- 1/2 cup chopped nuts

Grate potatoes. Combine next 5 ingredients. Add milk to well-beaten eggs; blend with potatoes. Pour into greased 1-quart casserole. Top with nuts. Bake at 325° for 1 hour. Serve warm.

Mrs. Fannie Petty, *Secret Recipes of Telephone Pioneers, Volume I*
South Carolina Chapter No. 61

# Pink Cloud

- 8 ounces cottage cheese
- 1 3-ounce package strawberry gelatin
- 1 11-ounce can mandarin oranges, drained
- 1 7-ounce can crushed pineapple, drained
- 12 ounces whipped topping

Combine cottage cheese and dry gelatin in bowl; mix well. Stir in oranges and pineapple. Fold in whipped topping. Chill overnight. Yield: 8 servings.

Friend of the Pioneers, *Lawfully Good Eating*, Dixie Chapter No. 23

# Christmas Strudel

1/2 c. butter
1/2 c. vanilla ice cream
2 c. flour
1 lb. jar apricot jam
1 c. chopped pecans
1 pkg. white raisins

Soften butter and ice cream in a large bowl. Add 2 cups of flour and mix to dough stage. Roll out dough into an oblong shape. On a sheet of plastic wrap place dough (you might want to roll dough out on plastic). Cover with another sheet of plastic and roll into a log (cake roll). Refrigerate overnight.

Preheat oven to 350 degrees. Unroll dough. Remove top plastic cover, In a small bowl, combine jam, nuts and raisins. Spread an even layer over dough. Carefully reroll dough and separate from bottom sheet of plastic. When completely rolled turn seam down. Place on greased sheet. Cut slits halfway through log about 1 inch apart. Bake at 350 degrees for 50 minutes.

Rose Ann Towers
*A Tablespoon of Pioneering and a Teaspoon of Horses and the Handicapped*
Florida Gold Coast Chapter No. 83

# Twinkie Treat

Hostess Twinkies
1 can pie filling (any flavor)
8 oz. Dream Whip
Coconut (optional)
Pecans (optional)

Layer a casserole dish or deep cake pan with Hostess Twinkies. The size of the pan determines the number of Twinkies needed. Pour pie filling over Twinkies. Sprinkle with coconut or pecans if desired. Spread Cool Whip over pie filling. Refrigerate overnight and serve.

Any flavor pudding may be substituted for the pie filling. Try using sliced bananas and banana pudding. *Delicious!!*

Judy Bourque, *Pots, Pans and Pioneers, Volume IV*
Louisiana Chapter No. 24

## A Helpful Hint

Save colories by topping desserts with lightly sweetened nonfat sour cream instead of whipped cream.

# Cakes

FIRST IN SERVICE - FIRST IN FLIGHT
NORTH
CAROLINA
CHAPTER 35
PIONEERS FOR SPECIAL PEOPLE

## *Cherry Chocolate Chip Angel Food Cake*

**1 Duncan Hines angel food cake mix**
**2 unbeaten egg whites**
**1 small jar maraschino cherries, chopped fine**
**1 c. mini chocolate chips**
**1 tsp. almond extract**

Follow directions on the box for the angel food cake, adding 2 egg whites and the liquid from the cherries as part of the water in the recipe. When all are well beaten and ready for the pan, add the chopped cherries and mini chips. Bake as directed.

Delicious served unfrosted or with whipped cream.

Ruth Odom, *Dogwood Delights Volume II*, Dogwood Chapter No. 84

## *Raw Apple Cake*

**1½ c. Wesson oil**
**2 c. sugar**
**3 eggs**
**3 c. cake flour**
**1 tsp. soda**
**3 c. chopped dates**
**1 tsp. salt**
**1 tsp. baking powder**
**1 tsp. cinnamon**
**1 tsp. cloves**
**1 c. chopped nuts**
**3 c. raw apples, chopped**

Beat eggs with Wesson oil and sugar. Add flour, sifted with other dry ingredients. Mix thoroughly. Add dates, nuts and apples. Mix thoroughly. Bake in tube pan for 1½ hours at 325°. Good!

Elizabeth Dodds, *Bell's Best*, Mississippi Chapter No. 36

## *Apple Dapple Cake*

**2 cups sugar**
**1¼ cups oil**
**4 eggs**
**2 cups self-rising flour**
**3 cups finely chopped apples**
**1 cup chopped pecans**
**1 teaspoon cinnamon**
**1 teaspoon vanilla extract**

Cream sugar and oil in mixer bowl until light and fluffy. Add eggs, flour, apples, pecans, cinnamon and vanilla. Beat until smooth. Pour into greased Bundt pan. Bake at 325 degrees for 1 hour to 1¼ hours or until cake tests done. Yield: 16 servings.

**Approx Per Serving:** Cal 385; Prot 4 g; Carbo 42 g; Fiber 1 g; T Fat 24 g; 54% Calories from Fat; Chol 53 mg; Sod 214 mg.

Lola Duffey, *Calling All Cooks three*, Alabama Chapter No. 34

## Applesauce Cake

4 c. flour
1 tsp. allspice
2 c. brown sugar
1 Tbsp. cocoa
1/2 lb. dates
2 tsp. cinnamon
1 tsp. nutmeg
2 c. unsweetened applesauce
1 c. raisins
1/2 lb. figs
1/4 tsp. soda
Few grains of salt
1 c. Crisco
1 bottle maraschino cherries
1 c. nuts

Cream Crisco and sugar; stir in applesauce. Mix dry ingredients; sift into the creamed Crisco and sugar mixture. Flour the fruits and nuts; stir into batter. Pour into a well greased paper lined and floured pan. Bake in a moderate oven (350°). Bake 2 1/2 hours.

Mattie Hammack, *Kentucky Kitchens, Volume I*
Kentucky Chapter No. 32

## Apricot Nectar Cake

1 pkg. Duncan Hines lemon supreme cake mix
3/4 c. oil
1 c. apricot nectar
1/2 c. sugar
4 eggs

Mix all ingredients together. Bake at 325° for 1 hour or until done. Cool cake about 30 minutes before icing.

**Icing:**

2 c. powdered sugar
Juice of 2 lemons

Mix and glaze the cake.

Martha Lewis, *Bell's Best 2*, Mississippi Chapter No. 36

### A Helpful Hint

The top of a layer cake won't slip as you frost it if you hold it in place with a wire cake tester or thin skewers inserted through all layers. Remove the tester just before completing the job.

# Avocado Cake

City: Miami. Approximate year created: 1955. Relative obtained from: Mother.

1 1/3 c. sugar
1/2 c. butter or oleo
2 eggs
1 c. mashed avocado (ripe)
1/2 tsp. cinnamon
1/2 tsp. allspice
1/2 tsp. nutmeg
1/2 tsp. salt
1 1/2 tsp. soda
1/3 c. buttermilk
1/2 c. chopped dates
1/2 c. chopped nuts
1/4 c. raisins
1 1/2 c. flour

Cream sugar, butter, eggs, and avocado; beat. Add spices, salt and soda; add buttermilk, nuts, etc. Add flour; mix well. Pour in 9x13 inch pan and bake at 300° for 1 hour.

**Preparation time:** 1 1/2 hours.
**Cooking time:** 1 hour at 300°.
**No. of servings:** 20 pieces.

Mrs. Dorothy Terwilliger, *A Taste of Pioneering*, Florida Gold Coast Chapter No. 83

# Better than Sex Cake

1 box yellow cake mix
1 box instant vanilla pudding mix
1/2 c. oil
1/2 c. water
6 oz. pkg. chocolate chips
1 German's chocolate bar, grated
8 oz. sour cream
4 eggs

Mix cake mix, pudding mix, oil, water, sour cream and eggs together. Grate chocolate bar and add along with chocolate chips to mixture. Mix by hand. Bake in a tube pan in a 350° oven for 55 minutes. Frost.

**Frosting:**

1 stick butter
1 (8 oz.) pkg. cream cheese
1 box powdered sugar
1 tsp. vanilla
1/2 c. pecans

Cream butter and sugar together and add powdered sugar, vanilla and pecans. Frost cake and then sprinkle grated German's chocolate on top of cake.

Bill Dean, *Kentucky Kitchens, Volume I*, Kentucky Chapter No. 32

# *Black Magic Cake/7 Minute Frosting*

**1 3/4 c. flour**
**2 c. sugar**
**3/4 c. Hershey's cocoa**
**2 tsp. baking soda**
**1 tsp. baking powder**
**1 tsp. salt**
**2 eggs**
**1 c. strong black coffee (or 2 tsp. in 1 c. boiling water)**
**1 c. buttermilk or sour milk (1 tbsp. vinegar in 1 c. milk)**
**1/2 c. vegetable oil**
**1 tsp. vanilla**
**7 Minute Frosting (recipe follows)**

Preheat oven to 350 degrees.

In large mixing bowl combine flour, sugar, cocoa, baking soda, baking powder and salt. Beat in eggs, coffee, buttermilk, oil and vanilla. Beat well. (Batter will be thin.)

Pour into greased and floured round pans. Bake at 350 degrees for 35 to 40 minutes or until cake springs back to touch in center. Remove from oven. Cool, then remove cake from pan to rack and allow to cool completely before frosting. Just tell the kids to wait — and that includes you George!!

**7 Minute Frosting:**

**2 egg whites, room temp.**
**1 1/2 c. sugar**
**1/8 tsp. salt**
**1/3 c. water**
**2 tsp. light corn syrup**
**1 tsp. vanilla**

In the top pan of a double boiler (with water at a gentle boil) begin beating egg whites then add the next 4 ingredients. Beat for 7 minutes (over boiling water) or until thick and smooth. Remove from boiling water and add vanilla. Keep beating until vanilla is well incorporated. Frosting should be really thick and smooth at this point. Cool slightly but don't wait too long.

Denise Cowles
*A Tablespoon of Pioneering and a Teaspoon of Horses and the Handicapped*
Florida Gold Coast Chapter No. 83

## *A Helpful Hint*

For an easy orange frosting, use vanilla frosting mix, substituting orange juice for the water and adding grated orange rind.

## Butterfinger Cake

1 2-layer package yellow cake mix
1 8-ounce jar caramel ice cream topping
1 14-ounce can sweetened condensed milk
2 large Butterfinger candy bars, crushed
16 ounces whipped topping

Prepare and bake cake mix using package directions for 9x13-inch cake pan. Pierce cake several times with handle of wooden spoon. Mix topping and condensed milk in bowl. Pour over cake. Sprinkle with half the candy crumbs. Spread with whipped topping. Sprinkle with remaining crumbs. Chill until serving time. Yield: 15 servings.

**Approx Per Serving:** Cal 401; Prot 5 g; Carbo 63 g; Fiber 1 g; T Fat 15 g; 34% Calories from Fat; Chol 10 mg; Sod 329 mg.

Dot Johnson, *Calling All Cooks three*, Alabama Chapter No. 34

## Chocolate Lovers' Chocolate Cake

1 2-layer package devil's food cake mix
1/2 cup water
1/2 cup oil
1/2 cup packed brown sugar
4 eggs
1 1/3 cups milk chocolate chips, melted
1 cup sour cream
1 tablespoon baking cocoa
1 teaspoon vanilla extract
Confectioners' sugar

Combine cake mix, water, oil and brown sugar in bowl; mix well. Add eggs 1 at a time, mixing well after each addition. Add melted chocolate chips and sour cream; mix well. Spoon into greased bundt pan. Bake at 350 degrees for 55 minutes. Combine baking cocoa, vanilla and confectioners' sugar in bowl. Add enough water to make of glaze consistency. Pour over hot cake. Yield: 16 servings.

Patti Stephens, *Lawfully Good Eating*, Dixie Chapter No. 23

# Cradle Cake

2 c. plain flour
1 Tbsp. baking powder
1/4 tsp. salt
4 eggs, separated (room temperature)
2 c. sugar, divided
2 (1 oz.) sq. semi-sweet chocolate, melted with 2 Tbsp. water for garnish
8 pecan or walnut halves for garnish
1 c. finely chopped pecans or walnuts
1 (1 oz.) sq. unsweetened chocolate, grated
1/2 c. butter or margarine, softened
1 tsp. vanilla
3/4 c. milk

Grease 9 or 10 inch tube pan. Line bottom with waxed paper; set aside. Stir together flour, baking powder and salt; set aside.

In medium bowl, beat egg whites until soft peaks form. Gradually beat in 1 cup sugar until stiff, glossy peaks form. Fold in nuts and grated chocolate. Spread mixture on bottom and 3/4 up sides of pan as though lining it.

In large bowl, cream butter and 1 cup sugar. Beat in egg yolks and vanilla until well blended. Stir in flour mixture alternately with milk. Pour into pan, making sure it is surrounded by meringue on all sides and lower than top of meringue. Bake in preheated 325° oven for 65 to 75 minutes. *Do not invert.* Cool on rack for 25 minutes. Turn out on serving plate. Garnish with melted chocolate and nuts.

Mrs. James (Janie) F. Mathis, *Dogwood Delights Volume II*
Dogwood Chapter No. 84

*Reading to children at Christ the King Center.* (North Carolina Chapter No. 35)

# Creole Cake

1/4 c. ground chocolate
1/2 c. butter or oleo
3 eggs, separated
3/4 tsp. soda
1/2 c. hot coffee
1 1/2 c. brown sugar
2 c. cake flour
1/3 c. sour cream

Blend chocolate with hot black coffee. Cool. Cream butter with sugar. Add egg yolks, 1 at a time, beating after each addition. Add coffee mixture. Add flour. Mix soda in sour cream, add to batter. Beat egg whites until stiff and fold into batter. Bake in 2 greased and floured layer pans at 350° for 30 minutes or 1 long pan about 45 minutes. Prepare the following Creole Frosting.

### Creole Frosting:

1 tsp. instant coffee
1/3 c. soft butter or oleo
1 egg yolk
1/4 c. hot water
2 c. powdered sugar

Dissolve instant coffee in hot water, add butter and beat thoroughly. Add sugar and egg yolk. Beat well. Allow to stand for awhile before putting on cake.

Marie Pamplin, *Pots, Pans & Pioneers II*, Louisiana Chapter No. 24

# German Chocolate Upside-Down Cake

1 cup chopped pecans
1 cup coconut
1 2-layer package German chocolate cake mix
1/2 cup margarine, softened
8 ounces cream cheese, softened
1 1-pound package confectioners' sugar

Combine pecans and coconut in small bowl. Sprinkle in greased 9x13-inch cake pan. Prepare cake mix using package directions. Pour into prepared pan. Cream margarine and cream cheese in mixer bowl until light and fluffy. Add confectioners' sugar; beat until smooth. Spread over batter. Bake at 325 degrees for 1 hour. Cool.
Yield: 15 servings.

**Approx Per Serving:** Cal 570; Prot 5 g; Carbo 82 g; Fiber 1 g; T Fat 27 g; Chol 17 mg; Sod 285 mg.

Molly Alexander, *Carolina Cooking*, North Carolina Chapter No. 35

# *Mississippi Mud Cake*

1 cup butter
1/2 cup baking cocoa
2 cups sugar
4 eggs, slightly beaten
1 1/2 cups flour
Pinch of salt
1 1/2 cups chopped nuts
1 teaspoon vanilla extract
1 1-pound package confectioners' sugar
1/2 cup milk
1/3 cup baking cocoa
1/4 cup butter or margarine, softened
Miniature marshmallows

Combine 1 cup butter and 1/2 cup baking cocoa in saucepan. Cook over low heat until butter melts. Remove from heat. Add sugar and beaten eggs; mix well. Add flour, salt, nuts and vanilla; mix well. Spoon into greased 9x13-inch cake pan. Bake at 350 degrees for 35 to 45 minutes or until cake tests done. Combine confectioners' sugar, milk, 1/3 cup baking cocoa and 1/4 cup butter in bowl, mixing until of frosting consistency. Sprinkle marshmallows over top of hot cake. Spread chocolate frosting over top. Yield: 12 servings.

Mary Mims, *Lawfully Good Eating*, Dixie Chapter No. 23

# *Chocolate Potato Cake*

2 c. flour
3 tsp. baking powder
3/4 c. shortening
2 c. sugar
3 eggs
1 c. warm, mashed Irish potatoes
2 1/2 sq. melted chocolate
3/4 c. milk
1 tsp. vanilla
1 c. chopped nuts

Sift flour, measure and add remaining dry ingredients; sift twice. Cream shortening and sugar until light and fluffy. Add eggs one at a time, mixing well after each addition. Add potatoes and chocolate. Mix well. Add dry ingredients and milk alternately, starting and ending with milk. Add vanilla and nuts. Bake in 3 greased and floured 9-inch pans at 350° until toothpick comes out clean. Frost with favorite chocolate frosting or Seven Minute Icing.

Carrie Teasley, *Dogwood Delights*, Dogwood Chapter No. 84

# Milky Way Cake

**4 large Milky Way candy bars**
**1 stick butter**
**2 c. sugar**
**½ c. vegetable oil**
**4 eggs**
**2 tsp. vanilla**
**1 c. buttermilk**
**2½ c. plain flour**
**½ tsp. soda**
**1 tsp. salt**
**1 c. chopped pecans**

Melt candy bars and butter in double boiler and set aside to cool. Combine sugar, vegetable oil, eggs, and buttermilk. Stir well. Sift together flour, soda, salt and add to milk mixture. Add nuts and vanilla, then add all to cool candy mixture. Bake in 4 layers or oblong pan about 25 minutes at 350°.

## Topping:

**1½ to 2 large Milky Ways**
**1 stick butter**
**2 Tbsp. milk**
**½ box powdered sugar**

Melt candy and butter in double boiler and let cool until you can hold hand on bottom of pan. Add milk and powdered sugar. Mix well and pour over cake.

*Dogwood Delights*, Dogwood Chapter No. 84

# Milky Way Cake

**2 c. sugar**
**2½ c. flour**
**1¼ c. buttermilk**
**1 tsp. vanilla**
**8 Milky Way candy bars**
**1 tsp. soda**
**2 sticks margarine**
**4 eggs**
**1 c. broken pecans**

Melt candy and 1 stick butter in double boiler; set aside. Mix the remaining ingredients as in any other cake. Stir in candy and margarine. Mix well and pour in sheet cake pan. Bake at 350° for 1 hour.

## Icing:

**2½ c. sugar**
**1 c. milk**

Boil to soft ball stage; remove from heat and add 1 cup of marshmallow cream, 1 (6 ounce) package semi-sweet chocolate chips and 1 stick butter. Beat until smooth and cool. Spread on cake.

Evelyn Easley, *Dining with Pioneers, Volume I*, Tennessee Chapter No. 21

## Mounds Cake

Bake and cool 1 box devils food cake mix in 13x9 inch pan.

**Filling:**

**3/4 c. sugar**
**24 large marshmallows**
**1 c. milk**
**14 oz. coconut**

Heat until marshmallows melt. Add coconut; pour over cool cake.

**Topping—Mix in saucepan:**

**1/2 c. milk**
**1 1/2 c. sugar**
**1 stick margarine**
**3 Tbsp. cocoa**
**6 oz. chocolate chips**

Boil 1 minute. Beat until creamy. Pour over coconut mixture.

Shelia Heatherly, *Dining with Pioneers, Volume II*
Tennessee Chapter No. 21

## Surprise Inside Cupcakes

**1 pkg. chocolate cake mix**
**1 (8 oz.) pkg. cream cheese, softened**
**1/3 c. sugar**
**1 egg**
**Dash of salt**
**1 (6 oz.) pkg. semi-sweet chocolate pieces**

Mix cake according to directions. Spoon batter into paper lined muffin pans. Fill cups 1/2 full.

Mix cream cheese with sugar and beat in egg and salt. Stir in chocolate pieces. Drop 1 rounded teaspoon of cheese mixture into the middle of each cupcake. Bake as directed on cake mix box.

Shirley Cody, *Dogwood Delights Volume II*, Dogwood Chapter No. 84

## Texas Sheet Cake

- 3 sticks butter
- 8 Tbsp. cocoa
- 1 c. water
- 6 Tbsp. milk
- 2 c. flour (plain—not self-rising)
- 2 c. sugar
- ½ tsp. salt
- 1 tsp. baking soda
- 2 eggs
- ½ c. sour cream
- 1 box confectioners' sugar
- 1 tsp. vanilla
- 1 c. chopped pecans

Preheat oven to 350°. Bring to a boil 2 sticks butter, 4 tablespoons cocoa, and 1 cup water. Add to 2 cups flour, 2 cups sugar, ½ teaspoon salt, 1 teaspoon baking soda, 2 eggs, and ½ cup sour cream. Mix well. Pour into sheet cake pan. Bake at 350° for 20 to 25 minutes.

**Icing:** Bring to a boil 1 stick butter, 4 tablespoons cocoa, and 6 tablespoons milk. Add to 1 box confectioners' sugar, 1 teaspoon vanilla, and 1 cup chopped pecans. Mix well. Pour on cake as soon as you take out of oven. Let cool before cutting.

Loretta Guidroz, *Pots, Pans and Pioneers, Volume IV*
Louisiana Chapter No. 24

## Texas Sheet Cake

- 2 cups flour
- 2 cups sugar
- 1 tsp. soda
- 2 sticks margarine
- 4 Tbsp. cocoa
- 1 cup water
- ½ cup buttermilk
- 2 eggs
- 1 tsp. vanilla

Sift flour, sugar and soda. Melt margarine, cocoa and water and bring to a rapid boil. Pour over dry ingredients. Add buttermilk, eggs and vanilla. Mix well and pour into a greased and floured 17x11 pan and bake at 350 degrees for 15–20 minutes. While cake is cooking make icing.

**Icing:**

- 1 stick butter
- 4 Tbsp. cocoa
- 6 Tbsp. buttermilk
- 1 lb. 10X powdered sugar
- 1 cup chopped pecans

Bring to a boil butter, cocoa and buttermilk. WATCH! Then remove from heat. Add powdered sugar and beat. Add chopped pecans. Spread on cake while warm. Serves 24.

Carolyn Hanning, *Secret Recipes of Telephone Pioneers, Volume III*
South Carolina Chapter No. 61

# Tudor Turtle Cake

1 package German chocolate cake mix
1 14-ounce can sweetened condensed milk
3/4 cup melted butter
1 14-ounce package caramels
6 ounces semisweet chocolate chips
3/4 cup chopped nuts

Prepare cake mix according to package directions, using 1/3 cup sweetened condensed milk and half the melted butter; mix well. Pour half the mixture into greased and floured 9x13-inch cake pan. Bake at 350 degrees for 10 minutes. Heat caramels, remaining sweetened condensed milk and butter in saucepan until caramels are melted, stirring constantly. Pour over baked batter. Sprinkle with chocolate chips and nuts. Top with remaining batter. Bake for 20 minutes longer or until cake tests done. Frost with milk chocolate icing of your choice.
Yield: 12 servings.

Patricia J. Tudor, *Kentucky Kitchens, Volume II*
Kentucky Chapter No. 32

# Velvet Almond Fudge Cake

1 cup blanched slivered almonds
1 2-layer package chocolate fudge cake mix
1 4-ounce package chocolate instant pudding mix
4 eggs
1 cup sour cream
1/2 cup water
1/4 cup oil
1/2 teaspoon vanilla extract
1/2 teaspoon almond extract
2 cups chocolate chips

Chop almonds; place on baking sheet. Bake at 350 degrees for 3 to 5 minutes or until toasted. Sprinkle 1/2 cup toasted almonds in well-greased 10-inch tube pan. Combine cake mix, pudding mix, eggs, sour cream, water, oil and flavorings in large mixer bowl; mix well. Beat at medium speed for 4 minutes. Fold in remaining almonds and chocolate chips. Spoon into prepared pan. Bake at 350 degrees for 1 hour and 10 minutes or until cake pulls away from side of pan. Do not underbake. Cool in pan for 15 minutes. Invert onto wire rack to cool completely. Place on serving plate. Garnish with whipped topping.
Yield: 16 servings.

**Approx Per Serving:** Cal 401; Prot 6 g; Carbo 48 g; Fiber 2 g; T Fat 23 g; Chol 60 mg; Sod 273 mg.

Mrs. Charles A. Anderson, *Carolina Cooking*
North Carolina Chapter No. 35

# California Cake

1/4 teaspoon salt
1 cup sugar
1 teaspoon lemon extract
1/2 cup butter, softened
1 cup chopped pecans
1 17-ounce package pound cake mix
2 eggs
1 cup sour cream
1 15-ounce can pineapple tidbits, drained

Combine salt, sugar and lemon extract in bowl; mix well. Cut in butter until crumbly and moist. Stir in pecans. Prepare pound cake mix according to package directions using 2 eggs and substituting sour cream for milk. Pour into greased and floured 9x13-inch cake pan. Top with pineapple; sprinkle with crumb mixture. Bake at 325 degrees for 45 minutes or until light brown and cake tests done. Cool. Cut into squares. Yield: 15 servings.

**Approx Per Serving:** Cal 454; Prot 5 g; Carbo 60 g; Fiber 1 g; T Fat 23 g; Chol 52 mg; Sod 265 mg.

Elizabeth Stirewalt, *Carolina Cooking*, North Carolina Chapter No. 35

# Carrot Cake

1 1/2 c. oil
2 c. sugar
4 eggs
2 c. flour
3 c. grated carrots
1 tsp. salt
2 tsp. soda
2 tsp. cinnamon
1/2 c. coconut
1/2 c. raisins

Mix oil and sugar, then add eggs, 1 at a time, beating until thick. Next, add 1 cup flour, salt, soda, and cinnamon. Mix this well with oil, then add other cup of flour, carrots and coconut. Pour in 2 pans and bake at 250° until done (at least 2 hours).

**Icing:**

1 (8 oz.) pkg. cream cheese
1 stick oleo
1 box powdered sugar
1 tsp. vanilla
1 c. chopped pecans
Dash of salt

Mix cream cheese and oleo until soft, then add sugar, vanilla, salt, and nuts.

Rosemary Parker, *Calling All Cooks two*, Alabama Chapter No. 34

# Supreme Carrot Cake

2 cups sugar
4 eggs
1/2 teaspoon soda
2 teaspoons cinnamon
1 teaspoon vanilla extract
3 cups shredded carrots
1 1/4 cups oil
2 cups self-rising flour
Frosting

Combine sugar, eggs, soda, cinnamon, vanilla, carrots and oil in large mixer bowl. Beat at medium speed for 5 minutes. Add flour; mix well. Pour into 3 greased and floured 9-inch round cake pans. Bake at 350 degrees for 30 minutes. Remove to wire racks to cool. Spread frosting between layers and over top and side of cooled cake. Yield: 12 servings.

### Frosting for Supreme Carrot Cake

1 1-pound package confectioners' sugar
8 ounces cream cheese, softened
1/2 cup margarine, softened
1 teaspoon vanilla extract
1 cup chopped pecans
1 7-ounce can coconut

Cream confections' sugar and cream cheese in mixer bowl until light and fluffy. Beat in margarine and vanilla. Stir in pecans and coconut.

**Approx Per Serving:** Cal 887; Prot 7 g; Carbo 105 g; Fiber 3 g; T Fat 51 g; Chol 92 mg; Sod 500 mg.

Sybil P. Peele, *Carolina Cooking*, North Carolina Chapter No. 35

# Coconut Cake

1 pkg. white cake mix
1 tsp. baking powder
1 c. water
4 eggs
1/4 tsp. almond flavoring
1 pkg. instant coconut cream pudding mix
1/2 c. cooking oil
1 tsp. vanilla flavoring
1/4 tsp. butter flavoring

Add baking powder to cake mix and sift. Add pudding mix. Add water, oil, eggs and flavorings, blending well. Beat at high speed for 5 minutes. Bake in 3 greased and floured pans for 30 to 35 minutes at 350°. Frost with Seven Minute Frosting (page 327) and cover with grated coconut. May use spice cake mix and instant vanilla pudding. Ice with caramel icing.

Mrs. Dick Taylor, *Pots, Pans and Pioneers, Volume I*
Louisiana Chapter No. 24

# Coconut Black Walnut Cake

2 c. sugar
4 eggs
1 c. oil
1 c. buttermilk
1 c. coconut
1 c. black walnuts
1/2 tsp. salt
1/2 tsp. soda
1/2 tsp. baking powder
1 tsp. coconut flavoring
3 c. all-purpose flour

Blend together sugar, oil and eggs. Sift flour, salt, soda and baking powder. Add to first mixture with buttermilk. Add nuts, coconut and flavoring. Bake at 325° for 75 minutes in well greased, floured pan (tube pan). When cake is about finished baking, mix together:

2 c. sugar
1 c. water
4 Tbsp. margarine
3 tsp. coconut flavoring

Mix sugar, water and butter. Boil 5 minutes; remove from heat. Add flavoring. While cake is still hot, pour over cake and let stand 4 hours. Insert knife in cake as syrup is poured over cake.

Freddie Pesterfield, *Dining with Pioneers, Volume I*
Tennessee Chapter No. 21

*Collecting over 350 tons of books in Louisville telephone book recycling program.* (Kentucky Chapter No. 32)

# *Fresh Coconut Cake*

1 c. butter
2 c. sugar
3 c. cake flour
3 tsp. baking powder
1/2 tsp. salt
1 c. sweet milk
4 whole eggs
1 tsp. vanilla

**Filling:**

3 Tbsp. sugar
3/4 c. sweet milk
1/4 stick butter or margarine
1/4 c. coconut

**Icing:**

2 c. sugar
1 c. water
1/4 c. white corn syrup
2 egg whites, stiffly beaten
1 tsp. vanilla
1 large coconut, grated

Cream butter and sugar for at least 10 minutes. Sift flour, baking powder and salt together. Alternately add milk and flour to creamed mixture. Beat in 1 egg at a time. Add vanilla. Pour into 3 greased and floured 8 inch layer pans. Bake 25–30 minutes at 350°.

For a moist cake, make a filling by combining sugar, milk, butter and coconut. Heat almost to a boiling point and put mixture over each layer of cake.

Make a divinity icing of last 6 ingredients. Boil sugar, water and corn syrup until mixture spins a thread. Slowly pour boiled mixture over stiffly beaten egg whites. Add the vanilla. Continue beating until spreading consistency is reached. Heap icing and coconut between layers and on top and sides of cake.

Betty Di Palma, *Bell's Best 2*, Mississippi Chapter No. 36

## *A Helpful Hint*

Dress up prepared frosting mixes with some easy variations. For orange frosting, substitute orange juice for the water in a vanilla frosting mix and add a little grated orange rind. For lemon frosting, substitute lemon juice for half the water in a vanilla frosting mix. For mocha frosting, substitute cold coffee for the water in a chocolate fudge frosting mix.

# Rave Reviews Coconut Cake

1 (2 layer size) pkg. yellow cake mix
1 sm. pkg. vanilla instant pudding
1 1/3 c. water
4 eggs
1/4 c. oil
2 c. coconut
1 c. chopped walnuts or pecans

Blend cake mix, pudding mix, water, eggs and oil in large mixer bowl. Beat at medium speed 4 minutes. Stir in coconut and walnuts. Pour into 3 greased and floured 9 inch layer pans. Bake at 350° for 35 minutes. Cool in pans 15 minutes; remove and cool on racks.

## Coconut-Cream Cheese Frosting:

4 Tbsp. margarine
2 c. coconut
1 (8 oz.) pkg. cream cheese
2 tsp. milk
3 1/2 c. confectioners' sugar
1/2 tsp. vanilla

Melt 2 tablespoons margarine in skillet. Add coconut; stir constantly over low heat until golden brown. Spread coconut in paper towel to cool. Cream 2 tablespoons margarine with cream cheese. Add milk; beat in sugar gradually. Blend in vanilla; stir in 1 3/4 cups of the coconut. Spread on tops of cake layers. Stack and sprinkle with remaining coconut.

Donna Browning, *Kentucky Kitchens, Volume I*
Kentucky Chapter No. 32

*Environmental project at Elaine Clark Center.*
(Dogwood Chapter No. 84)

## *Coconut Sour Cream Cake*

Make 1 package Duncan Hines butter flavored cake mix according to directions on package. I bake mine at 335° for 25 minutes. Cool and slice each layer in half for filling.

**Filling:**

**2 c. granulated sugar**
**2 (8 oz.) pkg. sour cream**
**2 (6 oz.) pkg. frozen coconut**

Stir well and put between split layers of cake. Save about a cup or little more for icing to go on top and sides. Set aside in freezer or refrigerator until ready to put icing on.

**Icing**: Take the saved filling; add 2 cups Cool Whip. Spread on cake. Keep cake in refrigerator.

Can make same cake and use drained (chilled) pineapple instead of coconut.

Mac McCuan, *Bell's Best*, Mississippi Chapter No. 36

## *Doodle Cake*

**2 cups self-rising flour**
**2 cups sugar**
**2 eggs**
**1 20-ounce can crushed pineapple**
**1½ cups sugar**
**½ cup margarine**
**1 5-ounce can evaporated milk**
**1 cup coconut**
**1 cup chopped pecans**

Combine flour, 2 cups sugar, eggs and pineapple in bowl; mix well. Pour into greased and floured 9x13-inch cake pan. Bake at 350 degrees for 25 minutes or until cake tests done. Combine 1½ cups sugar, margarine and evaporated milk in saucepan. Bring to a boil. Boil for 3 minutes, stirring constantly. Remove from heat. Stir in coconut and pecans. Pour over warm cake. Yield: 12 servings.

Judy Seeders, *Kentucky Kitchens, Volume II*, Kentucky Chapter No. 32

### *A Helpful Hint*

Substitute yogurt for milk, sour cream, butter or margarine in uncooked frosting.

# *Friendship Cake*

**1 can peaches with juice**
**2½ c. sugar**
**1½ c. starter**

Place in a gallon container, loosely covered. Leave at room temperature. Stir each day for 10 days.

*On tenth day, add:*
**1 large can chunk or grated pineapple**
**2½ c. sugar**

Stir each day for 10 days. On twentieth day, add: 2 (8 ounce) jars maraschino cherries, drained. Add no sugar. Stir each day for 10 days. On thirtieth day, drain mixture well. Divide juice into 1½ cups to give to friends. Should be 4 starters.

## Cake Recipe:

**1 box yellow cake mix**
**1 box vanilla instant pudding**
**1 c. chopped nuts**
**⅓ c. coconut**
**1½ c. drained fruit**
**⅔ c. cooking oil**
**4 eggs**
**1 c. raisins (that have been "plumped" in boiling water for 15 minutes and drained)**

Mix cake according to package directions. Stir in fruit and nuts. Bake in well greased and floured Bundt pan at 350° for 40 to 60 minutes.

You should have approximately 3 cups fruit remaining. This cake freezes well; should you want to use your fruit in cake. The brandied fruit is good as an ice cream topping or the following dessert.

Mix 1½ sticks melted margarine, 4 tablespoons sugar, 1½ cups flour and 1 cup chopped pecans. Spray 9x13 inch baking dish with Pam. Mixture is pressed firmly into dish and baked for 20 to 25 minutes or until golden brown, at 350°.

## Filling:

**1 large pkg. cream cheese**
**2 large pkg. Cool Whip**
**1 lb. powdered sugar**

Spread over cooled crust. Top with fruit. Dab with more Cool Whip and sprinkle with toasted pecans.

Margarete Miller, *Kentucky Kitchens, Volume I*, Kentucky Chapter No. 32

# Friendship Cake

1 2-layer package white cake mix
1½ cups Friendship Cake Starter
⅔ cup oil
4 eggs
1 cup chopped pecans

Combine cake mix, Friendship Cake Starter, oil and eggs in bowl; mix well. Stir in pecans. Pour into greased and floured bundt pan. Bake at 325 degrees for 1 hour. Cool in pan for several minutes. Invert onto serving plate. Yield: 12 servings.

**Approx Per Serving:** Cal 551; Prot 5 g; Carbo 82 g; Fiber 1 g; T Fat 24 g; Chol 71 mg; Sod 286 mg.

## Friendship Cake Starter

1 16-ounce can fruit cocktail
1 16-ounce can peaches
2½ cups sugar
1 20-ounce can pineapple tidbits
2½ cups sugar
1 8-ounce jar maraschino cherries
2½ cups sugar

Combine fruit cocktail with juice, peaches with juice and 2½ cups sugar in large glass jar; stir with wooden spoon until sugar is dissolved. Cover. Let stand at room temperature. Stir each day for 10 days. Add pineapple with juice and 2½ cups sugar; mix well. Stir each day for 10 days. Add cherries with juice and remaining 2½ cups sugar; mix well. Stir each day for 10 days. Store in refrigerator May store in refrigerator indefinitely. Yield: enough for 7 cakes.

**Approx Per Serving:** Cal 1021; Prot 1 g; Carbo 264 g; Fiber 2 g; T Fat <1 g; Chol 0 mg; Sod 15 mg.

Edna M. Barham, *Carolina Cooking*, North Carolina Chapter No. 35

## A Helpful Hint

Fruitcakes can be stored indefinitely. Wrap them in cloths soaked in brandy or wine and then in foil. Store them in an airtight container in a cool place.

# Light-as-a-Feather Gingerbread

- 2 cups flour
- 3/4 teaspoon salt
- 1/2 teaspoon soda
- 1 1/4 teaspoons baking powder
- 1 1/4 teaspoons ginger
- 1 1/4 teaspoons cinnamon
- 1/2 teaspoon cloves
- 1/2 to 2/3 cup oil
- 2 eggs
- 1 1/3 cups molasses
- 1/2 cup boiling water
- Lemon Sauce

Sift flour, salt, soda, baking powder, ginger, cinnamon and cloves into large bowl. Stir in enough oil to make mixture crumbly. Add eggs; beat well. Combine molasses and boiling water in bowl; mix well. Add 3/4 cup molasses mixture to flour mixture; beat until smooth. Add remaining molasses mixture, stirring just until well-mixed. Pour into greased 8-inch square baking pan. Bake at 325 degrees for 1 hour or until gingerbread tests done. Serve warm with Lemon Sauce.
Yield: 16 servings.

**Lemon Sauce**

- 2/3 cup sugar
- 1 1/4 tablespoons flour
- 1/8 teaspoon salt
- 1 1/4 cups boiling water
- 1 1/2 tablespoons butter, softened
- 1 1/2 tablespoons lemon juice

Combine sugar, flour and salt in saucepan; mix well. Stir in boiling water and butter. Bring to a boil, stirring constantly. Boil for 5 minutes. Stir in lemon juice.

**Approx Per Serving:** Cal 247; Prot 2 g; Carbo 36 g; Fiber <1 g; T Fat 11 g; Chol 30 mg; Sod 211 mg.

Sybil P. Peele, *Carolina Cooking*, North Carolina Chapter No. 35

# Gingerbread

- 4 cups flour
- 1 cup sugar
- 1 tsp. salt
- 1 tsp. soda
- 1 1/2 tsp. ginger
- 1 tsp. cinnamon
- 3 eggs
- 1 cup molasses
- 1 cup melted Crisco
- 1 cup buttermilk
- 1 cup seedless raisins

Mix and bake at 350° for 40 to 50 minutes.

Lois Oxendine, *Secret Recipes of Telephone Pioneers, Volume II*
South Carolina Chapter No. 61

# Harvest Loaf Cake

**Approximate year created:** 1966. **Brief history:** Pillsbury Bake Off. First cake I baked was taken to Westchester Telephone Office while being built. They had no snack bar—became their favorite. This recipe has been taken or sent to 15 different states—Do I say more.

**Cake:**

- 1¾ c. flour
- 1 tsp. soda
- 1 tsp. cinnamon
- ½ tsp. salt
- ½ tsp. nutmeg
- ¼ tsp. ginger
- ¼ tsp. ground cloves
- ½ c. butter (1 stick)
- 1 c. sugar
- 2 eggs
- ¾ c. canned or cooked pumpkin
- ¾ c. semi-sweet chocolate morsels
- ¾ c. finely chopped walnuts

**Spice Glaze:**

- ½ c. sifted confectioners' sugar
- ⅛ tsp. nutmeg
- ⅛ tsp. cinnamon
- 1 to 2 Tbsp. cream

Cake: Grease and flour 9x5x3 inch pan. Combine flour with soda, salt, and spices. Cream butter in large mixing bowl. Gradually add sugar; cream at high speed of mixer until light and fluffy. Blend in eggs, beating well. At low speed, add dry ingredients alternately with pumpkin, beginning and ending with dry ingredients. Blend well after each addition. Stir in chocolate chips and walnuts. Pour into pan. Bake at 350° for 65 to 75 minutes until cake springs back when touched lightly in center. Cool. Drizzle with glaze. Let stand 6 hours before slicing.

**Spice Glaze:** Combine confectioners' sugar, nutmeg and cinnamon. Blend in cream until the consistency of a glaze.

If using self-rising flour, omit salt. Reduce soda to ½ teaspoon.

If desired, 2 teaspoons pumpkin pie spice may be substituted for cinnamon, nutmeg, ginger, and cloves.

**Cooking time:** 65 to 75 minutes.
**No. of servings:** 1 large loaf.

Alice Moore, *A Taste of Pioneering*, Florida Gold Coast Chapter No. 83

## A Helpful Hint

Dust flour in greased cake pans with a new powder puff.

# Georgia Cake

1½ c. sugar
5 eggs
2 sticks margarine
1 box graham crackers
1 large can or pkg. coconut
1 c. finely chopped pecans
½ c. milk

Finely crush crackers and mix all ingredients. Pour into three 9-inch greased and floured pans. Bake 30–40 minutes at 350°.

**Filling:**

1 stick margarine
1 (No. 2) can crushed pineapple
1 c. chopped pecans
1 box confectioners' sugar

Drain pineapple. Save the juice and pour over the layers before icing. Mix pineapple and margarine. Heat, then cool. Add nuts and confectioners' sugar. Beat, then spread between layers and on top.

Carrie Teasley, *Dogwood Delights*, Dogwood Chapter No. 84

# Harvey Wallbanger Cake

Orange cake mix (2 layers)
3¾ oz. size vanilla pudding
4 eggs
½ c. orange juice
½ c. Liquore Galliano
2 Tbsp. vodka
½ c. cooking oil

In a large bowl, combine cake mix and pudding. Add eggs, oil, orange juice, Liquore Galliano and vodka. Beat on low speed of electric mixer for ½ minute; beat on medium speed for 5 minutes, scraping bowl frequently. Pour into greased and floured 10 inch Bundt pan. Bake at 350° for 45 minutes. Cool in pan for 10 minutes. Remove and pour on icing while cake is still warm.

**Icing:**

1 c. sifted confectioners' sugar
1 Tbsp. orange juice.
1 Tbsp. Liquore Galliano
1 tsp. vodka

Mix all of the preceding well.

Peggy Hunter, *Kentucky Kitchens, Volume I*, Kentucky Chapter No. 32

## Hummingbird Cake

3 cups flour
2 cups sugar
1 teaspoon salt
1 teaspoon baking soda
1 teaspoon cinnamon
3 eggs, beaten
1½ cups oil
1½ teaspoons vanilla extract
1 8-ounce can crushed pineapple
1 cup chopped nuts
2 cups chopped ripe bananas
1 cup butter, softened
16 ounces cream cheese, softened
2 1-pound packages confectioners' sugar
2 teaspoons vanilla extract
1 cup chopped nuts

Combine flour, sugar, salt, baking soda and cinnamon in large bowl. Add eggs and oil, stirring until moistened. Stir in vanilla, pineapple, 1 cup nuts and bananas. Pour into 3 greased 9-inch cake pans. Bake at 350 degrees for 25 minutes or until layers test done. Cool in pans for several minutes; remove to wire rack to cool completely. Cream butter, cream cheese, confectioners' sugar and 2 teaspoons vanilla in mixer bowl until light and fluffy. Spread over side and top of layers. Sprinkle with additional nuts. Yield: 12 servings.

Jane Snider, *Lawfully Good Eating*, Dixie Chapter No. 23

## Hummingbird Cake

2 c. chopped bananas, optional
8 oz. can crushed pineapple
1 c. chopped apple
1 c. chopped nuts
2 c. plain flour
2 c. sugar
3 eggs
1¼ c. oil
1½ tsp. vanilla flavoring
1 c. coconut
1 tsp. salt
1 tsp. cinnamon
1 tsp. soda

Mix dry ingredients in one bowl. Mix liquid in another. Combine the two and bake in a bundt pan at 350° for 1 hour, 10 minutes.

Icing:

8 oz. pkg. cream cheese
1 box powdered sugar
1 stick margarine or butter
1 tsp. vanilla

Beat all ingredients until creamy.

Irene Foster, *Pioneers Pots and Pans—1985 Cookbook*
North Florida Chapter No. 39

## Huntsville Bar Cake

2 c. sugar
1 stick butter or oleo
1/2 c. shortening
4 eggs
2 c. all-purpose flour
1/2 tsp. soda
1/2 tsp. baking powder
1/4 tsp. salt
1 c. buttermilk
1 tsp. vanilla
1/2 tsp. butter flavor (opt.)
Rum Syrup

Cream sugar, butter and shortening until smooth and creamy. Add one egg at a time, beating after each. Add mixture of dry ingredients alternately with buttermilk, beginning and ending with dry ingredients. Stir in vanilla and butter flavor. Bake in greased, floured pan in preheated 325° oven for 30 minutes or until cake tests done. Let cool in pan. Pierce cake several times across top with toothpick and drizzle with Rum Syrup.

**Rum Syrup:**

1 c. sugar
1/2 c. water
1 tsp. rum flavor or 1/4 c. rum

Combine sugar and water; bring to boil Cool; add rum flavor or rum. When cool, drizzle over pierced cake.

Julia Stuart, *Pots, Pans and Pioneers III*, Louisiana Chapter No. 24

## Italian Cream Cake and Frosting

1 stick margarine
1/2 cup vegetable shortening
2 cups sugar
5 egg yolks
2 cups plain flour
1 tsp. soda
1 cup buttermilk
1 tsp. vanilla
1 cup chopped pecans or walnuts
5 egg whites
1 cup flaked coconut

Beat egg whites; set aside. Cream margarine and shortening. Add sugar and beat smooth. Add egg yolk and beat. Combine flour and soda. (Sift flour 3 times.) Add alternately with buttermilk the flour-soda mixture. Stir in vanilla. Add coconut and nuts. Fold in egg whites. Pour into three 9-inch greased pans. Bake at 350 degrees for 25 minutes.

**Frosting:**

**8-oz. pkg. cream cheese**
**1 box 10X sugar**
**½ stick margarine**
**1 tsp. vanilla**
**¾ to 1 cup pecans, chopped**

Beat cream cheese and margarine until smooth. Add sugar and vanilla. Mix well and frost top and sides of cake. Sprinkle with nuts.

Eva Perry, *Secret Recipes of Telephone Pioneers, Volume III*
South Carolina Chapter No. 61

# Carolina Jam Cake

**1 cup margarine, softened**
**1 cup sugar**
**6 eggs**
**1 large jar blackberry jam**
**1 small jar strawberry jam**
**3 cups unsifted, self-rising flour**
**1 Tbsp. soda**
**2 tsp. each cinnamon and allspice (ground)**
**½ tsp. ground cloves**
**1 cup and a tad buttermilk**
**Maple flavoring**

Preheat oven 350 degrees. In mixer bowl beat margarine and sugar until creamy. Add eggs, one at a time, stirring well after adding each one. Stir in jams. Stir together dry ingredients. Add alternately to jam mixture with buttermilk. Mix well. Bake in 3 greased pans, lined with wax paper. Bake 40–50 minutes. Cool until cold to touch.

**Maple Frosting:**

**6 cups sifted confectioners' sugar**
**1 8-oz. pkg. cream cheese, room temperature**
**dash salt**
**2 Tbsp. milk**
**2 tsp. maple flavoring**

Beat cheese until fluffy. Add sugar, salt and flavoring with 1 tsp. milk, mixing well. If you wish frosting thinner, you may add more milk, teaspoon at a time. Yummy! Yummy!

Sarah Connell, *Secret Recipes of Telephone Pioneers, Volume III*
South Carolina Chapter No. 61

# *Kentucky Jam Cake*

**1¾ cups flour**
**1½ cups sugar**
**1 teaspoon soda**
**1 teaspoon baking powder**
**½ teaspoon salt**
**1 teaspoon cinnamon**
**1 teaspoon nutmeg**
**1 teaspoon allspice**
**½ teaspoon cloves**
**3 eggs**
**1 cup oil**
**1 cup blackberry jam**
**1 cup buttermilk**
**1 teaspoon vanilla extract**
**1 cup finely chopped pecans**

Combine flour, sugar, soda, baking powder, salt and spices in large mixer bowl; mix well. Add eggs and oil, beating well. Add jam, buttermilk and vanilla; beat for 8 minutes. Stir in pecans. Pour into 3 greased and floured 9-inch cake pans. Bake at 350 degrees for 40 minutes or until cake tests done. Cool in pans. Remove to serving plate. Spread Vanilla Frosting between layers and on top and side of cake. Yield: 16 servings.

## Vanilla Frosting

**¼ cup margarine, softened**
**½ teaspoon salt**
**2 teaspoons vanilla extract**
**¼ cup milk**
**3 cups confectioners' sugar**

Combine margarine, salt, vanilla, milk and 1 cup confectioners' sugar in bowl; mix well. Add remaining confectioners' sugar; beat until smooth and creamy.

Georgia B. Flora, *Kentucky Kitchens, Volume II*
Kentucky Chapter No. 32

# *Mama's Jam Cake*

1 c. brown sugar
$1/2$ c. oleo or butter
2 eggs
2 c. cake flour
1 c. blackberry jam with seeds
1 Tbsp. baking soda
2 Tbsp. cocoa
$1 1/4$ c. buttermilk
$1 1/2$ tsp. allspice
$1/2$ tsp. cinnamon
$1/2$ tsp. cloves
$1/2$ tsp. vanilla
1 tsp. lemon flavoring
$1/2$ c. raisins
$1/2$ c. chopped pecans

Cream brown sugar and oleo; add beaten eggs. Mix all dry ingredients; add to sugar mixture. Add buttermilk, vanilla and lemon flavoring. Now, add jam, raisins and nuts; mix well by hand. Pour into 2 cake pans and bake at 350° for 20–25 minutes or until done. It's best iced with caramel icing.

Lorene Elkins, *Pots, Pans and Pioneers III*
Louisiana Chapter No. 24

# *Julekaker*

(Norwegian Christmas Cake)

2 eggs
$1 1/4$ c. milk
$1/4$ lb. butter or margarine
3 c. plain flour
2 c. raisins
2 pkg. dry yeast
1 c. sugar
3 tsp. ground cardamom

Beat eggs in medium sized bowl. Mix raisins and all dry ingredients together in a large bowl. Heat butter and milk until lukewarm and add carefully to the egg mixture. Add the liquid mixture to the dry ingredients. Pour into a large buttered loaf pan. The mixture should fill the pan more than halfway. Bake at 350° for 45 minutes or until done. Test with a toothpick.

Mickey Fennelly, *Dogwood Delights*, Dogwood Chapter No. 84

## Lady Baltimore Cake

1 c. shortening
1½ c. sugar
5 eggs
Pinch of salt
1½ c. milk
3 tsp. baking powder
3 c. flour

Cream sugar and shortening. Mix baking powder with flour and salt. Add eggs, one at a time, saving 2 yolks for filling. Alternate milk with flour. Bake at 350° for 45 minutes. If you want a white cake, use only egg whites.

**Frosting:**

2 egg yolks
2 c. sugar
3 Tbsp. flour
1½ c. milk
1 Tbsp. butter
1 c. pecans
1 c. raisins
1 c. coconut

Combine beaten egg yolks, sugar and flour. Add milk and butter. Cook in double boiler until thick. Remove from heat; add pecans, raisins, and coconut. Mix well. Frost cake after cool.

Kathryn Garrett, *Dogwood Delights*, Dogwood Chapter No. 84

## Love Cake

8 egg whites
1 c. sweet milk
1 c. butter or oleo
1 tsp. lemon extract
2 c. sugar
3 tsp. baking powder
3 c. flour

Cream butter and sugar. Sift baking powder with flour and add alternately with milk. Beat egg whites stiff and add to mixture. Add lemon flavor. Mix well and bake in floured and greased cake tins at 350° until done.

**Icing:**

8 egg yolks
1 c. coconut
1 c. pecans, chopped
1 c. butter
1 c. raisins
1 c. sugar

Beat egg yolks very lightly. Put butter and sugar in the top of a double boiler. As soon as the butter melts, mix with sugar; add egg yolks and cook until thick. Take from fire and add pecans, coconut and raisins. Ice cake. Sprinkle top with dry coconut.

Betty Harman, *Pots, Pans and Pioneers, Volume I*
Louisiana Chapter No. 24

# 1–2–3–4 Cake

1 c. shortening
1 c. milk
2 c. sugar
3 c. flour
3 tsp. baking powder
4 eggs
1 tsp. vanilla

Cream shortening and sugar. Separate eggs; add beaten yolks to mixture and beat well. Add flour and baking powder alternately with milk. Add vanilla; fold in stiffly beaten egg whites. Bake in tube pan at 325° for approximately 1 hour 10 minutes, or may be baked in two 9 inch layer pans.

Mary Norris, *Calling All Cooks*, Alabama Chapter No. 34

# Orange Slice Cake

1 c. butter or oleo
2 c. sugar
1 tsp. soda
2 small cans coconut
1 small pkg. dates, chopped
2 c. pecans, chopped
4 eggs
1/2 c. buttermilk
1 3/4 c. plain flour
2 Tbsp. grated orange peel
2 c. candy orange slices, chopped

Mix as any other cake. Bake at 250° until done in tube pan. (It takes a little longer to bake this cake than other cakes; test after 1 hour.)

Glaze:

2/3 c. fresh orange juice
1 2/3 c. powdered sugar

Mix and pour over hot cake. Leave in pan until completely cool.

Yvonne Roberson, *Bell's Best*, Mississippi Chapter No. 36

## A Helpful Hint

For a frosted cake with a nice appearance, brush loose crumbs from layers and place 1 layer rounded side down on plate. Spread with frosting and add remaining layer rounded side up. Frost side of cake with up and down motions of spatula and frost top last, adding swirls as desired.

## Tiny Orange Cupcakes

1/2 cup shortening
1 cup sugar
2 eggs, at room temperature
2 cups flour
1 teaspoon soda
1/2 teaspoon salt
2/3 cup buttermilk
1/2 teaspoon vanilla extract
2/3 cup chopped pecans
Juice and rind of 3 oranges
1 1/2 cups sugar

Cream shortening and 1 cup sugar in mixer bowl until light and fluffy. Add eggs; beat well. Sift flour, soda and salt together. Add to creamed mixture alternately with mixture of buttermilk and vanilla, beating well after each addition. Stir in pecans. Fill ungreased miniature muffin cups 1/3 full. Do not overfill muffin cups. Bake at 375 degrees for 10 to 12 minutes or until tops spring back when touched. Combine orange juice and rind with remaining 1 1/2 cups sugar in saucepan. Cook until sugar dissolves, stirring constantly. Spoon hot gaze over hot cupcakes in muffin cups to fill cups. Cool in pans. Loosen edges with knife; remove to serving plate. May be frozen between layers of waxed paper.
Yield: 84 servings.

**Approx Per Serving:** Cal 56; Prot 1 g; Carbo 9 g; Fiber <1 g; T Fat 2 g; Chol 5 mg; Sod 26 mg.

Ovid Smith, *Carolina Cooking*, North Carolina Chapter No. 35

## Better Than Sex Cake

1 box yellow cake mix (without pudding in mix)
1 22-oz. can crushed pineapple with juice
1 cup sugar
1 6-oz. pkg. vanilla pudding mix (not instant)
1 9-oz. container Cool Whip
1 can coconut

Prepare cake by directions using 9x13 pan. Bake at 350 degrees until done. Remove and punch holes all over surface of cake with fork. While cake bakes, mix together pineapple and sugar, heat until sugar dissolves. Spoon the mixture over baked cake after holes are punched. Make up pudding mix and cook. When thick, spoon over cake. Chill. When chilled, spread cake with whipped cream. Sprinkle coconut over top. Keep refrigerated.

Betty O. Hayes, *Secret Recipes of Telephone Pioneers, Volume III*
South Carolina Chapter No. 61

# Celestial Snow Cake

3/4 cup oil
4 eggs
1 11-ounce can mandarin oranges
1 cup chopped pecans
1 2-layer package yellow butter cake mix
1 cup confectioners' sugar
1 8-ounce can crushed pineapple
8 ounces whipped topping
1 cup sour cream

Combine oil, eggs, undrained mandarin oranges, pecans and cake mix in bowl; mix well. Spoon into 2 greased and floured 9-inch cake pans. Bake at 375 degrees for 20 to 25 minutes. Cool in pans for 10 minutes. Remove to wire rack to cool completely. Combine confectioners' sugar, undrained pineapple, whipped topping and sour cream in bowl; mix with spoon. Spread between layers and over top of cake.
Yield: 16 servings.

Dawson County Sheriff's Department, *Lawfully Good Eating*
Dixie Chapter No. 23

# Pineapple Upside Down Cake

1 stick butter
1 c. dark brown sugar
1 (1 lb. 4 oz.) can sliced pineapple
Maraschino cherry halves
1 c. water
1 pkg. Duncan Hines pineapple supreme cake mix
1/2 c. Crisco oil
4 eggs
1 (6 oz.) box Jell-O instant pudding (vanilla or pineapple)

Melt butter in a 13x9 inch pan; sprinkle brown sugar evenly in pan. Drain pineapple slices; arrange slices and cherry halves on the sugar mixture. Mix cake mix, pudding, water, oil and eggs; blend until moistened. Beat 2 minutes at medium speed; do not overbeat. Pour batter over fruit. Bake at 350° for about 50 minutes or until tests done with toothpick. Let stand 5 minutes to allow topping to set. Turn upside down onto large platter.

Jacque Lamille, *Pots, Pans and Pioneers III*, Louisiana Chapter No. 24

# Pistachio Nut Cake

**3/4 c. chocolate chips**
**3/4 c. chopped nuts**
**1 pkg. pistachio nut pudding mix**
**1 pkg. yellow cake mix**
**1/2 c. sugar**
**1/2 c. oil**
**1 c. water**
**5 eggs**

Grease tube pan and sprinkle nuts and chocolate chips in bottom of pan. Blend and mix above ingredients for 2 minutes in electric mixer at medium speed. Take out 1 cup of batter and mix with one 5 ounce can chocolate syrup. Pour batter into cake pan, then pour over the 1 cup batter around the top. Bake 1 hour at 350°.

Dora T. Tidwell, *Bell's Best 2*, Mississippi Chapter No. 36

# Basic Pound Cake

**2 cups flour**
**2 cups sugar**
**1 cup butter, softened**
**6 eggs**
**1/8 teaspoon salt**

Combine flour, sugar, butter, eggs and salt in mixer bowl. Beat at high speed for 6 minutes. Spoon into greased and floured tube pan. Bake at 300 degrees for 1 1/2 hours. Cool in pan for 10 minutes; remove to wire rack to cool completely. Frost as desired or serve with fresh fruit. Yield: 16 servings.

**Approx Per Serving:** Cal 283; Prot 4 g; Carbo 37 g; Fiber <1 g; T Fat 14 g; 43% Calories from Fat; Chol 111 mg; Sod 158 mg.

Eulala Morrison, *Calling All Cooks three*, Alabama Chapter No. 34

# Pound Cake

**5 eggs**
**1/2 c. shortening**
**2 sticks butter**
**3 c. sugar**
**3 c. flour**
**1/4 tsp. baking powder**
**1/4 tsp. salt**
**1 c. milk**
**1 1/2 tsp. vanilla, lemon or almond extract**

Beat 5 eggs in a small bowl. Cream together shortening, butter and sugar. Add eggs to creamed mixture and cream again. Sift together dry ingredients and add alternately with milk to creamed mixture. For flavoring, add 1 1/2 teaspoons vanilla, lemon or almond extract, or a combination. Bake in greased and floured tube pan at 325° for 1 1/2 hours.

Sara C. Smith, *Bell's Best*, Mississippi Chapter No. 36

## Bourbon Pound Cake

**Brief history:** I've baked this pound cake for special occasions for many years. It stays moist and always a hit anytime I've served it.

**1 lb. butter**
**2¾ c. sugar**
**8 eggs, separated**
**⅓ c. bourbon**
**1 tsp. almond extract**
**3 c. flour**

Cream butter with 2 cups sugar. Add egg yolks one at a time; beat thoroughly after each. Combine all liquids and add alternately with flour. Beat egg whites; add ¾ cup sugar and continue beating until stiff. Fold into batter. Grease bottom, not sides, of tube pan. Pour batter into pan and bake 1¼ hours in 350° oven. Can be removed from pan immediately.

**Preparation time:** 25 minutes.
**Cooking time:** 1¼ hours.

Jo Ames, *A Taste of Pioneering*, Florida Gold Coast Chapter No. 83

## Butter Pound Cake

**2½ cups plain flour**
**½ cup self-rising flour**
**4 eggs**
**3 cups sugar**
**1 cup milk**
**1 tbsp. vanilla flavoring**
**2 sticks butter (½ lb.)**

Cream butter and sugar. Beat in eggs, one at a time. Gradually alternate flour and milk at slow speed. Add vanilla flavoring. Serve plain or for nut cake, fold in two cups of favorite nuts before baking. Pour in bundt pan and bake 1 hour at 350°.

This is a never fail cake—Beginners can make a perfect cake.

Lucille Garrett, *Secret Recipes of Telephone Pioneers, Volume II*
South Carolina Chapter No. 61

### A Helpful Hint

To prevent a soggy or heavy cake, be sure that layers, filling and frosting are completely cool before assembling cake.

## Cream Cheese Pound Cake

**3 sticks butter, softened**
**3 c. sugar**
**6 eggs**
**3 c. plain flour**
**1 (8 oz.) pkg. cream cheese, softened**
**1 Tbsp. lemon or vanilla flavoring**

Whip cream cheese and butter together. Add sugar, blend well. Add eggs alternately with flour, beating well after each addition. Add flavoring. Pour batter into greased and floured Bundt pan. Bake at 350° for 1½ hours.

Ann Flint, *Pots, Pans & Pioneers II*, Louisiana Chapter No. 24

## Mama's Hershey Bar Pound Cake

**2 sticks margarine**
**2½ c. cake flour**
**1 c. buttermilk**
**1 c. chopped pecans**
**6 small bars (1.45 oz.) plain Hershey bar milk chocolate**
**2 c. sugar**
**4 eggs**
**½ t. vanilla**

Put 2 T. flour in nuts and let sit. In mixer bowl, soften margarine and Hershey bars, add sugar, mix. Add eggs, one at a time, mixing. Add buttermilk and mix. Add flour slowly. Mix well. Add vanilla, mix. Add chopped nuts and mix. Cook in 350° preheated oven for about 1 hour. Any questions—call mama.

Connie Cribb, *Taste of Dixie*, Dixie Chapter No. 23

## Diabetic Pound Cake

**2 c. flour**
**1 tsp. soda**
**2 eggs**
**3 large ripe bananas**
**1½ c. pecans or mixed nuts**
**1 c. raisins**
**½ c. corn oil**
**1½ Tbsp. liquid sugar substitute**
**1 tsp. vanilla**
**4 Tbsp. buttermilk**

Sift flour and soda. Add oil and sugar substitute; mix well until light. Beat eggs. Add rest of ingredients. Beat until well mixed. Combine with first mixture. Stir well. Pour into a loaf pan and bake at 350° F. for 25 minutes. Makes 20 servings.

Betty Sapp, *Dogwood Delights Volume II*, Dogwood Chapter No. 84

## Five-Flavor Pound Cake

1 cup butter, softened
1/2 cup shortening
3 cups sugar
1 teaspoon coconut extract
1 teaspoon rum extract
1 teaspoon vanilla extract
1 teaspoon butter extract
1 teaspoon lemon extract
5 eggs, well beaten
3 cups flour
1/2 teaspoon baking powder
1/4 teaspoon salt
1 cup evaporated milk

Cream butter, shortening and sugar in large mixer bowl until light and fluffy. Add flavorings; beat well. Beat in eggs. Sift flour, baking powder and salt together. Add to creamed mixture alternately with evaporated milk. Spoon into greased and floured 10-inch tube pan. Bake at 325 degrees for 1 1/2 hours. Cool in pan for 10 to 15 minutes. Invert onto serving plate. Yield: 16 servings.

**Approx Per Serving:** Cal 435; Prot 6 g; Carbo 57 g; Fiber 1 g; T Fat 21 g; Chol 102 mg; Sod 180 mg.

Mrs. F. H. Waldrop, *Carolina Cooking*, North Carolina Chapter No. 35

## Million Dollar Pound Cake

1 lb. butter or oleo
3 c. sugar
6 eggs
4 c. flour
3/4 c. milk
1 tsp. almond extract
2 tsp. vanilla flavoring

Cream together butter and sugar, adding sugar gradually. Add eggs, 1 at a time. Add vanilla and milk.

Bake at 325° for 1 hour and 40 minutes in a well greased and floured tube pan. This recipe makes a large cake. Do not be tempted to make half of it. You will be sorry because it is so good.

Serves 24.

Ella Mae Vances, *Pioneers Pots and Pans—1985 Cookbook*
North Florida Chapter No. 39

### A Helpful Hint

Add 1/2 cup mayonnaise to any 2-layer cake mix for moistness.

## 125 Year Old Black Walnut Pound Cake

1/2 lb. margarine
1/2 cup Crisco
5 eggs
3 cups plain flour
1 cup evaporated milk
1 cup chopped black walnuts
3 cups sugar
1 tsp. vanilla
1 tsp. baking powder
1/2 tsp. black walnut flavoring (I usually use 1/4 tsp. black walnut flavoring)

Preheat oven to 325 degrees. Cream margarine and shortening. Add sugar and beat until light and fluffy. Add eggs, one at a time, beating well. Mix 1/4 cup of flour with nuts. Sift remaining flour with baking powder and add alternately with milk. STARTING AND ENDING WITH FLOUR. Fold in floured nuts. DO NOT BEAT. Bake in greased and floured tube pan for 1 hour and 20 minutes or until done.

Delores Morgan, *Secret Recipes of Telephone Pioneers, Volume III*
South Carolina Chapter No. 61

## Christmas Prune Cake

1 cup margarine, softened
1 1/4 cups sugar
2 eggs
2/3 cup buttermilk
1 teaspoon baking soda
1 1/2 cups flour
1 teaspoon nutmeg
1 teaspoon cinnamon
1/2 teaspoon cloves
1/2 teaspoon allspice
1/4 teaspoon salt
1 1/2 cups stewed prunes
1 cup raisins
1 1/2 cups candied cherries
1 1/2 cups chopped candied pineapple
1 cup chopped walnuts

Cream margarine and sugar in mixer bowl until light and fluffy. Beat in eggs 1 at a time. Add mixture of buttermilk and baking soda; mix well. Sift flour, nutmeg, cinnamon, cloves, allspice and salt together. Add to creamed mixture alternately with prunes, raisins, cherries, pineapple and walnuts, mixing well after each addition. Spoon into greased and floured tube pan. Bake at 300 degrees for 1 hour or until wooden pick inserted in center comes out clean. Cool in pan for 10 minutes; remove to wire rack to cool completely. May bake in loaf pans if preferred. May double recipe or omit cloves. Yield: 24 servings.

**Approx Per Serving:** Cal 306; Prot 3 g; Carbo 51 g; Fiber 2 g; T Fat 11 g; 32% Calories from Fat; Chol 18 mg; Sod 160 mg.

Elaine Pass, *Calling All Cooks three*, Alabama Chapter No. 34

# *Red Velvet Cake*

1 tablespoon vinegar
1 teaspoon soda
1 cup shortening
1½ cups sugar
2 eggs
2 ounces red food coloring
2 teaspoons baking cocoa
1 cup buttermilk
2½ cups flour
1 teaspoon salt
1 teaspoon vanilla extract
Red Velvet Frosting

Combine vinegar and soda in small bowl; mix well. Cream shortening and sugar in mixer bowl until well blended. Add eggs; beat well. Combine food coloring and cocoa in small bowl; mix well. Add to shortening mixture. Add buttermilk alternately with mixture of flour and salt; mix well. Add vanilla and vinegar mixture; mix well. Pour into 2 greased and floured 8-inch cake pans. Bake at 325 degrees for 30 minutes. Remove to wire rack to cool. Split layers into halves crosswise. Spread Velvet Frosting between layers and on top and side of cake. Yield: 16 servings.

### Red Velvet Frosting

5 tablespoons flour
1 cup milk
1 cup butter, softened
1 cup sugar
1 teaspoon vanilla extract

Combine flour and milk in saucepan; mix well. Simmer until thickened, stirring constantly. Cool. Cream butter and sugar in bowl until light and fluffy. Add vanilla and flour mixture; beat until of spreading consistency.

Peggy Graviss, *Kentucky Kitchens, Volume II*, Kentucky Chapter No. 32

# *One-Step Spice Cake*

1 cup oil
3 eggs
¾ cup applesauce
2 cups self-rising flour
2 cups sugar
1 teaspoon cinnamon
1 teaspoon allspice
1 cup chopped pecans

Combine oil, eggs, applesauce, flour, sugar, cinnamon, allspice and pecans in mixer bowl; mix well. Spoon into greased and floured tube or bundt pan. Bake at 350 degrees for 1 hour. Cool in pan for 10 minutes; remove to wire rack to cool completely. May substitute 1 jar baby food prunes for applesauce if preferred. Yield: 16 servings.

**Approx Per Serving:** Cal 345; Prot 3 g; Carbo 40 g; Fiber 1 g; T Fat 20 g; 50% Calories from Fat; Chol 40 mg; Sod 211 mg.

Rosa Stoudemire, *Calling All Cooks three*, Alabama Chapter No. 34

# Scripture Cake

**1 Kings 19:6**

"...and he looked, and, behold there was a CAKE baked on the coals..."

**1 cup Judges 5:25**

"...she brought forth BUTTER in a lordly dish..."

**2 cups Jeremiah 6:20**

"...and the SWEET CANE from a far country..."

**6 Job 39:14**

"...which leaveth her EGGS in the earth..."

**A little Genesis 19:26**

"...and she became a pillar of SALT..."

**To taste Mark 16:1**

"...and Salome had brought sweet SPICES..."

**1 tablespoon I Samuel 14:25**

"...and there was HONEY on the ground..."

**2 cups I Kings 4:22**

"...and two clusters of RAISINS..."

**1 cup Genesis 26:20**

"...the WATER is ours and he...called the well Esek..."

**1 cup Numbers 17:8**

"...and blossomed blossoms and yielded ALMONDS..."

**1½ cups I Kings 4:22**

"...and Solomon's provisions for one day was thirty measures of fine FLOUR..."

Follow Solomon's advice for making good boys. Proverbs 23:24 "thou shalt BEAT him WITH A ROD and shalt deliver his soul from hell..."

## *Scripture Cake*

(in modern terms)

**1 c. butter**
**2 c. sugar**
**6 eggs**
**1/4 tsp. salt**
**1/4 tsp. sweet spices**
**1 tbsp. honey**
**2 c. figs, chopped**
**2 c. raisins, chopped**
**1 c. water**
**1 c. almonds, chopped**
**1 1/2 c. cake flour**

Cream butter and sugar. Combine all dry ingredients. Combine all liquid ingredients. Add the dry and liquid ingredients, in small amounts, alternately to the butter and sugar mixture, beating well.

Pour into buttered loaf pan. Bake for about 1 hour at 350 degrees (with all the rich ingredients, do not preheat oven).

Praise the Lord and pass the coffee.

Nathalee Barnes
*A Tablespoon of Pioneering and a Teaspoon of Horses and the Handicapped*
Florida Gold Coast Chapter No. 83

## *Liz Mays Fresh Strawberry Cake*

**1 yellow cake mix**
**2 boxes fresh strawberries**
**1 jar strawberry glaze**
**1 (8 oz.) cream cheese**
**1 large Cool Whip**
**1/2 c. powdered sugar**
**1/2 c. white sugar**

Bake cake as directed on box. Cut the 2 layers of cake with string to make 4 layers. Combine the cream cheese, Cool Whip and both sugars. Set aside until cake is cooled. Wash strawberries and cut thin. Mix with glaze. Put a layer of cream cheese mixture, then a layer of strawberry glaze mixture. Alternate each. Keep in refrigerator.

Imogene Davis, *Calling All Cooks two*, Alabama Chapter No. 34

# Easy Strawberry Cake

1 large box strawberry jello
1 large pkg. frozen strawberries, sliced
1 medium size Cool Whip
1 large angel food cake

Use pound cake pan. Tear ½ angel food cake into pieces. Put in cake pan. Mix jello with 2 cups hot water. Mix thawed strawberries with jello mixture. Pour ½ mixture over cake. Spread ½ Cool Whip on cake. Tear other ½ of cake into pieces. Pour remainder of jello mixture over cake. Refrigerate overnight. When ready to use, put cake pan into hot water a few seconds. This will loosen cake. Turn out on plate; top with remainder of Cool Whip.

Nila Swann, *Calling All Cooks*, Alabama Chapter No. 34

# Strawberry Pecan Cake

1 pkg. white cake mix
1 small box strawberry gelatin
1 c. salad oil
½ c. milk
4 eggs
1 c. frozen strawberries
1 c. coconut
1 c. chopped pecans

Combine cake mix and dry gelatin. Add other ingredients, adding eggs one at a time. Pour into 3 greased and floured cake pans and bake for 20–25 minutes in a 350° oven.

## Strawberry Frosting:

1 stick margarine
1 box confections' sugar
½ c. strawberries, drained
½ c. coconut
½ c. chopped pecans

Cream sugar and margarine. Add other ingredients and spread on cooled cake.

Sara F. Williams, *Dining with Pioneers, Volume I*
Tennessee Chapter No. 21

## A Helpful Hint

Cake flour is specially milled from selected winter wheats to make delicate, fine-textured cakes.

## *Sock-it-to-Me Cake*

**1/2 c. sugar**
**3/4 c. Wesson oil**
**4 eggs**
**3 tsp. cinnamon**
**1 box Duncan Hines yellow cake mix**
**1 (8 oz.) ctn. sour cream**
**3 tsp. brown sugar**
**1/2 c. chopped pecans**

Glaze:

**3 Tbsp. butter**
**1 tsp. vanilla**
**3 Tbsp. milk**
**1 c. powdered sugar**

Mix sugar, cake mix, sour cream, Wesson oil and eggs and pour 1/2 of mixture into tube pan. In a small bowl, mix brown sugar, cinnamon and chopped pecans. Over cake mix that is in pan, scatter 1/2 of brown sugar mix and swirl with knife blade. Pour remainder of cake dough in pan and scatter remainder of brown sugar mix over this and swirl again with knife blade. Bake in preheated 325° oven for 1 hour or until cake is done. While cake is warm, glaze.

**Glaze:** Brown mixture in saucepan.

Nervetta Fairchild, *Bell's Best*, Mississippi Chapter No. 36

## *Vanilla Wafer Cake*

**1 cup butter, softened**
**1 1/2 cups sugar**
**6 eggs**
**1/2 cup milk**
**1 12-ounce package vanilla wafers, crushed**
**1 cup chopped pecans**
**1 7-ounce package extra-fine coconut**

Cream butter and sugar in large mixer bowl until light and fluffy. Add eggs 1 at a time, beating well after each addition. Add milk alternately with vanilla wafer crumbs, beating well after each addition. Stir in pecans and coconut. Pour into well-greased and floured tube pan. Bake at 300 degrees for 1 1/2 hours or until cake tests done. Cool in pan for several minutes. Invert onto serving plate. Yield: 16 servings.

**Approx Per Serving:** Cal 415; Prot 5 g; Carbo 42 g; Fiber 2 g; T Fat 27 g; Chol 125 mg; Sod 238 mg.

Helen Marie Woods, *Carolina Cooking*, North Carolina Chapter No. 35

# Virginia Whiskey Cake

**Origin:** Adapted from an 18th Century Williamsburg recipe. **Country:** U.S.A. **City:** Williamsburg. **Relative obtained from:** Mother (Mrs. Lillian Nienke). **Brief history:** An old Virginia recipe that has been passed from generation to generation for at least the last 100 years in our family.

**1 c. granulated sugar**
**1 c. firmly packed brown sugar**
**1 c. butter**
**3 eggs**
**3 c. sifted cake flour**
**1/2 tsp. baking powder**
**1/2 tsp. mace**
**1 c. 100 proof bourbon whiskey**
**2 c. broken pecan meats**

Combine the sugars and cream with butter. Add well beaten eggs. Sift flour and mace; add alternately with whiskey. Add nuts. Bake in well greased or paper lined tube pan at 250° for 2 1/2 to 3 hours.

The cake should have a moist crumbly texture similar to a macaroon. Wrap in aluminum foil and store in cool place. (Do not freeze.) The cake cuts easier when cold, but should be served at room temperature. It will keep for 2 weeks or longer. Slices about 1/2 inch thick are best. Save the crumbs for parfaits or sundae topping.

For added flavor, add 1 tablespoon of Whiskey Sauce (1/2 cup light corn syrup, 1 tablespoon rum, 2 tablespoons whiskey) to cake about half an hour before serving. Whipped cream topping is optional.

**Preparation time:** 45 minutes.
**Cooking time:** 2 1/2 to 3 hours.
**No. of servings:** 20 to 25.

Mrs. Nita Brown, *A Taste of Pioneering*
Florida Gold Coast Chapter No. 83

# Caramel Icing

**1/2 c. buttermilk**
**2 c. sugar**
**3/4 c. oleo**
**1/2 tsp. soda**
**1 Tbsp. light Karo syrup**
**12 marshmallows (1 c. small)**

Mix all ingredients together and cook to firm ball stage; beat well and pour on cake. This is a simple, easy caramel icing. No more burnt sugar to make caramel.

Lou Sparks, *Bell's Best*, Mississippi Chapter No. 36

# Pies

NEW ERA PIONEERS
NORTH FLORIDA CHAPTER #39
TELEPHONE PIONEERS OF AMERICA
174465
1875
1911

# Angel Pie

1 c. chocolate cookie crumbs
3 Tbsp. melted margarine
1 env. unflavored gelatin
1/4 c. cold water
1/4 c. boiling water
1 tsp. vanilla
1/4 tsp. aniseed
3 egg whites
1/2 c. sugar
1 c. heavy cream, whipped

Combine cookie crumbs and melted butter. Set aside 1 tablespoon crumb mixture for garnish. Press remaining crumbs into a 9 inch pie pan; chill. Soften gelatin in cold water; add boiling water, vanilla and aniseed; stir to dissolve gelatin. Beat egg whites until soft peaks form; add sugar, 1 tablespoon at a time; beat well after each addition. Beat until stiff peaks form. Fold in gelatin, then fold in whipped cream. Refrigerate until mixture starts to set, then spoon into crumb crust. Sprinkle top with reserved crumbs; chill until set. Serves 6.

Cristy Lewis, *Kentucky Kitchens, Volume I*, Kentucky Chapter No. 32

# Crumb Crust Apple Pie

4 cups sliced apples
1/3 cup butter
1 cup sugar
1/2 cup water
3/4 cup flour
1/2 tsp. cinnamon

Butter a baking dish or pie pan, put in sliced apples and pour water over them. Sprinkle on cinnamon generously. Work together flour, sugar and butter until crumbly. Spread this over the apple mixture and bake slowly, uncovered, until the apples are tender and the crust is brown. Serve warm with whipped cream or ice cream.

Sara Simpson, *Secret Recipes of Telephone Pioneers, Volume II*
South Carolina Chapter No. 61

# Fried Apple Pies

3 c. all-purpose flour
1½ tsp. salt
1 c. shortening
½ c. cold water
8 oz. dried apples
3 c. water
½ c. sugar

Prepare pastry by mixing flour and salt; cut shortening into flour until size of small peas. Sprinkle 1 tablespoon water and toss with fork and push aside until all dough is mixed. Roll to ⅛ inch thick and cut into 6 inch circles. Place 2 tablespoons apples (cooked about 45 minutes to an hour in 3 cups water; ½ cup sugar added after cooking). Fry in heavy skillet in shortening at 375° about ⅛–¼ inch deep. Fry 3–4 minutes on each side. Drain on paper towel. Sprinkle with powdered sugar, if desired. Makes 12. Just like grandma's!

Claudia Parsons, *Bell's Best*, Mississippi Chapter No. 36

# Brown Sugar Custard Pie

2 c. brown sugar, packed
¼ c. margarine
3 Tbsp. flour
1 tsp. ground cinnamon
¼ tsp. cream of tartar
1/16 tsp. salt
3 eggs
3 c. milk
1 tsp. vanilla
2 unbaked (8 inch) pie shells

Cream brown sugar and margarine until light and fluffy. Mix flour, cinnamon, cream of tartar and salt. Add eggs and beat well; add to brown sugar and butter mixture. Slowly beat in milk and vanilla. Pour into pie shells. Bake in 375° oven for about 40 minutes or until a knife inserted in the center comes out clean. Cool.

Lora Martin, *Kentucky Kitchens, Volume I*, Kentucky Chapter No. 32

## A Helpful Hint

Add spices such as cinnamon, nutmeg, ginger or cloves to your pie pastry to add interest to your fruit and custard pies.

## Buttermilk Pie

1½ cups sugar
1 tbsp. flour, plain
3 eggs, beaten
1 tsp. vanilla
1 cup buttermilk
1 stick melted oleo

Mix and pour into unbaked pie shell. Bake at 315° till "shaky" in 9-inch pie pan. Serve hot or cold.

Jennie Lancaster, *Secret Recipes of Telephone Pioneers, Volume II*
South Carolina Chapter No. 61

## Caramel Pie

1 can Eagle Brand milk
1 graham crust
1 small Cool Whip
1 tsp. vanilla
⅓ c. pecans

Preheat oven to 425°. Pour milk into empty pie plate. Cover with foil. Place in shallow pan of hot water. Bake for 1 hour or until thick. Cool. Add vanilla and chopped pecans. Pour into crust. Put Cool Whip on before serving.

Deloris Rinker, *Pots, Pans and Pioneers, Volume IV*
Louisiana Chapter No. 24

## Cherry Pie

2 cans cherry pie filling
½ cup butter or oleo
⅔ cup light brown sugar
⅔ cup plain flour
1½ cups quick cook oatmeal

Cream sugar and butter, add flour and oatmeal. Empty cherry pie filling in 9x12 baking dish, top with above mixture. Bake 35 or 40 minutes at 375°. Serve with dip of ice cream. Can be made ahead of time, when ready to serve, reheat with foil over top. Recipe serves 8.

Mrs. Reuben Anderson, *Secret Recipes of Telephone Pioneers, Volume II*
South Carolina Chapter No. 61

## Chocolate Pie

2 squares baking chocolate
2 tbsp. butter
1/3 cup flour
1 cup sugar
1/4 tsp. salt
2 1/2 cups milk
3 eggs, separated
3/4 tsp. vanilla
Baked 8 inch pie shell
1/3 cup sugar
Chopped nuts, if desired

Melt chocolate and butter over hot water in top of double boiler. Mix flour, sugar and salt and stir into chocolate; add milk slowly and stir constantly until mixture is fully thickened, about 15 minutes. Beat egg yolks well, stir in a little of the chocolate mixture, then pour into rest of hot mixture and cook 2 minutes, stirring constantly. Remove from heat, cool partially and stir in vanilla. Pour into pie shell. Beat egg whites until stiff. Swirl meringue over pie filling so it touches edge of crust all around. Sprinkle with chopped nuts and place in moderate oven (350°) 12 to 15 minutes or until golden brown. Very good!

Mae Jeter, *Secret Recipes of Telephone Pioneers, Volume II*
South Carolina Chapter No. 61

## Chocolate Pie

1/2 cup flour
2 tablespoons baking cocoa
1 1/4 cups sugar
1 egg
2 cups water
1/2 cup margarine
1 teaspoon vanilla extract
1 baked 9-inch pie shell
8 ounces whipped topping

Combine flour, cocoa and sugar in double boiler. Add egg, water, margarine and vanilla; mix well. Cook for 5 minutes or until thickened, stirring constantly. Let stand to cool. Pour into pie shell. Spread with whipped topping. Yield: 8 servings.

**Approx Per Serving:** Cal 472; Prot 4 g; Carbo 55 g; Fiber 1 g; T Fat 27 g; 51% Calories from Fat; Chol 27 mg; Sod 272 mg.

Hazel E. Campbell, *Calling All Cooks three*, Alabama Chapter No. 34

# Cocoa Cheesecake Pie

**8 ounces cream cheese, softened**
**1/3 cup baking cocoa**
**1/2 cup sugar**
**1 teaspoon vanilla extract**
**1/8 teaspoon salt**
**2 eggs**
**1 9-inch chocolate crumb pie shell**
**Sour Cream Topping**

Beat cream cheese in mixer bowl until fluffy. Add baking cocoa, sugar, vanilla and salt; mix well. Beat in eggs 1 at a time. Pour into chocolate pie shell. Bake at 325 degrees for 25 minutes. Spread Sour Cream Topping over pie. Bake for 10 to 15 minutes longer or until set. Cool. Chill in refrigerator for 3 hours or longer. Yield: 8 servings.

### Sour Cream Topping

**1 cup sour cream**
**2 tablespoons sugar**
**1/2 teaspoon vanilla extract**

Combine cream cheese, sugar and vanilla in bowl; mix well. Yield: 8 servings.

Athens-Gainesville Council, *Lawfully Good Eating*
Dixie Chapter No. 23

# Old-Fashioned Chocolate Pie

**3 eggs**
**1 1/2 c. sugar**
**1/4 c. cocoa**
**1/4 c. corn starch**
**1 1/2 c. sweet milk**
**1 tsp. vanilla flavoring**

Cream egg yolks and sugar; add cocoa and corn starch, then add milk and flavoring. Put in a double boiler and cook. Stir while cooking. When it turns to a dark brown and thick, it's done. Put in cooked pie shell. Beat whites and add the sugar. Put on top of pie and brown.

Mary Alice Neal, *Calling All Cooks two*, Alabama Chapter No. 34

## A Helpful Hint

Always prick the bottom and side of a pie shell which is baked before filling to prevent puffing. Brush the bottom with 1 egg white beaten with 1 tablespoon water just before the shell has finished baking to keep it from becoming soggy when filled.

## Original Chocolate Pie

1 cup sugar
1/3 cup cornstarch
1/3 cup baking cocoa
1/8 teaspoon salt
2 cups milk
2 egg yolks, beaten
1/4 cup butter
1/2 teaspoon vanilla extract
1 baked 9-inch pie shell
2 egg whites
2 tablespoons sugar

Combine 1 cup sugar, cornstarch, cocoa and salt in mixer bowl. Beat in 1/4 cup milk until creamy. Beat in remaining milk and egg yolks. Pour into saucepan. Cook until thickened, beating constantly with mixer. Remove from heat. Beat in butter and vanilla. Pour into pie shell. Beat egg whites with 2 tablespoons sugar until stiff peaks form. Spread over filling. Bake at 325 degrees until golden brown. Recipe may be doubled. May substitute flour for cornstarch or 1/2 cup evaporated milk and 1/2 cup water for 1 cup milk. Yield: 8 servings.

**Approx Per Serving:** Cal 363; Prot 6 g; Carbo 49 g; Fiber 2 g; T Fat 17 g; 42% Calories from Fat; Chol 77 mg; Sod 261 mg.

Pattie Smith, *Calling All Cooks three*, Alabama Chapter No. 34

## Favorite German Chocolate Pies

3/4 cup coconut
2 unbaked 10-inch pie shells
3/4 cup chopped pecans
3 1/2 cups sugar
1 1/2 teaspoons cake flour
1 teaspoon cornstarch
2 eggs
1/2 cup melted margarine
2 ounces unsweetened chocolate, melted
2 cups evaporated milk
1 teaspoon vanilla extract
1/8 teaspoon salt

Sprinkle coconut over bottom of pie shells. Sprinkle pecans over coconut. Combine sugar, cake flour and cornstarch in mixer bowl. Add eggs, margarine and chocolate; beat until well blended. Add evaporated milk gradually, mixing constantly. Stir in vanilla and salt. Spoon into prepared pie shells. Bake at 350 degrees for 40 minutes or until set. Yield: 12 servings.

**Approx Per Serving:** Cal 605; Prot 7 g; Carbo 80 g; Fiber 2 g; T Fat 31 g; Chol 47 mg; Sod 349 mg.

Virginia S. Smith, *Carolina Cooking*, North Carolina Chapter No. 35

## *Refrigerator Chocolate Pie*

**½ cup butter**
**1 cup flour**
**1 cup chopped nuts**
**8 ounces cream cheese, softened**
**1 cup confectioners' sugar**
**1 cup whipped topping**
**3 4-ounce packages chocolate instant pudding mix**
**3 cups cold milk**
**1 cup whipped topping**
**¼ cup chopped nuts**

Melt butter in 9x13-inch baking dish in 350-degree oven. Add flour and 1 cup nuts; mix well. Spread evenly in baking dish. Bake at 350 degrees for 15 minutes. Cool. Combine cream cheese and confectioners' sugar in mixer bowl; mix well. Fold in 1 cup whipped topping. Spread over crust. Chill in refrigerator. Combine pudding mix and milk in bowl; beat well. Spread over cream cheese layer. Top with 1 cup whipped topping; sprinkle with remaining ¼ cup nuts. Chill in refrigerator until serving time. Yield: 12 servings.

Edna Hensler, *Lawfully Good Eating*, Dixie Chapter No. 23

## *Girdle Buster Pie*

**2 cups Oreo cookies, crushed**
**½ stick margarine, melted**
**1 small can evaporated milk**
**2 Tbsp. margarine**
**½ cup sugar**
**2 squares semi-sweet chocolate**
**½ tsp. vanilla**
**1 quart vanilla ice cream**
**Non-dairy whipped topping**

Mix crushed cookies and margarine and press into pie plate. Heat the next four ingredients until thick. Add vanilla, stir and let cool. Soften ice cream and spread over crust. Put cool sauce mixture over ice cream. Place in freezer 10 minutes. Remove and top with non-dairy whipped topping. Freeze.

Edna Gray, *Secret Recipes of Telephone Pioneers, Volume III*
South Carolina Chapter No. 61

# Chocolate Chip Pie

- 1 stick margarine
- 1 c. sugar
- ½ c. flour
- 3 eggs, well beaten
- 1 tsp. vanilla
- 1 (6 oz.) pkg. semi-sweet chocolate chips
- ½ c. chopped nuts
- 1 unbaked pie crust (don't cook in advance)

Combine sugar and flour. Melt margarine and cool. Add to flour and sugar with eggs and vanilla. Add chocolate chips and nuts to mixture; pour in pie shell. Bake in conventional oven at 375°; reduce heat to 350° after 10 minutes and finish baking.

C. Juandell Stogsdill, *Dining with Pioneers, Volume I*
*Tennessee Chapter No. 21*

# Aunt Lula's Coconut Pies

- 1¼ cups sugar
- 5 tablespoons cornstarch
- 4 cups milk
- 5 egg yolks, beaten
- 1 teaspoon vanilla extract
- 2 tablespoons margarine
- 1½ cups flaked coconut
- 2 baked 9-inch pie shells
- 5 egg whites
- 10 tablespoons sugar
- ¼ teaspoon cream of tartar

Combine 1¼ cups sugar, cornstarch, milk, egg yolks, vanilla and margarine in double boiler. Cook over hot water until thickened, stirring constantly. Stir in coconut. Pour into pie shells. Beat egg whites in mixer bowl until soft peaks form. Add remaining 10 tablespoons sugar and cream of tartar gradually, beating until stiff peaks form. Spread over pie fillings, sealing to edges. Sprinkle with additional coconut if desired. Bake at 400 degrees until lightly browned.
Yield: 12 servings.

**Approx Per Serving:** Cal 426; Prot 7 g; Carbo 55 g; Fiber 2 g; T Fat 20 g; Chol 100 mg; Sod 266 mg.

Ramona K. Hedgpeth, *Carolina Cooking*, North Carolina Chapter No. 35

## *Mama's Coconut Pie*

**2 c. milk**
**$2/3$ c. sugar**
**$1/3$ c. flour**
**3 eggs, beaten well**
**Pinch of salt**
**1 can Angel Flake coconut**

Mix sugar and flour well. Add milk, eggs and salt. Stir until well mixed. Cook over low heat, stirring constantly, or cook in top of double boiler over boiling water until thick. Stir in coconut. Pour into baked 9 inch pie shell. Top with meringue.

**Meringue:**

**3 egg whites**
**6 Tbsp. sugar**

Beat egg whites until stiff. They should be glossy on top. Also, when you invert the bowl, they should remain in place. Fold in sugar gradually, using folding motion. Do not beat sugar in. Put on top of pie. Bake for 18 minutes at 350°.

Frankie Miller, *Bell's Best*, Mississippi Chapter No. 36

## *Quick Coconut Pie*

**$1/4$ cup butter, softened**
**1 tablespoon vanilla extract**
**1 cup sugar**
**$1/4$ cup buttermilk**
**3 eggs**
**1 3-ounce can coconut**
**1 unbaked 9-inch pie shell**

Combine butter, vanilla, sugar, buttermilk, eggs and coconut in mixer bowl; beat well. Pour into pie shell. Bake at 250 degrees for 1 hour or until golden brown. Yield: 8 servings.

**Approx Per Serving:** Cal 350; Prot 4 g; Carbo 41 g; Fiber 2 g; T Fat 19 g; 48% Calories from Fat; Chol 95 mg; Sod 215 mg.

Carolyn Brouillette, *Calling All Cooks three*, Alabama Chapter No. 34

### *A Helpful Hint*

Chill pastry for 4 to 12 hours before rolling out to ensure tender easy-to-handle pastry that won't shrink during baking.

# Grape Pie

Wash and stem blue Concord grapes. Remove skins and put into a bowl. Boil pulp for a few minutes to remove seeds (keep stirring). Remove from stove and put through sieve to remove seeds. Combine skins and pulp. You should have 3 cups.

*Add the following to the grape mixture:*

**1½ c. sugar**
**Dab of salt**
**3 Tbsp. Minute tapioca**
**2 tsp. fresh lemon juice**
**1 Tbsp. corn starch (mix like for gravy by using a little juice from mixture)**
**¾ c. chopped pecans**

Make pastry for 2 crust pie. Put bottom crust in 9 inch pie tin. Sprinkle 1 tablespoon flour and 1 teaspoon sugar on it. Add grape mixture. Put dabs of butter on top. Add top crust. Be sure to slit top crust for steam to escape.

Preheat oven to 400°. If pie starts getting too brown, turn down to 350°. Bake for about ½ hour to 35 minutes. It's really good! Bake in the fall while you can find Concord grapes.

This recipe was given to me by "Ma" Shay in Painesville, Ohio. She was the only person I ever knew to make it. She brought it to this country from the "old" country (Hungary). She didn't want it to die out. I make it quite often. I freeze the grape mixture while they are in season. If you like grapes, you'll *love it*.

Eudene H. Tindell, *Dogwood Delights Volume II*
Dogwood Chapter No. 84

*Raising the roof for Habitat for Humanity.* (North Florida Chapter No. 39)

# Grapefruit Chiffon Pie

1 env. unflavored gelatin
1/2 c. sugar
2 c. Ocean Spray Pink Grapefruit Juice Cocktail
1/3 c. orange juice (fresh, if possible)
1 tsp. grated orange peel
1 c. Cool Whip, thawed
Graham cracker pie crust

In a small saucepan, mix gelatin and sugar. Add grapefruit juice, stir until dissolved. Bring to a boil on medium-high heat, stirring frequently. Remove from heat. Add orange juice and peel. Chill until soft set. Fold in Cool Whip, spoon into crust. Refrigerate several hours or overnight.

Dorothy Abel
*A Tablespoon of Pioneering and a Teaspoon of Horses and the Handicapped*
Florida Gold Coast Chapter No. 83

# Key Lime Pie

4 egg yolks
1 14-ounce can sweetened condensed milk
1/2 cup lime juice
1 baked 10-inch graham cracker pie shell
4 egg whites
1/4 cup sugar
1/2 teaspoon vanilla extract

Beat egg yolks and condensed milk in mixer bowl. Beat in lime juice gradually. Pour into pie shell. Beat egg whites until soft peaks form. Add sugar and vanilla gradually, beating well. Spread over pie, sealing to edge. Bake at 375 degrees for 5 minutes or until meringue is golden brown. Chill before serving. Yield: 8 servings.

Chuck Baker, *Lawfully Good Eating*, Dixie Chapter No. 23

## A Helpful Hint

To fit a crumb crust into a 9-inch pie plate, place the crumbs in the plate and press with an 8-inch pie plate. The crust will be shaped evenly between the 2 plates.

# *Key Lime Cream Pie*

**Approximate year created:** 1985.

**1 c. sugar**
**5 Tbsp. flour**
**1/4 tsp. salt**
**3 egg yolks**
**1/2 c. Key lime juice**
**1 tsp. lime rind, grated**
**1 1/4 c. milk**
**1 Tbsp. butter or oleo**
**3 egg whites, beaten**
**4 Tbsp. powdered sugar**
**4 Tbsp. coconut (optional)**
**1 baked (9 1/2 inch) pie shell**

Blend sugar, flour, and salt. Add yolks, juice, rind, and milk. Cook slowly; stir constantly until it just starts to bubble. Add butter; remove from heat. Mix powdered sugar with egg whites and beat until creamy. Fold into yolk mixture; pour into pie shell (see optional note which follows). Cool slightly; refrigerate. Garnish with whipped cream/lime slices.

**Optional:** Sprinkle with coconut and bake 10 minutes in 300° oven; cool slightly and refrigerate. (Lemon juice can be used for a great lemon cream pie.)

**Preparation and cooking time:** 30 minutes.
**No. of servings:** 10 to 12.

Rhonda Danielson, *A Taste of Pioneering*
Florida Gold Coast Chapter No. 83

*Huck Finn Fishing Rodeo for Handicapped Children.*
(Louisiana Chapter No. 24)

# *Lemon-Almond Tartlets*

Butter Cookie Dough:

**2½ cups all-purpose flour**
**½ cup butter or margarine**
**½ cup sugar**
**1 extra-large egg**
**1 tsp. vanilla extract**

Cut butter or margarine into flour until crumbly. Add sugar, egg and vanilla. Mix until blended. Dough will be slightly dry. Place on floured board and knead into a ball. Divide into two round flats and wrap in wax paper and refrigerate.

Lemon-Almond Filling:

**3 eggs**
**¾ cup sugar**
**1½ tsp. grated lemon peel**
**½ cup lemon juice**
**¼ tsp. almond extract**
**1 cup blanched almonds, finely chopped**

Beat eggs for filling until frothy. Blend in remaining ingredients. Preheat oven to 375 degrees. Break off small pieces of butter cookie dough and press into bottom and sides of 2 or 3 inch tart molds, making dough as thin as possible. Bake 12–15 minutes or until edges are lightly browned. Do not turn off oven. Cool tartlet shells slightly in molds. Prepare filling. Spoon into tartlet shells. Bake at 375 degrees 12–15 minutes until top is firm. Cool 5 minutes in molds. Remove tartlets from molds by pressing sharp knife into one edge and slipping them out. Cool.

Topping:

**2 cups sliced almonds**
**1½ cups apricot preserves**

Arrange almonds on top of tart. Press preserves through strainer into small saucepan and heat until melted. With a spoon or baster, carefully cover almonds with warm preserves. May be stored in a single layer at room temperature overnight. Makes 36.

Martha Lemond, *Secret Recipes of Telephone Pioneers, Volume III*
South Carolina Chapter No. 61

# Lemon Pie

For 8-inch pie:

1 cup sugar
$1^1/_4$ cups water
1 tablespoon butter or margarine
$^1/_4$ cup cornstarch
3 tablespoons cold water
3 egg yolks
2 tablespoons milk
6 tablespoons lemon juice
1 teaspoon grated lemon peel
1 baked 8-inch pastry shell
3 egg whites
6 tablespoons sugar
1 teaspoon lemon juice

Combine sugar, water and butter; heat until sugar dissolves. Blend cornstarch with cold water; add to hot mixture; cook slowly until clear, about 8 minutes.

Beat egg yolks with milk; slowly stir into cornstarch mixture. Cook 2 minutes, stirring constantly. Remove from heat. Add 6 tablespoons lemon juice and lemon peel. Cool. Pour into cooled baked shell.

Beat egg whites stiff but not dry; add sugar gradually; add 1 teaspoon lemon juice at the last. Spread meringue over cooled filling, sealing to the edges of pastry to avoid shrinking. Brown at 350° 12 to 15 minutes.

For 9-inch pie:

$1^1/_3$ cups sugar
$1^1/_4$ cups water
2 tablespoons butter or margarine
$^1/_3$ cup cornstarch
$^1/_2$ cup cold water
4 egg yolks
3 tablespoons milk
$^1/_2$ cup lemon juice
$1^1/_2$ teaspoons grated lemon peel
1 baked 9-inch pastry shell
4 egg whites
$^1/_2$ cup sugar
1 teaspoon lemon juice

Mrs. Dolores Hill, *Secret Recipes of Telephone Pioneers, Volume I*
South Carolina Chapter No. 61

# Lemon Meringue Pie

**1½ cups sugar**
**7 tbsp. cornstarch**
**Dash salt**
**4 egg yolks**
**1 tsp. grated lemon peel**
**2 tbsp. butter or margarine**
**½ cup lemon juice**
**1 baked 9 inch pie shell**
**4 egg whites**
**1 tsp. lemon juice**
**6 tbsp. sugar**

In saucepan, combine 1½ cups sugar, cornstarch and salt. Stir in water. Bring to boiling over medium heat, stirring constantly until thick. Remove from heat, add egg yolks. Bring to a boil, cook for 1 minute. Remove from heat; add butter and lemon peel. Slowly stir in lemon juice. Cool to lukewarm. Pour into cooled baked pie shell. Beat egg whites with 1 tsp. of lemon juice until soft peaks form. Gradually add 6 tbsp. of sugar, beat until stiff. Spread meringue over pie filling.

Seal edges to keep from shrinking. Bake 10 to 15 minutes at 350° for browning. Glass pie pan is recommended. Cool thoroughly before serving. "Enjoy." Recipe serves 6.

Constance M. Gunther, *Secret Recipes of Telephone Pioneers, Volume II*
South Carolina Chapter No. 61

*Potting 15,000 seedlings with much excitement and resolve.* (Alabama Chapter No. 34)

# Mystery Pie

20 Ritz crackers, crushed
1 c. sugar
1 c. pecans, chopped
3 egg whites
1 tsp. vanilla
Whipped cream

Mix crackers, nuts and 1/2 cup of sugar. Beat egg whites until stiff. Add remaining 1/2 cup sugar and vanilla. Fold in cracker and nut mixture. Pour in buttered pie pan. Bake at 350° for 30 minutes. Let cool and top with whipped cream to serve.

Wylene Durden, *Dogwood Delights*, Dogwood Chapter No. 84

# Pat-a-Shoe Pie

Shell:

1/4 c. butter
1/2 c. flour
2 eggs
1/2 c. water
1/8 tsp. salt

Filling:

1 (3 oz.) pkg. instant Jell-O pudding and pie filling
1 1/2 c. cold milk
1 Tbsp. brandy
1 pt. fresh blueberries
1 c. whipping cream

First, make the pate a chou. In small pan, melt butter; add water and heat to boiling. Add all at once the flour and salt and stir until paste leaves sides of pan and forms a ball. Transfer paste to small mixer bowl and beat. Add eggs, one at a time, and beat until very smooth. Using a wet rubber spatula, spread paste in greased 9-inch pie plate covering bottom evenly and only halfway up sides. Bake in preheated oven at 400° for 5 minutes. Cool. Prepare pudding and as soon as it thickens, pour into cooled pie shell and refrigerate. Wash and pick over blueberries and roll them on a paper lined cake pan to absorb excess moisture. Put berries in a dry bowl, add a tablespoon of brandy and toss to coat berries. With slotted spoon, carefully lift out berries and tumble them on top of filling. Whip the cream, if desired, with 1 teaspoon of confectioners' sugar, and spread on pie. Refrigerate at least 6 hours before serving. Serves 6.

Ralph V. Campbell, *Dogwood Delights*, Dogwood Chapter No. 84

## Peach Meringue Pie

1/2 cup margarine, softened
1 cup sugar
1/8 teaspoon salt
2 tablespoons flour
3 egg yolks, lightly beaten
1 cup sliced fresh peaches
1 unbaked 9-inch pie shell
6 tablespoons sugar
1/8 teaspoon salt
3 egg whites

Cream margarine and 1 cup sugar in mixer bowl until light and fluffy. Add 1/8 teaspoon salt and flour; mix well. Fold in egg yolks. Stir in peaches. Spoon into pie shell. Bake at 400 degrees for 8 minutes. Reduce oven temperature to 325 degrees. Bake for 25 to 30 minutes longer or until filling is firm and browned. Let stand until cool. Sprinkle 6 tablespoons sugar and 1/8 teaspoon salt over egg whites in mixer bowl. Beat until stiff and glossy. Spread over pie, sealing to edge. Bake at 325 degrees for 15 to 20 minutes or until lightly browned. Let stand until cool. Yield: 8 servings.

**Approx Per Serving:** Cal 398; Prot 4 g; Carbo 49 g; Fiber 1 g; T Fat 21 g; 47% Calories from Fat; Chol 80 mg; Sod 346 mg.

Velvo Chaney, *Calling All Cooks three*, Alabama Chapter No. 34

## Peanut Butter Pie

2/3 c. sugar
2 1/2 Tbsp. cornstarch
1 Tbsp. all-purpose flour
1/2 tsp. salt
3 c. milk
3 slightly beaten egg yolks
1/4 c. crunchy peanut butter
1 Tbsp. butter
1 (9 inch) baked pastry shell
3 egg whites
1/4 tsp. cream of tartar
6 Tbsp. sugar
1/2 tsp. vanilla

Combine first 4 ingredients. Add milk and cook over low heat, stirring constantly, until smooth and thick. Remove from heat; add a small amount of the hot mixture to egg yolks and return to hot mixture. Boil for 1 minute longer, stirring constantly. Add peanut butter and butter. Stir until blended. Cool slightly.

Pour into shell while warm. Top with meringue. Beat egg whites with cream of tartar till soft peaks form. Beat in sugar, 1 tablespoon at a time, till hard peaks form. Add vanilla and spread over warm filling. Bake for 12 to 15 minutes at 350°.

Joyce Runyan, *Calling All Cooks two*, Alabama Chapter No. 34

## Jimmy Carter Pie or Peanut Butter Pie

1/2 c. crunchy peanut butter
8 oz. cream cheese
1 c. powdered sugar
1/4 c. milk
1 carton whipped topping (9 oz.)
1 graham cracker pie crust
1/2 c. mini-chocolate chips (if desired)

Soften cream cheese (room temp.). Beat until fluffy and add peanut butter and sugar. Add milk slowly, mix well. Fold in topping and sprinkle with peanuts. Chill till firm.

Peggy Dempsey, *Taste of Dixie*, Dixie Chapter No. 23

## Buttermilk-Pecan Pie

1 cup chopped pecans
1 unbaked 10-inch pie shell
3 tablespoons flour
1/4 teaspoon salt
1/2 cup butter, softened
2 cups sugar
2 teaspoons vanilla extract
3 eggs
1 cup buttermilk

Sprinkle pecans in pie shell. Sift flour and salt together. Cream butter in mixer bowl. Add sugar 1/2 cup at a time, beating well after each addition. Stir in vanilla. Beat in eggs 1 at a time. Add flour mixture gradually, mixing well after each addition. Add buttermilk; mix well. Pour over pecans. Bake at 300 degrees for 1 hour. This pie is not as rich as some pecan pies. Yield: 8 servings.

**Approx Per Serving:** Cal 577; Prot 7 g; Carbo 68 g; Fiber 1 g; T Fat 32 g; 49% Calories from Fat; Chol 112 mg; Sod 376 mg.

Mrs. A. T. Vaughn, *Calling All Cooks three*, Alabama Chapter No. 34

### A Helpful Hint

You can substitute an equal amount of smooth or crunchy peanut butter for the shortening in your pastry recipe. It is a taste treat and handy when you have no shortening.

# Pecan-Cheese Pie

1 (8 oz.) pkg. cream cheese, softened
1/3 c. sugar
1 egg
1 tsp. vanilla extract
1/4 tsp. salt
1 unbaked 9 inch pastry shell
1 1/2 c. chopped pecans
1 c. light corn syrup
1/4 c. sugar
3 eggs, beaten
1 tsp. vanilla extract

Combine cream cheese and 1/3 cup sugar in a large bowl; beat at high speed of an electric mixer until fluffy. Add 1 egg, 1 teaspoon vanilla, and salt; blend well. Pour into pastry shell. Sprinkle with pecans. Set aside.

Combine corn syrup and remaining ingredients, stirring well. Pour over cream cheese mixture. Bake at 375° for 35 to 40 minutes until set. Cool completely. Chill until time to serve.

Grace Malone, *Dogwood Delights Volume II*, Dogwood Chapter No. 84

# Southern Pecan Pie

1/2 cup sugar
2 tablespoons melted butter
3 eggs, beaten
1 cup dark corn syrup
1 teaspoon vanilla extract
1/4 teaspoon salt
1 cup chopped pecans
1 unbaked 9-inch pie shell

Combine sugar, butter and eggs in medium bowl; mix well. Stir in corn syrup, vanilla, salt and pecans. Pour into pie shell. Bake at 350 degrees for 45 minutes or until set. Yield: 6 servings.

**Approx Per Serving:** Cal 580; Prot 6 g; Carbo 75 g; Fiber 2 g; T Fat 30 g; Chol 117 mg; Sod 377 mg.

Phyllis Cox, *Carolina Cooking*, North Carolina Chapter No. 35

## Sure-Set Pecan Pie

**½ cup sugar**
**3 tablespoons butter, softened**
**¼ cup flour**
**¼ teaspoon salt**
**3 eggs, beaten**
**1 cup light corn syrup**
**2 teaspoons vanilla extract**
**1 cup chopped pecans**
**1 unbaked 9-inch pie shell**

Cream sugar and butter in mixer bowl until light and fluffy. Add flour, salt, eggs, corn syrup and vanilla; mix well. Stir in pecans. Pour into pie shell. Bake at 350 degrees for 45 to 50 minutes or until knife inserted near center comes out clean. Yield: 8 servings.

Approx Per Serving: Cal 466; Prot 5 g; Carbo 61 g; Fiber 1 g; T Fat 24 g; 45% Calories from Fat; Chol 91 mg; Sod 306 mg.

Charles Clark, *Calling All Cooks three*, Alabama Chapter No. 34

## Pineapple Millionaire Pie

**2 c. sifted powdered sugar**
**¼ lb. margarine or butter, softened**
**2 large fresh whole eggs**
**⅛ t. salt**
**¼ t. vanilla**
**1 c. crushed pineapple, well drained**
**2 baked 9-inch pie crusts**
**1 c. heavy cream**
**½ c. sifted powdered sugar**
**½ c. chopped pecans**

Cream together 2 c. sifted powdered sugar and butter with electric mixer. Add eggs, salt and vanilla. Beat until light and fluffy. Spread mixture evenly into baked pie crusts, then chill. Whip cream until stiff. Blend in ½ c. powdered sugar. Fold in pineapple and pecans. Spread this mixture on top of base mixture and chill thoroughly. Yield: 2 9-inch pies.

Chris Pace, *Taste of Dixie*, Dixie Chapter No. 23

### A Helpful Hint

For fresh fruit pies all year, prepare several pie fillings in season and freeze them in pie plates lined with foil. Transfer to plastic bags when frozen. Just place a frozen filling in a baked pie shell and let thaw when ready to serve.

# Aunt Haley's Sister's Pies

1 can Eagle Brand milk
1 (8 oz.) Philadelphia cream cheese
juice of 2 lemons or 1/4 c.
1 (#) can crushed pineapple
1 can drained Mandarin oranges
1 large Cool Whip

Mix together well, then add 1 (#2) can crushed pineapple, 1 can Mandarin oranges, drained. Add 1 large container of Cool Whip, pecans (if desired). Pour into 2 graham cracker crusts. Will keep 2 weeks in the refrigerator.

Anna Campbell, *Pioneers Pots and Pans—1985 Cookbook*
North Florida Chapter No. 39

# Pumpkin Praline Pie

1 unbaked 10-inch pie shell
5 tablespoons unsalted butter, softened
1/2 cup packed light brown sugar
3/4 cup chopped walnuts
1/2 cup sugar
1 tablespoon unflavored gelatin
1 teaspoon cinnamon
1/2 teaspoon ginger
1/2 teaspoon nutmeg
1 1/2 cups eggnog
3 egg yolks
1 16-ounce can mashed pumpkin
3 egg whites
1/4 teaspoon cream of tartar
1/4 cup sugar
1 cup whipping cream

Bake pie shell at 450 degrees for 10 minutes. Cream butter and brown sugar in mixer bowl until light and fluffy. Stir in walnuts. Spread mixture in bottom of pie shell. Bake for 5 minutes or until sugar bubbles. Cool on wire rack. Combine 1/2 cup sugar, gelatin, cinnamon, ginger and nutmeg in saucepan. Add eggnog and egg yolks; mix well. Cook over medium heat until thickened, stirring constantly; do not boil. Remove from heat. Stir in pumpkin. Cool until thick enough to mound. Beat egg whites in large bowl until foamy. Add cream of tartar. Beat until soft peaks form. Add 1/4 cup sugar gradually, beating until stiff peaks form. Spoon over pumpkin mixture. Beat whipping cream in large bowl until stiff peaks form. Fold pumpkin with egg whites into whipped cream gently. Spoon into pie shell. Chill for several hours. Garnish with additional whipped cream and pecan halves.
Yield: 8 servings.

Patricia J. Tudor, *Kentucky Kitchens, Volume II*
Kentucky Chapter No. 32

## Sawdust Pie

1½ cups sugar
1½ cups coconut
1½ cups graham cracker crumbs
1½ cups coarsely chopped pecans
7 egg whites, unbeaten
1 unbaked 9-inch pie shell
Whipped cream
Bananas, sliced

Combine sugar, coconut, crumbs, pecans and egg whites in large bowl; stir until well mixed. Pour into pie shell. Bake at 350 degrees for 30 to 35 minutes or until set; do not overbake. Top with whipped cream and sliced bananas. Serve warm. Yield: 8 servings.

Ladonna Darnell, *Kentucky Kitchens, Volume II*, Kentucky Chapter No. 32

## Strawberry Glazed Pie

4 c. fresh strawberries
1 c. sugar (granulated)
¼ tsp. salt
3 tbsp. cornstarch
Red food coloring (optional)
1 tbsp. lemon juice
1 pkg. Lucky Whip
1 baked pie shell (deep dish)

Wash and hull strawberries, drain thoroughly. Arrange 2 cups of these berries over bottom of pie shell. (You can cut strawberries into bite size pieces—but whole berry is much more impressive presentation. —Edit.) Crush the remaining 2 cups of strawberries in a saucepan.

In a bowl mix together sugar, salt and cornstarch; stir into crushed berries. Heat slowly, stirring constantly. Cook until mixture thickens. (Add food coloring now, if desired.) Remove from heat; add lemon juice. Allow to cool.

Spoon mixture over strawberries in pie shell. Chill until filling sets. Top with Lucky Whip or whipped cream.

Lynn Newmaster
*A Tablespoon of Pioneering and a Teaspoon of Horses and the Handicapped*
Florida Gold Coast Chapter No. 83

# Strawberry-Ice Cream Pie

**Graham cracker crust**

**1/3 lb. graham crackers, crushed**
**3/4 stick oleo, melted**
**1/3 c. sugar**

Combine cracker crumbs and sugar; stir in melted oleo. Press into pie pan. Chill for 1 to 2 hours.

**Filling:**

**3 oz. lemon Jell-O**
**10 oz. frozen strawberries, almost thawed**
**1 pt. vanilla or strawberry ice cream**
**1 c. hot water**

Dissolve Jell-O with water. Stir in ice cream and beat; stir in strawberries. Add a few drops of red food coloring; beat for 1 minute. Chill for 1/2 hour, then pour into crust. Chill for 3 to 4 hours before serving.

Beverly Brodie, *Dogwood Delights Volume II*, Dogwood Chapter No. 84

# Black Walnut Pie

**2 egg whites**
**1 cup sugar**
**2 teaspoons baking powder**
**16 butter crackers, crushed**
**1 cup chopped black walnuts**
**1 teaspoon vanilla extract**
**1 unbaked 9-inch pie shell**
**1 cup whipping cream**
**2 tablespoons (or more) sugar**

Beat egg whites in mixer bowl until stiff. Add 1 cup sugar and baking powder gradually, beating constantly. Stir in cracker crumbs, walnuts and vanilla. Spoon into pie shell. Bake at 320 degrees for 20 to 25 minutes or until set. Beat whipping cream with 2 tablespoons sugar in mixer bowl. Spread over cooled pie. Chill until serving time.
Yield: 8 servings.

**Approx Per Serving:** Cal 460; Prot 7 g; Carbo 45 g; Fiber 1 g; T Fat 29 g; 56% Calories from Fat; Chol 41 mg; Sod 280 mg.

Bonnie Golden, *Calling All Cooks three*, Alabama Chapter No. 34

# Candy & Cookies

South Carolina Chapter 61

# Apricot Balls

$1^1/_2$ c. ground dried apricots
2 c. coconut, flaked
$^2/_3$ c. Eagle Brand milk

Mix well. Shape into balls. Roll in powdered sugar.

Mrs. Charles P. Toops, *Pioneers Pots and Pans—1985 Cookbook*
North Florida Chapter No. 39

# Kentucky Bourbon Balls

1 cup margarine, softened
1 14-ounce can sweetened condensed milk
$4^1/_2$ to 5 pounds confectioners' sugar
$^2/_3$ cup Kentucky Bourbon
Pecan halves
$^1/_2$ stick Para-Seal Wax
4 cups semisweet chocolate
$^1/_4$ cup butter

Cream margarine in mixer bowl until light and fluffy. Stir in condensed milk; mix well. Add sugar alternately with Bourbon, mixing well after each addition. Press 1 teaspoonful at a time around pecan half; shape into ball. Place on waxed paper-lined trays. Chill overnight. Melt paraffin in double boiler. Add chocolate and $^1/_4$ cup butter; stir until chocolate is melted and mixture is well blended. Dip Bourbon balls into chocolate mixture; place on waxed paper. Let stand until firm. Make coconut bonbons by omitting most of the Bourbon and the pecans and adding desired amount of coconut. Reduce confectioners' sugar as necessary. Yield: 16 dozen.

Wilma Sullivan, *Kentucky Kitchens, Volume II*, Kentucky Chapter No. 32

## A Helpful Hint

Make candy in a saucepan with 3 or 4 times the volume of the combined ingredients so the candy can boil freely without boiling over. Use a wooden spoon and a saucepan with a heavy bottom.

## Christmas Wreaths

**30 large marshmallows**
**1 stick butter**
**1 tsp. vanilla**
**2 tsp. green food coloring**
**3½ c. corn flakes**
**Red cinnamon candies**

Melt butter and marshmallows together in large saucepan over medium-low heat, stirring constantly. When completely melted, remove from heat and add vanilla and coloring. Mix well. Stir in *uncrushed* corn flakes until flakes are completely covered, but not broken. Allow to cool only enough to handle. Mixture will be very sticky and hard to handle, but take small portion (about 2 tablespoons) in hand and shape into 2½ inch wreaths. Place on waxed paper. While still warm, place cinnamon candies around on wreath for berry effect. I usually use about 5 per wreath. These will get firm as they dry but they need to be handled carefully. They are a little trouble but the end result is well worth it.

This might be formed into 1 large wreath for center piece.

Bob and Jo Fannin, *Dogwood Delights*, Dogwood Chapter No. 84

## Church Windows

**1 (12 oz.) pkg. semi-sweet chocolate chips**
**1 stick margarine**
**1 bag colored miniature marshmallows**
**1 can coconut**
**1 c. chopped pecans**

Melt chocolate chips and margarine; cool. Pour mixture over marshmallows and nuts. Use 4 pieces of wax paper. Divide mixture; with hands pat together. Make 4 rolls. Sprinkle coconut over rolls; roll in wax paper. Refrigerate 2 hours and slice.

Hazel Campbell, *Calling All Cooks*, Alabama Chapter No. 34

# *No-Fail Divinity*

4 c. sugar
3/4 c. water
3 egg whites
1/2 c. nuts
1 c. light corn syrup
Salt
1 tsp. vanilla

Mix sugar, corn syrup, water and salt in 2-quart casserole. Cook in microwave oven 19 minutes, stirring every 5 minutes. Candy thermometer should read 260°. If not, cook 1 or 2 minutes longer. While syrup cooks, beat egg whites very stiff in a large bowl. Gradually pour hot syrup over egg whites and continue beating at a high speed until thick and candy starts to lose its gloss. Beating may require about 12 minutes. Add vanilla and nuts to beaten mixture. Drop by teaspoons onto waxed paper. Candy may be tinted with food coloring for special occasions.

Dianne Lowe, *Dogwood Delights*, Dogwood Chapter No. 84

# *Ripple Divinity*

3 c. sugar
1/2 c. water
1/2 c. white Karo syrup
2 egg whites, stiffly beaten
1 tsp. vanilla
1 c. chocolate pieces

Combine sugar, water and Karo syrup into 2 quart saucepan. Cook over high heat to boiling point. Reduce heat and continue cooking until mixture reaches 240°. Slowly pour 1/3 of mixture over egg whites, beating constantly. Cook remaining syrup to 265° (hard ball stage). Then gradually add to first mixture. Beat until mixture will hold shape when dropped from a spoon. Add vanilla and fold in chocolate pieces. Drop from teaspoon onto waxed paper.

4 dozen pieces.

NOTE: Black walnuts or shredded coconut may be substituted for chocolate pieces if desired.

Vera Peyton, *Pioneers Pots and Pans—1985 Cookbook*
North Florida Chapter No. 39

## *A Helpful Hint*

Choose a cool dry day to make candy. Hard candies, divinities, fondants and nougats are especially sensitive to humid conditions.

## *Forever Ambers*

**1 lb. orange slices, chopped fine**
**1 7 oz. pkg. frozen coconut**
**2 c. condensed milk**
**1 t. vanilla**
**powdered sugar**

Combine all ingredients except powdered sugar and mix well. Spread on lightly oiled baking sheet and bake at 275° for 30 min. Remove from oven. While hot, form mixture into small balls and roll in powdered sugar. Place on cooling rack and cool.

Gladys Hardegree, *Taste of Dixie*, Dixie Chapter No. 23

## *Fantasy Fudge*

**3 c. sugar**
**3/4 c. margarine**
**2/3 c. evaporated milk (5 1/3 oz. can)**
**1 c. chopped nuts**
**1 (12 oz.) pkg. semi-sweet chocolate pieces**
**1 jar Kraft marshmallow creme**
**1 tsp. vanilla**

Combine sugar, margarine and milk; bring to a rolling boil, stirring constantly (mixture scorches easily). Remove from heat; stir in chocolate pieces until melted. Add marshmallow creme, nuts and vanilla; beat until well blended. Pour into a greased 13x9 inch pan. Cool; cut in squares.

*Bell's Best*, Mississippi Chapter No. 36

## *Microwave Fudge*

**1 box powdered sugar**
**1/2 c. Hershey's cocoa (dry)**

Mix well.

**1 stick margarine or butter**
**1/4 c. milk (just pour over mixture)**

Microwave on high for 2 minutes; stir vigorously and add 1 teaspoon vanilla and nuts, if desired.

Pour into greased pan and chill.

Dottie Jackson, *Pioneers Pots and Pans—1985 Cookbook*
North Florida Chapter No. 39

# *Martha Washington Balls*

**2 boxes confectioners' sugar**
**1 can Eagle Brand condensed milk**
**2 c. Angel Flake coconut**
**2 c. chopped pecans**
**2 sticks oleo**
**1 tsp. vanilla**
**Large pkg. chocolate chips**
**1 stick paraffin wax**

Mix sifted powdered sugar, condensed milk, coconut, chopped pecans, oleo and vanilla. Form into small balls; chill overnight. Melt large package chocolate chips and wax in top of double boiler over hot water. Dip balls with toothpicks into mixture. Put on waxed paper to dry. Makes 100 pieces or more.

**Note**: wax will catch on fire if it is melted directly over heat. Be sure to melt it over water in a double boiler.

Eleanor Johnson, *Bell's Best*, Mississippi Chapter No. 36

# *Sheriff's Peanut Brittle*

**3 cups sugar**
**1 cup light corn syrup**
**1½ cups water**
**1 cup peanuts**
**¼ cup margarine**
**1 teaspoon vanilla extract**
**2 tablespoons baking soda**

Combine sugar, corn syrup and water in saucepan. Cook over medium-high heat to 230 to 234 degrees on candy thermometer, spun thread stage. Add peanuts. Cook until peanuts are golden brown. Stir in margarine until melted. Stir in vanilla and baking soda until foamy. Pour onto buttered surface. Let stand until cool enough to handle. Pull with buttered hands until stiff. Break into pieces.
Yield: 18 to 24 servings.

W. G. Tallent, *Lawfully Good Eating*, Dixie Chapter No. 23

## *A Helpful Hint*

The hard-crack stage of candy making is reached when a drop of the mixture in cold water separates into hard threads that crack when pressed.

## Peanut Brittle

2 c. sugar
1 c. white Karo syrup
1/2 c. water
1/4 tsp. salt
2 c. raw peanuts
4 tsp. baking soda

In a large pan, bring all ingredients to a boil. Cook until hard crackle when dropped into cold water. Remove from heat and add 4 teaspoons baking soda. Stir vigorously till all soda is dissolved. It will foam up. Pour into greased 9x13 inch pan immediately. Do not spread with spoon, just let it spread itself. Let cool; remove from pan and break into pieces.

Lois Moman, *Calling All Cooks two*, Alabama Chapter No. 34

## Peanut Brittle

2 c. sugar
1 c. white Karo syrup
1/2 c. water
1 pt. shelled peanuts (fresh, unsalted)
1 tsp. paraffin shavings
1 tsp. soda

Mix all ingredients, except peanuts and soda. Bring to a boil; add peanuts. When peanuts stop popping, remove from heat; add 1 teaspoon soda. Pour onto a greased cookie sheet; do not stir. Let cool. Break into pieces.

Dot Doster, *Bell's Best*, Mississippi Chapter No. 36

*Pioneers working on Nature Trail at Rocky Bottom Camp for the Blind.* (South Carolina Chapter No. 61)

# *Microwave Peanut Brittle*

**1 cup sugar**
**1/2 cup white corn syrup**
**1 cup roasted, salted peanuts**
**1 tsp. margarine**
**1 tsp. vanilla**
**1 tsp. baking soda**

Stir sugar and syrup in 1/2 quart microwavable casserole dish and microwave on high, uncovered, for 4 minutes. Stir in peanuts and microwave, uncovered, on high 3 to 5 minutes.* Add margarine and vanilla. Blend well. Microwave, uncovered, 1 to 2 minutes. Add baking soda and stir gently until light and foamy. Pour onto greased cookie sheet (use margarine or Crisco, do not use "No stick cooking spry;" it will make the candy sticky on bottom). Cool and crack.

*Try using the lower amount of time first.

John Diamond, *Secret Recipes of Telephone Pioneers, Volume III*
South Carolina Chapter No. 61

# *Easy Pecan Rolls*

**16 oz. box vanilla wafers**
**16 oz. large marshmallows**
**2 1/2 c. pecans**
**1 can condensed milk**
**white powdered sugar**

Crush vanilla wafers into crumbs. Cut marshmallows with scissors and mix with crumbs. (Use butter on scissors to keep from sticking.) Add pecans and condensed milk. Mix well. Squeeze into balls and roll in powdered sugar.

Faye Boyette, *Pioneers Pots and Pans—1985 Cookbook*
North Florida Chapter No. 39

# *Cream Pralines*

**1 lb. brown sugar**
**1/8 tsp. salt**
**3/4 c. evaporated milk**
**1 Tbsp. butter**
**2 c. pecan halves**

Mix sugar, salt, milk and butter in pan. Cook until sugar dissolves. Add pecans and cook to soft ball stage, stirring entire time. Remove from heat. Cool 5 minutes. Stir rapidly until mixture is thickened. Drop by spoonfuls onto aluminum foil.

Teri Stricklen, *Pioneers Pots and Pans—1985 Cookbook*
North Florida Chapter No. 39

## New Orleans Pralines

3 c. sugar
1 c. light cream
1/4 tsp. salt
2 Tbsp. butter
2 tsp. vanilla
2 c. pecan halves

Combine 2 cups sugar, light cream, salt, and butter in large, heavy saucepan over low heat, stirring often. In a small, heavy saucepan, melt remaining 1 cup sugar over low heat. Pour the melted sugar into hot sugar-cream mixture very slowly, stirring constantly. Cook until candy thermometer registers 235° or soft ball stage. Remove from heat and stir in vanilla and nuts. Beat or stir until mixture begins to thicken. Drop rounded teaspoons onto foil or waxed paper until cool.

Joyce Teasley, *Dogwood Delights*, Dogwood Chapter No. 84

## Pecan Pralines

2 c. white sugar
1 c. evaporated milk
2 c. pecans
1 tsp. vanilla flavoring

Mix sugar, milk and vanilla. Cook very slowly for about 1 1/2–2 hours until soft ball stage is reached. Beat well and add pecans. Drop by tablespoonfuls onto waxed paper.

Jeanette English, *Pots, Pans & Pioneers II*, Louisiana Chapter No. 24

## Almond Cookies

2 c. flour
1 c. lard or butter
2/3 c. sugar
1 Tbsp. almond extract
1/3 c. fine crushed and blanched almond nuts (food processor works best)
1 egg
1/2 tsp. baking soda
1 tsp. baking powder
1/3 c. almonds for cookie centers
1/4 tsp. salt

Cream lard and sugar together. Add almond extract, egg, flour, crushed almonds, baking soda, baking powder, and salt. Knead dough until very smooth. Form into small balls. Press. Lay on ungreased cookie sheet 1 inch apart. Press on almond half gently, but firmly, in the center of each. Bake 15 to 20 minutes in 350° oven or until golden brown. Makes 4 dozen. Serve with hot Jasmin Tea.

Sarah A. Drewes, *Kentucky Kitchens, Volume I*, Kentucky Chapter No. 32

## Anise Cookies

3 eggs
$1\frac{3}{4}$ c. plain flour
$\frac{1}{2}$ tsp. salt
1 c. sugar plus 2 Tbsp.
$\frac{1}{2}$ tsp. baking powder
1 tsp. anise extract or 5 drops anise oil

Beat eggs on high speed for 10 minutes; add sugar and beat an additional 17 minutes. Add salt, flour and baking powder; add anise oil or extract. Beat about 3 minutes on low. Line cookie sheets with waxed paper. Drop by teaspoonful onto waxed paper, leaving space between for cookies to spread. Let set 8 hours. Bake at 325° for 8 to 10 minutes.

Mrs. Amy Clements, *Pots, Pans and Pioneers III*
Louisiana Chapter No. 24

## Boiled Cookies

2 cups sugar
$\frac{1}{2}$ cup baking cocoa
$\frac{1}{2}$ cup milk
$\frac{1}{2}$ cup butter or margarine
2 cups quick-cooking oats
2 cups chopped pecans
1 teaspoon vanilla extract

Combine sugar, cocoa, milk and butter in saucepan. Bring to a full rolling boil. Cook for 2 minutes. Remove from heat. Stir in oats, pecans and vanilla. Drop by spoonfuls onto waxed paper. Yield: 48 servings.

Ann Dunbrack, *Lawfully Good Eating*, Dixie Chapter No. 23

## Chocolate Oatmeal No-Bake Cookies

2 cups sugar
3 tablespoons baking cocoa
$\frac{1}{2}$ cup milk
$\frac{1}{2}$ cup butter
3 cups oats
2 tablespoons peanut butter
$\frac{1}{2}$ teaspoon vanilla extract

Combine sugar, baking cocoa, milk and butter in saucepan. Bring to a boil for 2 minutes, stirring constantly. Remove from heat. Add oats, peanut butter and vanilla; mix well. Drop by teaspoonfuls onto waxed paper-lined trays. Let stand until cool. Yield: 32 servings.

**Approx Per Serving:** Cal 113; Prot 2 g; Carbo 18 g; Fiber 1 g; T Fat 4 g; Chol 8 mg; Sod 30 mg.

Patricia L. Goodin, *Carolina Cooking*, North Carolina Chapter No. 35

## Date Balls

1 8-ounce package whole pitted dates, chopped
1/2 cup margarine
3/4 cup sugar
1 egg
1 cup chopped pecans
2 1/2 cups crisp rice cereal
Confectioners' sugar

Combine dates, margarine, sugar and egg in heavy saucepan. Cook over low heat until thickened and creamy, stirring constantly. Remove from heat. Stir in pecans and cereal. Shape into balls. Roll in confectioners' sugar. Place on waxed paper. Let stand until cool. Store in airtight container. Yield: 32 servings.

Jo Ann Goins, *Carolina Cooking*, North Carolina Chapter No. 35

## Humdingers

2 sticks margarine
1 c. sugar
8 oz. chopped dates
1 c. chopped pecans
2 c. Rice Krispies
2 tsp. vanilla

Melt margarine and sugar. Add dates. Cook for about 5 minutes, then add pecans, Rice Krispies, and vanilla. Shape into balls and roll in powdered sugar.

Frances M. Barnes, *Bell's Best 3*, Mississippi Chapter No. 36

*Pioneers assembling "Read to Me" packets to be donated to area hospitals.* (Mississippi Chapter No. 36)

# Mudball Cookies

6 tablespoons baking cocoa
2 tablespoons melted margarine
3 cups oats
3/4 cup nonfat dry milk
1 cup corn syrup
1/2 cup chunky peanut butter
2 teaspoons vanilla extract
1/2 teaspoon salt
1/2 cup seedless raisins

Combine cocoa, margarine, oats, dry milk, corn syrup, peanut butter, vanilla, salt and raisins in large bowl; mix well. Shape into balls. Store in airtight container at room temperature or in freezer. May press into 8x8-inch dish and cut into squares if preferred. Yield: 36 servings.

**Approx Per Serving:** Cal 94; Prot 3 g; Carbo 15 g; Fiber 1 g; T Fat 3 g; Chol <1 mg; Sod 67 mg.
**Dietary Exchanges:** Bread/Starch 1/2; Fat 1/2

"*Answering the Call of Those in Need*," Tennessee Chapter No. 21

# Cake Mix Cookies

1/2 c. oil
1 box cake mix (your choice)
2 eggs
1 small pkg. Jello (same flavor as cake)

Mix Jello and cake mix dry; add eggs and oil. Roll into small balls; flatten. Bake on cookie sheet for about 18 minutes in 350° oven.

Virginia Lowrey, *Pots, Pans and Pioneers III*, Louisiana Chapter No. 24

# Cheese Bars

1 2-layer package butter-flavored cake mix
1/2 cup melted margarine
1 egg
1 cup chopped pecans
8 ounces cream cheese, softened
2 eggs
1 1-pound package confectioners' sugar

Combine cake mix, melted margarine, 1 egg and pecans in bowl; mix well. Press into 9x13-inch baking pan. Mix cream cheese, 2 eggs and confectioners' sugar in bowl. Spread in prepared pan. Bake at 325 degrees for 1 hour. Cool in pan. Cut into squares. Yield: 24 servings.

Hilda Harrison, *Lawfully Good Eating*, Dixie Chapter No. 23

## Chess Squares

**1 box butter cake mix**
**1 stick butter**
**1 box powdered sugar**
**4 eggs, divided**
**1 (8 oz.) pkg. cream cheese**
**2 tsp. vanilla**

Mix cake mix, butter and 1 egg, press into 9x13-inch pan. Mix remaining ingredients and pour over cake mix. Bake at 350° for 30–40 minutes. Let cool and cut into squares.

Gayle Palermo, *Pots, Pans & Pioneers II*, Louisiana Chapter No. 24

## Chinese Chews

(Serves 10)

**1 c. flour**
**1 c. sugar**
**1 c. chopped dates**
**1 c. chopped nuts**
**1 egg**
**1 tsp. vanilla**
**1 stick butter, melted**

Combine all ingredients. Spread in greased pan. Bake 20–30 minutes at 325° to 350°. Cool and cut into squares.

Barbara G. Cobbs, *Dogwood Delights*, Dogwood Chapter No. 84

## Black-Eyed Susans

**1/2 cup butter, softened**
**1/2 cup sugar**
**1/2 cup packed brown sugar**
**1 egg**
**1 1/2 tablespoons warm water**
**1 teaspoon vanilla extract**
**1 cup peanut butter**
**1 1/2 cups flour**
**1/2 teaspoon salt**
**1/2 teaspoon baking soda**
**1/2 cup semisweet chocolate chips**

Cream butter, sugar and brown sugar in mixer bowl until light and fluffy. Add egg, water, vanilla and peanut butter; beat well. Add mixture of flour, salt and baking soda; mix well. Press through cookie press fitted with flower disc onto greased cookie sheet. Place chocolate chip in center of each. Bake at 350 degrees for 8 minutes or until light brown. Remove to wire racks to cool. Chill for 30 minutes or until chocolate centers are firm. Yield: 10 dozen.

Frances Hixon, *Lawfully Good Eating*, Dixie Chapter No. 23

## Chocolate No-Bakes

(So rich they can be served as candy)

*Blend together:*

¹⁄₄ c. butter or margarine, melted
¹⁄₂ c. confectioners' sugar
¹⁄₄ c. cocoa
1 egg, slightly beaten

*Stir in:*

2 c. finely crushed graham crackers
¹⁄₂ c. flaked coconut
¹⁄₂ c. finely chopped nuts

Press into 13x9x2 inch dish or pan. Chill. Melted ¹⁄₄ cup butter or margarine.

*Add:*

2 Tbsp. milk
1 tsp. vanilla
2 tsp. dry vanilla pudding mix (not instant)

Cook and stir until mixture thickens and boils. Remove from heat. Beat in 2 cups confectioners' sugar. Spread over first layer. Chill. Melt 6 ounces (1 cup) chocolate chips. Spread over top and chill. Cut into small bars for dessert or bite-size pieces for candy.

**Note:** Cuts easier before final chilling.

Walter Anderson, *Dogwood Delights Volume II, Dogwood Chapter No. 84*

## Chocolate-Caramel Layer Squares

1 (14 oz.) bag caramels
1 c. evaporated milk (divided ¹⁄₃ c. and ²⁄₃ c.)
³⁄₄ c. butter or margarine, softened
1 (18¹⁄₂ oz.) pkg. regular German chocolate cake mix
1 c. chopped pecans
1 (6 oz.) pkg. semi-sweet chocolate morsels

Combine caramels and ¹⁄₃ cup evaporated milk in top of a double boiler. Cook, stirring constantly, until caramels are completely melted. Remove double boiler from heat. Combine cake mix, remaining ²⁄₃ cup milk and butter, mixing with electric mixer until dough holds together; stir in nuts. Press half of cake mixture into a greased 13x9x2 inch pan. Bake in preheated 350° oven for 6 minutes. Sprinkle chocolate morsels over crust. Pour caramel mixture over chocolate morsels, spreading evenly. Crumble remaining cake mixture over caramel mixture. Return pan to oven and bake 15–18 minutes; cool. Chill 30 minutes; cut into small squares.

Helen McMullen, *Bell's Best* 2, Mississippi Chapter No. 36

## Coleman Christmas Cookies

**Origin:** Hilda Hanna Coleman. **Country:** U.S.A., North Carolina. **City:** Burlington. **Approximate year created:** 1936. **Relative obtained from:** Sister (Brenda Coleman). **Brief history:** Passed down through generations of Hilda Hanna Coleman's family from North Carolina.

- 1½ lb. pecans, shelled (24 oz.), broken up
- 1 lb. sliced glazed pineapple, cut into small pieces
- ½ lb. chopped candied cherries (4 oz. red, 4 oz. green), cut into fourths
- 1 lb. white or golden raisins
- 1 c. brown sugar
- 4 eggs, well beaten
- 3 c. plain flour
- ½ tsp. nutmeg
- 1 tsp. vanilla
- 1 tsp. soda
- ½ c. butter or margarine
- ½ c. cherry brandy (can use more)

In a large bowl or pot, beat sugar, butter and eggs together. Sift flour, soda and nutmeg together into mixture. This will get too thick for electric mixer; use large wooden spoon. Mix well. Add brandy, vanilla, fruit, and nuts; mix well. Chill overnight or a couple of hours. Drop by spoon onto greased cookie sheet. Bake for 10 to 15 minutes at 350°.

**Preparation time:** 1 hour.
**No. of servings:** 10 dozen cookies.

Shirley Tillman, *A Taste of Pioneering*
Florida Gold Coast Chapter No. 83

## Candy Kiss Cookies

**Origin:** Obtained from a friend. **Brief history:** Great for a Christmas cookie.

- 1 c. butter, softened
- 2 c. all-purpose flour
- ½ c. confectioners' sugar
- 1 tsp. vanilla extract
- 1 c. chopped pecans (fine)
- 36 Hershey's kisses

Cream butter, flour, and sugar together. Add vanilla extract and nuts. Roll dough into 1¼ inch balls. Roll balls around Hershey's kiss. Place on ungreased cookie sheet. Bake at 375° for 12 to 15 minutes or until cookies are set, not brown. Cool; roll in confectioners' sugar.

**Preparation time:** ½ hour.
**Cooking time:** 12 to 15 minutes.
**No. of servings:** 3 dozen.

Joyce Terry, *A Taste of Pioneering*, Florida Gold Coast Chapter No. 83

## Congo Bars

2/3 c. melted shortening
1 box (1 lb.) brown sugar
3 eggs
2 3/4 c. sifted flour
2 1/2 tsp. baking powder
1/2 tsp. salt
1 c. chopped walnuts
1 pkg. (6 oz.) chocolate bits

Blend melted shortening and brown sugar. Add eggs, 1 at a time, beating well. Add dry ingredients, blending well. Stir in nuts and chocolate or nuts and 1 cup of white raisins. Spoon the batter (it will be very thick) into a well greased and floured oblong pan (13x9x2 inches). Bake in a moderate oven 350° about 40 minutes until golden or until cake tester comes away clean. Cool in pan before cutting into squares or bars.

Priscilla Young, *Pioneers Pots and Pans—1985 Cookbook*
North Florida Chapter No. 39

## Greek Butter Cookies

2 cups butter, softened
1/2 cup confectioners' sugar, sifted
2 egg yolks
1 teaspoon vanilla extract
4 1/2 cups flour, sifted
1 teaspoon baking powder
1/2 cup (or more) confectioners' sugar

Cream butter in bowl for 10 to 15 minutes or until very light. Add 1/2 cup confectioners' sugar, egg yolks and vanilla; mix well. Stir in flour and baking powder. Shape dough into small crescents. Place 1 inch apart on 2 ungreased cookie sheets. Bake at 375 degrees for 15 minutes or until lightly browned. Place cookies carefully on waxed paper sprinkled with 1/4 cup confectioners' sugar. Cool thoroughly. Store in airtight container. Yield: 60 servings.

**Approx Per Serving:** Cal 98; Prot 1 g; Carbo 9 g; Fiber <1 g; T Fat 6 g; Chol 24 mg; Sod 58 mg.

Anne Beratis, *Carolina Cooking*, North Carolina Chapter No. 35

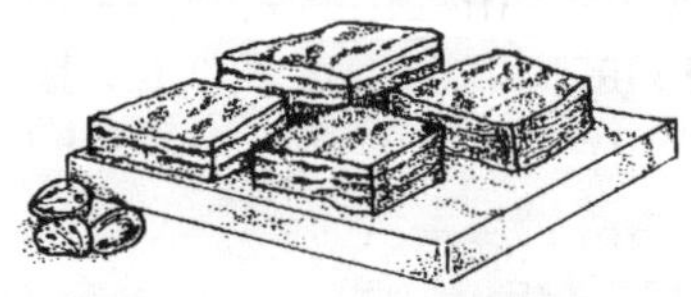

## *Gumdrop Cookies*

1 cup shortening
1 cup packed brown sugar
1 cup sugar
2 eggs, beaten
2 cups flour
1 teaspoon baking powder
1 teaspoon baking soda
1/4 teaspoon salt
2 cups oats
1 cup flaked coconut or chopped pecans
1 teaspoon vanilla extract
1 cup chopped gumdrops

Combine shortening, brown sugar, sugar, eggs, flour, baking powder, baking soda, salt, oats, coconut, vanilla and gumdrops in bowl; mix well. Drop by spoonfuls onto nonstick cookie sheet. Bake at 350 degrees for 10 minutes or until light brown. Yield: 100 servings.

Becky Davis, *Lawfully Good Eating*, Dixie Chapter No. 23

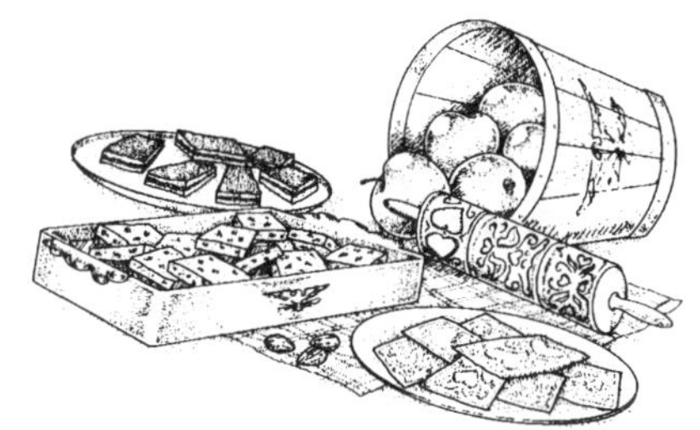

## *Lemon Squares*

1 2-layer package lemon cake mix
1 egg, beaten
1/2 cup melted butter
8 ounces cream cheese, softened
2 eggs
2 tablespoons lemon juice
1 1-pound package confectioners' sugar

Combine cake mix, beaten egg and melted butter in bowl; mix well. Press into 9x13-inch baking pan sprayed with nonstick cooking spray. Combine cream cheese, remaining 2 eggs, lemon juice and confectioners' sugar in bowl; mix well. Spread into prepared pan. Bake at 350 degrees for 40 minutes. Cool. Cut into squares. Garnish with additional confectioners' sugar. Yield: 15 servings.

**Approx Per Serving:** Cal 409; Prot 4 g; Carbo 65 g; Fiber <1 g; T Fat 15 g; Chol 76 mg; Sod 320 mg.

Katie Grist, *Carolina Cooking*, North Carolina Chapter No. 35

## Coconut-Lemon Squares

1 c. graham cracker crumbs
1 (14 fl. oz.) can sweetened condensed milk
1/4 c. melted butter
1/3 c. lemon juice
1/2 tsp. grated lemon rind
5 1/4 c. (12 oz.) Cool Whip, thawed
2 2/3 c. flaked coconut

Combine graham cracker crumbs and melted butter. Press firmly into bottom of a 9 inch square pan. Combine milk, lemon juice and rind in a large bowl. Fold in 3 1/2 cups of the whipped topping and 1 1/2 cups of the coconut. Spread mixture over crumbs. Sprinkle with remaining coconut. Chill for at least 2 hours. Cut into squares. Top with remaining whipped topping. Garnish with lemon slices and mint leaves if desired. Makes 9 servings.

Maxine Lawley-Sutherland, *Calling All Cooks two*
Alabama Chapter No. 34

## Diabetic Cookies

1 stick margarine
1/4 c. milk
1 sq. unsweetened chocolate
1 box chopped raisins
1 box ground dates
1 c. chopped nuts
1/2 c. peanut butter
1 tsp. liquid sweetener
3 c. quick oatmeal
1 tsp. vanilla

Cook chocolate, milk and margarine for 1 minute. Stir while cooking. Add remaining ingredients and mix with hands. Roll into walnut size balls. Do not bake. Can be frozen. Makes 40.

Eunice Thompson, *Dogwood Delights Volume II*
Dogwood Chapter No. 84

## Fruit Cake Cookies

1 lb. candied fruit
1 pinch of salt
1 can condensed milk
1/2 c. flour
2 c. pecans
1 (3 1/2 oz.) can coconut

Dredge fruit in flour. Add salt, nuts and coconut; mix well. Add milk; stir. Drop by teaspoonfuls on greased cookie sheet. Bake 25–30 minutes at 275°.

Marie Benfield, *Pots, Pans and Pioneers III*, Louisiana Chapter No. 24

## Hog Hedges

2 c. walnuts
1 c. dates
2 c. coconut
1 c. brown sugar
2 eggs, slightly beaten

Put nuts and dates through food chopper. Mix nuts and dates with 1½ cups coconut, sugar and eggs. Shape into rolls about ¾ inch thick, 1 inch wide, and 1 inch long. Roll in remaining ½ cup coconut. Place on ungreased cookie sheet and bake at 350° for 10–12 minutes.

Dot Swaitek, *Dogwood Delights*, Dogwood Chapter No. 84

## Lemon Delight Bars

½ cup margarine, softened
1 cup flour
¼ cup sugar
2 eggs
1 cup sugar
3 tablespoons lemon juice
2 tablespoons flour
½ teaspoon baking powder
Confectioners' sugar

Combine margarine, 1 cup flour and ¼ cup sugar in bowl; mix well. Press into 9x9-inch baking pan. Bake at 350 degrees for 10 minutes. Combine eggs, 1 cup sugar, lemon juice, 2 tablespoons flour and baking powder in bowl; mix well. Spread over baked layer. Bake for 20 minutes longer. Sprinkle with confectioners' sugar. Cool on wire rack. Cut into squares. Yield: 16 servings.

Betty Krueger, *Kentucky Kitchens, Volume II*, Kentucky Chapter No. 32

## Lemon Drops

1 box Betty Crocker white cake mix
½ lemon rind, grated
½ orange rind, grated
Juice of 1 lemon
Juice of 1 orange
¾ box confectioners' sugar (XXXX) sugar

Mix cake mix according to instructions on box. Bake in oven at 350° in greased and floured pans. (Use miniature muffin pans—Baker's Joy is good to use to grease and flour pans.) Have ready grated lemon and orange rinds, juice of lemon and orange, and XXXX sugar (sifted). (Do not mix until cakes are ready to be dipped.) Put on wax paper after dipped for glaze to dry. Turn muffins after dry on one side so other side can dry.

Helen Atherton, *Dogwood Delights Volume II*, Dogwood Chapter No. 84

# Nieman-Marcus Cookies

**2 cups butter, softened**
**2 cups packed brown sugar**
**2 cups sugar**
**4 eggs**
**2 teaspoons vanilla extract**
**4 cups flour**
**1 teaspoon salt**
**2 teaspoons baking powder**
**2 teaspoons baking soda**
**2/3 cup chocolate chips**
**1 8-ounce chocolate bar, grated**
**3 cups chopped pecans**
**5 cups oats, pulverized**

Cream butter, brown sugar and sugar in mixer bowl until light and fluffy. Stir in eggs and vanilla. Add flour, salt, baking powder and baking soda; mix well. Stir in chips, grated chocolate, pecans and oats. Shape into small balls. Place 2 inches apart on nonstick cookie sheet. Bake at 375 degrees for 6 minutes. Cool on cookie sheet for several minutes. Remove to wire rack to cool completely. Yield: 112 servings.

Linda Yates, *Lawfully Good Eating*, Dixie Chapter No. 23

# Nutty Fingers

**1 cup butter, softened**
**1/4 cup confectioners' sugar**
**2 cups flour**
**1 cup chopped pecans**
**1/4 cup confectioners' sugar**

Cream butter and 1/4 cup confectioners' sugar in bowl until light and fluffy. Stir in flour. Add pecans; mix well. Shape by 2 tablespoonfuls into 3-inch fingers on lightly greased cookie sheet. Bake at 350 degrees for 20 minutes. Roll warm cookies in remaining 1/4 cup confectioners' sugar. Cool on wire rack completely. Yield: 24 servings.

**Approx Per Serving:** Cal 148; Prot 2 g; Carbo 11 g; Fiber 1 g; T Fat 11 g; Chol 21 mg; Sod 65 mg.

Kim Parker, *Carolina Cooking*, North Carolina Chapter No. 35

## A Helpful Hint

If the dough for rolled cookies seems too soft, do not add more flour, as this will toughen the dough. Instead, chill it until it is firm and then roll a small amount at a time.

# Orange Slice Cookies

3 eggs, beaten
2 cups packed brown sugar
1 teaspoon vanilla extract
1 tablespoon water
2 cups flour
1 16-ounce package orange slice candy, chopped
1 cup coconut
1 cup chopped pecans

Combine beaten eggs, brown sugar, vanilla and water in bowl; mix well. stir in flour and candy. Add coconut and pecans; mix well. Drop by tablespoonfuls 2 inches apart onto lightly greased cookie sheet. Bake at 350 degrees for 25 minutes or until lightly browned. Cool on cookie sheet for 2 minutes. Remove to wire rack to cool completely.
Yield: 24 servings.

**Approx Per Serving:** Cal 231; Prot 2 g; Carbo 45 g; Fiber 1 g; T Fat 5 g; Chol 27 mg; Sod 32 mg.

Carolyn Austin, *Carolina Cooking*, North Carolina Chapter No. 35

# Over-That Cookies

1 stick oleo, melted
1 c. graham crackers
1 c. oatmeal
1 c. coconut
1 (6 oz.) pkg. chocolate or butterscotch chips
1 c. nuts
1 can Eagle Brand milk

Place by layers in baking dish. Pour Eagle Brand milk over it. Bake for 30 minutes at 350°. Cut in squares when cool.

Janice Howton, *Pioneers Pots and Pans—1985 Cookbook*
North Florida Chapter No. 39

## Carrie's Famous Cookies

**1 cup butter, softened**
**1 cup peanut butter**
**1 cup sugar**
**1 cup packed brown sugar**
**2 eggs**
**2 cups flour**
**1 teaspoon baking soda**
**1/4 teaspoon salt**
**1/2 cup chocolate chips**
**1 cup chopped pecans**
**1 1/2 cups flaked coconut**
**1 1/2 cups raisins**

Cream butter and peanut butter in mixer bowl until fluffy. Beat in sugar and brown sugar. Add eggs 1 at a time, beating well after each addition. Add mixture of flour, baking soda and salt gradually; mix well. Stir in chocolate chips, pecans, coconut and raisins. Drop by teaspoonfuls onto lightly greased cookie sheet. Bake at 350 degrees for 20 minutes or until light brown. Remove to wire rack to cool. Yield: 75 servings.

**Approx Per Serving:** Cal 108; Prot 2 g; Carbo 13 g; Fiber 1 g; T Fat 6 g; 50% Calories from Fat; Chol 12 mg; Sod 63 mg.

Carrie Thomas-Evans, *Calling All Cooks three*, Alabama Chapter No. 34

## Peanut Butter Fudge Bars

**Origin:** Family Cookbook. **Country:** U.S.A. **City:** Vero Beach. **Approximate year created:** 1950–1986.

**1 (6 oz.) pkg. semi-sweet chocolate pieces**
**1 (14 oz.) can sweetened condensed milk (not evaporated)**
**1/2 tsp. vanilla**
**2/3 c. butter or margarine, softened**
**1/2 c. peanut butter**
**1 c. firmly packed brown sugar**
**1 1/2 c. flour**
**1 c. quick-cooking rolled oats**

Preheat oven to 350°. Grease a 13x9 inch baking pan; set aside. In small saucepan, melt chocolate with condensed milk over low heat, stirring occasionally. Remove from heat; stir in vanilla. In large bowl, beat butter with peanut butter and sugar until blended. Stir in flour and oats until combined. Measure 1 cup and set aside. Press remaining oats mixture onto bottom of baking pan. Spread chocolate mix evenly over crust in pan. Crumble reserved cup of oats mix over top. Bake 30 to 35 minutes until topping is golden. Cool in pan on wire rack about 1 hour. Makes 24 bars.

R. W. Rhodes, *A Taste of Pioneering*, Florida Gold Coast Chapter No. 83

## Wilma's Peanut Butter Cookies

½ c. lard
½ c. butter
1 c. white sugar
1 c. brown sugar
1 c. peanut butter
2 eggs, beaten
3 c. flour (plain)
1 tsp. soda
½ tsp. salt
1 tsp. vanilla

Cream fat and sugar. Add peanut butter and mix well. Add eggs, then dry ingredients, sifted together. Add flavoring, mix well and shape into balls. Place about inches apart and press 2 ways with a fork to flatten. Bake in moderate oven (375° F.) until delicately browned.

Wilma Wilkins, *Pioneers Pots and Pans—1985 Cookbook*
North Florida Chapter No. 39

## Pecan Balls

½ c. butter
3 heaping Tbsp. confectioners' sugar
1 c. + 2 Tbsp. flour
1 tsp. vanilla flavoring
1 c. floured pecans
1 Tbsp. water

Cream butter and sugar; blend well. Add flour and nuts. Add flavoring and water last; blend well. Roll into balls the size of walnut. Bake on greased cookie sheet approximately 15 minutes. Roll balls in powdered sugar.

Lola E. Johnson, *Calling All Cooks*, Alabama Chapter No. 34

## Pecan Sandies

2 Tbsp. sugar
½ c. butter
1 tsp. vanilla
1 c. chopped nuts
1 c. plain flour
Pinch of salt

Cream butter, sugar, and vanilla. Add flour and mix well. Add pecans and roll in finger size rolls. Bake at 325° until slightly browned. Cool and roll in sifted powdered sugar. Makes 25 to 30 cookies.

Sandra Garrett, *Dogwood Delights Volume II*, Dogwood Chapter No. 84

# Persimmon Cookies

1 c. persimmon pulp
1 c. nuts
1 c. raisins
1 c. sugar
1/2 c. shortening
1 tsp. soda, dissolved in pulp
2 1/4 c. flour
1/2 tsp. cinnamon
1/2 tsp. cloves
1/2 tsp. nutmeg
1 egg

Cream shortening and sugar. Add egg, soda and persimmon pulp. Add dry ingredients, nuts and raisins. Drop with teaspoon on greased cookie sheet. Bake for 10 minutes in 350° to 375° oven. Makes approximately 90 cookies.

Dee Dee Millen, *Kentucky Kitchens, Volume I*, Kentucky Chapter No. 32

# Potato Chip Cookies

1/2 lb. butter
1/2 lb. margarine
1 c. sugar
2 tsp. vanilla
3 1/2 c. sifted all-purpose flour
1 (6 1/2 oz.) pkg. potato chips

Cream butter, margarine and sugar together until mixture is light and fluffy. Add vanilla, flour and potato chips which have been crushed. Drop by teaspoonfuls onto baking sheet and bake at 325° F. for 12 to 15 minutes.

**Preparation time:** 10 minutes.
**Cooking time:** 12 to 15 minutes.

Alice J. Wilson, *A Taste of Pioneering*
Florida Gold Coast Chapter No. 83

# Powdered Sugar Balls

2 sticks margarine
2 cups unsifted plain flour
1/2 cup powdered sugar
1 tsp. vanilla flavor
1 cup finely chopped nuts

Sqush margarine with hands, sqush margarine, flour, sugar and flavor together until mixed. Add nuts. Roll into little balls and put on ungreased cookie sheet. Bake about 15 minutes at 350°. When done lift out and shake in bowl with powdered sugar.

Dolores S. White, *Secret Recipes of Telephone Pioneers, Volume II*
South Carolina Chapter No. 61

# Quick Reunion Snacks

**1 cup butter (no substitutes)**
**1 cup chopped pecans**
**1 cup brown sugar**
**graham crackers**

Melt butter and brown sugar in heavy sauce pan or double boiler, add pecans and bring to boil, cooking for 2 minutes. Cover bottom of a greased 9x15 inch pan with graham crackers, spread with boiled mixture. Bake at 300° for 10 minutes. Do not break graham crackers, leave whole.

Grace Threatt, *Secret Recipes of Telephone Pioneers, Volume II*
South Carolina Chapter No. 61

# Raisin Oatmeal Cookies

**1 c. raisins**
**1/2 c. shortening**
**1 c. sugar**
**2 eggs**
**1/4 c. milk**
**1 2/3 c. oatmeal**
**1 1/2 c. flour**
**1 tsp. soda**
**1/2 tsp. salt**
**1 tsp. cinnamon**

Wash raisins in hot water and drain. Cream shortening with sugar, then add beaten eggs and milk. Combine with oatmeal and raisins and mix well. Add flour, sifted with soda, salt, and cinnamon. Beat thoroughly. Drop onto greased cookie sheet and bake about 12 minutes at 350°. Makes 4 dozen medium size cookies.

Betty Townsend, *Dining with Pioneers, Volume II*
Tennessee Chapter No. 21

## A Helpful Hint

Plan a cookie exchange as an easy way to get friends together. Each guest should bring one or more batches of cookies made from her favorite recipes, along with copies of the recipes and a container in which to take home the leftovers. The hostess should provide a choice of drinks.

# Sand Dabs

**2 c. flour**
**1 c. nuts**
**3/4 c. butter**
**Pinch of salt**
**4 Tbsp. sugar**
**1 Tbsp. vanilla**
**1 tsp. water**
**1/4 c. powdered sugar**

Cream together all ingredients except powdered sugar. Roll into balls or fingers and place on ungreased pan. Heat oven to 450°. Place small balls in oven for 3 minutes, then turn off heat and let remain 45 minutes. Pour into sack in which powdered sugar has been placed. Shake until covered with sugar.

Icing:

**2 c. sugar**
**1 stick margarine**
**1/2 c. milk**
**1/4 c. cocoa**

Mix and boil 2 minutes. Beat until starts to thicken, then spread on top of cookie.

Lillian Strickland, *Dogwood Delights*, Dogwood Chapter No. 84

# Sand Tarts

**1 cup butter, softened**
**6 tablespoons confectioners' sugar**
**2 cups flour**
**1 teaspoon vanilla extract**
**1 1/2 cups crushed pecans**

Cream butter and confectioners' sugar in mixer bowl until light and fluffy. Add flour and vanilla; mix well. Stir in pecans. Shape into 1-inch balls. Place on cookie sheet. Bake at 350 degrees for 15 minutes. Remove to wire rack to cool. Roll in additional confectioners' sugar.
Yield: 2 dozen.

Patsy Akers, *Kentucky Kitchens, Volume II*, Kentucky Chapter No. 32

## A Helpful Hint

Revive stale cookies by storing them with an apple wedge in an airtight container in the refrigerator for several days.

## Scones

1 pound margarine
1 cup confectioners' sugar
2 tsp. vanilla flavoring
3½ cups plain flour
1 cup chopped nuts

Mix margarine and sugar together. Add vanilla flavoring. Mix in flour. Add chopped nuts. Put in refrigerator overnight. Roll in "fingers." Bake at 350° until brown. Cool. Roll in confectioners' sugar (takes rest of box). Just as good after freezing.

Mae Jeter, *Secret Recipes of Telephone Pioneers, Volume II*
South Carolina Chapter No. 61

## Seven Layer Cookies

5 Tbsp. butter or margarine
1½ c. graham cracker crumbs
1 c. coconut
1 c. semi-sweet chocolate bits
1 c. butterscotch bits
1 c. chopped nuts
1 (15 oz.) can sweetened condensed milk

Put butter in 9 inch square pan in 325° oven. When butter has melted, spread crumbs evenly over butter. Now spread coconut, then chocolate bits, butterscotch bits, then nuts. Do not mix layers. Spread or pour condensed milk over all and bake at 325° for about 30 minutes (25 minutes if using glass dish). Cut into 1½ inch squares. Freeze well. Yield: 36 squares; double the recipe for a tea for 25.

Martha Minyard, *Bell's Best 2*, Mississippi Chapter No. 36

## Jeanne's Spice Cookies

¾ c. shortening or 1½ sticks oleo
1 c. sugar
1 egg
¼ c. molasses
2 c. sifted plain flour
2 tsp. baking soda
¼ tsp. salt
1 tsp. cinnamon
¾ tsp. cloves
¾ tsp. ginger
Powdered sugar

Preheat oven to 375°. Mix together the shortening, sugar, egg, and molasses. Add the flour, baking soda, salt, cinnamon, cloves, and ginger. Grease cookie sheet. Form dough into small balls. Bake 10 to 12 minutes. Roll in powdered sugar while still warm.

Joe DeFraites, *Pots, Pans and Pioneers, Volume IV*
Louisiana Chapter No. 24

# Drop Sugar Cookies

1 c. margarine or butter
1 c. granulated sugar
1 c. confectioners' sugar
1 c. oil
2 eggs
4 c. plus 4 Tbsp. flour
1 tsp. cream of tartar
1 tsp. soda
1 tsp. pure almond extract
1/2 tsp. salt

Cream margarine; add sugar and mix well. Add eggs, oil and almond extract; mix well. Add dry ingredients that have been sifted together and mixed well. Chill for several hours or overnight. Roll into walnut size pieces; put on ungreased cookie sheet; flatten with a small juice glass that has been dipped in granulated sugar and bake at 350° for 8 to 10 minutes. Yield: 6 dozen.

Betty Coogle, *Kentucky Kitchens, Volume I*, Kentucky Chapter No. 32

# Icebox Sugar Cookies

1/2 cup margarine, softened
1/2 cup sugar
1/2 cup packed brown sugar
1 egg, beaten
1 1/2 cups self-rising flour
1 teaspoon vanilla extract

Cream first 3 ingredients in bowl until light and fluffy. Add egg; mix well. Stir in flour. Add vanilla; mix well. Shape into three 1-inch logs. Chill, covered, overnight. Cut into 1-inch slices. Place on greased cookie sheet. Bake at 350 degrees for 10 minutes or until lightly browned. Yield: 24 servings.

**Approx Per Serving:** Cal 99; Prot 1 g; Carbo 15 g; Fiber <1 g; T Fat 4 g; Chol 9 mg; Sod 134 mg.

Phyllis Cox, *Carolina Cooking*, North Carolina Chapter No. 35

## A Helpful Hint

Do not use butter or margarine to grease cookie sheets, as it will burn easily and cause the bottoms of cookies to become too brown. Use shortening, spreading it evenly over the surface of the cookie sheet.

## Old Fashioned Southern Teacakes

**2 1/4 c. sifted flour**
**1/4 t. salt**
**2 t. baking powder**
**1/2 c. butter**
**1 c. sugar**
**2 eggs, beaten**
**1 t. vanilla**
**1 T. milk**

Sift flour, salt and baking powder together. Cream butter, sugar and eggs. Add vanilla, milk and dry ingredients. Blend well. Place dough on a lightly floured board, sprinkle a little flour over the dough and roll out to about 1/2 inch thick. Cut with cookie cutter. Place on cookie sheet and bake in a moderate oven at 350–375° for 12–15 min. or until lightly browned.

Sybil A. Mills, *Taste of Dixie*, Dixie Chapter No. 23

## Grandma's Tea Cakes

**1 egg**
**1 c. sugar**
**1/4 c. buttermilk**
**1 tsp. vanilla**
**2 c. flour**
**3 Tbsp. butter**
**1 tsp. soda**

Cream sugar and butter, add vanilla and egg; beat well. Sift dry ingredients and add alternately with buttermilk. Roll in small amount of flour and pinch off about 1 teaspoonful of dough at a time. Flatten with your hands. Place on lightly greased cookie sheet and bake for 10 minutes at 350°. For added flavor, use 1/2 teaspoon vanilla and 1/2 teaspoon lemon flavoring.

Jeanette English, *Pots, Pans & Pioneers II*, Louisiana Chapter No. 24

### A Helpful Hint

Pack homemade refrigerator cookie dough into clean 6-ounce frozen juice cans. Freeze until needed. Thaw for about 15 minutes, remove bottom of can and push dough up, using the top edge as a cutting guide.

# *1882 Charleston Benné Wafers*

**From the kitchen of:** Bess' Beans, Old City Market, Charleston, South Carolina. **Brief history:** When slaves first came to coastal areas of Georgia and South Carolina, they bought with them—as their most valued possession—a little handful of benne seed (Sesamum Indicum) which they believed held for them the secret of health and good luck.

Planted near the slave quarters of the early plantations, benne became a traditional part of "The Old South." Cooks in the "Big House" kitchens knew just how to use this rich, spicy, honey-colored seed to make delicious and exotic concoctions that have since been famous recipes of "dabuckra."

**1 c. benné seeds**
**2 c. flour**
**1/2 c. soft butter**
**1/2 c. brown sugar**
**1/2 tsp. salt**
**1/4 c. milk**
**1 tsp. baking powder**
**1 tsp. maple syrup**

Toast seeds. Sift flour, salt and baking powder in large bowl. Add butter; add benné seeds and all other ingredients. Use fork to stir in milk, perhaps a bit more. Roll 1/8 inch on floured board. Cut with quarter size cutter. Bake 10 minutes (watch) on greased sheet. Serves: 24.

Mrs. Charles V. Miller (Mrs. Dolores J. Miller), *A Taste of Pioneering*
Florida Gold Coast Chapter No. 83

*Volunteers at a Habitat site.* (North Florida Chapter No. 39)

# Children's Recipes

## *Out-of-This-World Cheesy Pretzels*

**1½ cups baking mix**
**½ cup milk**
**½ cup shredded Cheddar cheese**
**1 egg, beaten**
**½ teaspoon salt**

- Combine baking mix, milk and cheese in bowl; mix well.
- Roll into 8x12-inch rectangle on floured surface.
- Cut into 1x8-inch strips.
- Twist each strip into pretzel shape and place on greased baking sheet.
- Brush strips with beaten egg. Sprinkle with salt.
- Bake at 400 degrees for 20 to 25 minutes or until golden brown.
- Yields 1 dozen.

*Just Kid-ding Around*, Tennessee Chapter No. 21

## *Popcorn Fantasy*

**1 cup butter**
**1 16-ounce package marshmallows**
**8 cups popped popcorn**
**1 cup peanuts**
**1 cup "M & M's" Chocolate Candies**
**1 cup gumdrops**

- Heat butter and marshmallows in saucepan over low heat until melted and well blended, stirring constantly.
- Combine popcorn, peanuts and candies in bowl; mix lightly.
- Pour marshmallow mixture over popcorn; mix well.
- Press in 9x13-inch dish.
- Chill in refrigerator for several hours.
- Cut into squares.
- Yields 6 dozen.

*Just Kid-ding Around*, Tennessee Chapter No. 21

# *Peanut Butter-Stuffed Apples*

Apples
Peanut butter
Raisins
Granola
Wheat germ
Oats
Honey

- Remove cores from apple carefully. Do not cut apples into halves.
- Combine peanut butter with 1 or more of the remaining ingredients in bowl; mix well.
- Spoon 2 tablespoons peanut butter mixture into apples. Wrap in foil.
- These are great for camping. Eat them whole or sliced.

*Just Kid-ding Around*, Tennessee Chapter No. 21

# *Raggedy Ann Salad*

1 canned peach half
1/2 hard-boiled egg
4 small celery sticks
1 leaf curly lettuce
1/4 cup finely shredded cheese
1/4 maraschino cherry
Raisins

- Place peach in center of salad plate.
- Position egg for head, celery for arms and legs and lettuce for skirt.
- Add cheese for hair, cherry for mouth and raisins for eyes, nose, buttons and shoes.
- Yields 1 serving.

*Just Kid-ding Around*, Tennessee Chapter No. 21

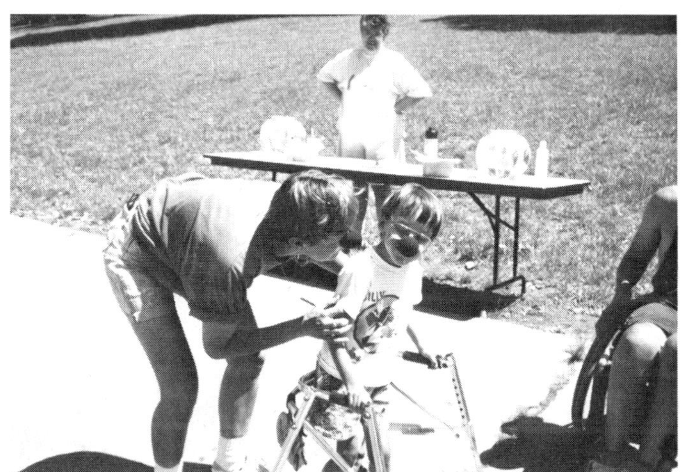

*Pioneers assisting a child at Easter Seals Camp.* (Tennessee Chapter No. 21)

## *Corn Dogs*

1 c. flour
2 tsp. baking powder
1 tsp. salt
1 c. milk
1 lb. wieners
1 c. corn meal
2 Tbsp. sugar
1 egg
2 Tbsp. shortening, melted

Sift together flour and corn meal, baking powder, sugar and salt. Beat egg slightly and add milk. Stir into dry ingredients. Add shortening. Dip wieners into batter, holding with a fork or skewer. Drain excess batter back into bowl. Fry in a wire basket in oil heated to 375° until golden brown. Drain on absorbent paper. Serve hot.

Helen Sykes, *Kentucky Kitchens, Volume I*, Kentucky Chapter No. 32

## *Fun in the Bun*

**1½ cups pancake mix**
**2 tablespoons sugar**
**½ cup cornmeal**
**1¼ cups milk**
**1 egg**
**1 pound hot dogs**
**Oil for deep frying**

Combine pancake mix, sugar, cornmeal, milk and egg in bowl; mix well. Insert 1 popsicle stick into each hot dog. Dip into batter, coating well. Deep-fry until golden brown. Serve with mustard dip.
Yield: 10 servings.

**Approx Per Serving:** Cal 268; Prot 9 g; Carbo 22 g; Fiber <1 g; T Fat 16 g; Chol 49 mg; Sod 785 mg.
Nutritional information does not include oil for deep frying.

Deni Dumford, *Carolina Cooking*, North Carolina Chapter No. 35

# *Jack-O'-Lantern Pizzas*

**4 English muffins, split**
**1 8-ounce can pizza sauce**
**8 slices cheese**

- Preheat oven to 400 degrees.
- Separate muffins. Toast until brown.
- Spread about 1 tablespoon pizza sauce on each muffin.
- Trim off corners of cheese slices to make circles to fit muffins.
- Cut jack-o'-lantern face in each circle; remove cutouts and place cheese circle on muffins. You may eat the cutouts if you wish.
- Place on baking sheet.
- Bake for several minutes until cheese is melted.
- Yields 8 servings.
- This recipe can also be baked in a toaster oven.

*Just Kid-ding Around*, Tennessee Chapter No. 21

# *Baked Spaghetti*

**1 pound ground beef**
**1/2 cup chopped onion**
**1 clove of garlic, chopped**
**1 16-ounce jar spaghetti sauce**
**Salt and pepper to taste**
**1 8-ounce package spaghetti**
**2 cups shredded Cheddar cheese**

- Preheat oven to 350 degrees.
- Cook ground beef with onion and garlic in skillet until ground beef is brown and crumbly, stirring frequently; drain.
- Mix in spaghetti sauce and add salt and pepper to taste.
- Simmer for several minutes, stirring several times.
- Cook spaghetti according to the package directions; drain well. Place in 9x13-inch baking dish.
- Ladle spaghetti sauce over spaghetti.
- Sprinkle cheese over top.
- Bake for 40 minutes.
- Yields 6 to 8 servings.

*Just Kid-ding Around*, Tennessee Chapter No. 21

# Quick Tuna-Mac

**1 14-ounce package macaroni and cheese mix**
**1 10-ounce can cream of mushroom soup**
**1/2 cup milk**
**1 6-ounce can tuna**
**2 cups potato chip crumbs**
**2 slices American cheese**

- Preheat oven to 350 degrees.
- Cook macaroni and cheese according to the package directions. Add soup, milk and tuna; mix well.
- Sprinkle half the potato chip crumbs evenly into greased 2-quart casserole. Spoon tuna mixture into casserole.
- Top with remaining potato chip crumbs. Cut cheese slices into thin strips; arrange strips in decorative pattern over top.
- Yields 6 servings.

*Just Kid-ding Around*, Tennessee Chapter No. 21

# Baked Salmon Loaf

**1 1/2 cups milk**
**1 slice bread, torn**
**1/4 cup butter**
**2 cups canned salmon**
**2 eggs**
**1/2 teaspoon salt**

- Preheat oven to 350 degrees.
- Combine milk, bread and butter in top of double boiler over boiling water.
- Heat until mixture is smooth and creamy, stirring frequently; remove from heat.
- Place salmon in bowl. Remove salmon bones carefully. Add eggs; mix well. Add milk mixture; mix well.
- Spoon into greased 5x9-inch loaf pan.
- Bake for 1 hour or until firm.
- Serve salmon hot or cold.
- Yields 6 to 8 servings.

*Just Kid-ding Around*, Tennessee Chapter No. 21

## Waffley Cheese Strata

**1 8-count package frozen waffles**
**2 tablespoons butter, softened**
**1 8-ounce package sliced cheese**
**6 eggs, beaten**
**3 cups milk**

- Toast waffles using package directions. Cool. Spread with butter.
- Arrange several waffles in single layer in 8x12-inch baking dish. Top with cheese slices.
- Repeat layers with remaining waffles and cheese slices.
- Beat eggs with milk in medium bowl. Pour over waffles and cheese carefully.
- Cover baking dish with plastic wrap.
- Chill in refrigerator for 3 hours or longer.
- Preheat oven to 325 degrees.
- Remove plastic wrap.
- Bake strata for 35 to 40 minutes or until golden brown.
- Let stand for 5 minutes. Cut into squares.
- Yields 6 servings.

*Just Kid-ding Around*, Tennessee Chapter No. 21

## Surprise Baked Beans

**1 8-ounce can apricots**
**2 16-ounce cans Beanee Weenees**
**1/2 cup chopped onion**
**2 tablespoons brown sugar**
**1 teaspoon dry mustard**

- Preheat oven to 350 degrees.
- Drain apricots. Place in large bowl; mash with fork.
- Add Beanee Weenees, onion, brown sugar and dry mustard; mix well.
- Spoon into greased 1 1/2-quart casserole.
- Bake for 1 hour or until bubbly.
- Yields 6 to 8 servings.
- **Pineapple Baked Beans:** Substitute crushed pineapple for apricots.

*Just Kid-ding Around*, Tennessee Chapter No. 21

# *Applesauce Spice Bread*

**1 2-layer package yellow cake mix**
**1 3-ounce package vanilla instant pudding mix**
**1/2 teaspoon cinnamon**
**1/2 teaspoon nutmeg**
**1 cup applesauce**
**1/2 cup raisins**

- Preheat oven to 350 degrees.
- Grease and flour two 5x9-inch loaf pans.
- Combine cake mix, pudding mix, cinnamon, nutmeg and applesauce in mixer bowl.
- Beat at low speed for 1 minute. Beat at high speed for 4 minutes.
- Pour into prepared loaf pans.
- Bake for 30 to 35 minutes or until you can stick a toothpick in the center and it comes out clean.
- Cool in pans for 15 minutes.
- Remove carefully from pans; place on wire racks.
- Cool completely before slicing.
- Yields 2 loaves.

*Just Kid-ding Around*, Tennessee Chapter No. 21

*Clowns entertaining kids at Special Olympic events.*
(Florida Gold Coast Chapter No. 83)

## *Cinnamon and Raisin Biscuits*

**2 cups self-rising flour**
**2 tablespoons sugar**
**1 teaspoon cream of tartar**
**5 tablespoons shortening**
**1 cup buttermilk**
**Melted butter**
**2 cups sugar**
**3 tablespoons cinnamon**
**1 tablespoon oil**
**1/4 cup raisins**

- Preheat oven to 375 degrees.
- Combine flour, 2 tablespoons sugar and cream of tartar in bowl.
- Cut shortening into mixture with pastry blender until mixture is crumbly.
- Add buttermilk; mix until mixture clings together and forms ball.
- Sprinkle a small amount of additional flour onto counter top. Roll dough into thin rectangle on floured surface with rolling pin.
- Brush with melted butter. Mix 2 cups sugar, cinnamon, oil and raisins in small bowl. Sprinkle over dough. Roll as for jelly roll; cut into 1 1/2-inch slices. Place on greased baking sheet.
- Bake for 15 minutes or until golden brown.
- Yields 6 to 8 servings.

*Just Kid-ding Around*, Tennessee Chapter No. 21

## *Muffins in a Hurry*

**2 cups self-rising flour**
**1 cup milk**
**1/4 cup mayonnaise**

- Preheat oven to 400 degrees.
- Grease 12 muffin cups
- Sift flour into bowl.
- Add milk and salad dressing; stir just until flour is moistened. Batter will be lumpy.
- Spoon enough batter into muffin cups to fill 2/3 full.
- Bake for 20 minutes or until golden brown.
- Serve muffins hot with butter.
- Yields 12 muffins.

*Just Kid-ding Around*, Tennessee Chapter No. 21

# *Light and Crisp Belgian Waffles*

**2 egg whites**
**2 egg yolks**
**2 cups milk**
**2 cups all-purpose flour**
**1/2 teaspoon salt**
**1 tablespoon baking powder**
**1/3 cup oil**

- Preheat Belgian waffle iron.
- Beat egg whites in mixer bowl with electric mixer at high speed until stiff peaks form. Set aside.
- Combine egg yolks, milk, flour, salt, baking powder and oil in large mixer bowl.
- Beat with electric mixer at low speed until ingredients are moistened.
- Beat at medium speed until smooth.
- Fold in egg whites gently with spatula.
- Pour 1/2 cup batter onto hot waffle grids; close waffle iron.
- Bake for 2 to 2 1/2 minutes or until waffle is golden brown and tests done.
- Repeat with remaining batter.
- Serve with favorite waffle toppings.
- Yields 18 waffles.

*Just Kid-ding Around*, Tennessee Chapter No. 21

# *Clown Face Sundae*

**1 scoop vanilla ice cream**
**1 ice cream cone**
**Chocolate chips**
**1 maraschino cherry**
**3 or 4 ice cream wafers**

- Place ice cream in center of serving dish.
- Press cone onto ice cream to resemble hat.
- Add chocolate chips for eyes and mouth and cherry for nose.
- Cut ice cream wafers into triangles. Press points of triangles into base of ice cream scoop to resemble collar.
- Yields 1 clown sundae.
- **Any-Flavor Clown:** Substitute your favorite ice cream flavor for vanilla.

*Just Kid-ding Around*, Tennessee Chapter No. 21

## Cinderella Cake

1 cup sugar
1/4 cup butter, softened
2 eggs, beaten
1/2 cup milk
1 1/2 cups flour
2 teaspoons baking powder
1 teaspoon vanilla extract

- Preheat oven to 350 degrees.
- Cream sugar and butter in mixer bowl until light and fluffy.
- Add eggs and milk; mix well.
- Sift flour and baking powder together.
- Add to creamed mixture; mix well. Blend in vanilla.
- Pour into greased and floured 9-inch cake pan.
- Bake for 45 minutes or until cake tests done.
- Cool in pan for 5 minutes. Remove to wire rack to cool completely.
- Frost with favorite frosting.
- Yields 8 servings.

*Just Kid-ding Around*, Tennessee Chapter No. 21

## No-Bake Fudge Cookies

1/4 cup butter
2 cups sugar
1/2 cup milk
1/4 cup baking cocoa
Pinch of salt
1 teaspoon vanilla extract
1/2 cup peanut butter
3 cups quick-cooking oats

- Melt butter in saucepan over low heat.
- Add sugar, milk, cocoa and salt; mix well.
- Bring just to the boiling point. Do not boil. Remove from heat.
- Add vanilla, peanut butter and oats; mix well.
- Drop by spoonfuls onto cookie sheet.
- Let stand until firm.
- Yields 3 dozen.

*Just Kid-ding Around*, Tennessee Chapter No. 21

# *Edible Play Dough*

**1 cup peanut butter**
**1 cup corn syrup**
**$1^1/_4$ cups confectioners' sugar**
**$1^1/_4$ cups dry milk powder**

- Combine peanut butter and corn syrup in large bowl; mix until smooth.
- Mix confectioners' sugar and dry milk powder in small bowl.
- Add confectioners' sugar mixture to peanut butter mixture; mix well. May add enough additional confectioners' sugar to make of consistency of play dough
- Let kids create yummy sculptures and then gobble them up.
- Yields $2^1/_2$ to 3 cups.

*Just Kid-ding Around*, Tennessee Chapter No. 21

*Newspapers in the Schools Literacy Project.*
(North Carolina Chapter No. 35)

# Index

The designation following the recipe title denotes the chapter contributing the recipe: **AL** Alabama Chapter No. 34; **DX** Dixie Chapter No. 23; **DG** Dogwood Chapter No. 84; **FLG** Florida Gold Coast Chapter No. 83; **KY** Kentucky Chapter No. 32; **LA** Louisiana Chapter No. 24; **MS** Mississippi Chapter No. 36; **NC** North Carolina Chapter No. 35; **NFL** North Florida Chapter No. 39; **SC** South Carolina Chapter No. 61; and **TN** Tennessee Chapter No. 21.

# *Order Information*

## Order *Servin' It Up* from any of the chapters on the following pages.

*Servin' It Up* is available with open-flat Wire-O binding from the North Carolina and South Carolina chapters. Smooth spine adhesive bound books are available from the remaining chapters.

The recipes selected for *Servin' It Up* represent only a small portion of those contained in the source cookbooks listed on the following order forms. If you would like to purchase one or more of the source cookbooks, please address your orders to the appropriate Telephone Pioneer chapter and enclose a check for the total amount. All prices include postage and handling.

### *Alabama Chapter No. 34*

| Quantity | | | Total |
|---|---|---|---|
| ______ | Servin' It Up | @ $10.50 | ______ |
| ______ | Calling All Cooks | @ $10.00 | ______ |
| ______ | Calling All Cooks two | @ $10.00 | ______ |
| ______ | Calling All Cooks three | @ $10.00 | ______ |

Name ______________________________

Address ______________________________

City/State/Zip ______________________________

Make check payable to: TPA - Alabama Chapter No. 34

Mail to: Telephone Pioneers of America, Alabama Chapter No. 34
Room 301-N, 3196 Hwy. 280 South, Birmingham, Alabama 35243
1-205-972-2724

### *Dixie Chapter No. 23*

| Quantity | | | Total |
|---|---|---|---|
| ______ | Servin' It Up | @ $10.50 | ______ |
| ______ | Lawfully Good Eating | @ $12.00 | ______ |

Name ______________________________

Address ______________________________

City/State/Zip ______________________________

Make check payable to: Dixie Chapter No. 23

Mail to: Telephone Pioneers of America, Dixie Chapter No. 23
151–100 Perimeter Center Place
Atlanta, Georgia 30346
1-404-391-4482

SWEET
16
Alabama
North Carolina
South Carolina
Tennessee
Kentucky
Georgia
Florida
Mississippi
Lousiana

## *Dogwood Chapter No. 84*

**Quantity** **Total**

_______ **Servin' It Up** . . . . . . . . . . . . . . . . . . . . . . . . . . . . @ $10.50 _______
_______ Dogwood Delights . . . . . . . . . . . . . . . . . . . . . . . . . @ $ 8.50 _______
_______ Dogwood Delights Volume II . . . . . . . . . . . . . . . . @ $ 9.50 _______

Name ______________________________________________

Address ____________________________________________

City/State/Zip _______________________________________

Make check payable to: Dogwood Chapter No. 84

Mail to: Telephone Pioneers of America, Dogwood Chapter No. 84
151–100 Perimeter Center Place
Atlanta, Georgia 30346
1-404-391-2680

## *Florida Gold Coast Chapter No. 83*

**Quantity** **Total**

_______ **Servin' It Up** . . . . . . . . . . . . . . . . . . . . . . . . . . . . @ $10.50 _______
_______ A Tablespoon of Pioneering and
a Teaspoon of Horses and the Handicapped . . . . @ $ 9.25 _______

Name ______________________________________________

Address ____________________________________________

City/State/Zip _______________________________________

Make check payable to: Telephone Pioneers - #83

Mail to: Telephone Pioneers of America, Chapter No. 83
6451 North Federal Hwy., Room 101B
Fort Lauderdale, Florida 33308
1-305-492-2802

## *Kentucky Chapter No. 32*

**Quantity** **Total**

_______ **Servin' It Up** . . . . . . . . . . . . . . . . . . . . . . . . . . . . @ $10.50 _______
_______ Kentucky Kitchens, Volume I . . . . . . . . . . . . . . . . @ $10.00 _______
_______ Kentucky Kitchens, Volume II . . . . . . . . . . . . . . . . @ $10.00 _______

Name ______________________________________________

Address ____________________________________________

City/State/Zip _______________________________________

Make check payable to: TPA - Kentucky Chapter No. 32

Mail to: Telephone Pioneers of America, Kentucky Chapter No. 32
P.O. Box 32410
Louisville, Kentucky 40232
1-502-582-8319

Alabama
North Carolina
South Carolina
Tennessee
Kentucky
Georgia
Florida
Mississippi
Lousiana
SWEET
16

## *Louisiana Chapter No. 24*

| Quantity | | | Total |
|---|---|---|---|
| ______ | **Servin' It Up** | @ $10.50 | ______ |
| ______ | Pots, Pans and Pioneers, Volume I | @ $ 9.00 | ______ |
| ______ | Pots, Pans & Pioneers, Volume II | @ $ 9.00 | ______ |
| ______ | Pots, Pans and Pioneers, Volume III | @ $ 9.00 | ______ |
| ______ | Pots, Pans and Pioneers, Volume IV | @ $ 9.00 | ______ |

Name ______________________________

Address ______________________________

City/State/Zip ______________________________

Make check payable to: TPA - Louisiana Chapter No. 24

Mail to: Telephone Pioneers of America, Louisiana Chapter No. 24
365 Canal Street, Room 1445, New Orleans, LA 70140

## *Mississippi Chapter No. 36*

| Quantity | | | Total |
|---|---|---|---|
| ______ | **Servin' It Up** | @ $10.50 | ______ |
| ______ | Bell's Best | @ $10.00 | ______ |
| ______ | Bell's Best 2 | @ $10.00 | ______ |
| ______ | Bell's Best 3 | @ $10.00 | ______ |

Name ______________________________

Address ______________________________

City/State/Zip ______________________________

Telephone No. ______________________________

Make check payable to: Telephone Pioneers of America

Mail to: Telephone Pioneers of America, Mississippi Chapter No. 36
P.O. Box 811, 110 Landmark Center, Jackson, MS 39205
1-601-961-1981

## *North Carolina Chapter No. 35*

| Quantity | | | Total |
|---|---|---|---|
| ______ | **Servin' It Up** (Wire-O bound) | @ $12.50 | ______ |
| ______ | Carolina Cooking | @ $12.00 | ______ |

Name ______________________________

Address ______________________________

City/State/Zip ______________________________

Make check payable to: North Carolina Chapter No. 35 TPA

Mail to: Telephone Pioneers of America, North Carolina Chapter No. 35
P.O. Box 30188, 606 Southern National Center
Charlotte, NC 28230
1-704-378-8478

North Carolina
South Carolina
Alabama
Tennessee
SWEET
16
Lousiana
Kentucky
Mississippi
Georgia
Florida

## North Florida Chapter No. 39

| Quantity | | | Total |
|---|---|---|---|
| _______ | **Servin' It Up** | @ $10.50 | _______ |
| _______ | Pioneers, Pots and Pans—1985 Cookbook | @ $ 6.75 | _______ |

Name ______________________________

Address ______________________________

City/State/Zip ______________________________

Make check payable to: Telephone Pioneers of America

Mail to: Telephone Pioneers of America, North Florida Chapter No. 39
Room 3AA1
301 West Bay Street, Jacksonville, FL 32202
1-904-350-4230

## South Carolina Chapter No. 61

| Quantity | | | Total |
|---|---|---|---|
| _______ | **Servin' It Up** (Wire-O Bound) | @ $12.50 | _______ |
| _______ | Secret Recipes of Telephone Pioneers, Vol. I | @ $ 8.00 | _______ |
| _______ | Secret Recipes of Telephone Pioneers, Vol. II | @ $ 8.50 | _______ |
| _______ | Secret Recipes of Telephone Pioneers, Vol. III | @ $10.00 | _______ |

Name ______________________________

Address ______________________________

City/State/Zip ______________________________

Make check payable to: Telephone Pioneers

Mail to: Telephone Pioneers of America, South Carolina Chapter No. 61
Room 201, 1600 Hampton St. Annex Bldg., Columbia, SC 29201
1-803-733-6453

## Tennessee Chapter No. 21

| Quantity | | | Total |
|---|---|---|---|
| _______ | **Servin' It Up** | @ $10.50 | _______ |
| _______ | Dining With Pioneers, Volume I | @ $ 9.75 | _______ |
| _______ | Dining With Pioneers, Volume II | @ $ 9.75 | _______ |
| _______ | Answering the Call of Those in Need | @ $ 7.75 | _______ |
| _______ | Just Kid-ding Around | @ $ 7.75 | _______ |

Name ______________________________

Address ______________________________

City/State/Zip ______________________________

Make check payable to: Telephone Pioneers - #21

Mail to: Telephone Pioneers of America, Tennessee Chapter No. 21
333 Commerce Street, Suite 107, Nashville, TN 37201-3300
1-615-214-6754

SWEET
16
Alabama
North Carolina
South Carolina
Tennessee
Kentucky
Georgia
Florida
Mississippi
Lousiana